Adobe Dreamweaver CS3
with ASP, ColdFusion, and PHP
Training from the Source

Jeffrey Bardzell and Bob Flynn

Adobe

Adobe Dreamweaver CS3 with ASP, ColdFusion, and PHP: Training from the Source

Jeffrey Bardzell and Bob Flynn

Adobe Press books are published by

Peachpit
1249 Eighth Street
Berkeley, CA 94710
510/524-2178
510/524-2221 (fax)

Find us on the Web at: www.peachpit.com.
To report errors, please send a note to errata@peachpit.com.
Peachpit is a division of Pearson Education.

For the latest on Adobe Press books, go to www.adobepress.com.

Copyright © 2008 by Adobe Systems, Inc.

Authors: Jeffrey Bardzell and Bob Flynn
Editor: Wendy Sharp
Production Coordinator: Myrna Vladic
Compositors: Rick Gordon, Emerald Valley Graphics / Debbie Roberti, Espresso Graphics
Indexer: Julie Bess, JBIndexing Inc.
Cover Design: Peachpit Press

Printed and bound in the United States of America

ISBN 13: 978-0-321-46106-3
ISBN 10: 0-321-46106-1

9 8 7 6 5 4 3 2 1

To Christian and Esther Briggs
(and guitar heroes everywhere)

To Yvonne, Mara and Tess.
You knew I'd eventually get this finished and come to bed.

Bios

Jeffrey Bardzell, Ph.D., is an Assistant Professor of HCI/Design and new media at the School of Informatics in Indiana University—Bloomington. He specializes in the aesthetics of software interfaces, amateur multimedia design communities, and digital creativity. His recent work explores the emergence of discourses and professionalization within so-called "amateur" multimedia communities, such as Second Life, Newgrounds, Facebook, and YouTube. Media forms include Flash animation, virtual fashion design, machinima, education, and viral videos.

Bob Flynn is the technology director for a couple niche graduate programs at the Indiana University Kelley School of Business. He is a Certified Advanced ColdFusion developer but does most of his programming in PHP working on volunteer projects for local non-profits. Bob is an active leader in the Web community at Indiana University where he is a user group manager and serves on a number of university-wide Web committees and initiatives. Bob lives with his wife Yvonne, daughters Mara and Tess, and trusty cat Peep in Bloomington, Indiana. Bob has lived and traveled throughout the former Soviet Union and Eastern Europe where he spread his love of Ultimate Frisbee to a willing populace.

Acknowledgments

First and foremost I want to thank Jeff Bardzell for luring me, unsuspecting, into these book projects. I have learned a lot and, despite the long hours, really enjoyed it. Jeff deserves the credit for the wonderfully cohesive project the book is constructed around and the thoughtful and thorough explanations that hold it all together. I am grateful to have had an opportunity to contribute to it, but I don't know that I would have been able to come up this solid of an idea in the first place.

No book is complete without the author acknowledging the care and guidance of their editor. Now I know why. My editor is, of course, more wonderful than any of theirs. Wendy Sharp has been cheerleader, task master, tower of patience and an expert of the subtle word change. There was not a single suggestion or correction she made that I could take issue with. Hers is not a job I envy, but it is one I would not have been able to do without.

Thanks go also to Paul Robertson, friend, colleague and fellow member of my user group until he was snatched away by Adobe. Paul answered my ASP questions and gave me a reality check a couple times I thought I knew better.

I would like to thank the readers of previous versions of the book who have posted their questions and problems on the Dreamweaver forums. I tried to iron out the wrinkles they found as I worked through the rewrite of this book. I'm sure I introduced a few of my own, but I have faith they will let me know if I did.

Finally I must thank my family. My wonderful wife Yvonne has been very supportive, never begrudging my need to hide myself away to work on the book and never forgetting to tell me to not stay up too late. My girls Mara and Tess, though still relatively young, understood that this project was something I was committed to doing and gave me the space I needed. Of course headphones also helped create that space, but hey, they deserve their space too.

Contents

Introduction

Adobe Dreamweaver has been the market leader in visual (X)HTML editors for years, combining ease of use, power, and unusually high quality code writing. But since version 1 was first released, the Web has changed. Numerous technologies have emerged as critical Web authoring tools, including JavaScript, databases, SQL, Java, WML, WSDL, cascading style sheets (CSS), XML, XSLT, CGI scripting, and above all, a group of server languages that enable developers to turn Web pages into powerful, data-driven, interactive Web applications: these include Adobe ColdFusion, Microsoft ASP and ASP.NET, as well as JSP and PHP. Without compromising its ease of use or the quality of code it has always generated, Adobe Dreamweaver has absorbed these technologies, not only making it possible to work with each of them in isolation, but also making it possible to build sophisticated applications combining these technologies.

Prerequisites

While Dreamweaver has managed to keep up with the rapid evolution of Web technologies, many developers have not fared so well. HTML, image editing, and CSS are one thing: document object models, for loops, relational data, concatenation, recordsets, cookies, and methods are something else. Yet for many of us, our careers depend on our ability to make the jump from static HTML to full-fledged dynamic Web applications—and that means gaining competence with several of the technologies listed in the previous paragraph.

That's where *Adobe Dreamweaver CS3 with ASP, ColdFusion, and PHP: Training From the Source* comes in. In a series of hands-on tutorials, you'll build competence in working with three dynamic application development languages: Microsoft ASP (VBScript) and Adobe ColdFusion Markup Language (CFML), and the open source PHP. Along the way, you'll also learn about database design, writing SQL queries, CSS, the XHTML standard, Ajax and more.

The book mixes enough hand-coding for you to become competent programming in these languages with extensive coverage of the dialog- and wizard-based server behaviors and pre-built application objects that Dreamweaver provides to speed up application development. The goal is not simply to build dynamic applications, but for you to gain a deep understanding about how they work, even when you are relying on GUI-based server behaviors.

The lessons assume the following:

- You have basic familiarity with your operating system, including using the menu system and file management.

- Dreamweaver CS3 is installed, and your system meets the requirements needed to run it.

- You are familiar with working in Dreamweaver, including the use of the Property inspector, various panels, and the main menu. You should also understand the site definition process and Site panel.

- You understand how XHTML code works, and you are familiar with its most common tags and attributes, such as the <p>, <table>, <tr>, <td>, <h1>, <h2>, and <img> tags. You should also understand common HTML concepts, such as absolute versus relative links, validly nested tags, and the difference between the document head and body.

Outline

This Adobe training course steps you through the projects in each lesson, showing you how to create database-driven, interactive Web applications in Dreamweaver CS3 using ASP, ColdFusion, and PHP. The curriculum of this course should take you 20 to 24 hours to complete and includes the following lessons:

Lesson 1: Introducing Newland Tours
Lesson 2: Preparing the Static HTML and CSS
Lesson 3: Dynamic Web Sites
Lesson 4: Passing Data Between Pages
Lesson 5: Sending Email From a Web Form
Lesson 6: Building a Tour Price Calculator
Lesson 7: Databases on the Web
Lesson 8: Completing the Price Calculator
Lesson 9: Filtering and Displaying Data Using Ajax
Lesson 10: Building the Tour Descriptions
Lesson 11: Building Search Interfaces
Lesson 12: Authenticating Users
Lesson 13: Managing Content With Forms
Lesson 14: Building Update Pages
Lesson 15: Hand-coding a Basic CMS

The Project Site

In the course of completing the book, you will build a site for a fictional travel tours company, called Newland Tours. Newland Tours offers travel tours to numerous countries throughout the world. Currently, tours are listed on a static HTML Web page. Unfortunately, new tours are added, old tours are removed, and tour details (especially their prices) change frequently. Newland Tours, having no dedicated Web developer on staff, is having trouble keeping the site up to date, and they are looking for a better way to keep content up to date on the Web. In addition, site users are complaining that tours are hard to find, as there is no way to search for tours short of scrolling through long pages of tour listings.

The solution, of course, is to store data about the tours in a database, and enable users to search database records over the Web. Likewise, as you will learn, Web forms can be used to update the database from any computer with access to the Internet. Of course, exposing the Newland Tours database to the general public (via Web forms) would not be a good security practice, so you'll also implement an authorization framework for the site, which blocks users from seeing pages unless they have logged in with the correct level of access.

Along the way, you'll build a number of common Web applications, including a price calculator, a Contact Us form that automatically generates an email message, search interfaces, and a forms-based content management system that enables Newland Tours employees to insert, update, and remove country profiles.

Elements and Format

Each lesson in this book begins by outlining the major focus of the lesson at hand and introducing new features. Learning objectives and the approximate time needed to complete all the exercises are also listed at the beginning of each lesson. The projects are divided into short exercises that explain the importance of each skill you learn. Every lesson will build on the concepts and techniques used in the previous lessons.

Tips: Alternative ways to perform tasks and suggestions to consider when applying the skills you are learning.

Notes: Additional background information to expand your knowledge, as well as advanced techniques you can explore in order to further develop your skills.

Boldface terms: New vocabulary that is introduced and emphasized in each lesson.

Menu commands and keyboard shortcuts: There are often multiple ways to perform the same task in Dreamweaver. Menu commands are shown with angle brackets between the menu names and commands: Menu > Command > Subcommand. Keyboard shortcuts are shown with a plus sign between the names of keys to indicate that you should press the keys simultaneously; for example, Shift+Tab means that you should press the Shift and Tab keys at the same time.

CD-ROM: The files you will need to complete the projects for each lesson are located in a folder named for the lesson: Lesson01, Lesson02, etc. The CD can be found in the back of the book. Inside the lesson folders are Start and Complete folders, which represent the state of the Newland Tours project at the beginning and ending of that lesson, respectively. After the first few lessons, which use the same files regardless of the server model you plan to use (ASP, ColdFusion, or PHP), the Start and Complete folders have subfolders for each server model—newland-asp, newland-cfm, and newland-php.

The files you will use for each of the projects are listed at the beginning of each lesson.

If You Get Stuck

One frustrating aspect of learning dynamic Web site development is the errors that you will encounter. A dynamic Web site is typically the fusion of many technologies, and some of them, especially ASP, ColdFusion, and PHP themselves, depend on the configuration of the server. If the server (or database) is not configured correctly, you will see error messages even if you entered all the code correctly in Dreamweaver. Worse, the error messages that you see are often hard to interpret (especially those in ASP), and in some cases, misleading.

The following are some strategies you can use to resolve these problems:

Use the files in the lesson's Complete folder. One reason these are provided is so that you can use them if something goes wrong with your files. You can also print out the code for your file and the one in the Complete folder for a comparison.

Consult Adobe's TechNote on common server errors (http://www.adobe.com/go/gntray_supp_kb). Verify that the page you are testing has all of the data that it needs. Some pages depend on the presence of form or querystring/URL variables to work. For example, a SQL query on a detail page might filter database records based on a querystring or URL variable that it is expecting from a related page. If you test that detail page directly, without going through the related page first, the data ASP, ColdFusion, or PHP is expecting won't be present, resulting in an error. Always test starting from an application's starting page, rather than a page in the middle of the process.

Try to determine whether the problem is due to code or configuration. With static XHTML development, if a page doesn't look right, it's almost always because of something in your code. When they see a server error, many beginners assume that they made a mistake in their code, and while that is possible, it's just as likely that there is a configuration problem, such as the wrong permissions, a service that's not available, or a missing data source name (DSN). The easiest way to test is to swap in the file from the Complete folder—if it doesn't work either, then your code is probably fine. Take up the matter with your server administrator.

Check the book's Web site. Because ASP, ColdFusion, and PHP errors are so common and hard to troubleshoot, the author and the editorial team took extra pains to ensure that the code in the book and on the CD-ROM are bug free. However, no book is completely without errors, and if we learn of any, we will post them on the book's page at http://www.bobflynn.info/books/.

Ask your questions in the appropriate Adobe Dreamweaver forums. Adobe has a number of free forums where anyone can go to ask questions or search previous posts. The forums are frequented by Adobe tech support staff and Dreamweaver/ASP/ColdFusion/PHP veterans and gurus, and you can often get an answer to your questions within a matter of minutes. To access the forums, visit http://www.adobe.com/support/forums/. I visit the Dreamweaver Application Development newsgroup periodically and pay special attention to posts that reference this book in the title. I cannot guarantee to provide support for every problem every reader might encounter, but the community in that forum is sufficient to help most people get what they need.

Know when to move on. While you should try to resolve any errors that you encounter, don't beat your head against the wall. The goal of the book is for you to learn dynamic Web site development, and not literally to build every aspect of the Newland Tours site. It's okay to move on without completing a lesson if you cannot resolve an issue. Just be sure that you understand the concepts behind every step.

About This Edition

This is the fourth edition of this book. In 2002, Jeffrey first wrote this book to bridge a gap he perceived between books and workshops on HTML and CSS on the one hand and resources on more serious scripting, such as ASP, ColdFusion, and PHP, on the other. He noticed that a lot of people wanted to graduate from static Web development to serious Web programming, but for a variety of reasons, were unable to make the leap.

This book was, therefore, designed to help veteran static Web developers overcome the various barriers to entry into more serious Web development. These barriers include the following:

- The difficulty of configuring a desktop for dynamic, database-driven development.

- Lack of comprehensible resources concerning the conceptual issues behind the new forms of programming (how is it even possible for a Web page to "see" a database?)

- The lack of a good entry point for the serious beginner to get into large and complex languages, such as ASP VBScript, ColdFusion Markup Language, or PHP scripts.

Based on the feedback and sales of the first three editions, the book achieved those goals. What people seemed to respond to was not the latest bells and whistles of ASP, ColdFusion, PHP, or even Dreamweaver, but rather the fact that the book made them successful in their transition to dynamic Web programming. Therefore, when Dreamweaver CS3 came out, the editorial folks at Peachpit/Adobe Press and I had a choice to make: Do we overhaul the contents to address the latest changes and upgrades in the various technologies, or do we stick with content that we know works?

For this revision, we are preserving the content that we knew was working while adding some contenton on key new technology that Dreamweaver makes easily accessible. The book has been updated to include the latest technologies, including upgrades in Dreamweaver, Web technologies (PHP and ColdFusion have changed since the last edition of the book and Spry has been developed to make the use of Ajax more accessible), and databases (MySQL has also changed in ways that affect the book). I have made changes to the directions and explanations and reconstructed all the exercise files for ASP, ColdFusion, and PHP, for both PC and Mac. Thus, the book is fully up-to-date with current versions of technologies at the time of publication.

Application security has always been an important aspect of Web development. Both Jeffrey and I felt this book needed to at least make you aware of some of the practices that threaten the security of your Website and database. As much as was possible in a book that is not dedicated to security, I have tried to add some best practices and simple strategies for securing your applications. Having said that, readers should seek out more research and resources dedicated to Web security and not treat this book as a comprehensive treatment of the subject.

At the same time, because the three main barriers to entry mentioned earlier have not changed much—configuration issues, conceptual explanations, and accessible entry into these scripting languages—the needs of readers and therefore the goals of the book have not changed much, and much of the text, exercises, and explanations have not changed substantially from earlier editions.

This decision to preserve a successful formula also means that if you have already completed an earlier edition of this book with earlier technologies, you probably don't need to buy or work through this book again. You should be ready to move on to books more specialized in the language(s) in which you are interested in working (ASP, ColdFusion, or PHP). Challenge yourself! You are beyond the transitional phase.

Adobe Training From The Source

The Adobe Training from the Source series is developed in association with Adobe, and reviewed by the product support teams. Ideal for active learners, the books in the Training from the Source series offer hands-on instruction designed to provide you with a solid grounding in the program's fundamentals. If you learn best by doing, this is the series for you. Each Training from the Source title is designed to teach the techniques that you need to create sophisticated professional-level projects. Each book includes a CD-ROM that contains all the files used in the lessons, completed projects for comparison and more.

Adobe Authorized Training and Certification

This book is geared to enable you to study at your own pace with content from the source. Other training options exist through the Adobe Authorized Training Partner program. Get up to speed in a matter of days with task-oriented courses taught by Adobe Certified Instructors. Or learn on your own with interactive, online training from Adobe University. All of these sources of training will prepare you to become a Adobe Certified Developer.

For more information about authorized training and certification, check out www.macromedia.com/go/training1

What You Will Learn

You will develop the skills you need to create and maintain your own Web sites as you work through these lessons.

By the end of the course, you will be able to:

- Update an existing site so that it uses maintainable, standards-compliant XHTML and CSS code

- Understand the limitations of the HTTP protocol, and how ASP, ColdFusion, and PHP work with it to enable Web applications

- Pass data between pages and make data persist over time, using form, querystring/URL, cookie, session, and application variables

- Collect and process information entered by users via Web forms

- Validate data entered into forms using both client-side (JavaScript) and server-side (ASP, ColdFusion, or PHP) code

- Write code to evaluate expressions and perform simple mathematical calculations

- Connect your Web site to a database, so that it displays database contents

- Filter data retrieved from a database

- Build search interfaces that enable users to access only the information they need

- Authenticate users and restrict access to pages

- Build content management systems that enable site owners to maintain Web content using Web forms, rather than HTML editors and FTP

- Hand-code common ASP, ColdFusion, and PHP scripts that you can reuse in future projects

- Learn core SQL statements, enabling you to build pages that interact with data in sophisticated ways

- Control the flow of scripts, using conditional statements and loops

- Work with Dreamweaver's server behaviors, Recordset dialog, and pre-built application objects to rapidly develop dynamic Web applications

Minimum System Requirements: Windows

- Adobe Dreamweaver CS3 (A 30-day trial version is available at http://www.adobe.com/downloads/.)

- Intel Pentium III processor or equivalent 800+ MHz

- Windows 2000 or Windows XP (Windows XP Pro recommended)

- 256MB RAM

- Firefox 1.0 or Internet Explorer 6.0

- Internet access (for Lesson 5 only)

- Access to a server capable of processing the desired application language, as follows:

  - ASP/VBScript users must have access to Microsoft Internet Information Services (IIS). IIS comes bundled with Windows 2000 and Windows XP Professional, so you can run it on your local system. Alternatively, you can connect to an IIS server over a network or over the Web via FTP.

  - ColdFusion users must have access to the ColdFusion application server in addition to a Web server, such as IIS, Apache, or ColdFusion's own standalone server. A single IP developer's edition of ColdFusion can be downloaded for free from http://www.adobe.com/downloads/.

  - PHP users must have access to a Web server, such as the open source Apache Web server, with the PHP module loaded. It is possible to run PHP in an IIS environment, though Apache is recommended for PHP. PHP on Apache can be run locally on Windows 2000 or Windows XP Pro. A PHP/MySQL installer for Windows is included on the CD.

Minimum System Requirements: Macintosh

- Adobe Dreamweaver CS3 (A 30-day trial version is available at http://www.adobe.com/downloads/.)

- 600 MHz Power Mac G3 Processor

- Mac OS 10.3 or 10.4

- 128 MB computer RAM (256 MB recommended)

- Firefox 1.0, Safari 1.0, or Netscape 6.0 or higher

- Internet access (for Lesson 5 only)

- Access to a server capable of processing the desired application language, as follows:

  - ASP/VBScript users must have network or Internet access to a Microsoft Internet Information Services (IIS) Web server. IIS and ASP cannot be run locally from a Macintosh.

  - ColdFusion users must have access to a ColdFusion server. You can connect to a ColdFusion-enabled server over a network or over the Internet. You can also run ColdFusion locally as a standalone server on the Mac. A single IP developer's edition of ColdFusion can be downloaded for free from http://www.adobe.com/downloads/.

  - PHP users must have access to a PHP-enabled Web server, such as the open source Apache. You can connect to a PHP-enabled Apache server over a network or over the Internet. In addition, Mac users can now run Apache with PHP locally, without having to connect to a separate server over a network or the Internet. A PHP/MySQL installer for Macintosh is included on the CD.

What You Will Learn

In this lesson, you will:

- Define a static site in Dreamweaver
- Work in the Dreamweaver environment to create and lay out a new page of content
- Explore the existing HTML code
- Learn about the client's needs
- Explore the completed project as it appears at the end of the book
- Outline a strategy for upgrading the site

Approximate Time

This lesson takes approximately 60 minutes to complete.

Lesson Files

Starting Files:

Lesson01/Start/newland/about.html
Lesson01/Start/newland/contact_text.txt
Lesson01/Start/newland/index.html
Lesson01/Start/newland/profiles.html
Lesson01/Start/newland/tours.html

Completed Files:

Lesson01/Complete/newland/contact.html

LESSON 1

Introducing Newland Tours

Compared to other established media—novels, TV dramas, radio pop music countdowns—the Web is young. Like all new media forms, it is constantly changing. These changes often mean that established Web sites need reworking. For example, many organizations are replacing attractive Web presence sites, that is, sites that establish a static presence on the Internet but do little else, with interactive sites that inform, entertain, sell merchandise, organize activists, and so on.

The home page of the Newland Tours site looks good enough, but certain parts of it, such as the weekly Traveler's Journal column (at right) require a lot of work to maintain.

Web designers and developers today increasingly face a different set of problems than they did a few years ago.

- Rather than creating brand-new sites, today's designers and developers need to maintain existing sites in the face of changing standards, new technologies, and evolving content.

- Modern Web sites should respond to users' needs, which often means that Web sites must react on-the-fly to user interaction.

- Web sites now not only serve as one-off interactions between a single customer-user and an organization; many now serve as virtual community spaces, such as newgrounds.com (amateur Flash animators), dailykos.com (political community), and whatifsports.com (fantasy sports community).

- Today's designers and developers often need to build content or workflow management systems, which facilitate the movement of site content maintenance from IT departments to non-technical business users by creating Web forms that post content.

Needs such as these raise a series of practical questions. What is the fastest way to update the look or structure of a site? How can one design a site so that a nontechnical content expert can contribute to it? How does one develop a site that customizes itself to the needs and interests of the user? How does one form a community out of the collection of visitors that come to the site? And finally, how does one accomplish all these goals at the same time?

In response to these issues, a whole new series of technology solutions have appeared as solutions to Web development problems: cascading style sheets (CSS), Adobe ColdFusion, ASP, SQL, database servers, XHTML, DHTML, XML, Web services, ADO, CDO, JavaScript, Flash, PHP, Java, .NET, XSLT, Ajax and more. Web development software, such as Adobe Dreamweaver CS3, has kept up so that developers can create sites using any of the technologies just mentioned. But for the HTML jockey of yesteryear, this onslaught of technical solutions may seem as problematic as the problems they purport to solve.

Increasingly, mastering many of these technologies is part of the core skill set of today's Web developers. The goal of this book is to set you well on your way to that mastery. The central project transforms a static Web site into an interactive, easy to maintain, and standards-compliant site. The site is for a fictional travel tour operator called Newland Tours. By the time you are done, site visitors will be able to get to the content they need quickly and easily. In addition, the non-technical users who own the site will be able to update it without having to know any HTML. These are ambitious but attainable goals; and thanks to Dreamweaver's tools and environment, they are easier to achieve than you might think.

In this lesson, you will get familiar with the book's starting and ending points. You'll open the site as it exists today within Dreamweaver. The first task will be to create a new page; imagine that before you start overhauling the site, the client needs you to create a missing page immediately. With this crisis resolved, you'll go over the site's shortcomings. These shortcomings can be divided into two categories: technical shortcomings, such as accessibility problems and underutilized stylistic features; and business shortcomings, where the site no longer meets the needs of its business. Finally, you'll hop onto the Web and see the completed version of the site.

Defining a Static Site

The Newland Tours site, as you are inheriting it, is a static HTML site. For this reason, you can easily pull it into Dreamweaver and start working on it.

Working with Web sites often involves hundreds or even thousands of individual files, including Web pages, images, cascading style sheets, multimedia assets, and more. These files are linked together via HTML. Unfortunately, a small typo can create ugly (or indecipherable to users) error messages and even block access to portions of your site. Dreamweaver provides many sophisticated site management tools to help ensure the overall integrity of your site, both during development and once it is launched. To take advantage of these features, you should first define a site, a process in which, at a minimum, you tell Dreamweaver where the site's root folder is located on your hard drive.

Defining a site has several benefits, many of which you will see quickly. It helps prevent broken links, automatically updating files site-wide if you move or rename a file. The Site Manager also enables you to perform site-wide operations, such as Find and Replace, which greatly boosts productivity. Another key advantage of the Site Manager is that it has built-in file uploading capabilities (including FTP), which means you can publish your files to the Web whenever you want, with the click of a single button. You can even synchronize local files (on your hard drive) and remote files (on the Web or a staging server), to ensure that the most up-to-date versions of the files are in the right place.

In this task, you'll define a regular, static site in the Site Definition dialog box, a process involving little more than giving the site a name and telling Dreamweaver where it is stored on the local disk. In a few lessons, once you've made appropriate preparations, you'll return to this dialog box and define a dynamic site. Dynamic site definition is a little more involved, and the additional overhead won't do us any good at this early stage. Fortunately, you can always change a site definition, so we've nothing to lose by defining a static site for now and getting right to work.

1 Create a new directory on your hard disk called dwcs3da.

You'll store the local version of the site in this folder.

2 Copy the newland folder (and its contents), found in the Lesson01/Start folder on the CD-ROM, into this new directory.

Often enough in real life, you'll inherit an existing site and be asked to upgrade it. With any significant upgrade, it's best to make a copy of the existing site and work on that. You should never directly edit a site in production (that is, the site that the public sees).

3 Open Dreamweaver CS3.

Once the files are visible in Dreamweaver, you should edit them exclusively in Dreamweaver. Any text editor can open any HTML file, and every operating system has a file-management utility (such as Macintosh Finder or Windows Explorer) that lets you move and delete files. But you should avoid using these tools, because any change is likely to foil Dreamweaver's Site Manager, and could cause broken links.

4 On the Start page, click the Create New Dreamweaver Site link.

✹ NOTE: You can also choose Site > Manage Sites and click the New button.

Though the files are on your hard disk, Dreamweaver doesn't yet see them. By defining a site, you enable Dreamweaver to see—and manage—the files. You define a site in the Site Definition dialog box. If the dialog you see doesn't look like the one in the screen shot, it's probably because you are in advanced view. Click the Basic tab near the top of the dialog to bring up the basic view shown in the screen shot.

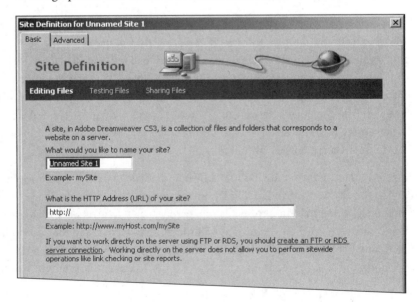

5 Enter *Newland Tours* in answer to the question "What would you like to name your site?", and click Next. There is no need to fill in the HTTP Address of the site at this time.

The Site Definition dialog's basic view uses a wizard-like approach.

▶ **TIP:** If you prefer the old-style Site Definition dialog better, you can access it by clicking the Advanced tab.

6 On the Editing Files, Part 2 screen, select "No, I do not want to use a server technology." Click Next.

Later in the book you will use a server technology. But by choosing No now, you get to skip several complex steps.

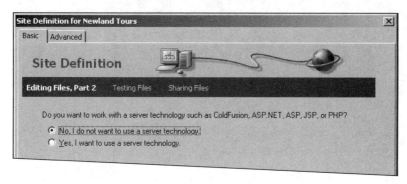

7 On the next screen, select the first option, "Edit local copies on my machine, then upload to server when ready (recommended)."

As a result of this decision, there will always be two sets of files for the site—one local (usually on your hard drive, though you can put it in a network folder if you want) and one remote (usually on a server). This is safer, because you always have at least one backup copy of your file. More importantly, it means that the files you work on will be stored on your hard drive, where customers will never see them.

Most professional sites work using a 3-tier setup. The local site contains all the files in development on the Dreamweaver user's hard drive. A staging server contains a mirror of the site used for testing and development purposes only. The public never sees content on the staging server, but it is a real Web server environment, which is typically identical or nearly identical to that of the production server. The production server is the public version of the site. Only tested, edited, polished, and approved files should be published on the production server.

8 Click the folder icon beside "Where on your computer do you want to store your files", and browse to the newland folder within the dwcs3da folder. Click Select to select the folder and return to the Site Definition dialog box. Click Next.

In this step you are defining the local site—this is where all the action takes place. Whenever you edit a file, you will be editing the file as it appears in the local site. The local site is generally not seen by the public, which means if you temporarily break the functionality of the site as you work, no harm is done.

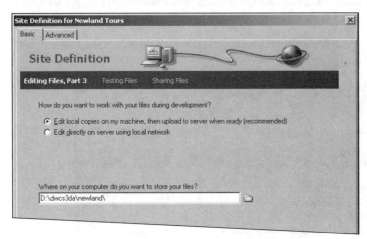

9 On the next screen, choose None in the drop-down menu.

Normally, you specify either a staging server or production server as the Remote site. When working with dynamic, database-driven content, a staging server is a necessity.

Later in the book, you will define a remote site, which you will use as a staging server. That staging server will be able to handle fully dynamic sites, which the local site you are defining can't do—as you'll see later. But for now, a remote site is an unnecessary complication.

✱ **NOTE:** There is no production server for the site you are building in this book because Newland Tours is fictional.

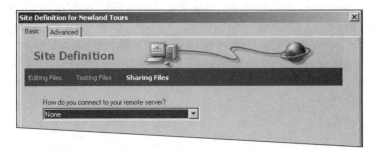

10 Click Next. Review the summary, and click Done.

When you are finished, a dialog box appears, indicating that Dreamweaver is building the site cache. Dreamweaver is analyzing all the files in the site, checking all the links, and storing them in memory. If you decide to rename a page or move an asset to a different folder, Dreamweaver will automatically update all of the files that link to the modified file. Once Dreamweaver has built the site cache, the dialog disappears on its own.

When you are finished, the Site panel (by default, in the lower-right corner of your screen) should be filled with files.

Creating the Contact Us Page

As is often the case with Web projects, before you can dig in and overhaul the Newland Tours site, you must address a more pressing need: the site's Contact Us page is missing and needs to be re-created.

This exercise is mainly intended as a crash course/quick review in the basics of creating and editing Web pages in Dreamweaver. If you are already comfortable with developing static pages in Dreamweaver, you can skip this exercise—the final result is on the CD in this chapter's Complete folder, as well as all subsequent chapters' Start folders. If you do skip this exercise, begin reading again several sections ahead, at *Assessing the Site: The Code*.

This quick exercise is only intended to give you a basis for working in the Dreamweaver environment. It is not intended as a comprehensive guide for developing static Web sites using Dreamweaver. For that, see *Adobe Dreamweaver CS3: Classroom in a Book* (Adobe Press) or *Adobe Dreamweaver CS3: Visual QuickStart Guide* (Adobe Press/Peachpit).

1 In the Files panel, double-click contact_text.txt to open the file in Dreamweaver. If the Files panel is not visible, choose Window > Files to show it.

As you can guess from the contents, this file contains all the text that needs to go on the Contact Us page.

This is a plain text file and not an HTML document. It doesn't contain any HTML tags, and though it appears formatted in Dreamweaver, if you were to view it in a browser, all the formatting would be lost and it would be collapsed into a single, large paragraph. The reason for the collapse is that browsers disregard white space—paragraph returns, spaces (beyond the first space used to separate words), and tabs. To create white space in a page displayed in a browser, you use HTML tags, such as the paragraph (<p>) tag. In the next few steps, you'll make a copy of an existing page in the site (about.html) and replace its contents with the contents of this file, format the contents using HTML, and save the page as contact.html.

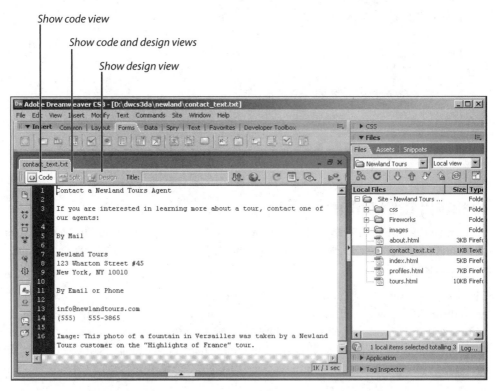

Notice that on the View toolbar, the Code button is selected, and the two buttons beside it, Split and Design, are grayed out. Because the document lacks any HTML, Dreamweaver can't open it in design view. You'll switch back and forth between code and design views often in this book.

2 Click anywhere in the text, and choose Edit > Select All. Choose Edit > Copy to place all the text on the clipboard.

The text is now ready to dump in the destination document—only you don't have a destination document just yet.

3 In the Files panel, double-click about.html to open it. If necessary, click the Design button to see the page rendered, as opposed to its code.

You'll use this page as a guide for creating the new page.

4 Choose File > Save As, and name the file contact.html.

You are about to modify this version of about.html. To ensure that you don't overwrite the original version, make a copy by using Save As and giving it a new name.

Each of the pages has a button in its navigation bar called Contact An Agent. Clicking that button loads contact.html, which until this moment didn't exist.

5 Drag to select everything from About Newland Tours down to and including the image caption. Press the Delete key.

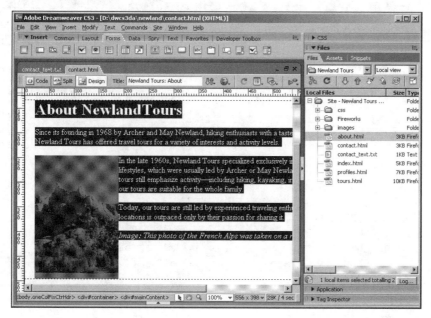

This content is unique to about.html. You'll replace it with the content on the clipboard.

After you press the Delete key, you'll notice that the image, which was placed inline with the rest of the text, is also deleted.

6   With the cursor blinking in the main (and now blank) content area of the page, switch into code and design views (henceforth referred to as split view), by clicking the Split button.

By working in both modes simultaneously, you can design visually and ensure that Dreamweaver writes the code the way you expect it to.

Notice that in code view, the cursor is located inside an <h1> tag. The <h1> tag tells the browser to render the enclosed contents using a Level 1 Heading. Below the document window, in the Property inspector, notice that the Format drop-down menu displays Heading 1. In other words, the Property inspector is showing what you've just seen in code view: the insertion point is formatted as a Level 1 Heading. If you paste in the contents on the clipboard now, all the content will be formatted as Level 1 Headings.

We will format the page title as a Level 1 Heading, but a more sensible choice for the body text would be the regular paragraph format, indicated by the <p> tag.

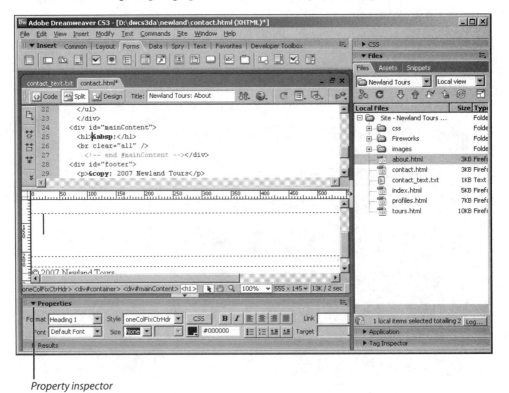

Property inspector

7   In the Format drop-down menu of the Property inspector, choose Paragraph.

In code view, notice that the <h1></h1> tags have been replaced with <p></p> tags. Now if you paste the contents on the clipboard, they'll be formatted as regular paragraphs.

8 If a   character entity appears between the <p></p> tags in code view, select and delete it.

This code acts as a placeholder and was put there by Dreamweaver when you deleted the original page contents.

```
22      </ul>
23      </div>
24   <div id="mainContent">
25      <p> </p>
26      <br clear="all" />
27      <!-- end #mainContent --></div>
```

9 With the cursor between the <p> and the </p> tags in the code half of the window, click in the design half of the window then choose Edit > Paste.

The text from contact_text.txt is pasted in, and is formatted the way it was in the original file. If you compare the text and code in design and code views, you'll see that Dreamweaver has automatically inserted line break characters (<br />) and paragraph tags to create the appearance of paragraph breaks, and converted quotation marks to their character entity ". If you had pasted in the code half of the window, there would have been no formatting and you would have had to manually insert the paragraph tags and line breaks.

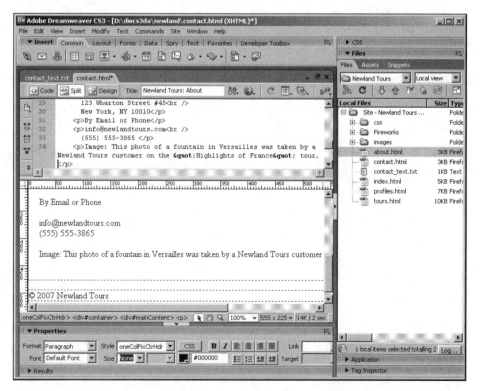

The content is in the new page but you have one last step before you're ready to finish formatting The page title still indicates that we are on the About page. This is easily remedied.

10 Select About in the Title field located at the top of the code window. Change it to *Contact an Agent.*

The title should now read Newland Tours: Contact an Agent.

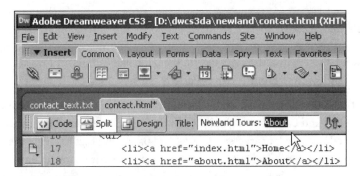

Formatting the Contact Us Page

While Dreamweaver did most of the formatting for you when you pasted the text into the design window, in this task, you'll finish formatting the text using some of Dreamweaver's layout features.

1 In design view, position the insertion point anywhere within the first paragraph, Contact a Newland Tours Agent. In the Property inspector's Format menu, choose Heading 1.

Notice that the page heading now looks like a page heading. In code view, you'll see that the <p> tag has been replaced with an <h1> tag for that paragraph.

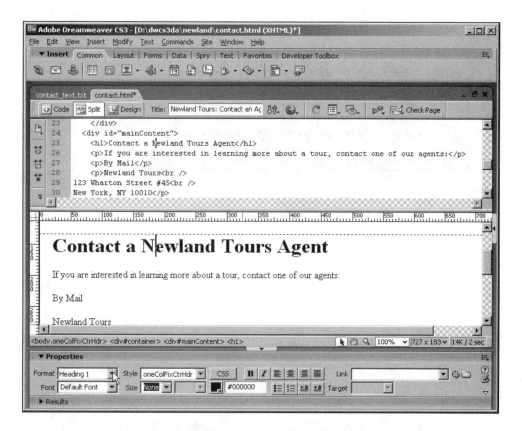

2 In design view, position the cursor just before If you are interested, and click the Insert Image button from the Common category of the Insert bar.

Images are inserted inline with the HTML and text that surrounds them, so it is important to choose the insertion point carefully.

Notice that beside the Insert Images button is a small arrow, indicating a drop-down menu. Clicking the arrow reveals many other image-related assets that you can insert from this menu, including image placeholders, interactive Fireworks HTML/images, rollovers, hotspots, and more. You won't use these features in this book, but be aware that they are there. Several other buttons in the Insert bar hide similar commands.

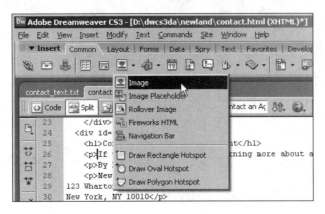

3 In the Select Image Source dialog, browse to fountain_versailles.jpg, in the site's images folder. Click OK.

In addition to enabling you to browse to the image, so Dreamweaver can write the correct path to it from contact.html, this dialog contains several other features and options. These include an image preview, information about the size and dimensions of the image, and options regarding the type of link, document or site root relative (it defaults to document relative, which is what you want).

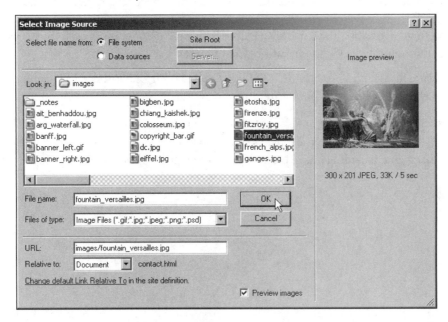

At the top of the dialog, there is an option, Select File Name From. Your choices are File system (that is, you browse to the file on your computer) or Data sources (that is, you dynamically pull the URL from a database); you'll work extensively with both approaches throughout the book. In this step, verify that File system is selected.

After you click OK, a dialog appears requesting accessibility information.

4 In the Alternate text field, type the following, *This photo of a fountain in Versailles was taken by a Newland Tours customer on the "Highlights of France" tour.* Leave the Long description field blank, and click OK.

In order to ensure that every element in your site, including images, is accessible to people with disabilities such as visual impairments, you need to insert a description of each image. This reminder dialog, which appears whenever you insert an image, was introduced in Dreamweaver 8. We will address the other images on the site in Lesson 2.

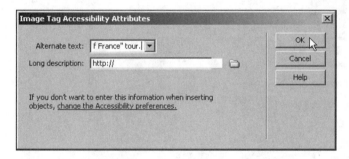

5 With the image selected on the page, use the Property inspector to change the image's Align setting to Left.

The default setting usually causes the image to render to the left of one line of text, with all other text wrapping beneath the image. The result is a considerable amount of wasted page space. By choosing Left (or its opposite, Right), the image is rendered so that text wraps around it.

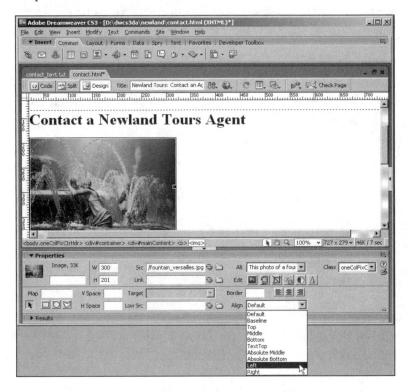

> ✱ **NOTE:** To make the screen shots easier to understand, I may occasionally switch among code, split, and design views. However, you should remain in split view throughout the book as your default view.

Expand Property inspector

> ✱ **NOTE:** If you do not see the Align setting drop-down menu in the Property inspector you may need to expand the panel.

6 Position the insertion point before the words By Mail, and click the Insert Table button from the Insert bar.

In this step, you are preparing to insert a table, which will hold information on how users can contact Newland Tours. While tables are no longer considered the best method for page layout, they are still appropriate for tabular data.

In the next steps, you will create a simple table that presents street address, email address, and phone number in a two-column format.

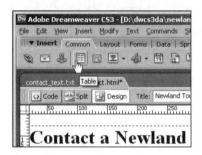

7 In the Insert Table dialog, specify 2 Rows, 2 Columns, a Table width of 400 pixels, a Border thickness of 1, Cell padding of 3, and Cell spacing of 0. In the Accessibility section, enter *Newland Tours contact information* as the Summary. Click OK.

These settings will result in a four-cell table that is 400 pixels wide. Cell padding measures the space between cell borders and cell contents. Cell spacing measures the distance between cells. When you fill out the Summary information, Dreamweaver adds a summary attribute to the <table> tag that screen readers use to give vision-impaired users a quick glance at what the table contains.

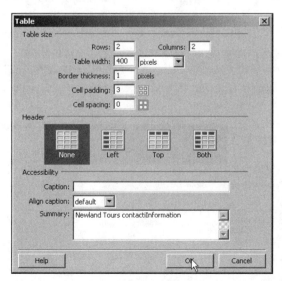

8 Triple-click the words By Mail to select the paragraph. Drag the selected paragraph (just those two words) into the top-left cell of the table. Likewise, triple-click to select and then drag the words By Email or Phone into the top-right cell. Use the same technique to move the paragraph with the mailing address into the lower-left cell, and the paragraph with the email and phone information into the lower-right cell.

Dreamweaver moves both the text blocks and all the enclosing tags into the appropriate cells.

The table is now complete. All that remains is to remove the superfluous white space below the table (if applicable), and to format the caption using italics.

9 Position the insertion point before Image: This photo…, and press Backspace (Windows) or Delete (Macintosh) as many times as necessary until the image caption appears just below the table.

The additional spaces are a relic of removing the original address paragraphs and placing them in the table. If you look in the code before you complete this step, you'll see a series of <p> </p> blocks. This is how Dreamweaver creates empty paragraphs. Modern browsers will not recognize opening and closing <p></p> tags with nothing in them. Dreamweaver therefore enters a space character as an empty placeholder. Because HTML ignores whitespace in code, Dreamweaver enters the character entity for the space character: , which stands for non-breaking space.

10 Triple-click anywhere in the caption line, and once it's selected, use the Property inspector to apply italics.

Italics help distinguish the caption from regular body text.

11 Save and close contact.html. Close contact_text.txt.

You are done designing the new page. In the real world, you would now publish the page to a Web server, but instead, you can turn your attention toward the more ambitious task of reworking the site.

Assessing the Site: The Code

In this task, you won't make any changes to the files; rather, you'll customize the Dreamweaver environment to make it more friendly to the kind of work we'll be doing, and then you'll explore the code in the index page of the start files so you can learn about its shortcomings.

These shortcomings will not show up at all if you view the page in a browser. That is, the page should look just fine in most major browsers. If the page looks fine in a browser, you might wonder how could the code have any shortcomings? The answer is that the starting code in this project is outdated and noncompliant with recent standards. We'll explore the significance of code and standards at the end of this task.

Often a Web redesign project will begin with outdated, noncompliant code, so you might as well learn how to spot it. Later, you'll learn how to fix it.

1 Double-click index.html in your file window to open it.

Depending on whether you did the Contact Us exercise, you may be viewing the document in design view (if you did not do the exercise) or split view (if you did do the exercise).

Back in the late 1990s, when the HTML editor market was crowded with editors that either did code well and design badly, or vice versa, the introduction of Dreamweaver, which excelled at both, was revolutionary. Many designers, knowing that Dreamweaver was writing clean HTML in the background, were content to design sites in design view and never worry too much about the code. But working exclusively in design view is a luxury of the past. If you are serious about Web development, and need to develop data-base-driven Web content, you have to get involved with the code.

2 If necessary, click the Split button.

Split view is a best-of-both-worlds feature. It gives you access to the code, so you can hand-edit code when necessary, even while it leaves the traditional design view open, which makes some kinds of edits, such as edits to body text, much easier than working in code view.

Show code and design views (split view)

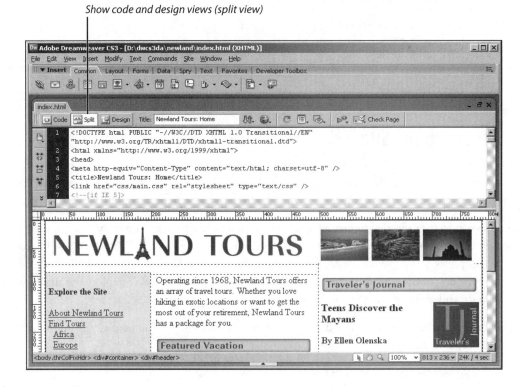

Split view is indispensable for working with dynamic sites. While Dreamweaver enables you to accomplish many tasks using wizard-based server behaviors and its built-in visual SQL builder, you still need to edit code directly. You'll also find that some edits are much faster in code view than they are in design view. Yet another benefit is that it will teach you code. While I assume if you are reading this book, you are familiar with HTML, you may have forgotten some of the details; for example, you might not remember all of the attributes of a given tag. Split view will help you master HTML. From now on (and for all your future projects), make split view your default view and avoid using either code view or design view alone unless you have a specific reason to do so. If that's the case, when done, remember to switch back to split view.

All of the problems specified in the subsequent steps in this task are revealed only in code view—they are all invisible in design view. Split view is already paying dividends.

TIP: Another benefit of working in split view is that you can easily find a piece of code in code view by clicking its corresponding object in design view. For example, to see the code for a given image, click the image. All of the relevant HTML will be centered in the window and highlighted in code view. This is especially helpful in pages with hundreds of lines of code.

Code automatically highlighted and centered

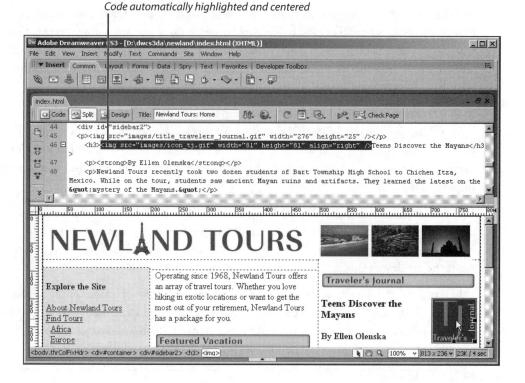

3 If necessary, turn on line numbering in code view by choosing View > Code View Options > Line Numbers.

✳ **NOTE:** You can also toggle line numbering on by clicking the Line Numbers button in the Coding toolbar running vertically down the left side of code view.

This setting displays line numbering beside the code in the code section of your screen. Line numbering makes it easier to communicate about portions of code to others. (I'll make use of line numbering quite often in this book.) It also makes troubleshooting much easier, because when they encounter problems, ASP, ColdFusion, and PHP send back error messages that specify the line number of the code that caused the problem.

4 Check for compliance with accepted accessibility practices.

For years many Web developers didn't address the needs of those with impairments that interfere with their ability to use sites. For example, users with visual impairments, which prevent them from seeing the site, had no way to access a site's content. Given that much of a site's content is text, a special kind of browser, called a screen reader, was developed that reads Web page content aloud. One problem with these readers, though, is that they have no way to articulate visual content, such as graphics. If these graphics communicate any important information about the site—and most graphics do—then users accessing sites using screen readers were missing out.

A simple way to enable screen readers to articulate all of the information on your page is to add text captions to describe the contents of images. If you put in a description of each image, including both graphics of substance (such as diagrams) and those used for mere decoration or even spacing, then users will never have to wonder if they're missing important information

You can accomplish this in code by adding an attribute to each image element that associates a text string with that image. The attribute in question is `alt`. To use it, you'd add `alt="A description of the image"` to each `<img>` tag in the document. The screen reader reads the `alt` description aloud and the user has access to the content.

When you scroll to line 26 of the current document, you'll see two images in the header div. These images are the Newland Tours banner and a single graphic holding three photos (the beach, forest, and mosque). As you can see, their `alt` attributes are missing, which means these images are inaccessible to users accessing the page with screen readers.

```
24   <div id="container">
25     <div id="header">
26       <img src="images/banner_left.gif" width="451" height="68" /><img src="images/banner_right.jpg"
     width="276" height="68" id="bannerRight" />
27       <!-- end #header --></div>
```

✱ **NOTE:** Adding the Image `alt` attribute is not the only accessibility concern. For example, to make pages accessible, you might add shortcuts at the top of the page that enable users to skip over navigation bars to the page content. Another code feature that undermines accessibility is the abuse of HTML tables. While there is nothing intrinsically inaccessible about HTML tables, their overuse breaks up content and may make it hard for a screen reader to present your page's content in a logical sequence.

The overriding goal of accessibility is to ensure that all users have equivalent access to all of your content. An extended discussion of accessibility is beyond the scope of this book, but you can learn more about it at Adobe's Web site: http://www.adobe.com/accessibility/

5 In the design half of split view, click anywhere in the text Explore the Site and look at the corresponding markup. Likewise, click anywhere in Teens Discover the Mayans and look at its markup.

The blandness of the text formatting is readily apparent. These pages use default browser styles for all the text! For most browsers, all text is in black Times New Roman, except for hyperlinks, which are the default blue (unvisited) and purple (visited). By relying on the defaults in this way, Newland Tours is unable to communicate its brand stylistically.

As a Web developer, you know that CSS makes it quick and simple to add stylistic flair to an entire site, while making it easier to maintain as a bonus. In the next chapter, you will create a CSS and apply it to this site.

Assessing the Site: Business Processes

Most Web redesign jobs occur because the current site no longer fits the business needs of the site owner. Common examples of a mismatch between the business needs and the site are as follows:

- The navigation is confusing. Site users can't find what they are looking for.

- Updating the site is too difficult. Many small businesses don't have large IT departments that can update their sites. A small-business owner may need to update site content, but lack the knowledge and tools to do so. The site begins to fall behind the business, or the business has to spend disproportionate money to pay for IT human resources.

- The look is outdated. Graphic design, like fashion, goes through cycles, and what was cutting-edge a few years ago may look stale today. An outmoded look communicates the wrong message to the business's target constituencies.

- The business wants to migrate certain services to the Web that are currently handled through other resources. Many clients want their sites to provide sufficient information to the public to decrease the number of phone calls coming in. For example, many companies deploy Web Knowledge Bases to decrease technical-support calls, while others provide online pricing and sales to decrease sales calls and/or to provide 24-hour service without hiring a whole night crew.

- The business is expanding or changing its offerings. If a business offers a whole new class of products or services, the Web site needs to reflect that. In such situations, adding a paragraph or two to an existing page isn't going to cut it. The site needs many new pages, requiring a new site map, navigation system, and so on.

This list, obviously, is not exhaustive, but it illustrates some of the relationships that exist between business processes and Web sites. In most cases, the client wants a site upgrade for many of these kinds of reasons. Ultimately, it is this information that should drive the entire site-revision process. It should enable you and your client to identify the scope of the upgrade, as well as each of the particulars about what you should do.

> **TIP:** Take the time to get this information from the client. Some clients are a little lazy about defining what they want. If you don't prompt them for more information, the site you deliver may not meet their needs. Do not expect them at that point to be self-critical enough to recognize that they were not sufficiently forthcoming: The burden is on you to work out all of this up front.

In this task, you'll take a guided tour of the site as it exists. Along the way, I'll role-play the client and point out some of the shortcomings of the site. In this way, this task represents meeting with the client and identifying how the site is out of sync with business needs and processes. As these problems are identified, solutions—the specific changes and enhancements that you need to make to the site—begin to materialize. This way, the primary force driving the site upgrade process is the needs of the client, and not something else, such as your own opinion about what the site could be or, as is too often the case, the hottest technology on the market.

1 Still viewing index.html, press F12 to open the site in a browser. Look over the main home page.

The F12 shortcut automatically opens the active file in a browser. You need to use this shortcut often, given that what the browser displays often varies from what you see in Dreamweaver, especially when you are working on dynamic content. The F12 shortcut is one of the most used keyboard shortcuts in all of Dreamweaver.

Traveler's Journal column

Graphically, the site design is not bad. The client is not intending to overhaul the look. This particular design is also used in several print advertisements, so the client wants the site to reinforce that branding. As we've already seen, the typography needs improving, and we'll use CSS to do that.

Aside from the design, the page has a significant practical problem. The column entitled "Traveler's Journal" needs to be updated about once a week. Sometimes the business owners update this column, other times travel agents update the column. Not everyone knows how to work with the code or upload the files to the site. In addition, the owner does not want to give out the password to enable people to upload new pages. Currently, the journal is written in a word processor and handed off to a travel agent who is able to revise and upload the pages. But this bottleneck prevents the site from being updated promptly, especially when that agent is busy or not in the office. The client would like to find a way to make the weekly posting of the Traveler's Journal easy enough for everyone to contribute to it, without compromising security.

2 In the navigation bar on the left side of the screen, click the About Newland Tours link.

Beyond the font issues, discussed previously, this page doesn't need to change. Its content is almost never changed, and the client is happy with it as-is. Aside from applying CSS styles to it, this is one page you won't change at all.

3 In the navigation bar at the top of the screen, click Find Tours. Scroll up and down the page, or use the internal navigation links near the top, to look over the tours.

This page is problematic in many different ways.

Let's start with the problems that the client faces with a page like this. Once again, the page is hard to maintain, because Newland Tours doesn't have an IT department. This issue is a serious problem from the client's point of view, because the content on this page is the primary source of information users have about the tours. The business problem that the client faces is that the tours change—some get added, some get removed. Worse, prices fluctuate so often that the client decided not to post them at the site, given the difficulty of keeping them up to date and the consequences if they were not. In addition, Newland Tours offers several more tours than listed here, but no one has had the opportunity to add them. This means that the client may be losing business, thanks to the difficulty of maintaining the Web site.

From the user's standpoint, the page is not very usable. It is extremely long, and it is hard to find tours of interest. There is no way to filter tours, other than checking out the tours listed in a particular region. For example, Newland Tours offers some tours that are exercise-intensive and others that are not; users have no way to filter out only those that are exercise-intensive. And, of course, the fact that the prices aren't listed doesn't give the users any way of knowing how much the tours cost, unless they make a phone call.

As developers, we should observe that much of the information on this page is structurally redundant. That is, every tour has a title, an image, a description, and so on. Such a predictable structure should make us think that this information would be better stored in a database and pulled in on the fly. This would simplify maintenance and create the possibility of filtering, which would enhance the page's usability.

4 In the navigation bar at the top of the page, click the Country Profiles button.

Almost every problem identified on the previous page also exists here. The page is hard to maintain, making it hard for Newland Tours staff to add countries to where they now offer tours. Users may incorrectly assume that Newland Tours doesn't offer any tours to, say, Italy, because it's not on this list. But since Newland Tours does offer a tour to Italy, the Web site is sending a counter-productive message to its users.

The problem also persists for users. Few users will want to learn about all of the countries that Newland Tours serves; they'll just want to see the ones they are interested in. Again, a simple filtering mechanism would make all the difference.

Another usability issue is that to go from a tour about Namibia's Etosha National Park to the Namibia country profile, the user has to scroll back up to the navigation bar, click Country Profiles, and scroll down to Namibia. It would be nice to automatically link from the Etosha National Park information to the Namibia country profile. But that would require extra coding using static HTML.

5 Return to the navigation bar, and click the Contact an Agent link.

This is the file that you developed earlier in the lesson to replace a version that was lost.

This simple table doesn't change very often, and it's easy enough to use. One thing about this page that the client doesn't like is that the email address appears on the page: About a week after the page was posted with this email address, spammers started flooding the account with weight loss, debt reduction, and other less savory messages.

Another problem is that some of Newland Tours' customers don't have email clients automatically configured or were confused when the email client opened.

The client would like some way for customers to be able to contact Newland Tours without having to rely on an email client configuration. Also, the client would like to find a way to discourage spammers from flooding the accounts with junk.

The solution, of course, is to use a Web form. A form is perfect because it demands very little of the user, and it is possible to hide the email address, which will prevent spam bots (automated programs that crawl the Web "harvesting" email addresses for spammers) from finding Newland Tours agents' email addresses. Forms also make it possible to send the email address to a different address depending on its contents. For example, if a form asks the user to select a region, you can create a script that sends an email of the form data only to the agent specializing in that region. You won't create that functionality in the course of this book, but by the time you are done, you should certainly have the wherewithal to do it.

A Glimpse of the Future

Though this lesson has yielded only a static Web page to show for itself, you have actually done more than you may realize, and you have worked through a step that is too often short-changed, with disastrous consequences. You've conducted a thorough assessment of the site, including code, business processes, and (indirectly) usability. You have a clear idea about what you need to do. For convenience, here is a summary of the site upgrade project goals:

- Improve site accessibility and usability

- Use CSS to improve site-wide visual style

- Store structured and/or frequently updated content in a database

- Provide search and/or filtering mechanisms to enable users to find tours and country profiles more easily

- Develop a Web form that enables users to contact Newland Tours staff, without having to use email

- Develop a series of Web forms that enable Newland Tours staff to add, update, and delete content stored in the database (remember that the content stored in the database is also the source material that appears on the Web site)

If some of this sounds a bit abstract, look at the final version of the site as it will appear at the end of the book.

1 Point your browser to http://www.bobflynn.info/books/DWCS3DA/final/.

The index page should look almost the same as the version you just opened in Dreamweaver. However, it is quite different behind the scenes. For example, the Traveler's Journal column is actually retrieved and formatted on the fly from a database. In addition, the text is formatted more nicely on this version of the page.

2 Click the Find Tours link in the navigation bar on the left side.

Instead of seeing the Find Tours page, as you expected, you are interrupted with a log-in screen. The previous site obviously had no such functionality. This was added because the client wanted users to register before accessing the site so the client has a way of learning about customers, as well as contacting them with offers and promotions. You can log in using the following credentials:

Email address: osiris@allectomedia.com

Password: osiris

✱ **NOTE:** This is a fictional account created for the purpose of giving readers access to the site without having to register. There is no such account, so please don't send email to it.

✱ **NOTE:** Once you authenticate, you are sent to the page you requested earlier.

3 Explore the site as much as you like.

At this point, I'll turn you loose and let you explore on your own. You will see that the site offers several methods of filtering content, linking to related content (from tours to country profile, for example), and even a price calculator utility.

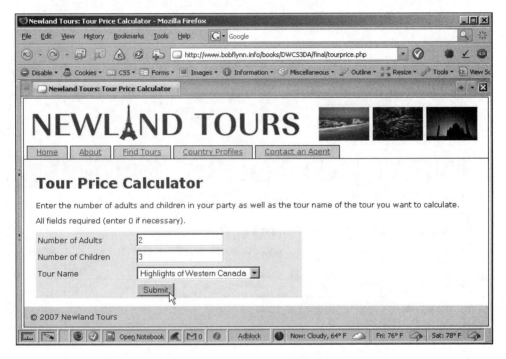

You'll notice that the Admin section is off-limits to the osiris@allectomedia.com account. As you'll see later, that section contains the content management system—that is, the Web forms that enable Newland Tours staff to update site content.

The accompanying screen shot shows one of these forms. Using this form, the staff can create a new Traveler's Journal entry just by filling out the form, following the directions that appear onscreen. As soon as the staff member clicks Submit, the database entry is added, and the staff member is redirected to the site's home page, where she or he will discover that the Traveler's Journal has already been updated on the public Web site in the split second between the time the Submit button was clicked and the index page was loaded.

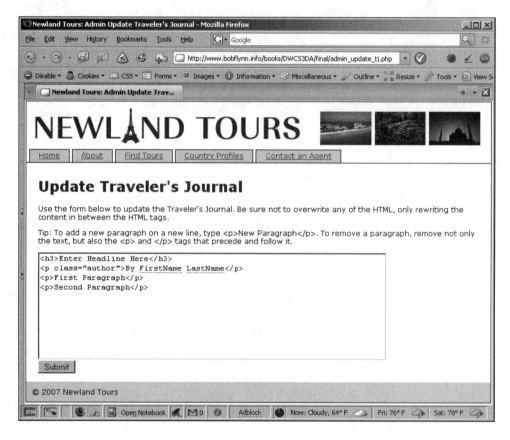

What You Have Learned

In this lesson, you have:

- Defined a static site in Dreamweaver (pages 5–9)

- Created a basic static page (pages 9–14)

- Formatted a page (pages 14–21)

- Assessed the existing code and identified several problems with it (pages 21–25)

- Compared the client's business needs with the current site and identified several short-comings (pages 25–32)

- Plotted out several site enhancements that will make it a better fit for the client's needs (pages 32–36)

- Previewed some of these enhancements, to get a better sense of what you'll be doing for the rest of the book (pages 32–36)

What You Will Learn

In this lesson, you will:

- Use Find and Replace to automate the process of ensuring that all images have alt descriptions

- Create and apply CSS styles to the site

- Build a reusable template for all new pages added to the site

- Enhance each page's accessibility with a hidden navigation element

Approximate Time

This lesson takes approximately 75 minutes to complete.

Lesson Files

Starting Files:

Lesson02/Start/newland/about.html
Lesson02/Start/newland/contact.html
Lesson02/Start/newland/index.html
Lesson02/Start/newland/profiles.html
Lesson02/Start/newland/tours.html
Lesson02/Start/newland/css/main.css

Completed Files:

Lesson02/Complete/newland/about.html
Lesson02/Complete/newland/contact.html
Lesson02/Complete/newland/index.html
Lesson02/Complete/newland/generic_ template.html
Lesson02/Complete/newland/profiles.html
Lesson02/Complete/newland/tours.html
Lesson02/Complete/newland/css/main.css

LESSON 2

Preparing the Static HTML and CSS

In the past, when designers were developing static HTML pages, they would often copy and paste several pages of plain text into Dreamweaver, and then go about the task of marking it up to make it presentable. In other words, roughing out the content preceded much of the design work, which came only at the end of the process.

That workflow is turned on its head when working with dynamic Web sites. The content that users see when they visit your site is often added to the HTML pages in the split second between the request for the page and its appearance in the browser. That means that you have to create your designs with placeholder content. In the dynamic Web site development workflow, then, you deal with design and presentation issues up front, and let the server model (ASP, Adobe ColdFusion, PHP, etc.) pour the right content into it.

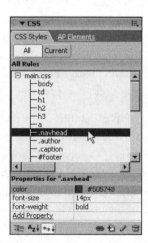

Use the improved CSS Styles panel to manage all your CSS styles, whether they're redefined HTML tags or custom CSS selectors.

After completing this lesson's tasks, you'll have specified nearly all of the stylistic and design information used in the Newland site. A few issues will come up during the application development stages—they always do—but by and large you'll nail down the main graphic design decisions by the end of this lesson. You'll begin by enhancing the accessibility of the site, by ensuring that all images have alternate descriptions (**alt** attributes). Next, you'll create and apply a Cascading Style Sheet, which controls most of the presentation issues in the site. Finally, you'll create an all-purpose page template that you can use as the basis for any new pages that you'll need to add to the site.

Automating Changes with Find and Replace

For years, HTML coders manually coded every aspect of every page, from the content to its formatting. This was tedious work, and error-prone to boot. One of the goals of this book is to show you how to leverage the power of Dreamweaver and server technologies to do much of the work for you, empowering you to create much more ambitious sites. One of the easiest ways to introduce automation into your workflow is to take advantage of Dreamweaver's Find and Replace dialog.

Word processor users are probably familiar with the Find and Replace function. Using a simple dialog, you specify the string that needs replacing and the string to replace it with. At its core, Dreamweaver's Find and Replace function works the same way. But Web sites are different from word processor documents—site content is spread out across files, strings can be either document text or document code, and so on. Dreamweaver's Find and Replace dialog offers a host of options that enable you to customize the tasks in ways that result in unbelievable productivity gains. Unfortunately, many Dreamweaver users don't realize how flexible the Find and Replace dialog is. For example, Find and Replace would be an ideal solution for changing a navigation bar sitewide, dealing with a company name change (e.g., a law firm that adds a new partner), or updating the address in every page's footer.

In this exercise, you'll sample some of its capabilities. The problem you need to address is the fact that most of the images in the site lack **alt** attributes, effectively making them inaccessible to a significant number of potential users. To solve this problem, you need to identify which <img> tags lack an **alt** attribute, and then you need to create **alt** attributes for these tags and supply the description for their corresponding images. Complicating the problem is the fact that images are dispersed across all of the images in the site.

This change is also hard to automate, since every image should have a different alt attribute. You'll use Find and Replace a couple of different ways in this task. First, you'll use it to add alt text to the four images that make up the banner on all of the pages. Second, you'll use it to find the remaining images that are lacking the alt attribute.

1 Open index.html.

2 Click the Eiffel Tower to select the left half of the Newland Tours banner in design view. Its corresponding HTML should be highlighted in code view. Right-click (Windows) or Control-click (Macintosh) over the highlighted code, and choose Copy from the context menu.

This method is about the fastest way that you can get the code for a given object onto the clipboard, which makes it convenient for pasting into the Find and Replace dialog or reusing on other pages. It works not just for images, but also for other objects, from image maps to Adobe Flash movies.

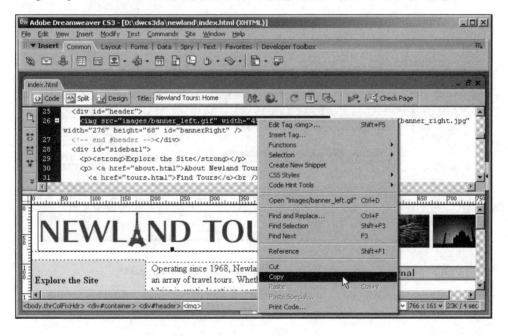

3 Press Ctrl+F (Windows) or Command+F (Macintosh) to open the Find and Replace dialog, remove any existing text (from previous searches) in the upper text area, and, if necessary, paste in the HTML code for the image.

Dreamweaver makes it possible to select the type of text string, whether HTML code, document text, or specific tags, for which you want to look. Since you were in code view when you activated the Find and Replace dialog, it defaulted to Source Code in the Search drop-down

▶ **TIP:** You can resize the Find and Replace dialog to accommodate long text strings.

4 In the Find In drop-down, select Entire Current Local Site. In the Search drop-down, select, if necessary, Source Code.

Dreamweaver is capable of performing a given find and replace operation throughout an entire site, rather than merely in the current open file(s). As a result, site-wide changes are quite fast and easy.

5 Paste the same HTML code in the Replace With (lower) text area. Somewhere inside the tag, add the following text: alt="Newland Tours Banner, Left."

The order of the attributes doesn't matter. Just make sure that the attribute is typed in lowercase and that the attribute's value is in quotation marks.

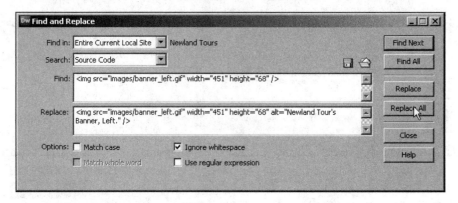

6 Click Replace All, and click Yes when the warning dialog appears.

The alt tag has now been updated for the left side of the banner throughout the site.

Dreamweaver automatically opens the Results panel with the Search tab activated to show you the matches for your search. Five matches are listed, one on each of the five pages in the site. The red underline indicates matched text.

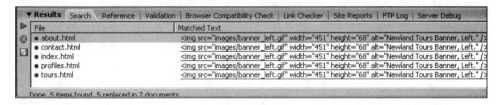

7 Repeat the preceding steps for the right-hand graphic on the banner (the three photos). The alt tag should read as follows: alt="Newland Tours Banner, Right." Click Replace All.

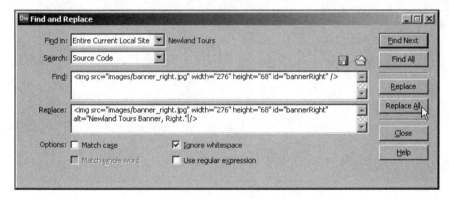

Both halves of the banner now have alt attributes in all five of the site's HTML documents.

> **TIP:** You can close the Results panel and recover screen space by right-clicking (Windows) or Control-clicking (Macintosh) the word Results and choosing Close panel group from the context menu.

The next step is to identify the remaining graphics that don't have an alt attribute. None of the remaining images appears on multiple pages, so you can't automate the replacement process with Find and Replace. Fortunately, you can automate the finding process, which will make it easy for you to identify the pictures still needing alt attributes.

8 Open Find and Replace again, verify Entire Current Local Site is selected, and choose Specific Tag from the Search drop-down menu. Choose img from the HTML Tag List drop-down menu. A new row for additional search criteria appears automatically, and it defaults to With Attribute. Change that to Without Attribute, and choose alt from the next drop-down menu. Don't worry about the Action row.

These settings tell Dreamweaver to find all instances of images that do not have an alt attribute. This should make it easy to ensure that you find all of the images without alt attributes. You don't need to specify anything in the action row, because you are taking no action. You are not replacing anything. You are simply using Dreamweaver tools to find tags that meet a certain criterion.

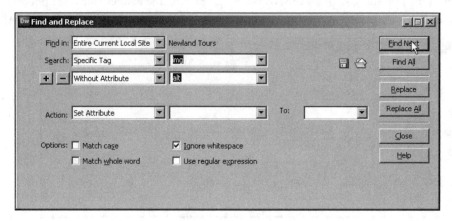

9 Press Find Next.

You will be taken automatically to an image without an alt tag. Which one you are taken to depends on the location of your cursor when you initiated the search.

10 Add alt attributes to each of the images you find on all of the pages except tours.html and profiles.html. Several of the images have captions or descriptive text embedded in them, so use those as a guide.

It doesn't matter all that much what you enter, so long as it is descriptive and conveys textually what the image conveys visually.

The reason you don't need to enter alt attributes on tours.html and profiles.html is that these pages will be upgraded to dynamic pages later in the book.

Caption   Corresponding alt attribute

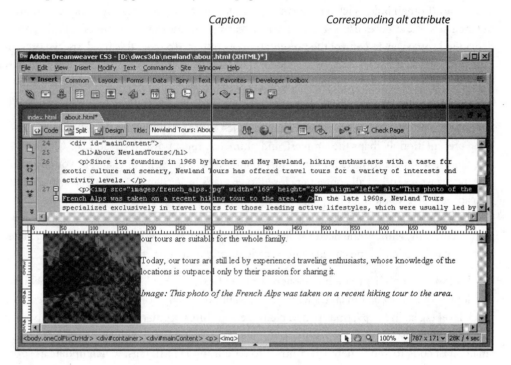

11 Save and close any open files.

Redefining HTML Elements with CSS

One of the advantages of HTML is that it includes a wide range of logical tags, flexible enough to describe the content of most basic documents. With its six built-in levels of heading (<h1>, <h2>, <h3>, and so on); tags for regular text (<p>); lists (<ol> and <ul>) and list items (<li>); tables (<table>, <tr>, <td>); block quotes (<blockquote>); address (<address>) tags and more, you can mark up documents quickly and in such a way that the tags actually describe the content and structure of the document. In addition, browsers recognize these styles and know how to render them. For example, content in the <h1> tag is large and bold with extra space above and below it, while content inside <p> tags is rendered in a normal body font, such as a 12-point system font.

Because every page relies on the browser for rendering, it might seem that all HTML pages would look the same. For example, every Level 1 Heading on the Internet might be in 18 point Times New Roman bold. Such a uniform appearance prevents organizations from differentiating themselves and bores users. For this reason, early on in the development of HTML, coders demanded some way to control the presentation of content. To meet this need, special presentation tags, such as the <font> tag, were added to the standard. The <font> tag has since fallen out of favor, largely because it is inefficient. It requires developers to add special formatting attributes to each and every paragraph that needs to diverge from the standard browser template.

With the emergence of CSS, developers have a much more powerful and flexible way of handling presentation. Perhaps the simplest, and ultimately most powerful, feature of CSS is that you can use it to tell browsers how to render standard HTML tags. For example, you can specify that the browser renders all content enclosed in <p> tags in Verdana 12 point black, and all Level 2 Headings as Verdana 16 point purple bold. What makes this so useful is that you specify these directions in one place, and every single <p> tag and <h2> tag in your site is automatically formatted correctly, without the need for any additional code. Further, if you make a change later to this small bit of code, the change will cascade throughout your entire site instantly.

In addition to the ability to define the appearance of existing HTML tags, CSS also enables developers to create custom styles which can be applied to any portion of text, whether it's a block level tag such as <p>, or a span of characters within a regular paragraph. The only catch to using these custom styles is that not only must you define them, you also have to add a small bit of code to apply them (in contrast to redefining HTML tags, which update as soon as you save the style). Conveniently, Dreamweaver enables you to apply custom CSS styles without having to type out the code manually, unless you want to.

Style rules are generally applied to three types of **selectors** — type (the HTML tags themselves), id (elements that are unique to a page or site) and class (elements that are used repeatedly). You will work with examples of all three.

The pages you have been working with already have a number of these custom styles defined for basic page layout and navigation. These styles are contained in an external style sheet that is attached to each of the site's pages. These positioning styles were generated using some of Dreamweaver CS3's built-in CSS page templates. A wide assortment of templates can be found in the New Document window (File > New). While you will work with this style sheet extensively in this lesson, an in-depth examination of the styles used for page layout is beyond the scope of this book.

The benefit of storing styles in an external style sheet is that multiple pages in the site can reference that same file, which means that a change made to the external file instantly affects every page that refers to it (which in the Newland Tours site will be every page in the site).

In the first task, you will create a series of CSS styles that redefine the most common HTML tags used in the site (type selectors). When you are finished, you will have formatted the vast majority of the text for the site—as it stands now and as it will stand at the end of the book. In the next task, you will create and apply custom styles, which will take care of some of the remaining needs (id and class selectors). Others will be added at appropriate times in the book. But for now, let's redefine the HTML elements to give the site the Newland Tours look.

1 Open index.html and choose Window > CSS Styles to open the CSS Styles panel (if necessary). Click the All button, if necessary.

You create and (in some cases) apply styles using the CSS panel. You can also access the same commands and any custom CSS classes from the Property inspector.

The CSS Styles panel displays styles applied to the selected tag (whatever your cursor happens to be in) or for the whole site, depending on whether the Current or All button is selected. You want to define some sitewide styles, so you need to have the All button selected.

The CSS Style buttons at the bottom of the panel are sometimes grayed out, unless you select the style name.

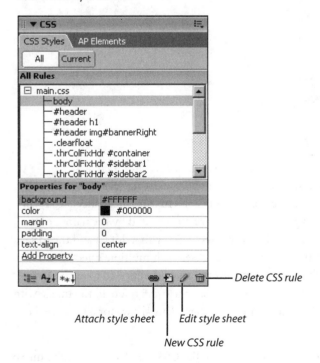

While your site's pages will use a single style sheet for its screen formatting styles, it is not uncommon to attach a second sheet to format the page for printing. A print style sheet can reformat the content to make it printer friendly. This site's tours.html page would be a good candidate for a print style sheet if the company wanted customers to treat it as a quick fact sheet of their tours.

The CSS panel has its own Properties window where it displays the individual properties applied to the chosen selector. It is one way to add to or edit the styles of individual selectors.

2 Expand the Properties window in the CSS panel if it is not already visible. Your cursor will turn to a double-headed arrow when you mouse over the Properties heading. Click and drag to resize the panel.

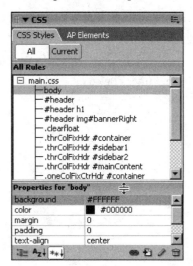

Our style sheet is called main.css. You can see a list of its existing selectors in the All Rules window. All three flavors of selectors already exist in this spreadsheet. You will either edit or add to each. The type selector rules are represented by the names of the HTML elements they will affect. The class selectors begin with a dot (.) and the id selectors begin with a # symbol. In the list you will see cases with multiple selectors for one set of style rules. #header h1, for example, means the rules are applied to any <h1> tag inside an element with id="header". #header img#bannerRight refers to the image with id="bannerRight" inside the element with id="header". This allows for a great deal of specificity when it is needed.

3 Select the body selector in the All Rules window of the CSS panel and click the Edit Style (pencil) icon at the bottom of the panel.

In this step, you are preparing to redefine the <body> tag. Since a type selector already exists for that tag we will edit its existing rules. If you look at its various categories you will see values such as background and text color already in place.

4 In the CSS Rule Definition for body in main.css dialog, in the Type category, select Verdana, Arial, Helvetica, sans-serif from the Font drop-down menu, and 12 pixels from the Size drop-down menu. Click OK.

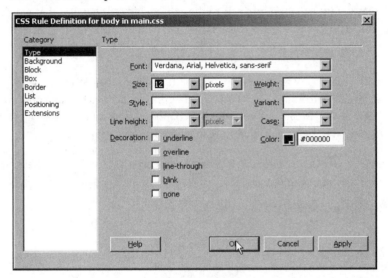

The text on index.html immediately updates to reflect the new style.

In this step, you are creating a default text setting for all of the text on the page. How does this work, since generally all text inside the <body> tag is also inside another set of tags, such as <p> or <h1>? The answer revolves around the concept of inheritance. Tags nested inside other tags inherit (theoretically) the styles of their parent tags. Since all page content appears within the <body> tags, all page content should inherit the CSS style information from those tags.

Does this mean that text inside an <h1> tag will now be formatted using 12 pixel Verdana? No, because browsers have a default set of formatting instructions for the <h1> tag. Where this formatting information conflicts with the formatting information in the <body> tag, it overrides it. Whether (and which) formatting is overridden is determined based on the order of precedence. In general, the closer a tag is to the text, the more heavily weighted are its formatting attributes. Since the content in an <h1> element is closer to the <h1> tags than it is to the <body> tags, the <h1> formatting takes precedence.

That's the theory, anyway. But browsers don't uniformly respect this CSS hierarchy, and sometimes formatting attributes get ignored when they shouldn't be. In practice you often have to define more information than you should have to in theory.

Due to varying implementations of CSS across browsers, you may discover with enough testing that regardless of the size you specify for the <body> tag, a browser may disregard it. The reason this happens is that some browsers ignore body formatting information if it conflicts with formatting information intrinsic to the <td> (table cell) tag. In other words, the formatting of the <td> tags in some browsers may override the size you specified in the <body> tag. But this is not a major problem: To fix it, you just need to redefine the <td> tag.

❋ NOTE: Whenever you create a new style, Dreamweaver actually opens the CSS file in the background. This enables you to edit your CSS file directly. Consider it also a learning opportunity: Look at the CSS code that Dreamweaver writes. Try changing some values or adding new properties. Use Dreamweaver's code hints to ensure that you get the syntax right.

5 Click New CSS Style, verify that the type is Tag, and Define in is set to main.css. Select td from the Tag drop-down menu, and click OK.

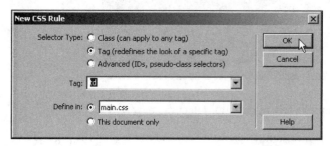

6 In the CSS Style Definition for td in main.css dialog, in the Type category select Verdana, Arial, Helvetica, sans serif as the font and 12 pixels as the size. Click OK to create the new style.

These are the same settings you associated with the <body> tag, and no change is visible in Dreamweaver, but you've added some insurance for older browsers. In Netscape 4.x, for example, text inside a <td> tag for some odd reason doesn't inherit the formatting from the <body> tag. This is a bug, of course, but a bug that millions of users likely still experience. You circumvent it with this step.

We need to redefine several more HTML styles using CSS, but index.html doesn't actually have that many styles, so in the next step, you'll open a different file.

7 Save and close index.html. Open tours.html.

This more structured document makes use of <h1>, <h2>, and <h3> tags as well as some plain-looking <a> elements. Let's spruce them up with some color.

8 Click the New CSS Rule button, and make the appropriate settings to redefine the h1 element, saving it in main.css. Once in the CSS Site Definition dialog, set the size to 24 pixels; the weight to bold; and the color to #505748. Click OK.

You should be getting comfortable creating style definitions at this point. The only new thing here is that you are specifying a color. You can click the color box to choose a color from a pop-up, or you can enter the color value directly.

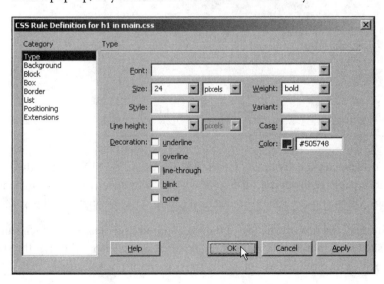

▶ **TIP:** Another way to select a color is to pick it up from somewhere else onscreen. To do so, click the color box pop-up, and then click with the eyedropper tool anywhere onscreen, and Dreamweaver will select that color. In this step, if you click any of the letters in the Newland Tours banner, the correct color value should appear automatically.

9 Redefine the <h2> tag using the following settings: Size = 20 pixels; Weight = bold; Color = #646482.

Look at the continent names on the page to see the results. They should appear dark purple.

10 Redefine the <h3> tag using the following settings: Size = 16 pixels; Weight = bold.

On the tours.html page, this setting affects the tour names. You'll probably notice little difference. We only redefine this HTML style to ensure it fits in consistently with the two headings you just defined.

11 Redefine the <a> tag using the following settings: Decoration = Underline; Color = #447832.

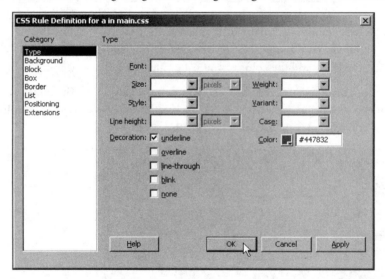

You probably know you can specify link colors in the <body> tag in HTML (or in the Dreamweaver Modify > Page Properties dialog). But, again, why specify the same information on every page, when you can specify it once in a CSS and have it apply to all pages?

When you are finished, the links at the top of the page should become green, which suits the color of the site better than the default blue color. The CSS Styles panel shows the six styles you have created or modified as well as the styles used for positioning.

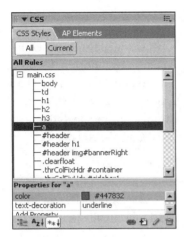

12 Save and close tours.html.

We are done redefining the main HTML tags used in the site. We have yet to create our custom styles—that's covered in the next section.

Take a quick look at the contents of the pages to verify that the styles have indeed been applied. If you are successful, not only will you see that the text is in Verdana and in the appropriate color, but you'll also see a series of styles listed in the CSS Styles panel.

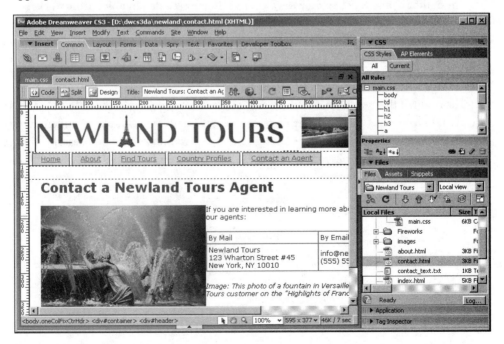

Creating and Applying Custom CSS Styles

By providing presentation specifications for HTML styles, you have quickly formatted the vast majority of your site, both as it stands now and as you will develop it during this book. Better yet, you've also optimized the site for maintenance, since to update the look of the site, you need only change the CSS file. You can do this using Dreamweaver's CSS Styles panel from any page in the site, and the settings update instantly throughout the site. If the site is already loaded on a server, all you need to upload is the updated CSS file; you do not need to re-upload each of the pages.

The only drawback to what you have done so far is that you've been limited to redefining the look of pre-existing HTML styles. You haven't created custom styles for text elements that aren't part of the HTML specification. For example, there is an author byline in the Traveler's Journal of the index page, but HTML has no <author_byline> tag. In this task, you will learn how to create and apply custom styles using class and id selectors.

1 Open index.html. Make sure you can see the Traveler's Journal section at the right side of the page.

The Traveler's Journal section is composed of three parts: a title, an author byline, and the body text of the article. The title is enclosed in a heading, and the body text is marked up in <p> tags, so in both cases the HTML markup represents the content reasonably well. The author byline is not so easy to categorize. It's represented in bold, using the <strong> tag. However, the author byline is bolded not because it is stronger, or more emphatic, than the surrounding text, but because it performs another function; it gives credit to the author. Again, since HTML doesn't have an <author_byline> tag, this is a good opportunity to create a custom CSS style.

The result of this new style, which we will call .author, will merely add bold to the element to which it is attached (in this case, a <p> tag), and it won't look any different in a browser than it does now. But making this change will make the code describe the text a little more meaningfully, and will make it easier to maintain across the site. You'll also see the concept of inheritance in action again.

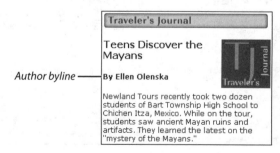

Author byline

2 Click New CSS Rule. In the New CSS Rule dialog, select Class in the Selector Type group, and verify that main.css is still specified in the Define in group. In the Name field, type .author. Click OK.

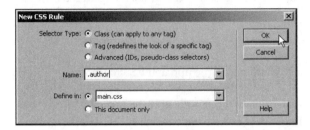

These settings should, at this point, all make sense to you, with one exception. Remember that class selector names begin with a dot (.). Class selectors do not redefine an HTML tag in its own right, as in "all <p> tags should look like XYZ," but rather they define an element (or elements) subordinate to an HTML tag. One practical application of this is that you can use a class to specify the appearance of some <p> tags, but not all of them. That makes sense in this particular case—only some paragraphs should be designated as author paragraphs.

Another benefit to classes is that they can be applied to different HTML elements. For example, not only could you apply the .author class to any <p> tag, but you could also apply it to a <span> or <div> tag.

3 In the CSS Rule Definition dialog, set the weight to bold and click OK.

You don't need to specify any other information here, such as the font face or size, because that information is already specified in a parent tag (in this case, the <body> tag). So all we need the style to do is inherit all of that presentation information and add bolding.

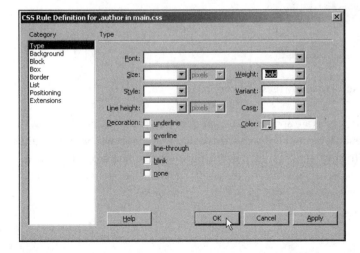

4 Create a new class called .navhead with the following settings: Size = 14 pixels; Weight = bold; Color = #505748.

This style will be used as the navigation header at the top of the navigation bar in the left-hand column of index.html.

5 Create a new class called .caption with the lone attribute of Style = italic.

This style will be used for all of the image captions used in the site. Currently, they are formatted using <em>, which most browsers render as italics. Again, .caption better describes that content than <em>, and creating this style gives us precise control over the presentation of all the captions in the site (or will, once we apply the style).

At this point, your CSS Styles panel should display the new style selectors you created, as well as the rules used for page layout that were in our starting file. You can organize the styles by clicking and dragging them up or down in the list.

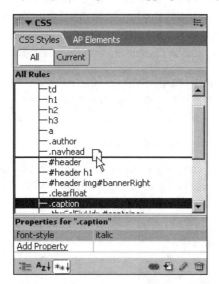

The next step, of course, is to apply these custom styles.

✳ **NOTE:** The order in which styles are applied is an important part of using CSS effectively. The order of your styles shouldn't be random, because rules lower in the list will be applied after rules higher in the list. The higher rules should define the most common properties, while the rules lower in the list can be applied to more specific situations. For examples and more information see http://www.w3.org/TR/REC-CSS1#cascading-order.

6 Back on the index.html page, click once anywhere in the Explore the Site text at the top of the navigation bar. Right-click (Windows) or Control-click (Macintosh) the <strong> tag in the tag selector at the bottom of the design window and choose Remove Tag from the context menu.

In this step, you are stripping the <strong> tag out of the code. It's no longer needed, since the .navhead class you created has bold already built in.

Make sure you are clicking in the tag selector, not in the text on the page.

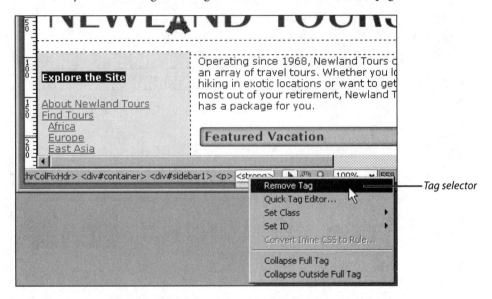

Tag selector

> **TIP:** The tag selector is a very useful tool for specifying which tag you want to affect in a Dreamweaver operation. One of the challenges when working with a graphical program to edit HTML code is that it is often hard to tell the editor which element in a group of nested elements you want to affect. For example, if you want to add background color to a string of text, how does the editor know that you are not actually trying to change the background color of a <td> cell that the string of text happens to be nested in?

> **TIP:** A related problem is getting Dreamweaver to display the version of the Property inspector that you want. Imagine you want to change the cellpadding attribute of a table used for page layout. How can you get the Property inspector to show the settings for the <table> element, rather than the settings for one of the dozens of elements nested inside it? The answer is the tag selector. Click anywhere on the page that's inside the attribute you are trying to affect, and then select the desired tag from the tag selector. The Property inspector shows settings for that tag, and the context menu provides several additional options for modifying it.

7 Click the <p> tag in the tag selector, and then click navhead in the Style drop-down menu in the Property inspector.

Not only does the heading update in design view, but the new style is reflected both in the source and in the tag selector itself.

Class attribute appears in html code

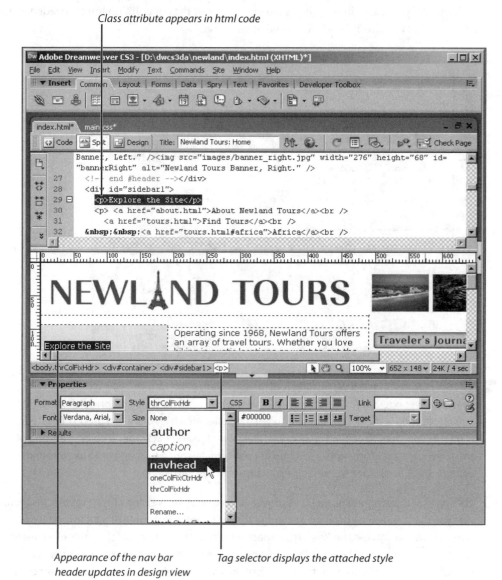

Appearance of the nav bar
header updates in design view

Tag selector displays the attached style

Let's take a moment to look at the code:

```
<p class="navhead">Explore the Site</p>
```

In the previous task, when you redefined HTML tags, the pages updated instantly, and you did not need to update the code. To apply a CSS class, however, you need to change the HTML code. Specifically, you add the class attribute to the desired HTML tag, and list the style name (without the dot) as the value of the attribute. The class is attached to the whole tag, and everything inside it, including text, images, and other tags, is affected by the style.

You cannot, therefore, attach a class to a portion of a tag. For example, if you wanted to attach the navhead style just to the word *Explore*, you could not do so by attaching the style to the `<p>` tag, because the style would be applied to everything else in the tag as well. However, you can get the same effect by creating a new tag around *Explore* and attaching the class to that tag. To do so, you'd use the inline tag `<span>` since it is used to create arbitrary inline containers that you can use to specify a part of a larger element. So, to complete the example, if for some reason you wanted to put just Explore in the .navhead style, the code would look as follows: `<p><span class="navhead">Explore</span> the Site</p>`.

8 Repeat Steps 6 and 7 to remove the `<em>` tag around the image caption beside the picture of the Japanese shrine, and then apply the .caption class to that paragraph.

The display in design view shouldn't change, since the `<em>` tag you are removing is represented with italics, and since the .caption style you are attaching specifies only italics. But you should see the changes reflected in the tag inspector and in the source code itself.

9 Remove the `<strong>` tags around the author byline (By Ellen Olenska), and attach the .author class to that paragraph.

Again, the page appearance won't change, but the class should be reflected in the tag inspector and in the source code.

You've created and applied a number of useful and meaningful classes. You can create classes wherever you need them, whether it's for a single instance in a page or many.

Id selectors serve a similar role but are intended only for unique items on a page. Like a class, ids are represented in the code as the attribute of a tag. Unlike classes, the id attribute is sometimes used in HTML code to give meaningful labels to unique elements in the document regardless of the existence of a corresponding CSS set of styles.

Not only is this practice part of writing good semantic HTML, it lays the groundwork for the future. It's similar to putting in extra conduit for wiring or plumbing when building a house. You may not need it at the time, but the conduits make your installation work easier should you later decide to finish the basement and put in a bathroom. Bear in mind that your pages may ultimately be viewed by more than just conventional web browsers; if your HTML is well-written, it can be more easily transformed for display on mobile devices, kiosks, etc.

10 Scroll to the bottom of the page and click once anywhere on the © 2007 Newland Tours text.

Notice that the `<p>` tag containing that text is inside of a `<div>` tag with an `id="footer"` attribute. You can use the id attribute because the footer is a unique element to the page. The groundwork has been laid in this site's pages for you to easily style the footer by creating an id selector and applying styles to it.

✱ **NOTE:** `<div>` is the block counterpart to `<span>`. Where `<span>` is used to create inline containers to which you assign styles, `<div>` gives you block containers for the same purpose. Inline means the element is in line with the text and pictures. Block elements are those that break the flow of the document, like headers, paragraphs or tables.

11 Click New CSS Rule. In the New CSS Rule dialog, select Advanced in the Selector Type group, and verify that main.css is still specified in the Define in group. In the Name field, type #footer. Click OK.

Id selectors are identified by using # instead of a dot before their name.

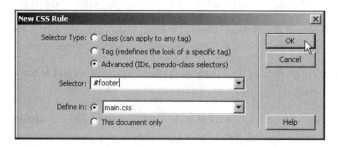

12 In the CSS Rule Definition dialog choose the Background Category and set the Background color = #DDDDDD. In the Box Category uncheck the Same for all checkbox under Padding and set the values to Top = 0, Right = 10 pixels, Bottom = 0, Left = 10 pixels.

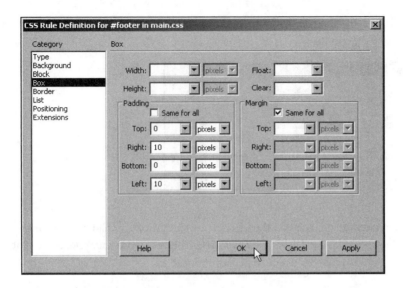

A gray background now appears behind the footer text and the text is pushed off the page margin but it doesn't really establish the footer as the end of the page. In fact, this in one area where CSS–rendering in different browsers can diverge.

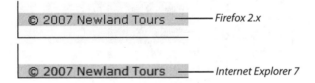

While this difference is subtle, some differences can be quite major. As you incorporate more CSS into your development you will find Dreamweaver a very useful tool not only for creating the styles, but for validating and troubleshooting your code as well. Dreamweaver CS3 includes a tool to check browser compatibility (File > Check Page > Browser Compatibility) and this tool is tied to Adobe's CSS Advisor site (http://www.adobe.com/go/cssadvisor).

CSS selectors can be combined to target specific elements in a document. You will use this technique to style the paragraph and the text contained in the footer. In the process you will also fix the difference in the rendering of the footer background.

13 Click New CSS Rule. In the New CSS Rule dialog, select Advanced in the Selector Type group, and verify that main.css is still specified in the Define in group. In the Name field, type #footer p. Click OK.

This syntax indicates that the rule will only apply to <p> tags contained inside the element with the id="footer" attribute.

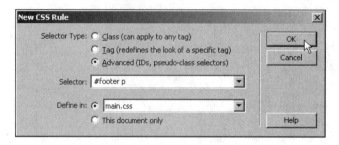

✱ NOTE: This syntax does not indicate that the <p> tag must be the direct child of the footer element, just a descendent at some level. However it is possible to write your selector so that it will only apply to a <p> tag that is a direct child of the footer.

14 In the Box Category uncheck the Same for all checkbox under Padding and set the values to Top = 10 pixels, Right = 0, Bottom = 10 pixels, Left = 0. Leave the Same for all checkbox under Margin checked and put 0 as the sole value.

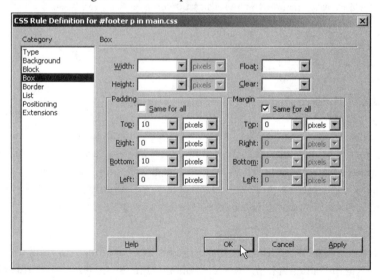

15 Save your changes and press F12 to preview in the browser.

By padding the top and bottom of the paragraph in the footer we are essentially using the content of the footer container to hold up its own walls, or more accurately its floor and ceiling. Your footer has now expanded to fill its space and it renders the same in most browsers.

© 2007 Newland Tours

16 Close index.html.

You've completed the design and presentation of index.html. All changes made to it from this point forward will affect its content and functionality, but not its design.

Of course, the site contains more than index.html. You have changes to make to about. html and contact.html before we move on. You won't need to update the classes on profiles.html or tours.html, because both pages will undergo fairly radical overhauls later in the book, and any effort expended now would be wasted.

17 Open about.html and contact.html, and replace the <em> tags with the .caption class in the captions on those two pages. Save both pages but leave them open for one more step.

The navigation in the interior pages is different than that on the home page. That's not good usability: consistency across a site is more comfortable for users. This issue should eventually be addressed, but you were hired by Newland Tours primarily for program-ming, not a complete redesign. You can add that to the list of recommendations you leave with the client at the end of the current project. Right now we're just going to add a simple bit of styling that will help users recognize where they are in the site. We're going to change the look of the navigation tab for the current page.

18 In about.html click on About in the navigation just under the page banner images.

Before creating a class to hold the styles for this change, let's examine what we are chang-ing. In code view you see that the navigation tabs on these internal pages are no more than an HTML unordered (or bulleted) list. This does not resemble default unordered list behavior though.

```
15    <div id="navigation">
16      <ul>
17        <li><a href="index.html">Home</a></li>
18        <li><a href="about.html">About</a></li>
19        <li><a href="tours.html">Find Tours</a></li>
20        <li><a href="profiles.html">Country Profiles</a></li>
21        <li><a href="contact.html">Contact an Agent</a></li>
22      </ul>
23    </div>
```

The relevant style selector does not jump out at you from the list in the CSS panel. This is another place where the tag selector comes in handy. The tag selector path <body.oneCol-FixCtrHdr> <div#container> <div#navigation> <ul> <li> indicates a list item inside an unordered list inside a div with an id of "navigation". Since ids are unique, this should be enough for us to find the style we are looking for.

19   In the CSS panel click .oneColFixCtrHdr #navigation ul li and examine the properties of this selector.

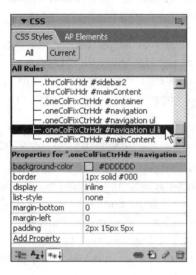

The properties show us how this normal unordered list has been turned into the set of navigation tabs. It is also instructive to look at the properties of the ancestor selectors .oneColFixCtrHdr #navigation ul and .oneColFixCtrHdr #navigation to see what role they play in the overall look of the navigation.

Our task is to simply override some of those style properties on an individual tab basis to create a unique look for the current tab.

20   Click in the About navigation tab and then click <li> in the tag selector. That will select the entire list element. Click New CSS Rule. In the New CSS Rule dialog, select Advanced in the Selector Type group, and verify that main.css is still specified in the Define in group. In the Name field, type .oneColFixCtrHdr #navigation ul li.currentTab. By using the tag selector most of this name should already be entered. Click OK.

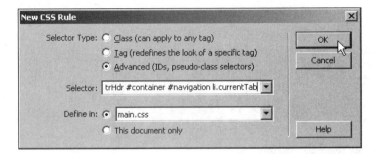

Even though you are creating a class, it is a complex selector so you need to use the Advanced Selector Type.

21 In the Background Category set the background color to #FFFFFF. In the Border Category uncheck all the Same for all checkboxes. Set the following properties for the Bottom only: Style = solid, Width= 1 pixel, Color = #FFFFFF.

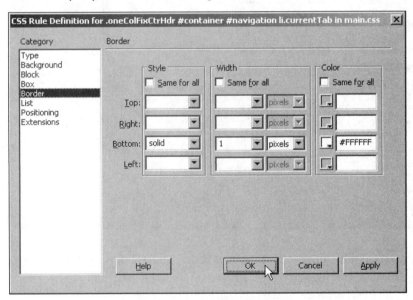

No change will be immediately apparent because, as with the classes we defined earlier in the chapter, this will not take effect until we have attached it to the appropriate HTML tag.

22 Click in the About navigation tab and then click <li> in the tag selector. Choose currentTab from the Style selector in the Properties panel.

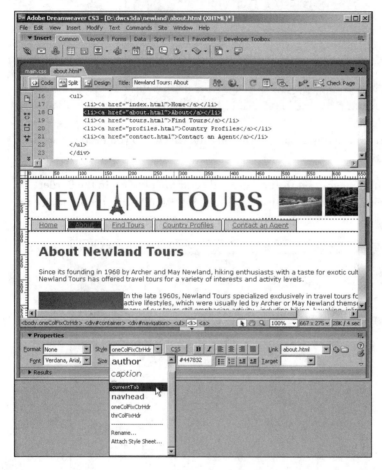

The About tab is now distinctive. This makes it easier for users to recognize the page they are on.

23 Repeat step 21 on contact.html. Click in the Contact an Agent navigation tab and then click <li> in the tag selector. Choose currentTab from the Style selector in the Properties panel. Save your changes and close all open documents.

Creating a Reusable Template

For the most part, the presentation aspect of the Newland Tours site is complete. As I mentioned, minor tweaks and additions will be necessary along the way, but by and large the site design is stable.

Once you reach this point in development, you should usually pause to create a generic site design template for all new files. For example, all of the pages within this site will share the same banner, basic layout, style sheet, and so on. Rather than re-creating all of that every time, if you create a generic page template, you can get straight to work.

In this task, you'll create such a template, which you will use throughout the rest of the book as the basis for all new pages in the site.

Before continuing, it's important to clarify that the template you are about to build is not a Dreamweaver Template file. Dreamweaver Templates enable designers to build page templates and then lock specified regions to prevent users from modifying their content. Other regions remain editable, so users can go in and change the content as needed without undermining the site look or navigation across pages. Dreamweaver Templates is a powerful feature, especially when combined with Adobe Contribute, enabling non-technical content experts to take control over page content and maintenance, while minimizing both their need for Web development skills and the chance that they will mess up the code. However, the word "template" used in this lesson and throughout the book is used in the common sense, not in the specialized sense of the Dreamweaver Templates feature.

1 Open about.html.

To create the template, you'll strip out all of the unique content from one of the pages of your site. Obviously, the fastest way to do that is to begin with the page that has the least unique content. The file about.html is the simplest page in the site, so it's a good place to start.

2 Choose File > Save As and save the file as generic_template.html.

Before you start destroying the content of your file, you should save it under a new name. Sooner or later, if you wait, you'll save over the source file and have to rebuild it from scratch.

3 Click to select the large photo of the French Alps and press Delete. Select the final two paragraphs of body text and the image caption, and press Delete.

All of this content is unique, so it needs to go. We'll deal with the title and the first paragraph of body text in a moment.

You may find that after Dreamweaver removed the content, it left some whitespace. We saw this before when moving the contact information into the table cells. There are empty <p> tags with non-breaking white spaces that can be removed.

4 Select the text About Newland Tours and replace it with *Page Title Goes Here.*

Placeholder text in your templates will make it faster to enter standard content and to ensure consistency across pages: For example, every page should have a title, and this title should be in the redefined <h1> style. By capitalizing each initial word, you remind yourself, or others working on the template, that page titles use initial capitalization.

5 Replace the first paragraph of body text with *Body Text Goes Here.* Press Delete several times, until all of the empty lines beneath the body text are removed.

6 Place your cursor anywhere in the About navigation tab. Click on <li.currentTab> in the tag selector. Remove the currentTab class attribute by changing the Style drop-down in the Properties inspector to None.

The page template should appear as in the screenshot.

7 Save generic_template.html.

Enhancing Accessibility with Invisible Navigation

In creating a page template, you spared yourself the redundant task of reconstructing the basic page content every time you want to create a new page. In this task, you'll extend a similar courtesy to visitors accessing your site via screen readers.

As you know by now, screen readers are browsers that read page contents out loud, so that users with visual impairments can still access the site. The problem is that screen readers start at the beginning of the page and work their way down. This means that visitors using screen readers will have to sit through a description of your navigation bar over and over again as they browse through the site.

In this task, you will implement an easy solution to this problem, using a tiny, invisible graphic and a link. This will enable these visitors to jump straight to the page's main content. And users accessing your site through traditional browsers need never know that this feature exists.

Here's how it works: You will insert a 1-by-1-pixel graphic and add a link to it that skips to the page title on each page. You will place this at the very top of the <body> element, so that it is the first element that a screen reader will encounter.

1 With generic_template.html still open, scroll to about line 10 in the code window. Place your cursor in the blank line between the opening <body> tag and the opening <div id="container"> tag.

```
 7   </head>
 8
 9   <body class="oneColFixCtrHdr">
10   |                                           ———— Insertion point
11   <div id="container">
12     <div id="header">
13       <img src="images/banner_left.gif" width
```

2 Click the Insert Image button in the Insert bar. Browse to spacer.gif in the images folder, and click OK.

The file spacer.gif is only 1-pixel in width and height, making it a fast download. In addition, that pixel is set to 100 percent transparency, so that it is invisible. Though it is invisible, it still has the two features you need most: the ability to add a hyperlink to it, and the ability to add an alt description.

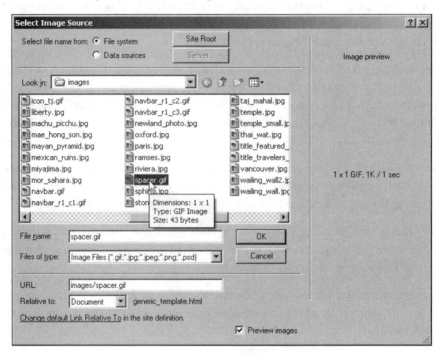

3 In the Alternate text field of the Image Tag Accessibility Attributes dialog that appears, type *Skip to main page content*.

You are using the alt attribute to provide directions to the user.

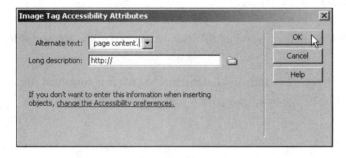

4 Position the insertion point just to the left of the word Page in the page title. Choose Insert > Named Anchor. In the Named Anchor dialog, name it *top*, and click OK.

Dreamweaver inserts the anchor in the code. Depending on your view settings, you may also see a yellow anchor icon beside the page title. This icon is a Dreamweaver visual aid only; it will not appear in a browser. One other visual aid is already on the page, for the image map in the navigation bar.

TIP: You can toggle these icons on or off by checking or unchecking View > Visual Aids > Invisible Elements.

Anchor icon

5 In the code half of split view, click anywhere inside the <img> tag immediately below the opening <body> tag.

While the image will appear for screen readers, you need to ensure the image does not appear in a regular web browser. Because the image is not easily visible and is 1 pixel in size, it is virtually impossible to select in design view, which is why you resort to code view instead.

Notice that when you click inside the <img> tag, the Property inspector updates to show the options for this image.

6 In the Link field of the Property inspector, type *#top* and in the Border field type *0*.

This option creates a link to the named anchor you entered a few minutes ago. If you had not removed the border the image would be highlighted as a link following this step.

You can see in code view that the `<img>` tag is now wrapped inside an `<a>` tag.

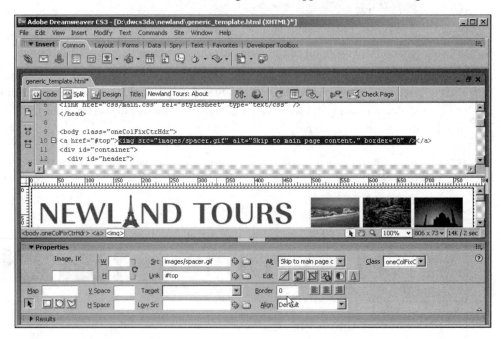

7 Save generic_template.html.

The template is ready to use.

8 In the code half of split view, copy the entire line below the `<body>` tag, which should include both the `<a>` and `<img>` tags that create the accessibility feature.

Though the template is ready for reproduction, the existing pages lack the accessibility feature that you just created. You can replicate it easily enough by pasting this line of code into each of the existing pages and inserting a named anchor at the top of each page.

```
9    <body class="oneColFixCtrHdr">
10 ▪ <a href="#top"><img src="images/spacer.gif" alt="Skip to main page content." border="0" /></a>
11   <div id="container">
12     <div id="header">
13       <img src="images/banner_left.gif" width="451" height="68" alt="Newland Tours Banner, Left." /><img
```

✳ NOTE: The following steps walk you through copying and pasting this line in each of the five existing files. But you should know a better way: If you are up to it, skip the remaining steps and use Find and Replace to update all five of the pages in one try. Also remember to use Find and Replace to insert the anchor tag as well.

9 Open about.html, and in code view, position the cursor between the opening `<body>` tag and the opening `<div id="container">` tag. Choose Edit > Paste.

If you haven't otherwise changed the code near the top of this document, the new code will go in line 10, just as in generic_template.html (and the image above).

This pastes the accessibility spacer graphic into the correct place on the page. Because it is invisible, you won't see it in design view.

10 In design view (or the design half of split view) position the insertion point just to the left of the page title (About Newland Tours), and press Ctrl+Alt+A (Windows) or Command+Option+A (Macintosh) to insert a named anchor. Once again, name it *top*, and click OK.

Obviously, for the link to work, the named anchor needs to be inserted!

11 Repeat Steps 9 and 10 for each of the remaining pages, except index.html.

Index.html has a different structure, so it won't work the same way. If you want to insert the accessibility spacer anyway, go ahead, but it's optional on this page.

What You Have Learned

In this lesson, you have:

- Used Find and Replace to automate changes sitewide (pages 40–45)
- Used Cascading Style Sheets to redefine several HTML tags used in the site (pages 45–53)
- Created custom CSS class, id and complex selectors and used them to apply styles to specific places on the page (pages 54–66)
- Created a generic template that you can use to generate future pages in the site (pages 67–68)
- Added an accessibility spacer image to enable users with screen readers to skip the navigation bar (pages 69–73)

What You Will Learn

In this lesson, you will:

- Learn foundational dynamic site concepts
- Choose a server model (ASP, Adobe ColdFusion, or PHP)
- Configure your computer to run a Web server with a server model (optional)
- Reconfigure the Newland Tours site definition for dynamic Web site production
- Develop a simple dynamic application

Approximate Time

This lesson takes approximately 60 minutes to complete.

Lesson Files

Starting Files:

Lesson03/Start/newland/about.html
Lesson03/Start/newland/contact.html
Lesson03/Start/newland/css/main.css
Lesson03/Start/newland/generic_template.html
Lesson03/Start/newland/index.html
Lesson03/Start/newland/profiles.html
Lesson03/Start/newland/tours.asp

Completed Files:

Lesson03/Complete/newland-asp/about.asp
Lesson03/Complete/newland-asp/contact.asp
Lesson03/Complete/newland-asp/css/main.css
Lesson03/Complete/newland-asp/generic_template.asp
Lesson03/Complete/newland-asp/index.asp
Lesson03/Complete/newland-asp/profiles.asp
Lesson03/Complete/newland-asp/test_form.asp
Lesson03/Complete/newland-asp/test_form_processor.asp
Lesson03/Complete/newland-asp/tours.asp

✳ **NOTE:** If you are using ColdFusion or PHP, and you want to access the completed files, then use the mirror folder (newland_cf or newland_php) included on the CD. All of the file names are the same, except the extension is .cfm or .php rather than .asp.

LESSON 3
Dynamic Web Sites

You have reached a significant milestone in the revision of the Newland Tours site. You have created and marked up a new page, created custom styles for the entire site, built a template, and enhanced the site's accessibility. Glancing at the site in a browser, it may not seem like you've accomplished two lessons' worth of work. But you know what important things are going on behind the screen: You've laid the foundations for a standards-compliant, flexible, maintainable site.

Beginning with this lesson, you'll cast aside (for the most part) traditional, static Web development, and move into database-driven, interactive, dynamic site development. Before you can start developing, though, you need to work through some prerequisites, of both a conceptual nature and a technical nature. By the end of this lesson, you'll have an idea of how dynamic sites work, and what they are created to do; you'll have Adobe Dreamweaver configured to work with dynamic data; and you'll have created your first page that uses dynamic content.

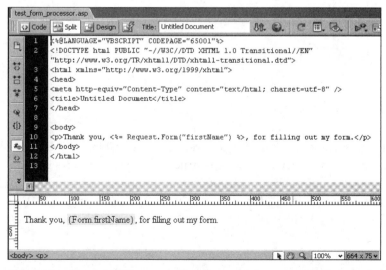

Developing dynamic Web pages often means mixing and matching regular text with placeholder variables.

75

Dynamic Web Site Basics

In the preceding lessons you explored several concepts that are critical to dynamic site development. One of these is the separation of content and presentation. The site content at this point is handled exclusively by XHTML, while the cascading style sheet (CSS) handles the presentation. You have also explored the concept of merging two different documents (an HTML page and a CSS) on the fly to create something different than either of the two source documents alone. These concepts are fundamental to creating dynamic Web sites.

To understand these interactions, and to prepare you for the tasks ahead, let's take a moment to analyze the relationship among the three different major sources of information that make up every Web page: the content (text, images, etc.), the structure (the document hierarchy, such as headings and body text), and the presentation (the colors, font sizes, positioning, and other cosmetic effects).

In earlier versions of HTML, text, markup, and presentation code all exist in the same place: the HTML document itself. In a meaningful way, the document that a developer creates on her or his hard drive is the same as the document viewed in a browser by the site visitor. This simple relationship is shown in the following figure.

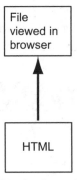

Presentation, Logic, and Content

As a result of the upgrades you made in Lesson 2, the relationships have changed: You have separated a document's presentation from its structure and content. Presentation information is now stored in the CSS. Document content is stored as text within the XHTML markup, which also provides the document structure. Only when the XHTML document and the CSS are merged is the "real" page created. This new relationship is represented in the following figure.

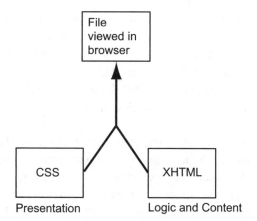

Beginning with this lesson, you are going to add yet another layer of sophistication to this relationship—one that's more profound and more powerful even than migrating from HTML to XHTML and CSS. Specifically, when you add database content to the site, you will separate the content from the structure. What this means is that all three levels—presentation, structure, and content—are quasi-independent of each other, which means you can make radical changes to one without needing to make changes to another. The relationship—and the basic blueprint for the rest of the book—is shown in the following figure.

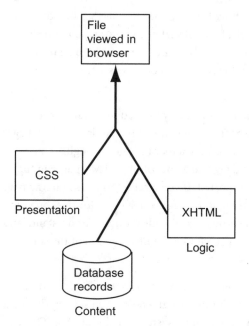

HTML cannot separate content from document structure. Even in its fifth major revision as XHTML 1, HTML is ultimately intended to mark up a plain text document. It cannot process scripts, evaluate expressions, do math, interact with a database, or send and receive information to or from a user. Yet separating structure from content requires, at times, each of these abilities and more. To accomplish these tasks, you need to give HTML some help, and this is where server-side technologies such as Microsoft ASP, Adobe ColdFusion, and PHP fit in.

> ✱ **NOTE:** A style sheet language (think CSS on steroids), XSLT (eXtensible Stylesheet Language for Transformation) is capable of looping, data conversion, and much more. One of its most useful features is its ability to convert one type of XML document (for example, a proprietary XML language developed for internal use) to another type of XML document (such as a standard type of XML document that can be shared with others), and vice versa. In spite of its utility, XSLT is not as powerful or flexible as server-side applications built using ASP, ColdFusion, or PHP.

Server technologies like ASP, ColdFusion, and PHP (and there are others, including JSP and ASP.NET) are able to handle programming tasks such as evaluating expressions, doing math, and processing scripts. In addition, they are capable of interacting with data sources, including databases, structured text files, and in some cases XML data. They also have special abilities that pertain only to the Web, such as the ability to collect data sent by the user and control the information that gets sent back to the user.

But there's a catch. Browsers are limited to handling HTML, CSS, and JavaScript—they don't understand server scripts (by server scripts, I am referring to code written in ASP, ColdFusion, PHP, and so on). Whatever the server sends to the browser has to be in standard HTML. All server scripts must be processed on the server and output as standard HTML before they get sent to the browser.

To put it more plainly, to view a page with dynamic content, you need to run the page through a server capable of processing the code. This is in contrast to standard HTML pages, which you can view directly in a browser, regardless of whether they go through a server. You can open Internet Explorer or Netscape and browse to any of the HTML pages in the Lesson03/Start folder, and they will display as expected. If you attempt to browse to the pages in the Lesson03/Complete folder, you'll discover that the pages don't open (or they open in Dreamweaver, rather than in the browser). The browser sees code it doesn't understand, and refuses to open the file. This is why, in Lesson 1, you viewed the final version of the site at bobflynn.info, rather than from the CD.

Normally when we think about servers on the Web, we use the term server to refer to the computer that holds the HTML file. This server is properly named the Web server. The most common Web servers include Apache, used on Unix/Linux systems, including Mac OSX;

Apache for Windows and Microsoft Internet Information Services (IIS), which is used on Windows Web servers.

In addition to the Web server, you will probably use other servers to deliver dynamic data. You may use a database server, such as MySQL or Microsoft SQL Server. You may also use an application server, which processes server scripts. ColdFusion is an application server. The application server that processes ASP scripts is actually built into IIS, so you might say that IIS is a hybrid Web and application server. PHP is an application server that runs as a module inside of Apache.

Choosing a Server Model

You know already that there are several common server-side languages. This begs the question (often asked by those new to dynamic site development), "which server model should I use?" The following list summarizes the main functions, pros, and cons of each:

Active Server Pages (ASP): ASP is a Microsoft technology that ties together its IIS (Internet Information Services for Windows 2000 and XP) servers with VBScript (Visual Basic Script) for dynamic Web site development (you can also use Microsoft's implementation of JavaScript, JScript). ASP is free and built into all IIS servers, which means that virtually all Windows users can develop ASP sites for free with little configuration. Its code, VBScript, can be somewhat daunting for those with little to no programming experience. ASP is being replaced with Microsoft's ASP.NET (see below).

ColdFusion: ColdFusion is Adobe's server technology. Its tag-based syntax is much easier to use than VBScript, and it certainly requires fewer lines of code. Most designers find it the most accessible of all the server models. Newbies aside, ColdFusion is a powerful language that makes dynamic site development rapid. The disadvantage to Adobe ColdFusion is that it is not free, though the boost to productivity it affords usually means it pays for itself. It is also extremely easy to set up and configure. At the time of this writing there are others developing ColdFusion engines, including some free and open-source versions.

PHP Hypertext Processor (PHP): A recursive acronym, PHP is a fast-growing server model for a variety of reasons. As an open-source solution, it is free and ties in well with other excellent open-source products, including the Apache Web server and MySQL database management system. The code is comparable in difficulty to that of ASP—possibly a little easier. PHP 5 is now out and being used more widely. It has been upgraded to add more object-oriented programming and XML features for advanced programmers, but the core functionality and syntax are quite similar to PHP 4. For our purposes either version is fine.

ASP.NET: The Web authoring portion of the .NET phenomenon, ASP.NET is a technology that has proven to be a quick and powerful Web development language. Like its predecessor ASP, it runs on any Microsoft IIS server on Windows 2000 and beyond. ASP.NET is conceptually and architecturally different from classic ASP, ColdFusion, and PHP. If you have no prior experience with programming, getting started with ASP.NET would not be much different than getting started with ASP, ColdFusion or PHP. If you have had experience with those languages or even JavaScript, you will need to do some adjusting to work with ASP.NET effectively. ASP.NET supports numerous development languages, but by far the two most prevalent are Visual Basic.NET and C#.

Java Servlet Pages (JSP): JSP is the Java-based solution to dynamic Web site development, requiring a Java server (such as a J2EE server) to interpret the code. JSP is fast, providing impressive response times. It is also extremely powerful—certainly the most powerful solution until the appearance of .NET, and certainly powerful enough to compete head-on with .NET. But its code, once again, is daunting for those new to dynamic Web site development.

This book provides coverage of ASP classic (hereafter just ASP), ColdFusion, and PHP. However, this is not specifically an ASP, ColdFusion, or PHP book. The book is designed to initiate readers into the concepts and practices of building database-driven, dynamic Web sites using Dreamweaver CS3. You will learn lots of code and coding concepts along the way, and you will also make use of Dreamweaver's server behaviors to speed up and simplify development. When you are done, you will have a solid sense of what's possible, how several different technologies merge to create dynamic pages, and how to plan and build sites that use these technologies effectively. You will not be an ASP, ColdFusion, or PHP expert, but you should be able to get a code-oriented, non-beginner's ASP, ColdFusion, or PHP book and understand it well enough to push forward and develop ambitious Web projects.

Having summarized the advantages and disadvantages of the various server models, I'll let you in on a secret. Web developers seldom choose based on rational criteria, such as which model fits their needs better than another. I certainly have rarely had that opportunity. In reality, the choice is usually driven by the available technology, your budget, the technologies used in an existing site, and the skills and experience of the available human resources. Going a step further, unless you develop for one organization and one organization only, and you intend to stay there for a very long time, you probably don't have the luxury of learning just one. I initially learned ColdFusion and ASP simultaneously, because both were required for different projects I was working on.

Side by Side with ASP, ColdFusion, and PHP: A Strategy for Learning

Don't be alarmed at the prospect of learning all three at the same time. The truth is, in the majority of situations, if you need to add a block of ASP to handle some functionality, then you would also need to add an equivalent block of ColdFusion or PHP to handle the same functionality. And the hardest part is not the syntax of one or the other type of code, but rather understanding what data is available, where it is available, and deciding how to get it to do what you want. If you know that much, the syntax isn't hard.

For this reason, this book uses ASP, ColdFusion, and PHP side by side. While you don't need to develop the same site three times to use all three server models, you should make an effort to understand all three sets of code. That is, if you decide to develop in ColdFusion, don't just skip the ASP and PHP code. Take a moment to see how the ASP and PHP code accomplishes the same thing as the ColdFusion code. If you can understand how all three code blocks accomplish the same task, you will accelerate your mastery of Web programming.

For example, the following three code snippets perform the same function: They output (or display) a value that the user entered in an XHTML form field, called "firstName."

In ASP:

```
<p>Thank you, <% Response.Write(Request.Form("firstName")) %>, for your
submission.</p>
```

In ColdFusion:

```
<p>Thank you, <cfoutput>#form.firstName#</cfoutput>, for your submission.</p>
```

In PHP:

```
<p>Thank you, <?php echo $_POST['firstName']; ?>, for your submission.</p>
```

Let's review the similarities between these three code snippets.

- All use a special set of tags to indicate server markup. ASP uses <% and %>, ColdFusion uses <cf[tagname]> and </cf[tagname]>, and PHP uses <?php and ?>.

- All indicate that they are outputting data: ASP uses Response.Write, ColdFusion uses <cfoutput>, and PHP uses echo.

- All make explicit reference to the variable name (firstName).

- All specify that this is a form/POST variable (form variables, as discussed later, are sent using POST): ASP uses Request.Form("firstName"), ColdFusion uses #form.firstName#, while PHP uses $_POST['firstName'].

- Neither contains any additional code beyond these four points.

You don't need to memorize this code; there won't be a quiz on it, and you'll get plenty of practice with it later. The point for now is to see the deep similarity between what the three snippets are doing: All are requesting a form variable named firstName, and outputting it in the middle of a string of otherwise regular XHTML code. The differences between the three code snippets are therefore completely cosmetic: a matter of syntax and a matter of looking up something in a reference. The hardest part is understanding in the first place that you can capture a value entered in a form and send it back mixed in with plain-old XHTML code.

Throughout the book, then, I will present all three sets of code side by side. In all cases, I will deconstruct what the code blocks are doing, so you should understand exactly what is going on. All you have to do is read the three sets of code, and see how each accomplishes in its own way the functions that I outline in the main text.

But before you start getting neck-deep in code, you need to configure your system for dynamic site development.

Redefining the Newland Tours Site for Dynamic Development

Configuring Dreamweaver to work with dynamic Web sites is somewhat more complicated than configuring it to work with static Web sites. Either way, you use the Site Definition dialog to configure the site. What makes defining dynamic sites so difficult, then, is external to Dreamweaver: To develop dynamic sites, you need access to (and permissions on) a bona fide Web server, with (if applicable) an application and/or database server.

This may be a new workflow for many readers. In the past, you may have developed a site locally on your hard drive, and then uploaded it to the production (or public) server when you were ready to publish. When developing dynamic Web sites, you can still develop locally on your hard drive, but you also need access to a development server. Only when you have completed the site using the development server do you upload it to the public Web server.

✱ **NOTE:** The only difference between a development Web server and a regular Web server is that the development server is not publicly accessible. But from a technical standpoint, a development server is identical to a regular Web server: It processes and outputs code in the same way.

You can connect to servers in two different ways: You can set up servers on your local machine and develop everything on your machine, or you can develop using a remote machine, such as a network server or using FTP to a machine out on the Web, such as at your ISP.

If you want to work locally, then you first need to spend some time configuring your computer (instructions follow). If you want to work remotely, then you don't have to do any configuration to your machine, but you will need several pieces of information from your server administrator to configure Dreamweaver to work with that machine.

Depending on your setup, you'll need to work through the lesson as follows:

- If you are developing locally, read the section immediately following, *Developing with a Local Server*.

- If you are developing remotely, skip to the section, *Developing with a Remote Server*, later in the lesson.

- Once you have finished the appropriate section, regardless of the server model or configuration you set up, you need to configure Dreamweaver to work with the server and server model you have chosen; this topic is discussed in the section, *Defining a Dynamic Site in Dreamweaver (All Users)*.

Developing with a Local Server

Developing with a local server has advantages and disadvantages. Benefits of developing locally include the following:

- Control and autonomy over your own computer: You never have to go through a server administrator.

- No need for an Internet or network connection throughout development.

- No lag time for logging in, authenticating, and transmitting data over a network.

The primary disadvantages to developing locally are the following:

- Running a server opens your computer to security risks, and the less you know about what you are doing, the more vulnerable you are to attacks, viruses, hacks, and worms.

- If you have a problem with configuration, or something is not working as expected, you are usually on your own.

> **TIP:** The best way to protect your server from hacks, viruses, and worms is to run Windows Update (Windows) or Software Update (Macintosh) regularly—at least twice a week—and to install all the security patches. This is especially important for Windows users, because Windows is far more commonly targeted by malicious code. Windows Update can be found in the Start Menu, while Macintosh Software Update can be found in the System Preferences.

If you decide to develop the Newland Tours site locally, then you must choose the server model you want to use and configure your system accordingly. Use the bolded headings below to select the directions that meet your needs. When you are finished, skip directly to the section later in the lesson entitled, *Defining a Dynamic Site in Dreamweaver (All Users)*.

✴ **NOTE:** Macintosh OS X users developing locally have only two choices: PHP, using the Apache Web server or ColdFusion. Macintosh OS 9 users as well as OS X users who want to develop ASP sites can do so, but not locally. They will have to connect to a remote server that is already running these technologies.

Setting Up a Local Environment for IIS/ASP

ASP users need to ensure that Internet Information Services (IIS) is installed and running on their system. IIS comes free with Windows 2000 and XP Pro.

✴ **NOTE:** Windows XP Home users are likewise out of luck: Microsoft officially states that if you need a Web server, you must use Windows XP Professional.

Depending on how Windows was first installed, you may already have IIS up and running. To determine whether you have IIS installed, look in Control Panel > Administrative Tools (Windows XP users need to switch to Classic View to see this option). If you see an icon in the list called Internet Information Services, then it is already installed. To verify that it is running, double-click the icon, and in the left side of the dialog, navigate down to Web Sites. In the right pane, you should see Default Web Site listed, and beside it, you should see the word Running. If it says Stopped, click the Start button to restart it.

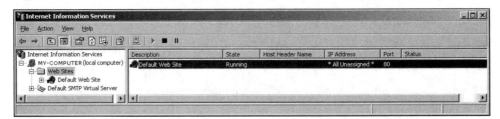

To install and run IIS, follow these steps:

1 Use the Add/Remove Programs utility in the Control Panel, and from there, select Add/Remove Windows Components.

It takes Windows a couple minutes to analyze your machine and determine what is already installed. Once it has built a profile, you will see the Windows Components Wizard.

2 From the list, check Internet Information Services, and click Next.

The default setup should work fine for our purposes, so no further customization is needed. Once you click Next, Windows installs and starts IIS.

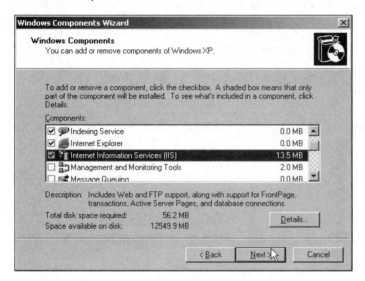

3 To confirm that the installation was successful, return to Control Panel > Administrative Tools and check for Internet Information Services and verify that the status of the Default Web Site is "running".

Setting Up a Local Environment for ColdFusion

Setting up ColdFusion locally for development purposes is easy, thanks to its installer.

1 Download the latest version of the free developer edition of ColdFusion from http://www.adobe.com/go/coldfusion/.

After a few moments, the installation begins.

2 Select your language, read through the information, and click Next twice to proceed through the Introduction and License agreement sections.

These sections both contain important information, so don't just skip them.

3 In the Install Type screen, you are prompted to enter your serial number. If you do not have one, check the Developer Edition checkbox and click Next.

You can use the Developer Edition indefinitely for free. The key limitation is that it can only be tested from the local machine. That is, if a different computer on your network attempts to access a ColdFusion Web page that is powered by the Developer Edition, the user will see an error indicating that the maximum number of IP addresses has been exceeded.

If you were installing the Enterprise edition of the ColdFusion server, you would have a serial number, and the limit of one machine would be lifted.

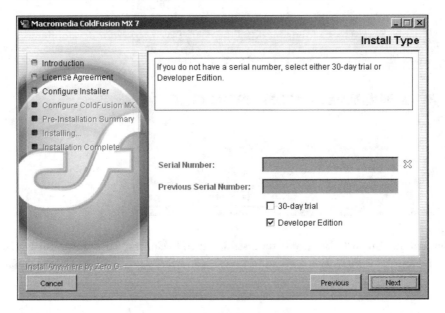

4 In the Install Configuration screen, leave the default at Server configuration. Click Next.

The other two options are for configuring a ColdFusion server to run on top of a J2EE server.

5 Click Next again in the Sub-component Installation screen, leaving the three boxes checked.

Here you are installing all the subcomponent services of ColdFusion, as well as some additional documentation. For a local install, unless you have a good reason otherwise, it is a good idea to do a complete install.

6 Accept the default and click Next in the Choose Install Directory screen.

This screen enables you to specify where the ColdFusion application files are installed.

7 In the Web Server Selection screen, choose Built-In Web Server (if you are not running a Web server, such as IIS or Apache), or (if you are running a Web server) choose Configure Web server connector for ColdFusion and verify that your server is listed in the Web Servers/Sites box.

As an application server, ColdFusion is not intended to fulfill the role of a Web server. On a real production site, another server, such as IIS or Apache typically fulfills this role.

In the development environment, one may not have a bona fide Web server available. Adobe enables you to let ColdFusion fulfill the role of Web server for development purposes if you need; to activate it, choose built-in Web server.

If you already have a Web server installed, such as IIS or Apache, you can let that continue as your main server, and enable ColdFusion to connect to it, so that when that Web server sees ColdFusion code that it does not understand, it knows to send it to the ColdFusion application server for processing.

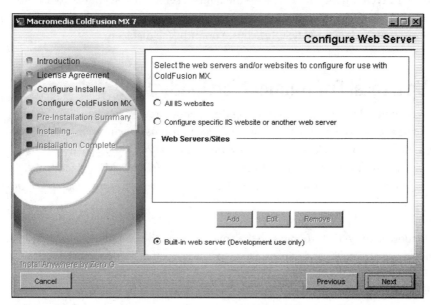

Your choice here ultimately affects the URL you use to view ColdFusion pages, which is important when configuring Dreamweaver later in the lesson.

8 Continue to finish the wizard, which is self-explanatory from this point forward.

❇ NOTE: During the installation, you will twice be asked to enter a password, once for the server administrator and once for RDS. They can be the same password. Do not forget this password! You will need it to configure the ColdFusion server, and you will also need it to access ColdFusion from within Dreamweaver during development time.

The installation process may take several minutes to run, as it installs the ColdFusion server and starts it up.

When you are finished, a browser opens, which lets you into the ColdFusion administrator application. This application is itself running in ColdFusion. You'll need to click Next a couple more times and wait a few more moments as ColdFusion finalizes the setup process. When you are dumped into the ColdFusion administrator application, you have finished the setup and can begin developing.

Installation on Mac OS X is quite similar to the installation on Windows. For local development I recommend working with the built-in server. If you choose to use Apache for the Web server there are good online resources for setting it up, including the "ACME Guide" (*Apache/ColdFusion/MySQL/Eclipse*) on http://acidlabs.org.

Setting Up a Local Environment for Apache/PHP

In the past, setting up a local environment using the open-source Apache and PHP setup could be difficult and frustrating for Windows and Macintosh users who were unfamiliar with Unix systems. But the situation is improving; several WAMP (*Windows/Apache/MySQL/PHP*) installers are now available for Windows and recently a free MAMP (*Macintosh/Apache/MySQL/PHP*) installer also became available. These are perfect for local development and for our purposes.

❇ NOTE: Windows users with IIS running on their machines may be tempted to only install the PHP module directly into IIS, and skip installing Apache altogether. This approach is certainly workable, but it has a drawback: Very few ISPs that offer PHP have it running on an IIS server. That is, PHP is almost invariably paired with Apache. Since it is generally desirable for your development environment to resemble, as closely as possible, your eventual production environment, it is worth installing Apache. Also, it is good practice, just to familiarize yourself with the Apache environment—the permissions structures, the commands, the interface, and so on.

Installing Apache, MySQL and PHP for Windows

There are a number of good WAMP installers available and most are free. The best I've found is called WAMP5.

■ **NOTE:** The following instructions assume that IIS is not already running as the local Web server. Setup and configuration varies if Apache is not the only Web server.

1 Go to the following URL, read the instructions, and click the Download link for the latest version of WAMP5: http://wampserver.com/.

At the time of this writing, the most current production release was 1.7.0

2 Double-click the installer file, which will be called something like wamp5_1.7.0.exe to launch the installation wizard.

The installer file is on your hard drive, in the directory you saved it in the preceding step.

3 Complete the installation wizard. Accept the default installation location unless you prefer to place the files in a specific location.

The WAMP5 installer is entirely self-explanatory, with one possible exception: the Auto Start screen. I typically do not have programs automatically start when I start my machine. It slows start-up time and affects overall performance. I like to start them manually when I am ready to do my development. Click Next without checking the Auto Start box.

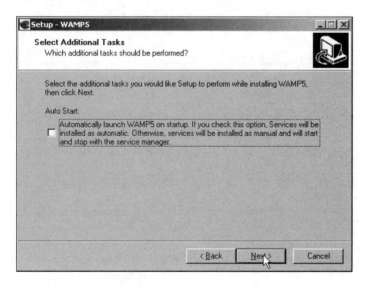

The installer will ask you where you would like to put the root of the web server. Again, I recommend the default location.

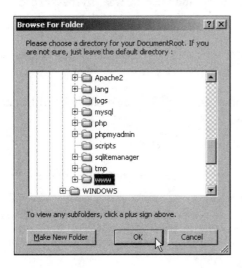

4 To verify the successful installation of your server, open a browser and go to the following location: http://localhost/

You should see a placeholder page, as follows.

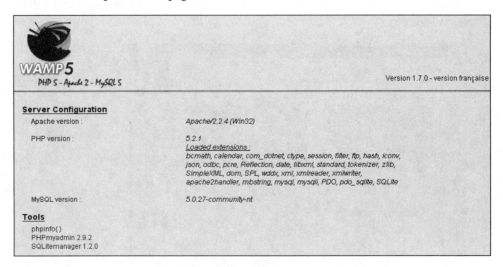

You have successfully installed Apache, PHP and the MySQL database and are ready to write code.

Installing Apache, MySQL and PHP for Mac OS X

Until recently setting up a local MAMP (*M*acintosh/*A*pache/*M*ySQL/*P*HP) environment was somewhat involved. Nature abhors a vacuum and so does the technical world. A company called Living-e has developed an excellent MAMP installer in both professional and free editions. The free edition serves our needs nicely.

✱ **NOTE:** Apple has a useful site for configuring the Mac for Web development: http://developer. apple.com/internet/macosx/intro.html. There are other fine online resources for MAMP development. Among them are http://phpmac.com, http://MacDevCenter.com and http://entropy. ch/software/macosx/.

1 Go to the following URL and download the latest version of MAMP http://www.mamp. info/. You do not need the power of MAMP-Pro for the purposes of this book.

At the time of this writing, the most current production release was 1.4.1

2 Unpack the installer file and double-click the .dmg file to mount the disk image. Drag the MAMP folder into your Applications folder.

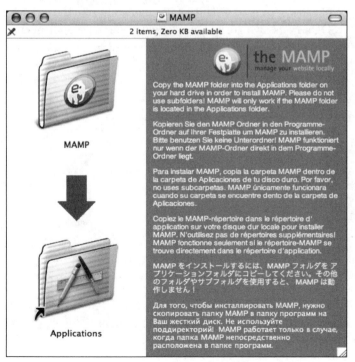

Macintosh installers are deceptively simple. They typically involve dragging the application folder into your computer's Applications folder. The actual installation often takes place when you launch the application for the first time.

3 Launch MAMP from within its folder.

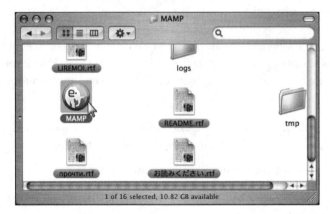

When the MAMP control panel appears it will take a few moments until the status lights for the Apache and MySQL servers turn green. Once they do, your development environment is ready to go. The MAMP start page should open in your default browser.

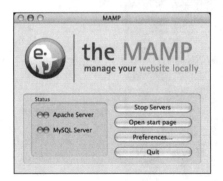

Leave the MAMP Preferences set at their default values. You'll use these values when defining your development environment in Dreamweaver later in the chapter.

In the next steps, you'll turn Personal Web Sharing off. This is good for security purposes but also ensures that the Apache and MySQL servers you just installed don't conflict with other software you might have installed.

4 Open System Preferences and click the Sharing folder.

The Sharing folder is used to control file sharing, Web services, FTP access, printer sharing and firewalls, among other features.

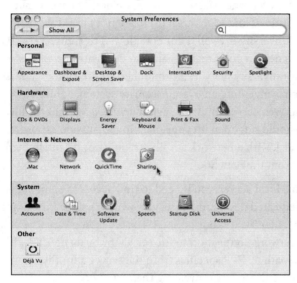

5 In the Services tab of the Sharing folder, ensure that Personal Web Sharing is not checked. If it is, select it and click Stop.

For security reasons it is a good idea to disable all of the sharing services unless you have a specific need to have one enabled.

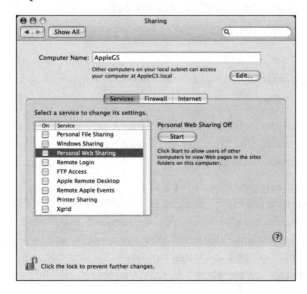

Developing with a Remote Server

The local server configuration is not for everyone. Macintosh users obviously have no access to ASP on IIS. Furthermore, many Windows and Macintosh users are not permitted to install and run Web servers. Even behind a university firewall, I am not allowed to run servers. The reason for this is security. Web servers need regular maintenance to deal with the viruses and security holes that make corporate or university networks vulnerable. To prevent, or at least minimize, the chance of infiltrators circumventing an overall security system, administrators often forbid users from installing Web servers on their own machines. Most of the local development tools presented above should not open up your machine to outside exposure if configured properly. If in doubt, check with a network administrator or only launch them when your machine is disconnected from the network.

Obviously, if you don't have access to a local server, you'll need to find access to some other development server. This may be a dedicated development server (which is what I use at the university), or it may be a nonpublic folder inside your public Web server. You can access the server over a network, if you have a network connection to the server, or by using FTP. Either way, you will need to get the network path or FTP specifics from the server administrator before you can continue and define your site in Dreamweaver. The server needs to be IIS (for ASP development), or have Apache or IIS installed with ColdFusion installed (for ColdFusion development), or the PHP module loaded (for PHP development).

In addition to an account, and permission to add and remove files and folders within that account, you'll also need one of the following pieces of information from the site administrator:

- The path to the folder on the network, which could look like one of the following:

  \\webdev.bigcompany.com\your_site\
  \\serverName\your_site\

✱ NOTE: If you have network access to a server, you should map a network drive to your account on that server.

- The FTP information to access the site, including the Host Name/Address, which is usually an IP address (and looks something like 123.12.123.12) and a username/password combination to access your account on that server.

The preceding information is enough to give you access to upload your content to those folders. But you will also need some way to browse the content. Specifically, you need a URL to access your content on the server. Typically, the URL will look something like http://webdev.bigcompany.com/your_site/ or http://serverName/your_site/. When you migrate your site into production, the production URL (in this example) would be http://www.bigcompany.com/your_site/. The important thing to look for is a complete URL that includes http://. Only your server administrator can give you this information.

Defining a Dynamic Site in Dreamweaver (All Users)

Regardless of which section above applied to you, use the following steps to define your site in Dreamweaver. Before you begin, you must have access to a fully configured Web server, with the desired application server/module loaded and running.

1 With the Newland site open in Dreamweaver, choose Site > Manage Sites. In the Manage Sites dialog, make sure Newland Tours is selected, and click Edit.

Remember, the Newland Tours site is already defined. You don't need to start from scratch. You just need to add the remote and testing server information to the existing site.

2 In the Site Definition for Newland Tours dialog, click the Advanced tab. Then select the Remote Info category from the Category list on the left side. From the Access drop-down menu, make a selection and enter the appropriate information in the fields that appear, using the guidelines below.

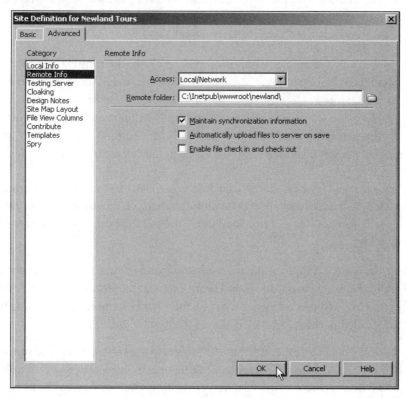

If you are developing on a computer with a local version of IIS installed (ASP or ColdFusion via IIS), choose Local/Network from the Access drop-down menu. Next to the Remote Folder field, click the browse button, and browse to the C:\Inetpub\ wwwroot\ folder. Click the Add New Folder button to create a new folder, called newland. Double-click this folder to select it as the Remote folder.

> **✱ NOTE:** The Inetpub/wwwroot folder is IIS' root Web folder on your system. When you browse to your site (http://localhost/), you will be served pages from this folder.

If you are developing on a computer with a local version of the stand-alone ColdFusion Web server, choose Local/Network in the Access drop-down menu. Next to the Remote Folder field, click the browse button, and browse to the C:\CFusionMX7\wwwroot\ folder. Click the Add New Folder button to create a new folder, called newland. Double-click this folder to select it as the Remote folder.

> **✱ NOTE:** The CFusionMX7/wwwroot folder is the stand-alone ColdFusion server's root folder on your system. When you browse to your site (http://localhost:8500/), you will be served pages from this folder. (Note also that ColdFusion 8 was in beta at the time of this writing. If you're using ColdFusion 8, rather than MX7, your folder name will vary.)

If you are developing on a computer with a local version of Apache running using the W/MAMP installer configured above, choose Local/Network in the Access drop-down menu. Next to the Remote Folder field, click the browse button, and browse to the C:\ wamp\www\ folder (Windows) or to HD:Applications:MAMP:htdocs folder (Macintosh). Click the Add New Folder button (Windows) or New Folder button (Macintosh) to create a new folder, called newland. Double-click this folder to select it as the Remote folder.

> **✱ NOTE:** The C:\wamp\www\ folder is Apache's root folder on Windows. The HD:Applications: MAMP:htdocs folder is Apache's root folder on Macintosh. When you browse to your site (by default http://localhost/ on Windows, http://localhost:8888/ on Macintosh), you will be served pages from this folder.

If you are developing on a computer that has a network connection to the server, choose Local/Network in the Access drop-down, and browse to your folder on the server. Most likely, this appears in a mapped network drive. Use the Choose Remote Folder dialog to add a new folder called newland, and select that as the Remote folder.

If you are developing on a computer that has FTP access to the server, first make sure that there is a folder in your account called newland. Then, in Dreamweaver's Site Definition dialog, select FTP from the Access menu, and type the IP or Web address in the FTP Host field. Enter the path to the newland folder in the Host Directory field. Then fill in the Login and Password fields. When you have done all this, click the Test button to make sure you have configured it all correctly.

3 From the Category list at left, select Testing Server. From the Server Model menu, select ASP VBScript, ColdFusion, or PHP MySQL, depending on which server model you have decided to use. In the Access menu, and also any options that appear beneath it, enter the same information you used in the previous step.

✱ **NOTE:** Do not choose ASP JavaScript. Though the server model works fine in general, it is incompatible with most of the code you will use in this particular book.

For the Newland Tours site, the Remote site and the Testing Server site are essentially the same. The difference is that the Remote site exists to enable Dreamweaver to save files to the correct folder, while the Testing Server enables Dreamweaver to test files after they have been processed on the server, so you can verify that they actually work.

4 In the URL Prefix field near the bottom of the Testing Server category tab, enter the site's URL.

If you are using IIS locally on your computer (all ASP and some ColdFusion users), enter http://localhost/newland/.

If you are running ColdFusion locally as a stand-alone server without IIS, enter http://localhost:8500/newland/.

If you are running Apache locally in Windows, enter http://localhost/newland/; on a Macintosh , http://localhost:8888/newland/.

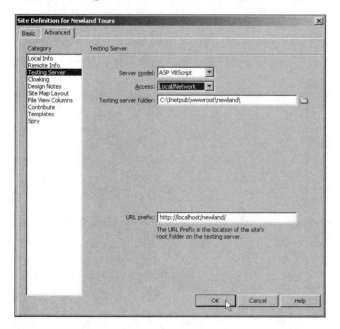

✱ **NOTE:** As indicated earlier, the word *localhost* is a shortcut that activates the Web server on your computer, and tells it to look in the server's root folder (the wwwroot folder for IIS and the stand-alone ColdFusion Web server, or htdocs for Apache on Macintosh and www for Apache on Windows), in which you created a newland folder in a previous step.

If you are using a remote server, whether through a network or through FTP, enter the server's URL, which the site administrator should have given you. It probably looks something like http://www.bigcompany.com/newland/.

Either way, the URL prefix must begin with http:// and should not have any drive letters (such as h:\) anywhere in it. Also note that the slashes in the URL are forward slashes, not backslashes.

➤ **TIP:** If the site doesn't display properly later in the lesson, the URL prefix is the first place you should look when troubleshooting. If this information is wrong, you will not be able to browse your site and see it in action, even if all your code is correct and your server and server models are correctly configured and running.

5 Click OK to save and close the dialog, and then click Done to close the Edit Sites dialog.

The site is now redefined and should be ready for dynamic development.

6 One at a time, right-click (Windows) or Control-click (Macintosh) each of the HTML files in the Site panel, choose Edit > Rename, and change the extension from .html to .asp, .cfm, or .php as appropriate. Whenever the Update Files dialog appears, click Update.

Changing the extension is required when you upgrade to dynamic sites, because the server uses the extension to determine whether to process any special code on the page.

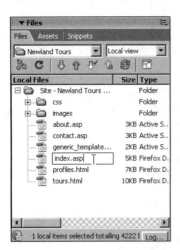

When you change the extension, all of the links that point to that page are broken. Dreamweaver's site manager catches this and fixes the problem when you choose Update.

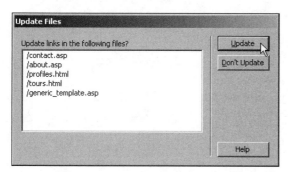

7 Click once on the top-level folder, and click the Put File(s) button.

This uploads the entire site to the remote folder and testing server.

✱ **NOTE:** If a dialog appears asking whether you want to Put the entire site, click OK.

8 Change the Files panel to remote view. Click once to select index.asp, index.cfm, or index. php in the Site window, and press F12 (Windows) or Option-F12 (Mac).

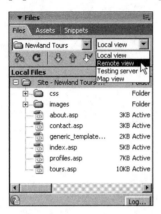

Pressing F12 or Option-F12 tests the site as it runs through the server. This test results in either good news or bad news. If you can see the Newland Tours index page, then you have correctly configured the site, and you are ready to start developing. If you get an error message or the site doesn't display properly, then something has gone amiss. To troubleshoot, take a second look at the URL prefix. Also, use Windows Explorer or Macintosh Finder to make sure that the files really were uploaded to the remote site. If you are still hung up, talk to your site administrator, who should be able to help you resolve this problem.

Site URL displays in address bar

Building a Simple, Dynamic Application

You have now tested the site going through the remote server, and—assuming you saw index. asp, index.cfm, or index.php in your browser—you have everything correctly configured. But nothing in the Newland site is actually dynamic yet. At this point, you've done all the work and haven't seen any of the benefits. In this task, you will create a very simple dynamic application, which will reward you with a taste of what's to come, both conceptually (how dynamic sites work) and behaviorally (the sequence of steps needed to create the functionality).

Creating the Input Page

You're going to build a page containing a Web form that asks users their names. Then they will click Submit, at which point they will be redirected to a second page, which will display the name they entered. No, this application doesn't exactly push the limits of ASP, ColdFusion, or PHP. It does, however, introduce you to building forms, dealing with dynamic data, and distinguishing between server-side and client-side code.

1 With the Newland site open, choose File > New. Choose ASP VBScript, ColdFusion, or PHP as the Page Type and <none> for Layout. Set DocType to XHTML 1.0 Transitional. Click Create.

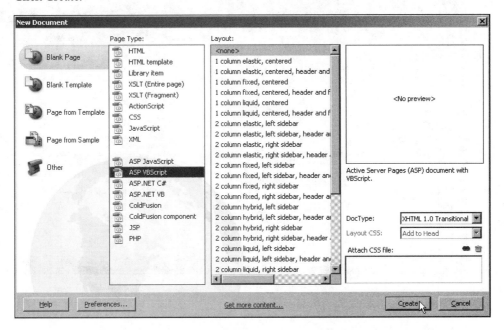

In this step, you are creating a new dynamic page. By specifying the type of dynamic page, you tell Dreamweaver what code to use when you use Dreamweaver's ready-made server behaviors, which extension to use when you save the file, and in some cases, which additional code to add to the document header.

ASP users will see `<%@LANGUAGE="VBSCRIPT" CODEPAGE="65001"%>`; this line specifies whether you are using VBScript and JScript, either of which you can use with ASP. For the exercises in this book, though, you must work with VBScript. ColdFusion and PHP don't have multiple scripting languages, so a new ColdFusion or PHP page has no equivalent for this line.

2 Click anywhere in the design window, select the Forms category in the Insert panel, and click the Form button to insert a form.

You have just added a basic form to your page.

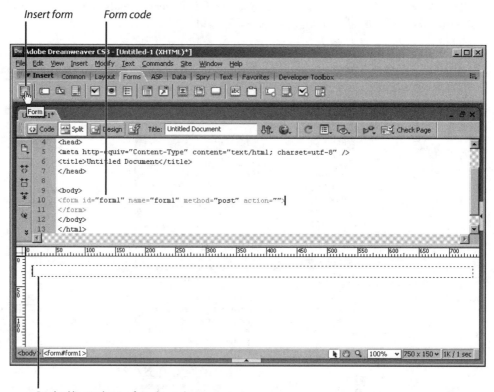

Insert form   Form code

Dashed line indicates form boundaries

The red dashed line indicates the form's boundaries. This will not appear in the browser; it is there just to help you know where the form begins and ends on the page.

3 Click the Text Field button. In the Input Tag Accessibility Attributes dialog, label the button *First Name* and click OK. Click the Button button, and in the Input Tag Accessibility Attributes dialog, click Cancel.

Here you've added two form elements, a text input field into which users can type, and a Submit button.

Dreamweaver has become more proactive about encouraging developers to design according to Web standards and accessibility guidelines, as you can see from the accessibility dialog encountered twice in this step.

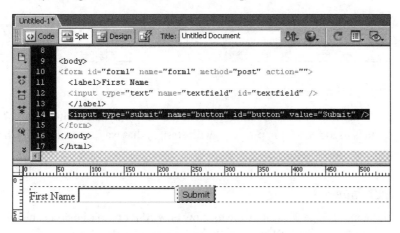

4 Click the text field, and in the Property inspector, name the field *firstName* and press Tab or Enter/Return.

You will use this name to retrieve the value in ASP, ColdFusion, or PHP in a few minutes. Always give your form fields meaningful names. Code is hard enough to write as it is—don't make it worse by sticking with Textfield1, Textfield2, and Textfield3, which Dreamweaver inserts by default.

You press Tab or Enter/Return to apply a setting entered in the Property inspector.

5 Click <form#form1> in the tag selector, to activate the Property inspector for the form. Name the form *frm_name*, and type *test_form_processor.asp* (or *.cfm* or *.php*) in the Action field.

The Action field points to the page (or other resource) that contains the script that can process the form data. It is always a URL. In this case, it points to a URL that doesn't exist, because you haven't created test_form_processor.asp (or .cfm or .php) yet. The method should be set to POST. I'll explain what POST means in a later lesson.

> ✳ **NOTE:** Henceforth, I will assume you can figure out your own extensions. It wastes space and insults your intelligence for me to specify "(or .cfm or .php)" every time I refer to a file. I will always use .asp, so if you are using ColdFusion, just use the .cfm extension instead, and if you are using PHP, use the .php extension instead.

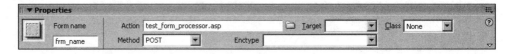

6 Choose File > Save As and name the file *test_form.asp*.

This is a throwaway file that you are creating just to test a simple dynamic site feature. I often prefix such files used for testing purposes with "test_"; that way, when I am finished, I can easily find and remove them.

Creating the Output Page

You have completed the input page. Now it's time to show how ASP or ColdFusion can collect that information, insert it into regular XHTML code, and return it to the client browser.

1 Create a new dynamic page.

See Step 1 from the previous task if you forgot how.

2 Save the new file as *test_form_processor.asp*.

I often use the suffix "_processor" for pages that exist to process some sort of data. This page will process the data entered by the user in the form.

3 In design view, type *Thank you, , for filling out my form*. With the cursor anywhere inside this paragraph, choose Paragraph from the Format menu in the Property inspector.

Eventually, this text will say, "Thank you, [whatever the user's first name is], for filling out my form." Most of the sentence is just static text. The dynamic part will be the actual value of the first name, which will be pulled in from the form.

By selecting Paragraph as the Format, you wrap the text string in <p></p> tags.

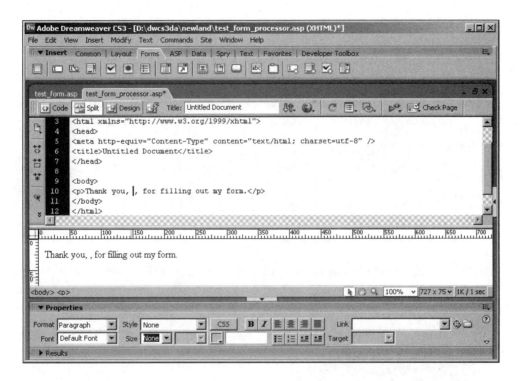

4 Position the cursor in between the commas, where you would enter someone's name. Open the Bindings panel (Window > Bindings).

The Bindings panel is used to specify all of the data that is available to the page. Data is typically stored in a name-value format. In this particular case, the name is firstName. The value doesn't yet exist—it won't exist until someone fills out the form. Remember also that this value comes to the page from a form on the test_form.asp page. Other possible sources besides forms (and you'll get quite familiar with these later) include the URL, a recordset (data retrieved from a database), a cookie, and more. But this time, it's from a form.

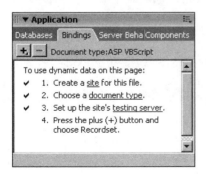

5 Click the + button to add a new binding. From the menu, choose Request Variable (ASP) or Form Variable (ColdFusion and PHP). In the resulting dialog, for ASP, select Request. Form in the Type Menu and type *firstName* in the Name field, or for ColdFusion or PHP type *firstName* in the Name field. Click OK.

The first screen shot shows the Request Variable dialog, which ASP users see, while the second one shows the Form Variable dialog, which ColdFusion and PHP users see.

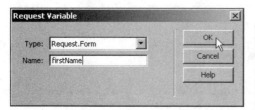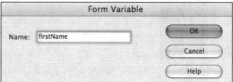

The Bindings panel is updated to show the firstName variable. The screen shot shows what the Bindings panel looks like in ASP. It looks slightly different in ColdFusion and PHP (the word Request is replaced with Form, and the word Form.firstName is replaced with firstName).

You might be wondering what exactly you've just accomplished. If you take a look at your code, you'll see that you haven't changed the document at all: The code is the same as it was before you opened the Bindings panel. What you've done is use Dreamweaver's graphic interface to tell Dreamweaver how to write a block of dynamic code.

Back at the beginning of the chapter, I listed three code snippets side by side: one each in ASP, ColdFusion, and PHP. The code in those snippets specified a variable (firstName); its origin (a form); and what to do with it (output it to XHTML). What you've just done in the Bindings panel is specify that logic in a way that Dreamweaver can understand and translate into code.

For ASP, you specified a Request variable. In ASP, the Request object is used to retrieve information from a given location. In the dialog, you then specified Request.Form, which tells ASP to look in the Request object for the variable in a form. Finally, you specified the name of the variable itself. You have provided a road map for Dreamweaver/ASP to find the value of the firstName variable.

For ColdFusion and PHP, you specified a variable in the form scope, which is sufficient for ColdFusion or PHP to look in the right place (no need to worry about Request objects and such). Then you provided the name of the variable. Again, to summarize, you have provided a road map for Dreamweaver/ColdFusion or PHP to find the value of the first-Name variable.

At this point, though, you have told Dreamweaver only *how* to find the variable. You haven't actually *asked* it to find that variable; nor have you asked Dreamweaver to do anything with that value once it has it.

6 Make sure that the variable Form.firstName (ASP) or firstName (ColdFusion/PHP) is selected in the Bindings panel, and click the Insert button at the bottom.

A blue highlighted {Form.firstName} appears on the page, in between the commas. Blue highlighted text signifies the presence of dynamic content in Dreamweaver. The text won't appear blue when viewed in a browser. For that matter, it also won't display {form. firstName}, either: It will display instead the user's first name.

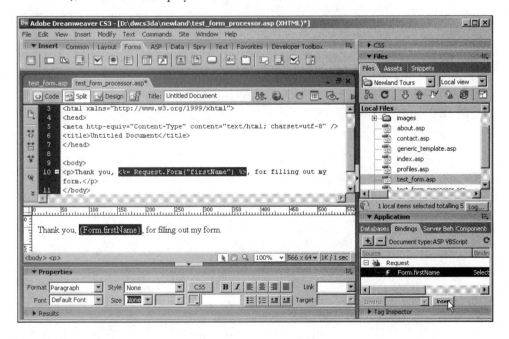

✱ **NOTE:** Though {Form.firstName} looks like code, it's actually pseudocode. It appears the same regardless of server model. One assumes Adobe used pseudocode to create a generic and descriptive language to communicate what was actually specified in the dynamic content. That's fine as long as you don't attempt to use that syntax to write code.

If you look in the actual code, you should see that `<%= Request.Form("firstName") %>` (ASP), `<cfoutput>#form.firstName#</cfoutput>` (ColdFusion), or `<?php echo $_ POST['firstName']; ?>` (PHP) has been added. These are the same snippets I showed you earlier in the chapter, with one small exception in the ASP code.

The way to tell IIS to output an expression is to use the Response object. The most common use of the Response object is `Response.Write()`. This is a command that tells IIS to insert whatever's inside the parentheses into the document. With a few nuances, `Response.Write()` is more or less the equivalent of `<cfoutput>` or echo. `Response.Write()` is so popular that it has a shortcut. When you see an ASP code block that begins `<%=` rather than simply `<%`, it means `<% Response.Write()`. In other words, the following two lines of code mean the exact same thing:

```
<% Response.Write(Request.Form("firstName")) %>
<%= Request.Form("firstName") %>
```

To summarize what you have done in the last two steps, you told Dreamweaver/ASP, Dreamweaver/ColdFusion, or Dreamweaver/PHP how to find the firstName variable, using the Bindings panel's + button. Then, you inserted that binding onto the page, which told ASP, ColdFusion, or PHP how to find the variable and also to display the current value of the variable.

7 Save and close all open documents. In the Site panel, hold down the Shift key and select both test_form.asp and test_form_processor.asp. Click the Put File(s) button in the toolbar at the top of the panel.

You can't test the site unless you run it through a server, and your server is not your local site. To test your site, you have to upload, or Put, your file to the server. If you receive a message asking about dependent files, check the box asking not to be shown the question again, then click No as there are no dependent files.

TIP: This is a step I forget about time and time again. If you get an unexpected error during development, your first point of troubleshooting should be to verify that you uploaded all of the requisite files.

8 Select test_form.asp in the Site panel, and press F12 to test it in a browser. When the page loads, type your first name in the field and click Submit.

You are redirected to the test_form_processor.asp page. As I hope you anticipated, the first name you entered in the form now appears on the screen.

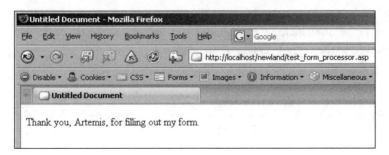

9 Still in your browser, choose View > Source (or your browser's equivalent). Look at the line enclosed in <p> tags.

This is the interesting part. The dynamic code has been completely removed! The code for this page is that of a static XHTML Web page. Even the dynamic part, the first name, looks as though it were hard-coded in there. But of course, you know it wasn't.

```
Source of: http://localhost/newland/test_form_processor.asp - Mozilla Firefox

File   Edit   View   Html Validator   Help


<!DOCTYPE html PUBLIC "-//W3C//DTD XHTML 1.0 Transitional//EN"
"http://www.w3.org/TR/xhtml1/DTD/xhtml1-transitional.dtd">
<html xmlns="http://www.w3.org/1999/xhtml">
<head>
<meta http-equiv="Content-Type" content="text/html; charset=utf-8" />
<title>Untitled Document</title>
</head>

<body>
<p>Thank you, Artemis, for filling out my form.</p>
</body>
</html>
```

Our review of the output code brings up a critical concept. The page you code in Dreamweaver is different from the page the user sees in a browser, even though they both have the same name (and still, of course, a great deal in common).

The difference between the two versions of the page is that all of the original page's ASP/ColdFusion/PHP code is processed and removed, with its output values written into the XHTML as regular XHTML.

The two versions of the page also share some similarities: All of the standard XHTML code written into the original, including the <body> and <p> tags, and most of the text, are passed unchanged to the output version of the page.

What You Have Learned

In this lesson, you have:

- Learned about the relationships between presentation, document logic, and content (pages 76–79)
- Explored the pros and cons of five major server models (pages 79–82)
- Set up a local Web server and server model (pages 82–93)
- Defined a dynamic site in Dreamweaver (pages 95–100)
- Developed a Web form (pages 101–104)
- Created a page that collected and displayed data from the Web form (pages 104–110)

What You Will Learn

In this lesson, you will:

- Learn about HTTP, and how it enables developers to create dynamic sites

- Discover the difference between GET and POST

- Encode and retrieve querystrings or URL variables

- Encode and retrieve cookies

- Create a cookie using dynamic data

Approximate Time

This lesson takes approximately 75 minutes to complete.

Lesson Files

Starting Files:

Lesson04/Start/newland/about.asp
Lesson04/Start/newland/contact.asp
Lesson04/Start/newland/generic_template.asp
Lesson04/Start/newland/index.asp
Lesson04/Start/newland/profiles.asp
Lesson04/Start/newland/test_form.asp
Lesson04/Start/newland/test_form_ processor.asp
Lesson04/Start/newland/tours.asp

Completed Files:

Lesson04/Complete/newland/about.asp
Lesson04/Complete/newland/animal_home_ page.asp
Lesson04/Complete/newland/animal_ questions.asp
Lesson04/Complete/newland/contact.asp
Lesson04/Complete/newland/generic_ template.asp
Lesson04/Complete/newland/index.asp
Lesson04/Complete/newland/profiles.asp
Lesson04/Complete/newland/test_form.asp
Lesson04/Complete/newland/test_form_ processor.asp
Lesson04/Complete/newland/test_form_ processor_cookies.asp
Lesson04/Complete/newland/tours.asp

LESSON 4

Passing Data Between Pages

The hallmark feature of dynamic Web pages is that the contents displayed in the browser are not coded in the page, as in static HTML, but rather are inserted into the page on the fly as it is served. The implication of this is that the core skill in developing dynamic Web applications consists of knowing how to capture and embed data, so the data can be inserted into Web pages when they are served.

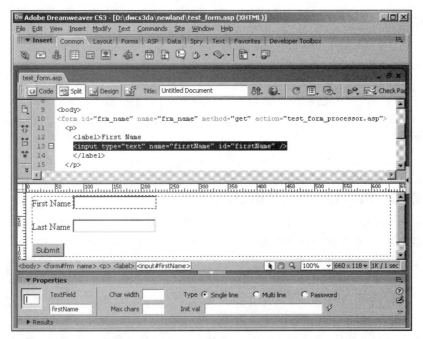

In this lesson you will pass data from a URL into a cookie on the user's hard drive to create persistent dynamic data.

At the end of the preceding lesson, you got a taste of this process, when you displayed the first name that users entered on a form on a different page. To accomplish this task, you used ASP, Adobe ColdFusion, or PHP code to capture the firstName variable and inserted it inline into regular XHTML code. Though it was a simple little application, the form-to-Web transfer you achieved at the end of Lesson 3 is representative of a good portion of dynamic site development.

You probably already know that there's a lot more to dynamic Web site development than forms and form variables. You know that you can embed database content in a Web page, and you have probably also heard of cookies, which store little bits of information on client computers for later use. Building dynamic Web pages, then, usually means working with several different types of data, coming from different sources, and outputting them into a standard XHTML page.

In this lesson, you will explore two other ways of capturing and embedding data in Web pages (also called binding). In doing so, you will discover how similar each of these approaches to binding data is to the other, from the perspective of coding. And yet you will also see that each approach offers unique benefits. You will not do anything for Newland Tours in this lesson; nor will the files be particularly attractive or useful in themselves. But they will teach you quite a bit about the core skill of binding data to Web pages.

As you learn these approaches to binding data, you'll also learn more about the Web's HTTP protocol. The nature of this protocol shapes the ways we bind data to Web pages, and understanding HTTP basics takes a lot of the mystery out of the inner workings of dynamic Web pages. As the book progresses, in addition to form, database, and cookie data, you'll learn several more ways to bind data to Web pages, and when and why to use each technique.

Understanding the HTTP Protocol

Pages on the Web are transferred using HTTP (the HyperText Transfer Protocol). This protocol specifies how users (or, in many cases, systems) make requests of servers over the World Wide Web, and how these servers respond to these requests. Understanding the basics of this protocol will help you understand how dynamic pages work.

At its core, HTTP is a transactional system. A client sends a request to a server, and the server sends a response back to the client. One part of the request is the URL, or Uniform Resource Locator. When you click a link in a browser, a request is sent to the server that contains the desired file.

What most people don't realize is that the client's computer sends a lot more to the server than simply the URL request. It also sends quite a bit of information about itself, including the browser (referred to as the user agent), username, IP address, file types it can accept (such as GIF and JPEG), and several sources of data. The request contains a header and a body; most of the information just specified is sent in the header. The reason people don't realize this is happening, of course, is that the header is not visible to the user.

Once the server receives the request, it responds if it can. It looks at the requested document, and if that document has any server-side code on it (such as ASP VBScript, ColdFusion Markup Language, or PHP code), the server processes those instructions. When it is finished, it removes the server-side code and combines the output from the server-side code along with the XHTML in the document, and sends it all back to the client in the body of the response. The response, like the request, has a header, which contains information for the client system (such as the document size and type and the date and time of the response). About all a user can see of this transaction are the URL and the output XHTML page.

The following figure represents an HTTP transaction. Solid rectangles show documents visible to the user, while dashed rectangles represent documents hidden from the user.

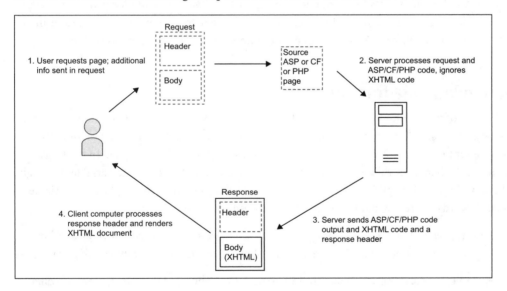

If you wondered at the end of Lesson 3 exactly how test_form_processor.asp gained access to the data that the user entered in the form on that page, the request is your answer. The first-Name variable and its value were sent in the body of the request message when you clicked the Submit button. In other words, the hidden portions of the HTTP request and response messages make it possible to send data values back and forth between the client and server, which makes them available to ASP, ColdFusion, or PHP scripts on the server. It also means, as you'll see in this lesson, that the server can send data back to the client with directions to store the data in a cookie.

Before we start looking at how to take advantage of HTTP to facilitate dynamic Web development, there is one more vital behavior you need to know about the protocol: Once the server sends its response to the client, it forgets about the entire transaction. That is, if the client makes a second request of the server, the server has no idea that this is the same client who made a request a moment ago. For this reason, HTTP is known as a *stateless protocol*.

The statelessness of HTTP is a significant problem for those developing Web applications. If the Web forgets who you are in between every request, how can you get through the successive screens of an online shopping cart? If you have a multipart survey, how can you ensure that the data entered on page 1 is inserted into the database along with the data entered on page 4? You have seen online shopping carts and probably taken multipage surveys, so you know there are solutions to these problems.

It is hard to develop dynamic Web sites without an awareness of the request-and-response transaction and the statelessness of HTTP. Binding data to pages takes place within this context, and the differences between querystring (or URL) variables and form variables, GET and POST, and setting and retrieving cookies—all of which you are about to become familiar with—are considerably less obscure when you understand how they relate to HTTP.

Retrieving Data from the URL

At the end of the previous lesson, users filled out a short form and submitted it to a page that displayed the value they entered in the form. As you know from the preceding section, the variable sent from the form to the test_form_processor.asp page was enclosed in the body of the request. There are other ways to send data between pages. You can send variables through URLs, cookies, and (depending on your server technology) session and application variables. In other words, there are many ways to share data among pages.

The logical question that follows from this is, why are there so many different ways, and how do you know which one to use? The answer is that each has unique capabilities and limitations.

For example, the form variable you sent in Lesson 3 in the body of the request sent the data from the form page to the page that processed and displayed the information. One limitation of this approach is that once the server completes this transaction, it forgets the firstName name-value pair. So although it outputs the user's first name to that page, if the user goes to a different page, the server no longer knows the value of the firstName variable, which means that this name-value pair is no longer available to your code.

In this task, you'll pass data from the form to the test_form_processor.asp page in a different way: You'll use a querystring. A *querystring* is a list of variables appended to the end of a URL. You have probably noticed as you surfed the Web that sometimes URLs are quite long and seem to contain much more information than the page address; that information is a querystring. Let's modify the Web form you created in Lesson 3 so that it sends information using a querystring, rather than a form variable.

1 Open test_form.asp.

At the moment the form is somewhat minimalist.

2 In design view, position the insertion point anywhere inside the text First Name and click on <label> in the tag selector. Next set the Property inspector's Format setting to Paragraph. Position the insertion point after the text field, and press Enter/Return to create a new blank line. Insert a new text field, and in the accessibility dialog, label it *Last Name*. With the new text field selected, use the Property inspector to name it *lastName*.

In this step, you are adding and formatting a second form field. Just because you are placing content in a form doesn't mean you can't format it as needed. You can insert just about any valid HTML element inside of a form.

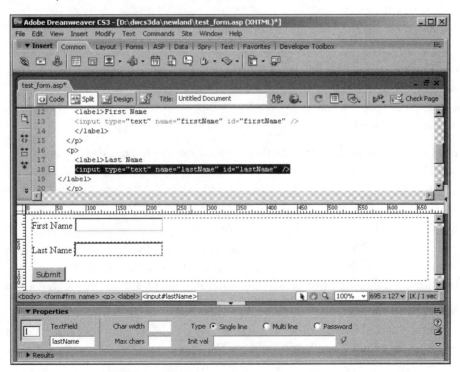

3 Click `<form#frm_name>` in the tag selector to select the whole form and also to bring up the form options in the Property inspector.

The easiest way to modify an element's attributes—especially an element with several child elements, such as the `<form>` element—is to select it in the tag selector.

4 In the Property inspector's Method drop-down menu, select GET.

By default, the value is set to POST, which you left alone in the previous lesson. By changing the method from POST to GET, you are changing the way that the data is sent to test_form_processor.asp. With POST, the data is sent in the request body, as discussed before. But with GET, the data will be sent as a querystring, which means that the firstName and lastName name-value pairs are appended to the URL, as you will see in a moment.

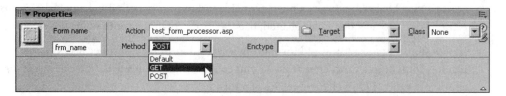

5 Save and close test_form.asp. Open test_form_processor.asp.

You need to modify the test_form_processor.asp page because the dynamic text on that page is looking for the firstName value to come to the page as a form variable. Now that you have changed POST to GET, the firstName value won't be available as a form variable; it will be available only as a querystring. That means that you have to return to the Bindings panel and define a new binding.

6 In the Bindings panel, for ASP click the New Binding (+) button, choose Request Variable, and in the Request Variable dialog specify Request.Querystring as the type. Type *firstName* as the name. For ColdFusion and PHP, click the New Binding (+) button, choose URL variable, and enter *firstName* as the name. Click OK.

"Querystring" and "URL variable" are two variations of the same thing: a variable appended to the URL. There are some subtle differences between the way ASP and ColdFusion handle these types of variables, but for the purposes of this book, we'll treat them as if they are no more than two different names for the same thing.

When you are finished, the change should be reflected in the Bindings panel. The screen shot is for ASP. ColdFusion and PHP users will see two categories of variable: Form (with firstName nested inside) and URL (with firstName nested inside).

7 Repeat Step 6 to add a Request.Querystring/URL Variable for the lastName variable.

Again, the Bindings panel should update, and you should now see three variables defined: two versions of firstName and one of lastName.

It might seem odd to have the same variable—firstName—listed twice. But as far as ASP, ColdFusion, and PHP are concerned, these are two completely different variables. One is a form variable, and is only retrievable from the body of the HTTP request. The other is a querystring variable, which is only retrievable from the URL itself. This concept—where variables are available only in a designated place—is known as variable scope. A variable's scope includes the place(s) where the variable exists, and excludes the places it does not. The lastName variable exists only as a URL querystring. If ASP, ColdFusion, or PHP looks for it in the request body, it won't find it: The request body is outside of the querystring scope.

Scoping variables is a fundamental task in any programming language. Without it, you would have no way of ensuring that data is available when you need it and that two different pieces of data don't inadvertently share the same name. It also speeds up processing as it helps the server narrow down its search for the variable, much like the zip code helps the post office narrow the search for your house.

By changing the form's method from POST to GET, you change the firstName variable's scope. By making these changes in the Bindings panel, you gave your server-side code access to the appropriate scope. There are many more scopes than form and querystring variables (as you doubtless noticed when working in the Bindings panel), but conceptually, they all work the same way.

8 Click to select the blue-shaded {Form.firstName} dynamic text on the page, and then in the Bindings panel, select QueryString.firstName (ASP) or URL > firstName (ColdFusion and PHP) in the Bindings panel, and click Insert.

When you are finished, you should see a new blue-shaded dynamic text block that contains {QueryString.firstName} (ASP) or {URL.firstName} (ColdFusion and PHP).

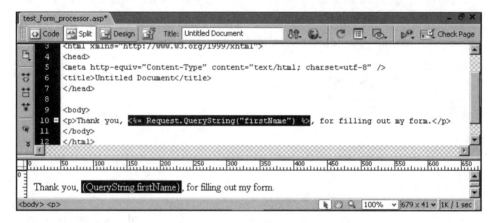

Now that you understand scope, you probably also can read Dreamweaver's dynamic text pseudocode. The curly braces {} represent a dynamic code block, and inside is listed the scope, followed by a period, followed by a variable name. Dreamweaver pseudocode gives you quick access to the scope and name of all dynamic text.

Looking beyond the pseudocode at the real code, you should see <%= Request. QueryString("firstName") %> embedded in the HTML on the ASP page, <cfoutput>#URL. firstName#</cfoutput> on the ColdFusion page, and <?php echo $_GET['firstName']; ?> on the PHP page.

✱ NOTE: In ColdFusion, values enclosed in #pound signs# are variables that ColdFusion must resolve before outputting. In the preceding example, if you omitted the pound signs, ColdFusion would write: Thank you, URL.firstName, for filling out my page. By adding the pound signs, ColdFusion knows it needs to evaluate the variable—in this case, by outputting whatever value is stored in the firstName variable in the URL.

9 Position the insertion point after the firstName block, insert a blank space, and bind the QueryString.lastName or URL.lastName variable to the page by selecting it in the Bindings panel and clicking Insert.

The two variables should appear side by side, so that the output displays the user's entire name.

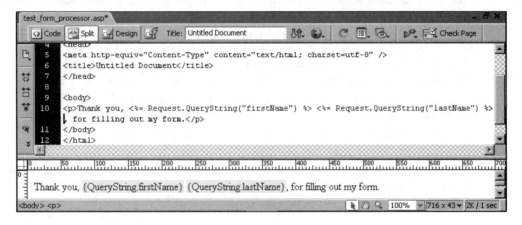

10 Save test_form_processor.asp, and in the Site panel, Shift-select test_form.asp and test_form_processor.asp and click the Put File(s) button.

Remember, you can't test your files unless you upload them to the server.

11 Click test_form.asp in the Site panel, and press F12 to test in a browser. Enter your first name and your last name, and click Submit.

As you've anticipated, the page now thanks you using your first and last name.

✳ NOTE: If the first and last names run together, which seems to happen in ASP but not ColdFusion or PHP, insert a non-breaking space character ( ) between the two dynamic blocks in test_form_processor.asp.

Of more interest, though, is the URL. Appended to the page address is a question mark followed by three name-value pairs:

```
http://localhost/newland/test_form_processor.asp?firstName=Ghengis&lastName=
➥Kahn&button=Submit
```

The appended three variables are the querystring. The output first and last names are pulled directly out of the URL. This URL appears the same, regardless of server model, because querystrings are a part of HTTP itself, rather than a dynamic Web page technology.

Generally, you should use POST, rather than GET, to send form data to be stored in a database, because with POST the data is not visible to the user. Also, you can embed quite a bit more data in the request body using POST than you could in a URL using GET. But for the sake of this exercise, GET is sufficient. As you will see momentarily, though, querystrings have some advantages that form variables don't.

✦ **NOTE:** Just because data in the form scope is not visible to the user doesn't mean it is secure! The data is sent unencrypted with the request, and anyone snooping on the lines can read in clear text the name-value pairs in the form scope.

12 Close your browser. In Dreamweaver's Site panel, click test_form_processor.asp, and press F12.

This time, when you test the page, it lacks the querystring data that ASP, ColdFusion and PHP are expecting, because you closed the browser and flushed that data from memory. Interestingly, ASP and PHP handle this problem differently than ColdFusion. ASP and PHP display, "Thank you, , for filling out my form." ColdFusion only gets as far as "Thank you, " before giving an error message stating that "Element FIRSTNAME is undefined in URL." It was expecting your firstName variable in the URL scope and did not find it.

One of the challenges of dynamic site development is to make sure that no user enters a page without all of the data that the page needs to process. If this happens, the result is often an error that confuses and frustrates users. The solution to this problem is twofold: Prevent users from accessing pages without sufficient data in the first place, and if that fails, catch the error and redirect users to an all-purpose error page that enables them to notify the Webmaster, which is better than them seeing a cryptic ASP, ColdFusion, or PHP error message. We'll use several different types of validation during the course of this book to prevent users from accessing pages without the required data.

> **TIP:** Error messages and the information they contain can be very useful during development. The ColdFusion error mentioned above told us that a variable our page was expecting was not there. That would point us in the right direction if we were troubleshooting. ASP, ColdFusion and PHP each have their own mechanism for enabling debugging output. I encourage you to explore debugging for your development. However it should never be enabled in a production environment. It gives too much useful information to those who may want to compromise your system. For more on how to set up debugging in your development environment, see:
>
> ASP: http://www.microsoft.com/technet/prodtechnol/WindowsServer2003/Library/ IIS/3c7830b4-df5c-41a2-9890-c201eb774c89.mspx?mfr=true
>
> ColdFusion: http://livedocs.adobe.com/coldfusion/7/htmldocs/00001717.htm#1165152
>
> PHP: http://us.php.net/manual/en/ref.errorfunc.php

Sending Data with Hyperlinks

The querystring's open display of data, though a problem for confidential information, has certain benefits. One of them is that you can embed data in hyperlinks. That is, you can collect information from users without requiring them to fill out a form. In this task, you will build a simple page, which, though a bit silly superficially, exhibits a couple of key dynamic Web site concepts in action.

You will build a two-page mini-application that lets each user specify whether she or he is a cat person or a dog person. The first page contains two links—one for cats and one for dogs. The interesting thing about these links is that they both point to the same page. The links are differentiated in that each has a querystring appended to it with the chosen animal preference. On the second page, dynamic text is output, based on the selected link. If you first choose one animal, and then go back and choose the other, it will appear as if you went to two different pages, while in fact you went to only one, with different dynamic text values displaying.

This is an important concept. Think about a large e-commerce site, such as Amazon. Rather than having a different page for every single book they sell, they have only one product detail page, and the page is populated dynamically when the user selects a book. In other words, dynamic pages enable developers to drastically reduce the number of pages they must create and maintain, while simultaneously expanding the amount of content that their pages can show.

So set aside the impracticality of this application for the time being. It forms the basis of the site maintenance functionality that you'll build later in the Newland site.

1 Choose File > New, and create a new dynamic page using ASP/VBScript, ColdFusion, or PHP.

By choosing the correct document type in this dialog, you ensure that Dreamweaver will write the correct type of code for your site.

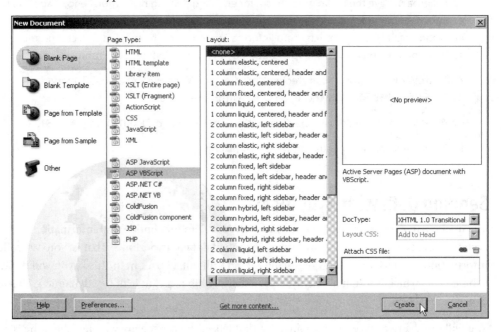

2 In design view, type the text shown in the accompanying figure. Format the first line as an <h1> heading and the second two as body paragraph elements <p>. Change the page title to *Animal Questions*.

In this step, you are marking up just the static portion of the application.

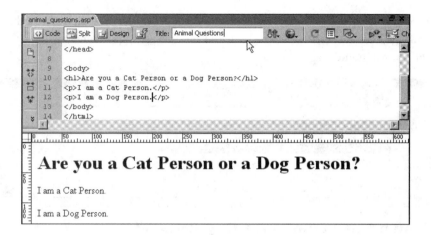

3 Save the file as animal_questions.asp. Then choose File > Save As and save the page again, this time as animal_home_page.asp.

Here you are both saving the file and creating a second page based on the first.

4 Still in animal_home_page.asp, replace the existing heading with *The Person Home Page*, and replace the first statement with *You are a person*. Remove the second statement. Change the page title to *Person Home Page*.

Again, you are setting up the static portion of this page. As it now stands, it's nonsensical. In a moment, it will make more sense when you add functionality that will place Cat or Dog before the word person in each paragraph.

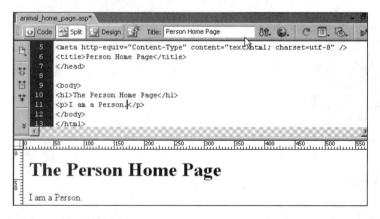

5 Open animal_questions.asp. Double-click to select the word Cat in the second paragraph. In the Link field of the Property inspector, type the following: *animal_home_page. asp?mypet=Cat*.

Here you are manually adding a querystring to the URL. When the user clicks this link, both the URL and the querystring will be sent, and the querystring's contents will be available on animal_home_page.asp.

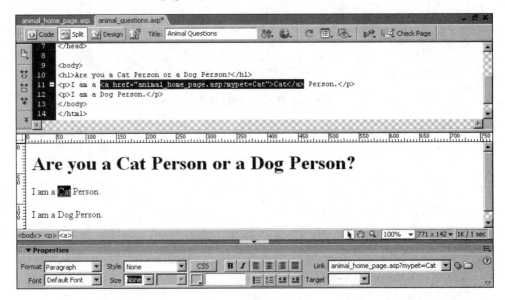

6 Repeat Step 5 to add a link to the word Dog, with the appropriate querystring added to the link. Save and upload (Put) the file.

You are finished with this page.

7 Return to animal_home_page.asp. In the Bindings panel, add a QueryString/URL variable named *mypet*.

This is the variable that you coded into the each link's URL on the previous page. But you set each one to a different value—Cat or Dog. In this step, you are using the Bindings panel to retrieve this name-value pair.

8 Position the cursor just ahead of Person in the heading. Click the mypet variable in the Bindings panel, and click Insert. Add another instance of this variable before the word "person" in the body paragraph. Save and upload the page.

The application is complete.

9 Select animal_questions.asp in the Site panel, and press F12 to test the application.

In turn, click both Cat and Dog, so you can see that the page does indeed change.

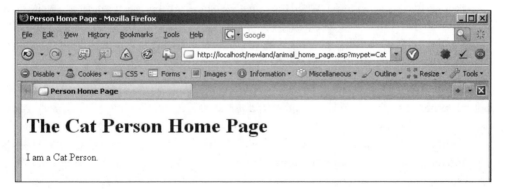

As you can see, animal_home_page.asp is a template that can hold any content. You could easily add links on animal_questions.asp for iguanas, tropical fish, and pythons, and animal_home_page.asp would function without any changes to the code. And this is the ultimate power of dynamic Web pages: You can present infinite content—as well as add to or change that content—without having to redo the XHTML pages. Change the content in the source, and the update takes place seamlessly in the output XHTML page.

Setting and Retrieving Cookies

Up to this point, you've seen different ways to use forms and simple links to collect user data, to make that data available to another page, and to make use of it on that page. In spite of their differences, though, form and querystring variables have something important in common: Each is good for sending data from one page to another, but after that they vaporize into the forgetfulness of HTTP.

When you build Web applications, you will often want certain pieces of data to persist beyond a single request/response transaction, and forms and querystrings won't do for that. However, other variable types do persist beyond a single transaction. How is that possible, given the limitations of HTTP? The answer is that their data is stored in memory or on a hard drive—the user's or the server's—and retrieved or set as a part of every request/response transaction that requires that data.

One such variable type is the *cookie*. Cookies are tiny text files that are written onto user's hard drives. You can save cookies on user's hard drives and retrieve them across multiple pages. In this manner, you can maintain state in spite of the stateless HTTP protocol.

> ✳ **NOTE:** Many users are concerned about cookies and security. In many instances, this concern is unfounded, since cookies can't be used to infect a computer with a virus, and the only site that can read a cookie is the site that set the cookie. However, cookies persist on a computer's hard drive, regardless of which actual user is logged in. Thus, storing credit card information in a cookie becomes dangerous when the user is working from a public terminal or a workstation that is shared with other colleagues. Developers should either not store anything sensitive in a cookie, such as a credit card number or a password, or the site should at least provide users with the option of whether to save the information to their hard drive.

In this task, you will learn how to set and retrieve cookies. You'll use the form application again, but this time, when the form is submitted and users are redirected to test_form_processor. asp, their first and last names will be stored in cookies on their hard drives. Then, you'll create a third page that requests these values—without using form or querystring variables—to demonstrate how the firstName and lastName variables can persist beyond a single HTTP request/response transaction.

1 Open test_form_processor.asp.

As you'll recall, this page is expecting the firstName and lastName variables to appear as a querystring; in fact, it outputs these values in the page's lone line of text: "Thank you, {QueryString.firstName} {QueryString.lastName}, for filling out my form."

In a moment, you'll capture those same values, not for the purpose of outputting them in body text, but rather to save them as cookies to the user's hard drive.

2 In code view, place the insertion point just before the <!DOCTYPE> tag (line 2 in ASP and line 1 in ColdFusion and PHP). Press Enter/Return a few times to add some blank space.

The blank lines should precede the <DOCTYPE> tag.

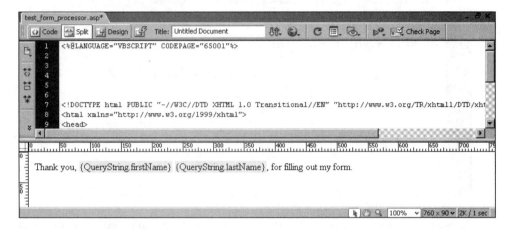

In a moment you will manually add some code, so you need to make space for it. Notice that you're adding the code before the HTML document proper, which begins with the <DOCTYPE> element. Server code is often placed outside the HTML document, which makes it easier to find and edit. And don't forget: When the page is output from the server to the client, the server code is stripped out, so users will never see this code.

✴ **NOTE:** In PHP, any time you attempt to send content back to the browser via a header—and setting cookies is one example of this—you must add this script before the first line of XHTML code, or you will see an error along the lines of "cannot add header information." The simple solution to this problem is to put such content at the very beginning of the file.

3 Type the code block below, as appropriate.

In ASP:

```
<%
Response.Cookies("firstName") = Request.QueryString("firstName")
Response.Cookies("firstName").Expires = Date+30
Response.Cookies("lastName") = Request.QueryString("lastName")
Response.Cookies("lastName").Expires = Date+30
%>
```

In ColdFusion:

```
<cfcookie name="firstName" expires="never" value="#url.firstName#">
<cfcookie name="lastName" expires="never" value="#url.lastName#">
```

In PHP:

```php
<?php
setcookie('firstName', $_GET['firstName'], time() + (60*60*24));
setcookie('lastName', $_GET['lastName'], time() + (60*60*24));
?>
```

```
1   <%@LANGUAGE="VBSCRIPT" CODEPAGE="65001"%>
2
3   <%
4   Response.Cookies("firstName") = Request.QueryString("firstName")
5   Response.Cookies("firstName").Expires = Date+30
6   Response.Cookies("lastName") = Request.QueryString("lastName")
7   Response.Cookies("lastName").Expires = Date+30
8   %>
9
10  <!DOCTYPE html PUBLIC "-//W3C//DTD XHTML 1.0 Transitional//EN" "http://www.w3.org/TR/xhtml1/DTD/xht
11  <html xmlns="http://www.w3.org/1999/xhtml">
12  <head>
13  <meta http-equiv="Content-Type" content="text/html; charset=utf-8" />
14  <title>Untitled Document</title>
15  </head>
```

Before discussing the particulars of this code, I'd like to point out that there is no visual way to write a cookie using Dreamweaver, so you have to write the code yourself. While Dreamweaver can help you develop dynamic Web sites, you have to be willing to do some hand-coding if you really want to build dynamic sites. If you've been studying the code, you probably already understand how the code works.

Though the syntax varies markedly when you compare ASP, ColdFusion, and PHP, all three sets of code work the same way. They create two new cookie variables, one named firstName and the other named lastName. As before, we are naming two completely different variables with the same names (QueryString.firstName and Cookies.first-Name, with a comparable pair for the last name), but their different scopes prevent any possible confusion. Both specify expiration dates (30 days from today in ASP, never in ColdFusion, and one day for PHP). Finally, all three specify the new cookie variable's value as the current value of QueryString.firstName and QueryString.lastName.

In other words, the values of the new cookie variables are dynamically set. Not only can you set variables to static, hard values, such as Cat or Dog, but you can also create variables to hold contents drawn from other variables. Here, the cookie variables are dynamically set with the contents of the querystring/URL variables.

4 Back in design view, create a new paragraph below the existing one, and type *Check cookie*. Link the word cookie to a page named *test_form_processor_cookies.asp*. Save and upload this page.

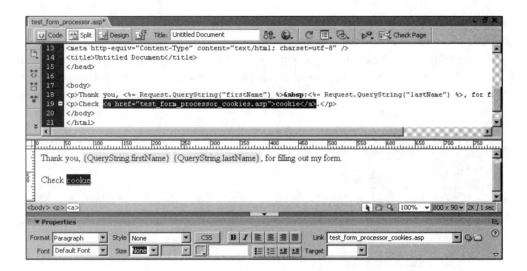

This new page, test_form_processor_cookies.asp, doesn't exist yet, but you'll create it in a moment.

Before you create this new page, based on what you have learned so far in this lesson, can you guess what you'll need to do to display the two cookie variables on that page?

5 Create a new dynamic, XHTML-compliant page, and save it as *test_form_processor_cookies.asp*.

Creating new dynamic pages should be familiar to you now.

6 In design view, type *Hi, !*.

Typing text to be used with dynamic pages often looks bizarre, because a portion of the text is hard-coded, and a portion of it is going to be loaded dynamically.

✱ **NOTE:** Because your text is coming from two different sources (static XHTML and a dynamic data source), be sure to double-check your grammar and punctuation, to ensure that the text works as a unit once it is all assembled.

7 In the Bindings panel, click the New Binding (+) button. ASP users should choose Request Variable, and then specify Request.Cookies and firstName. ColdFusion and PHP users simply choose Cookie Variable and type *firstName* in the dialog.

Adding cookie bindings is just like adding querystring and form bindings.

8 Repeat Step 7 to add the lastName cookie to the Bindings panel.

As ever, the Bindings panel updates to show you the variables that you've added.

One difference in the Bindings panel between ASP and ColdFusion/PHP is that ASP displays variables on a page-by-page basis, whereas the bindings that ColdFusion users created on other pages are available throughout the site. The practical consequence is that while an ASP user's Bindings panel at this point shows only the two cookie variables, a ColdFusion or PHP user's Bindings panel at this point shows all of the bindings you have created for the site.

9 Position the insertion point before the exclamation point, select Cookies.firstName (ASP) or Cookie > firstName (ColdFusion/PHP) in the Bindings panel, and click Insert. Repeat to add the last name as well.

At this point in the lesson, you should be familiar with this routine.

✱ **NOTE:** As before, ASP users will have to insert   between the two variable blocks to avoid run-on names.

10 Save and upload the page. Click test_form.asp in the Site panel, and press F12 to test. Fill out the form, click Submit, then follow the Check cookie link.

As you would expect, it works. Even though the data started on the first page, you got it to display on the third. The information was pulled not from the URL or the request body as form variables, but rather from your hard drive.

✱ **NOTE:** Because HTTP is limited to request/response transactions, the server does not have direct access to the hard drive, so the cookie variables are passed from the hard drive to the server through the request. However, the source value itself is on the hard drive.

11 Close your browser. Return to Dreamweaver, select test_form_processor_cookies.asp in the Site panel, and press F12.

Earlier when you did this experiment with test_form_processor.asp, it didn't work, because there was no data in the querystring—that data was lost as soon as you closed your browser. ASP and PHP left the text blank, while ColdFusion threw an error. But when you try the same experiment using cookies, even though you closed the browser, the data persisted, because it was saved on your hard drive as a cookie. As you can see, cookies are a powerful way to create a set of persistent data that you can access across multiple pages throughout the site.

What You Have Learned

In this lesson, you have:

- Learned about HTTP's request/response transaction model (pages 114–116)
- Captured and displayed data embedded in a querystring (pages 116–123)
- Collected user data and output dynamic results using links and querystrings (pages 123–127)
- Written the code to cause ASP, ColdFusion, and PHP to set cookie variables (pages 128–130)
- Retrieved and output data stored in cookies (pages 131–133)

What You Will Learn

In this lesson, you will:

- Configure IIS, ColdFusion or PHP to send email messages, if you are developing locally

- Use mail objects to generate an email from a Web page

- Create a form to collect data from the user

- Populate the email message with form data

- Deploy client-side form validation

Approximate Time

This lesson takes approximately 60 minutes to complete.

Lesson Files

Starting Files:

Lesson05/Start/newland/contact.asp
Lesson05/Start/newland/generic_template.asp
Lesson05/Start/newland/index.asp

Completed Files:

Lesson05/Complete/newland/contact.asp
Lesson05/Complete/newland/messageSent.asp
Lesson05/Complete/newland/generic_ template.asp
Lesson05/Complete/newland/index.asp

Sending Email from a Web Form

You are now experienced at sending data between pages in several different ways. Sending data between pages is helpful to users, because it creates a cohesive experience. Sending data is even more useful for Web site owners, since it allows them to offer customized services via the Web based on choices users make. In a word, sending data between pages enables a group of pages to function together as a single unit—no mean accomplishment given the forgetfulness of the HTTP protocol.

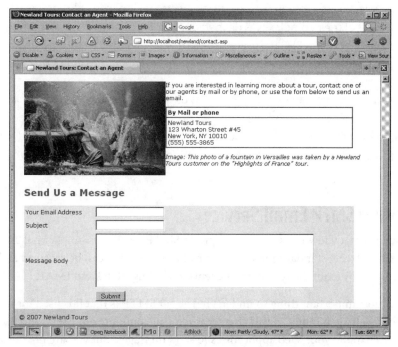

You'll use the data collected from this form to generate an email message to yourself.

Though passing data between pages is useful, pages are not the only places you'll need to send your data. Sometimes, you'll want to send it to an information storage warehouse, such as a database. Other times, you'll want to send the information directly to a reader. In this lesson, you'll see how to collect information from the user at the Newland Tours Web site and send it to a Newland Tours travel agent. (Of course, since Newland Tours doesn't really exist, you'll have to settle for sending the messages to yourself to test the functionality.)

In this lesson, you'll learn how to configure your system to send email messages, if you are running Internet Information Services (IIS), Adobe ColdFusion or PHP locally.

In addition to configuring a mail server, if applicable, you will make use of special mail objects. You may have heard the term "objects," as in "object-oriented programming," and not known exactly what that means. When working with ASP, you encounter many objects and have to deal with the initially unfamiliar syntax.

Objects can be intimidating to those new to programming. But the truth is, the objects in object-oriented programming (OOP) are conceptually modeled on tangible objects in the real world. That is, the whole point of OOP is to make programming easier, more approachable, and easier to maintain. But at first, you may feel that objects are unnecessarily complex. This, despite the fact that most of their complexity is deliberately hidden, even as their power is made available to you. ColdFusion and PHP users don't have to work explicitly with objects the way ASP users do, but objects are never far: sometimes they are hidden in the underlying code.

This lesson requires some hand-coding. Again, as user-friendly as Dreamweaver's interface is, sometimes you have to go behind the page design, behind the wizards and dialogs, and type your own code. Don't worry: I assume you have no programming experience and will walk you through it step-by-step with detailed explanations.

Introducing SMTP Email Service

The mail service that you will use in this chapter is SMTP. SMTP, or Simple Mail Transfer Protocol, is an Internet standard for sending email messages that can be received and correctly interpreted by a number of different clients, including POP3 and IMAP.

Perhaps the most important thing to understand about SMTP is that it is used for sending mail, not for receiving it. Thus, in this chapter when you configure your server to use SMTP mail, you are enabling your Web applications to send messages. But you are not creating a full-fledged email service. There are extensions and other solutions that enable you to make your local workstation able to send and receive messages, but doing so is beyond the scope of this book.

The goal in this lesson is to make it possible to generate messages from within your Web applications and send them over the Internet—a useful capability, as you will soon see.

Configuring Your System to Send SMTP Email Messages

Before you can send email from within a Web application, you need to ensure that the server hosting the application can send email. Some of you are using IIS locally to develop ASP pages, some are using ColdFusion locally, some are using PHP locally, and some are connecting to remote servers that have any combination of ASP, ColdFusion, and/or PHP. Depending on how you are connecting to your server, you need to follow a different set of steps in this task, as outlined in the following list:

- ASP users developing locally with IIS (Windows 2000 or Windows XP Professional) should read the section, *Configuring IIS to Send Email (ASP Users)*.

- ColdFusion users developing locally should skip ahead to the section, *Configuring ColdFusion to Send Email*.

- PHP users developing locally with Apache should skip ahead to the section, *Configuring PHP to Send Email*.

- ASP, ColdFusion, or PHP users developing on remote servers (using a mapped network drive or FTP) need to verify with their server administrator that the server is SMTP email-enabled, and likewise verify that their folder on that server has permission to send SMTP email messages. Once verified, skip ahead to the section, *Writing the Code to Send a Message*.

✱ **NOTE:** Web and mail (SMTP) servers present an attractive target to those wishing to exploit computers connected to the Internet. Regardless of the language you are using, if you are developing locally you should shut down the server whenever you are not working on it.

✱ **NOTE:** Due to security concerns some system administrators will have measures in place that will prevent your local server from using the SMTP server. If that applies to your system, you will not be able to successfully test sending email messages in this lesson. Do not spend too much time troubleshooting the problem. The thing to take away from this lesson is how to write the functionality. In a production environment the system administrator will have the SMTP set up for you.

Configuring IIS to Send Email (ASP Users)

You should read this section if you are using ASP on a local copy of the IIS server (Windows 2000 or XP Pro). Chances are your system is already configured to use SMTP email, but you should verify that. If for some reason SMTP service is not installed, you'll need to install it, following the steps provided below.

1 Open the Windows Control Panel, and access the Add/Remove Programs dialog. Click the Add/Remove Windows Components button.

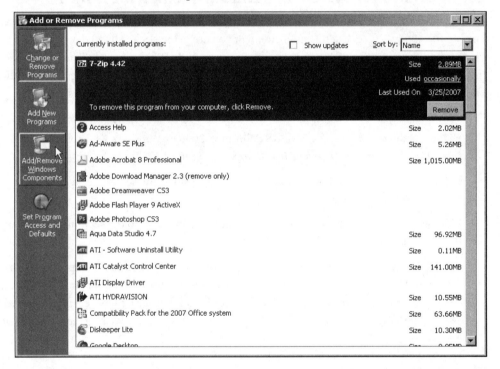

When you click the Add/Remove Windows Components button, a second dialog, the Windows Components Wizard, appears.

As you probably know, you not only maintain installed programs through the Add/Remove Programs portion of the Control Panel, but you also maintain the installation and configuration of Windows. Since IIS is a part of Windows 2000 and Windows XP, you can add and remove its installed components through this dialog.

2 In the Windows Component Wizard, click to select Internet Information Services (IIS), and click the Details button.

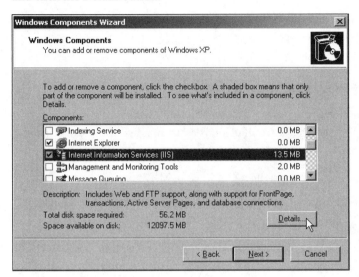

The Internet Information Services (IIS) dialog opens. Use this dialog to install and uninstall IIS components, including SMTP service.

3 Scroll down (if necessary) and verify that SMTP Service is checked.

If it is already checked, then SMTP outgoing email service is already installed.

If it is not checked, then SMTP is not installed. When you check it, Windows will install it and start it for you.

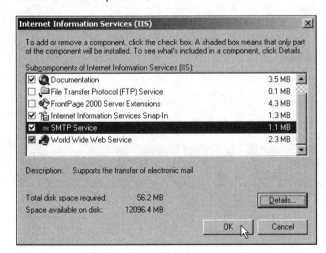

4 Click OK to accept the changes in the Internet Information Services (IIS) dialog, and then click Next to have Windows finish the installation.

At this point, outgoing SMTP mail service is installed. You can skip ahead to the section, *Writing the Code to Send a Message.*

Configuring ColdFusion to Send Email

You should read this section if you are using ColdFusion locally on your workstation. Configuring outgoing SMTP service for ColdFusion is easily handled using ColdFusion's Administrator application.

1 From the Start menu, open Macromedia > ColdFusion MX7 > Administrator.

The path within your Start menu may vary, if you have customized it , or are using ColdFusion 8.

When the page opens, you'll need to log in. Once you do, you will see the ColdFusion administrator. You use this page for a number of ColdFusion administration settings, and you'll use it later in the book to create a **datasource**, which will enable you to use database content on the Newland Tours page.

✳ **NOTE:** At the time of this writing the latest release version of ColdFusion is 7.0.2. While ColdFusion is now part of the Adobe family of products the installer still places ColdFusion in a folder labeled "Macromedia" by default.

2 Click the Mail link from the left navigation bar, in the Server Settings category.

You see a page containing several settings for the mail server. You can leave all of them, with the exception of the Internet or IP address of your outgoing mail server, at their defaults.

3 In the Mail Server field, enter the Internet or IP address of your outgoing mail server.

If you are not sure of your outgoing mail server's address, look inside the account settings of your email software. The Internet or IP address should be located there.

For example, in Outlook Express, look in Tools > Accounts. Select your email account, and click Properties. Click the Servers tab, and copy the address in the Outgoing mail (SMTP) field. The menus and commands in other email clients may vary, but the outgoing Internet or IP address information should be available somewhere in the interface.

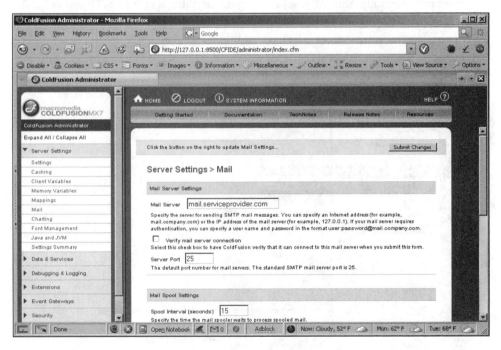

4 Click the Submit button at the top or bottom of the page.

ColdFusion updates the settings, and as long as the SMTP address you entered is valid, it will work as expected.

Configuring PHP to Send Email

You should read this section if you are using PHP locally on your workstation. Both Windows and Macintosh systems are configured through the php.ini file, which contains the settings for the PHP engine running on your server. In this section, you will update this file's SMTP server settings, as appropriate for either a Windows or Macintosh system.

Windows

You access the php.ini file via the WAMP5 control panel in your system tray. Your system tray is the area in the lower right corner of your screen. The WAMP5 control panel resembles a car's speedometer.

1 Click the WAMP5 control panel. Go to the Config files folder and select php.ini to open it in your default text editor.

You see a text file that starts with a warning about your installation being for development purposes only. You will just be changing the address of the SMTP server for the purposes of relaying mail sent from here. As mentioned previously, the administrators of your outgoing mail server may have additional security measures in place to prevent its use by servers such as this.

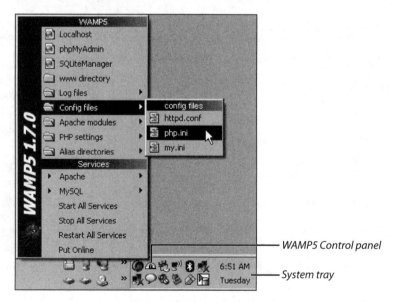

WAMP5 Control panel

System tray

2 Search for SMTP in the configuration file. Once you locate it, enter the Internet or IP address of your outgoing mail server.

```
[mail function]
; For win32 only.
SMTP = mail.serviceprovider.com

; For win32 only.
sendmail_from = yourname@yourserver.com
```

3 Save your changes and close the file. Return to the WAMP5 Control panel and choose Restart All Services.

In order for your changes to take effect, your server must be restarted.

Macintosh

The php.ini file of your MAMP installation is located in the application's folder.

1 Open Applications/MAMP/conf/. This folder will contain both php4 and php5 configuration folders. If you have not changed the default installation, open the php5 folder and open the php.ini file contained within.

✱ **NOTE:** You can confirm the version of PHP your MAMP installation is using by checking the PHP tab under Preferences.

2 Search for SMTP in the configuration file. Once you locate it, enter the Internet or IP address of your outgoing mail server.

3 Save your changes and close the file. Launch the MAMP Control panel and click the Stop Servers button. Once both lights have gone red the button will change to Start Servers. Click it again.

In order for your changes to take effect, your server must be restarted.

Writing the Code to Send a Message

In this task, you will create a page that sends an email message to your email address. The content of the message will be hard-coded initially. That is, if you send yourself 20 messages, they'll all have the same subject and body content. Once you have verified that it works, you can build a front-end form for the mail message and change the hard-coded values to dynamic form values.

1 Open generic_template.asp, choose File > Save As, and name the new file *messageSent.asp*.

This new file will do the work of generating and sending the email message and will inform the user that the message has been sent.

2 Replace the placeholder title with *Message Sent*. Replace the title with *Newland Tours: Message Sent*. Replace the placeholder body text with *Your message has been sent. You should hear from us within two days*. Insert a new paragraph with the text *Return to Newland Home*, and link the word Home to index.asp.

You can see the payoff for having created the template already. The new page literally takes seconds to create and customize.

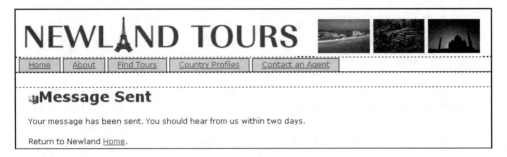

What's lacking at this point is the functionality that will generate and send the email. Before dealing with this issue, let's pause for a moment to discuss objects. Many modern computer languages—including most languages used for Web programming—contain them, so it's a good concept to master.

Understanding Objects, Methods, and Properties

Programming languages are developed to solve certain problems or enable certain functionalities—they don't just pop up from nowhere. For example, ActionScript was created to enable developers to get the most out of native Flash capabilities and features. For this reason, several features of ActionScript are unique to Flash, and these features distinguish ActionScript from languages similar to it, such as JavaScript.

ASP, ColdFusion, and PHP are no different. Each was designed to enable dynamic Web site functionality within the context of HTTP. Their respective developers knew that you would want to do certain tasks, such as send data between pages, connect to databases, and generate email messages. To simplify these tasks, each language includes built-in objects. Objects are generic entities created for the purpose of simplifying a given task. For example, ASP's Message object makes it easy to create and send new mail messages from within ASP.

✳ NOTE: Strictly speaking, the Message object doesn't belong to ASP, but rather to a larger class of objects built into Windows 2000 and XP, and available to IIS. This nuance has little consequence for our purposes, and I only mention it here for accuracy.

To use an object, you must first create an **instance** of it. If you've ever used a Library in Adobe Flash, Fireworks, or Dreamweaver, you are already familiar with the relationship. The object, or more properly, **class**, exists in potential only; you can't directly use the class itself. When you make an instance of it, you make a unique copy of that class, but you also customize it for its surroundings. You might think of it as the difference between the scientific definition of homo sapiens on the one hand, and an individual person on the other. All members of homo sapiens have height, hair color, and weight attributes. But these values differ for each person.

Most object classes have built-in features. Generally, these fit into three categories: events, properties, and methods. Some objects even have child objects with their own events, properties, and methods.

- **Events** can be thought of as built-in triggers, indicating when a certain kind of thing has happened. To use the homo sapiens example, "upon waking up" or "when one becomes thirsty" are events, or triggers, which often (though not necessarily) cause other behaviors to happen ("throw alarm clock" and "drink some water" might be typical responses to the events mentioned earlier). On the Web, common events include when the page loads, when the user clicks the submit button, and when an active text field loses focus.

- **Properties** are descriptive attributes. For a person, height, hair color, birthday, current location, and weight are all properties.

- **Methods** are what the object can do. Humans can walk, dance, sing, and sleep; each of these would be a method of the homo sapiens.

When you create an instance of an object, you often define its properties. When you want something to happen, you call one or more of its methods, in response to one of its events.

Finally, when you create an object instance, you usually need to give it a unique ID, or name. This name enables the script to keep track of it, since you can usually use multiple instances of the same object in the same script or document. Once again, humans have names for the same reason—names help us identify and refer to each other.

To summarize, you can achieve specific kinds of functionality in scripts by using built-in objects. To use an object, you must create an instance of it. To enable the script to properly identify your instance, you give it a unique name. Finally, to make use of the instance (and accomplish your task), you set its properties and call its methods in response to events.

In the steps that follow, ASP users will write a script in which they can see each of these steps in action. ColdFusion and PHP users will discover that their respective languages hide much of this complexity, though traces of it are still visible.

The following steps are separated to reflect the different stages of using an object.

✱ NOTE: These steps continue from the last task, *Writing the Code to Send a Message.*

3 Using the code view, position the cursor at the beginning of line 1 and press Enter/Return several times.

In this step, you are merely making room for a new script.

4 ASP and ColdFusion Users Only: To instantiate and give identity to a new mail object, enter the following code:

For ASP:

```
<%
theSchema="http://schemas.microsoft.com/cdo/configuration/"
Set cdoConfig=server.CreateObject("CDO.Configuration")
cdoConfig.Fields.Item(theSchema & "sendusing")=2
cdoConfig.Fields.Item(theSchema & "smtpserver")="your.SMTP.server.com"
cdoConfig.Fields.Update
set cdoMessage=Server.CreateObject("CDO.Message")
cdoMessage.Configuration=cdoConfig
%>
```

For ColdFusion:

```
<cfmail>
</cfmail>
```

ASP users: Be sure to replace the italicized code "your.SMTP.server.com" with the name or IP address of your actual SMTP server. This is most likely the same server as the one listed for outgoing email in your email client, such as Microsoft Outlook Express.

The ColdFusion code is fairly self-explanatory: These two tags tell ColdFusion to create a new mail object. It still needs help before it's useful, but at least you've created it. Behind the scenes, ColdFusion also gives this mail object a unique ID, so in this simple step you have accomplished several tasks.

The ASP code is (not surprisingly) somewhat more cryptic. In the first code block, you provide the information ASP needs to actually connect to the mail server. It's cryptic, to be sure, but you should be able to use it as-is on any modern Windows server.

The second code block in ASP, which you'll add to momentarily, instantiates the Message object.

```
1   <%
2   theSchema="http://schemas.microsoft.com/cdo/configuration/"
3   Set cdoConfig=server.CreateObject("CDO.Configuration")
4   cdoConfig.Fields.Item(theSchema & "sendusing")= 2
5   cdoConfig.Fields.Item(theSchema & "smtpserver")="mail.serviceprovider.com"
6   cdoConfig.Fields.Update
7   set cdoMessage=Server.CreateObject("CDO.Message")
8   cdoMessage.Configuration=cdoConfig
9   %>
10
11  <!DOCTYPE html PUBLIC "-//W3C//DTD XHTML 1.0 Transitional//EN" "http://www.w3.org/TR/xhtml1/DTD/xhtml
12  <html xmlns="http://www.w3.org/1999/xhtml">
13  <head>
14  <meta http-equiv="Content-Type" content="text/html; charset=utf-8" />
15  <title>Newland Tours: Message Sent</title>
16  <link href="css/main.css" rel="stylesheet" type="text/css" />
17  </head>
```

5 Customize the instance so that it can send desired information to the proper email address. To do so, add the following code just above the closing %> (ASP) or </cfmail> (ColdFusion). PHP users: Enter the line of PHP below, in the empty space you created in Step 3 above.

For ASP, enter the following code, substituting yourname@yourserver.com with your actual email address:

```
cdoMessage.From="yourname@yourserver.com"
cdoMessage.To="yourname@yourserver.com"
cdoMessage.Subject="This is the message subject"
cdoMessage.TextBody="This is the message body"
cdoMessage.Send
```

Then, ASP users should add two new lines, as follows:

```
Set cdoMessage=Nothing
Set cdoConfig=Nothing
```

For ColdFusion, amend the <cfmail> tag so that it reads as follows, substituting yourname@yourserver.com with your actual email address:

```
<cfmail from="yourname@yourserver.com" to="yourname@yourserver.com"
➥subject="This is the Message Subject">
```

ColdFusion users should then add a new line between the opening and closing `<cfmail>` tags. Type:

```
This is the message body.
```

For PHP, type the following code:

```
<?php
$to = "yourname@yourserver.com";
$subject = "This is the message subject";
$body = "This is the message body";
$headers = "From: yourname@yourserver.com\n";
mail($to,$subject,$body,$headers);
?>
```

The first four lines store the recipient, subject, body, and sender in variables, which are then plugged into the `mail()` method in the last line. Of course, you could skip the variables and drop the values directly into their parameter slots in the `mail()` function, but doing so makes it a little harder to read. The "\n" at the end of the From line is the new line character. It's used to separate the From: line from others, like CC:, in the headers.

All three languages require you to specify who the message is from, to whom it is being sent, the subject, and the body text itself.

ColdFusion uses easy-to-read attribute="value" syntax. The body of the message appears between the `<cfmail>` tags (as opposed to inside the opening `<cfmail>` tag, like the other attributes). The action of the message—the fact that you want to send it—is implied in ColdFusion.

✳ **NOTE:** For ASP, you call the Send method, which means that you are explicitly telling ASP to send the message. Before doing that, you populate a number of the Message object's properties, including the sender and recipient's email addresses, as well as the subject line and message body. After invoking the Send method, you destroy both the `cdoMessage` and `cdoConfig` objects. In doing so, you make it possible for the page to send a different message using the same objects in the future.

✳ **NOTE:** Anytime you create a form that will send mail or interact with your database you should take security precautions to ensure that the data being entered is from the source you expect. Spammers will attempt to exploit your email form by posting to it from their own sites. Code in the language of your choice that will test the origin of your form posts is not difficult to locate on the Web. A detailed treatment of these precautions is beyond the scope of this book.

The completed script for ASP looks as follows (you are free, of course, to insert blank lines into the code to make it more readable):

```
<%
theSchema="http://schemas.microsoft.com/cdo/configuration/"
Set cdoConfig=server.CreateObject("CDO.Configuration")
cdoConfig.Fields.Item(theSchema & "sendusing")= 2
cdoConfig.Fields.Item(theSchema & "smtpserver")="your.SMTP.server.com"
cdoConfig.Fields.Update
set cdoMessage=Server.CreateObject("CDO.Message")
cdoMessage.Configuration=cdoConfig
cdoMessage.From="yourname@yourserver.com"
cdoMessage.To="yourname@yourserver.com"
cdoMessage.Subject="This is the message subject"
cdoMessage.TextBody="This is the message body"
cdoMessage.Send
Set cdoMessage=Nothing
Set cdoConfig=Nothing
%>
```

```
1   <%
2   theSchema="http://schemas.microsoft.com/cdo/configuration/"
3   Set cdoConfig=server.CreateObject("CDO.Configuration")
4   cdoConfig.Fields.Item(theSchema & "sendusing")= 2
5   cdoConfig.Fields.Item(theSchema & "smtpserver")="mail.serviceprovider.com"
6   cdoConfig.Fields.Update
7   set cdoMessage=Server.CreateObject("CDO.Message")
8   cdoMessage.Configuration=cdoConfig
9
10  cdoMessage.From=Request.Form("emailAddress")
11  cdoMessage.To="yourname@yourserver.com"
12  cdoMessage.Subject=Request.Form("subject")
13  cdoMessage.TextBody=Request.Form("messageBody")
14  cdoMessage.Send
15
16  Set cdoMessage=Nothing
17  Set cdoConfig=Nothing
18  %>
19
20  <!DOCTYPE html PUBLIC "-//W3C//DTD XHTML 1.0 Transitional//EN" "http://www.w3.org/TR/xhtml1/DTD/xhtml
21  <html xmlns="http://www.w3.org/1999/xhtml">
22  <head>
```

The completed script for ColdFusion looks as follows:

```
<cfmail from="yourname@yourserver.com" to="yourname@yourserver.com"
➥subject="This is the Message Subject">
This is the message body.
</cfmail>
```

6 Save and Put the file on your remote server. Click anywhere in the document and press F12 to test it.

When your browser opens, you should see the message indicating that the message has been sent. If you see an error message, and you've double-checked the spelling in your code, there is something wrong with your server's mail configuration. If you are using a staging or production server with your work or ISP, contact the server administrator for troubleshooting.

If you are working on a stand-alone machine running IIS, you can try to troubleshoot on your own. In this instance, troubleshooting this issue may be more trouble than it's worth. The point is that you should understand the code and know that it will work on a production server, provided that it is configured to allow email to be sent. But dropping everything to spend potentially several frustrating hours debugging your server is not the most effective way to learn dynamic Web development; you might just want to move on.

Now for the acid test: Check your email. You should have a received a message, like the one shown in the screenshot, except with your own email address. Needless to say, this is not the most exciting email message you've ever received, and since it's hard-coded to contain that text, it's not likely to improve.

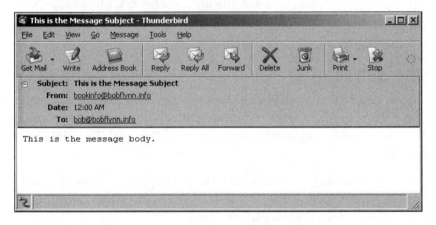

If you did not receive the message, then one of several things could have gone wrong. Possibly, there is a typo in your code. Alternatively, you may have a configuration issue (see the following tip). It is also possible that your ISP doesn't allow server-generated mail to pass through its system, which means that even though you have done everything right, your ISP is blocking it. It is also possible (in fact, this has happened to me more than once in writing this chapter) that spam filters intercept the message that *was* successfully sent and delivered and silently drop them in a Junk filter or quarantine!

Again, if you are running all of this locally and you cannot get it to work, I encourage you to simply pretend it worked and move on. The truth is, in a production setting this code works like a charm, so you have little to gain in troubleshooting your local server configuration.

> **TIP:** If you are having trouble sending mail and want to troubleshoot, here are some leads. Users with IIS might check Control Panel > Administrative Tools > Services and make sure that Simple Mail Transport Protocol is listed as Started. You can also look in Control Panel > Administrative Tools > Internet Information Services (XP) or Internet Services Manager (Windows 2000), select the computer with the server, and explore the Default SMTP Virtual Server's properties. If you are using ColdFusion, most likely you did not enter the correct Internet or IP address of your outgoing SMTP mail server.

7 Close messageSent.asp.

Now that you have the messaging itself working, you need to make it useful by putting meaningful content into the message. To do that, you will use a form to collect the message data from the user and then send that data to the mail object, which in turn will send it (ostensibly) to Newland Tours staff.

Creating the Web Form

In this task, you will create a form to collect data from the user, and you will send that data to messageSent.asp. Before you continue and start reading through the steps, however, test your knowledge. How do you send data to messageSent.asp? Should you use GET or POST? What fields should the form contain?

1 Open contact.asp. In design view, change the table on the page containing the mailing, phone, and email information so it appears as in the screenshot. Also, change the first body paragraph so it reflects the new page structure.

One benefit of placing your email address in server-side code is that spammers will have no access to it. If you put your email address on the page, as in the current version of the site, spammers' automated email address harvesting tools have easy access to it and can (and will) add it to their lists. By switching to a mail-based form, you keep your email address more private.

2 Position the insertion point below the image caption, and insert a line break by holding the Shift key and typing Enter/Return. Next choose Insert > Form > Form to create a new form. Without moving the insertion point, choose Insert > Table, providing the following settings. Click OK.

Rows:	4
Columns:	2
Width:	95 Percent
Border Thickness:	0
Cell Padding:	3
Cell Spacing:	0

People often forget that they can put all sorts of HTML inside tables, which enables you to present your form in a more structured way.

3 Insert two text fields, one text area, and a Submit button in the right column of the table; in the accessibility attributes dialog, select No Label Tag. In the first three cells of the left column, enter the following text: *Your Email Address, Subject, Message Body*.

In this step, you are building the presentation of the table. You are not yet dealing with its data—e.g., naming the fields you have created or worrying about the form's action statement. You will get to those shortly.

✳ NOTE: To stay focused on dynamic application building, in this task you are building a form using HTML tables for layout. Ideally, you should only use tables for tabular data. CSS can be used to style and position the input tags and their labels. By using the outdated tables approach, you have to skip over the <label> tags, which enhance accessibility. As mentioned earlier, CSS positioning is beyond the scope of this book. To learn how to lay out and style Web forms the right way, I recommend reading the chapter, "Making an Input Form Look Good" in Eric Meyer's book, *Eric Meyer on CSS* (New Riders) or visiting http://alistapart.com and reading one of the many articles on forms.

▶ TIP: Sometimes Dreamweaver has screen redraw problems when you add or remove large contents to or from table cells. For example, during this step, the dashed border of the form may appear to cut through the table. Remember, though, that this is merely a screen refresh problem: There is nothing wrong with the underlying code. To see how the page really looks at any time, click one of the enclosing <div> tags in the tag selector, which forces Dreamweaver to redraw the table.

4 Select the <table> tag in the tag inspector, and use the Property inspector to change its bgcolor (background color) attribute to #EEEEEE, which is a light gray.

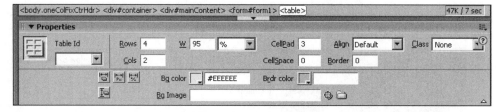

The gray background sets apart the form from the rest of the page, while also drawing attention to its text fields, which suddenly appear much whiter.

5 Insert a Heading 2 element above the table that reads, *Send Us a Message*.

The form itself is conspicuous, but until you label it, its purpose is not.

The effects of this and the preceding steps are visible in the accompanying screenshot.

6 In turn, select each of the first two text fields and name them *emailAddress* and *subject* in the Property inspector. Select the text area and name it *messageBody*, and specify its Char Width as 55 and its Num Lines as 6.

In this step, you take care of much of the behind-the-scenes logic—giving each field a meaningful ID, which will make it easier to collect that data on messageSent.asp.

By customizing the text area, you make it easier for users to enter a longer message than the default text area settings made convenient.

7 Select <form#form1> in the tag selector, and in the Property inspector, name it *frm_message*. In the Action field, type *messageSent.asp*. In the Method drop-down, select POST.

Hopefully you had anticipated the Action and Method settings at the beginning of this task. As a review, they mean that the form will call messageSent.asp and include the data entered in the form in name-value pairs in the body of the HTTP request.

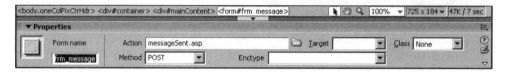

8 Save, close, and upload contact.asp.

The form is ready. To make use of it, though, you'll need to load the form values dynamically into the mail object.

Emailing Dynamic Form Values

Having worked through Lessons 3 and 4 and having sent form data from one page to another, you can probably complete this task without the steps printed here. Indeed, I challenge you to try it, only referring back if you get stuck or have a problem. Don't forget to come back for the final section, *Client-Side Form Validation*.

But before you put the book down and give it a go on your own, I want to point out the full complexity of what you are about to do. You have learned how to send and capture data using different scopes—cookies, form, querystrings, and so on. You have learned how to display dynamic text, using ASP's Response.Write(), ColdFusion's <cfoutput>, and PHP's echo. In this lesson, you learned about objects, and in particular, how your server model has objects dedicated to sending SMTP email. Individually, passing data between pages and mail objects have nothing to do with each other.

But in this final task of the lesson, you will bring together these two disparate techniques to create a specific functionality not explicitly built into ASP or ColdFusion. You have created your own application by combining different tools and technologies (HTML, HTTP requests, and ASP/ColdFusion/PHP communication objects). In a way, this convergence stands metaphorically for all of dynamic Web site development: You combine different objects and techniques to empower the user to make use of information and communication tools in an open-ended way.

1 Open messageSent.asp in code view.

Design view won't help you here, since the code you need to change isn't even visible on the page.

2 Find the sender email address in the mail code, and replace it with the appropriate form variable, as follows:

For ASP, change the from line, so it reads as follows:

```
cdoMessage.From=Request.Form("emailAddress").
```

For ColdFusion, replace the from attribute of the `<cfmail>` tag so that it reads as follows:

```
from="#form.emailAddress#"
```

For PHP, change the header line, so it reads as follows:

```
$headers="From: " . $_POST['emailAddress'] . "\n";
```

Rather than always printing your email address in the From portion of your email, the message will now indicate that it is from whatever value is entered in the form.

The . in the PHP code is used to concatenate, or glue together, strings. In this case, you need to construct a string of text of the following form: `"From: user@mailhost.com\n"`. But you don't know the email address until the form is processed, and you have to plug it in on the fly. What this means is that two parts of the line are hard-coded (unchanging or static) strings: `"From: "` and `"\n"`. Another part is dynamic: `$_POST['emailAddress']`. Because these are different kinds of code, we have to signify to PHP that they are different, and yet also that after it is done evaluating the expression (that is, figuring out what the email address is), it needs to stick them all together into a single string, thus completing the `$headers` variable and returning it to standard, processable form.

3 Continue through the code, replacing the hard-coded subject and messageBody values with the form data for each of those values.

Because there is no field for users to enter the recipient's email address, and because for testing purposes it needs to come to you, you will leave your own email address hard-coded as the recipient. The final code blocks should be as follows:

In ASP:

```
<%
theSchema="http://schemas.microsoft.com/cdo/configuration/"
Set cdoConfig=server.CreateObject("CDO.Configuration")
cdoConfig.Fields.Item(theSchema & "sendusing")= 2
cdoConfig.Fields.Item(theSchema & "smtpserver")="your.SMTP.server.com"
cdoConfig.Fields.Update
set cdoMessage=Server.CreateObject("CDO.Message")
cdoMessage.Configuration=cdoConfig
cdoMessage.From=Request.Form("emailAddress")
cdoMessage.To="yourname@yourserver.com"
cdoMessage.Subject=Request.Form("subject")
cdoMessage.TextBody=Request.Form("messageBody")
cdoMessage.Send
Set cdoMessage=Nothing
Set cdoConfig=Nothing
%>
```

```
1   <%
2   theSchema="http://schemas.microsoft.com/cdo/configuration/"
3   Set cdoConfig=server.CreateObject("CDO.Configuration")
4   cdoConfig.Fields.Item(theSchema & "sendusing")= 2
5   cdoConfig.Fields.Item(theSchema & "smtpserver")="mailserver.yourmailserver.com"
6   cdoConfig.Fields.Update
7   set cdoMessage=Server.CreateObject("CDO.Message")
8   cdoMessage.Configuration=cdoConfig
9
10  cdoMessage.From=Request.Form("emailAddress")
11  cdoMessage.To="yournamE@yoursever.com"
12  cdoMessage.Subject=Request.Form("subject")
13  cdoMessage.TextBody=Request.Form("messageBody")
14  cdoMessage.Send
15
16  Set cdoMessage=Nothing
17  Set cdoConfig=Nothing
18
19  %>
20
21  <!DOCTYPE html PUBLIC "-//W3C//DTD XHTML 1.0 Transitional//EN" "http://www.w3.org/TR
```

In ColdFusion:

```
<cfmail from="#form.emailAddress#" to="yourname@yourserver.com" subject=
➥"#form.subject#">
#form.messageBody#
</cfmail>
```

In PHP:

```php
<?php
$to = "username@yourserver.com";
$subject = $_POST['subject'];
$body = $_POST['messageBody'];
$headers = "From: " . $_POST['emailAddress'] . "\n";
mail($to,$subject,$body,$headers);
?>
```

4 Save and upload the page, and test the functionality by completing the form, clicking Submit, and checking your email.

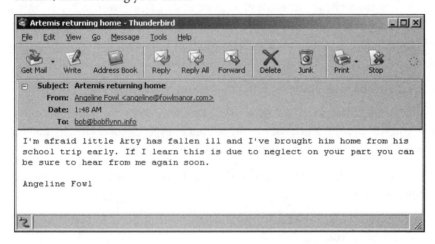

If, rather than seeing the values you entered, you see form.subject as the subject, or form. messageBody as the body, then you probably forgot to remove the quotation marks around the dynamic variables (ASP and PHP) or you forgot to include the pound signs ## (ColdFusion).

Client-Side Form Validation

Depending on what you entered in the form when you tested it, you may have exposed a problem. The form does not verify that users enter the correct type of data. For example, you could enter anything as the email address—nothing verifies that it meets the username@ domain.com format. But Newland Tours staff won't be able to respond to messages if users forget to enter their entire email address, which could result in lost business.

In this task, you will use a simple Dreamweaver behavior that verifies the user entered the correct type of information. This verification is called **form validation**, and it comes in two varieties: client-side and server-side validation.

- Client-side validation verifies that data entered in the form meets the needs of the page from within the browser, the moment the user presses the Submit button and before the HTTP request is sent.

- Server-side validation occurs in a script on the server after the HTTP request is sent. Each form of validation has its own strengths and limitations.

In this task, you will deploy client-side form validation, using a Dreamweaver behavior. This behavior writes JavaScript that ensures the user entered the correct information. If the user didn't, an alert pop-up appears, preventing further progress. If the user does enter the correct information, the JavaScript lets the page proceed as programmed.

1 Open contact.asp and in design view, select the Submit button.

You want the form validation to kick in as soon as the user clicks the Submit button. Therefore, you will attach the behavior to the Submit button. The user clicking that button becomes the event that triggers the validation script.

2 In the Behaviors panel (Window > Behaviors), click the Add Behavior (+) button, and choose Validate Form from the list.

This behavior enables you to enter a few parameters in a dialog box and then writes the requisite JavaScript for you.

3 In the Validate Form dialog, select the first item in the list, check the Required box, and select the Email Address radio button in the Accept group.

Here you are specifying that the user must fill in the emailAddress field of the form, and that what the user types in must be in the proper email format.

* **NOTE:** This validation verifies only the proper email syntax. It does not ensure that the particular email address actually exists, let alone attempt to verify that it belongs to the current user.

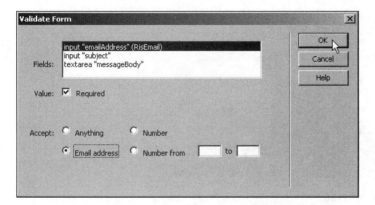

4 In turn, select each of the remaining two items in the list, and check the Required box. Leave the Accept radio setting at Anything.

Here you are forcing the user to enter a subject and body text, but you are not specifying any particular format.

The completed dialog displays (RisEmail) beside the first item, and (R) beside the remaining two.

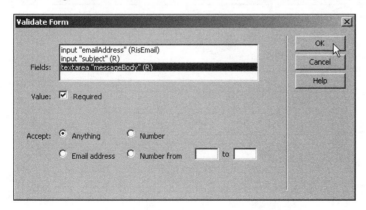

5 Click OK.

This applies the behavior to the Submit button.

6 Save, upload, and test the functionality, by leaving a field blank or by entering a non-email address in the Email address field, and press Submit.

If you break one of the validation rules, you'll see a JavaScript alert dialog. Correct the error, submit the form, and check your email.

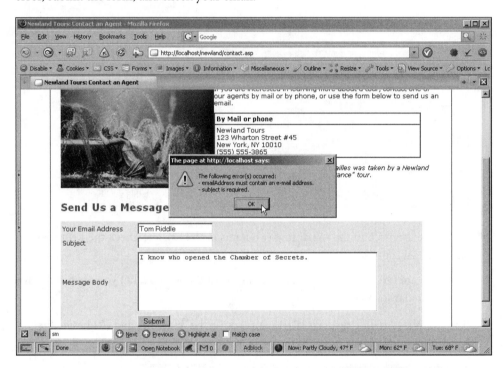

What You Have Learned

In this lesson, you have:

- Configured your server for SMTP message service (pages 137–144)

- Learned about objects, methods, and properties (pages 145–147)

- Made use of two ASP objects (CDO.Configuration and CDO.Message), a ColdFusion tag that makes use of an object (<cfmail>), and a PHP function (mail()) (pages 147–152)

- Caused the server to generate an email message with hard-coded values (pages 150–151)

- Built a form to collect message data from the user (pages 152–156)

- Dynamically loaded user-entered data into the email message (pages 156–159)

- Applied client-side form validation to ensure the integrity of the generated message (pages 159–162)

What You Will Learn

In this lesson, you will:

- Create a simple self-service application
- Collect and manipulate form data
- Display data, using a built-in function to format it as currency
- Deploy server-side form validation
- Use a conditional HTML region

Approximate Time

This lesson takes approximately 120 minutes to complete.

Lesson Files

Starting Files:

Lesson06/Start/newland/generic_template.asp
Lesson06/Start/newland/contact.asp
Lesson06/Start/newland/css/main.css

Completed Files:

Lesson06/Complete/newland/tourprice.asp
Lesson06/Complete/newland/tourprice_ processor.asp
Lesson06/Complete/newland/css/main.css

LESSON 6

Building a Tour Price Calculator

One of the most significant benefits of dynamic Web sites is that they are capable of including self-service applications. Self-service applications are a win-win situation for businesses and customers alike. Customers don't have to go to the trouble of calling a number, pressing a sequence of numbers ("please press 3, now"), and sitting interminably on hold ("your call is important to us"), only to learn that office hours ended three hours ago. Businesses decrease incoming calls, which decreases long-distance phone charges and hours, and yet they can still serve customers 24 hours, 7 days a week.

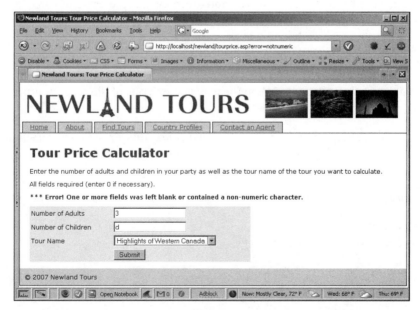

Your application both enables users to build customized estimates and ensures that they enter the correct information, displaying an error message inline if they do not.

In this lesson, you will build a tour price calculator, which enables users to obtain an estimate for the cost of a tour based on the number of adults and children going on the tour. You'll use ASP, Macromedia ColdFusion, or PHP to multiply the tour price by the number of adults and children to come up with the estimate. This estimate will be output using correctly formatted currency.

The calculator won't have full functionality until the end of Lesson 8, however, because part of it uses price amounts drawn dynamically from a database. But in this lesson, you'll build the majority of the application and temporarily hard-code the price values while you nail the functionality.

But that's not all you'll do. You'll also extend your skills with form validation, this time writing custom ASP, ColdFusion, or PHP code to handle form validation on the server side, rather than the client side, as in Lesson 5. You'll see how to use ASP, ColdFusion, or PHP to create a region of the page that displays conditionally: If the user does not fill in the form, an error message, written inline in HTML, appears that was hidden before.

Creating the Pages

To begin the application, you'll create the two pages needed for it to work and rough out the static content. Once that is in place, you can add the individual pieces of functionality one at a time. Until then, though, you're doing just plain HTML authoring.

1 Open generic_template.asp, and save it as *tourprice_processor.asp*, and then save it again as *tourprice.asp*.

You have created two pages based on the template, and one of the pages, tourprice.asp, is open in Dreamweaver.

2 In the toolbar, change the page title to *Newland Tours: Tour Price Calculator*. In the main document, change the page banner so it reads *Tour Price Calculator*. Then type the following text as the body text:

Enter the number of adults and children in your party as well as the tour name of the tour you want to calculate.

All fields required (enter 0 if necessary).

Beneath this text you will create a form, but for now, this file is done.

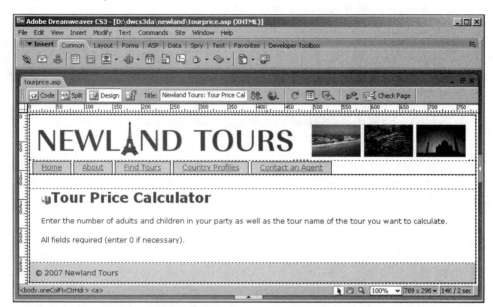

3 Save and close tourprice.asp. Open tourprice_processor.asp.

Creating the second page is much like creating the first.

4 In the toolbar, change the page title to *Newland Tours: Tour Price Calculator*. In the main document, change the page banner so it reads *Tour Price Calculator*. Then type the following text as the body text:

The estimated cost of your tour is XXX.

Prices include hotel, accommodation, and travel expenses during the tour. They do not include airfare to the starting destination.

Calculate another tour.

Contact one of our qualified agents.

Later in this lesson, the placeholder text string XXX will be replaced with the amount output from the ASP/ColdFusion/PHP script.

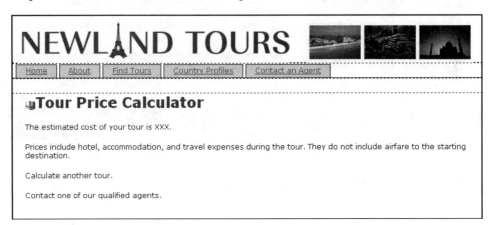

✱ **NOTE:** In this exercise, as in the previous exercises where we have processed a form, we have created a form page and a processing page. Using conditional logic, sometimes referred to as flow control, you can have the form and the processing page be the same page. The decision to do so is based on business need, security and desired user experience. We will not attempt it here, but you should be aware of it as a possibility. Later in this lesson you will learn to use basic if/else conditional logic.

5 Select the XXX placeholder text, and click the B button in the Property inspector to apply bolding to the text.

Just because the eventual output will be generated dynamically using ASP doesn't mean that you can't format the text the way you want it to appear.

6 Select the word Calculate, and use the Property inspector to link it to tourprice.asp. Select the word Contact and link it to contact.asp.

Visually, aside from the placeholder text, this page is ready. You'll add two significant pieces of functionality to it later in the lesson—server-side form validation and the tour price calculation itself—but these functionalities will be created with scripting and will be invisible to the user.

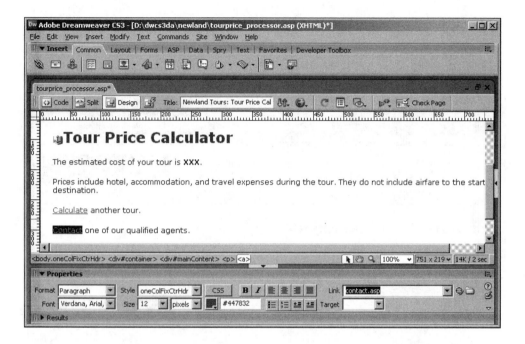

7 Save and close tourprice_processor.asp.

Building the Form

In this task, you will build the form that users will fill out to provide the calculation script with sufficient information to create the estimate. The form that you are about to build has two items of note. It includes an embedded table, used for formatting. You saw this technique in Lesson 5 when you built the contact form. The other item of note is the use of a drop-down menu.

1 Open tourprice.asp. Position the insertion point at the end of the All fields required line, after the period. Using the Forms tab on the Insert bar, click the Form button. In the Property inspector, name the form *frm_tourprice*, specify tourprice_processor.asp as its Action, and verify that POST is selected as its Method.

Without any fields or submit button, the form cannot do anything, but it's a start.

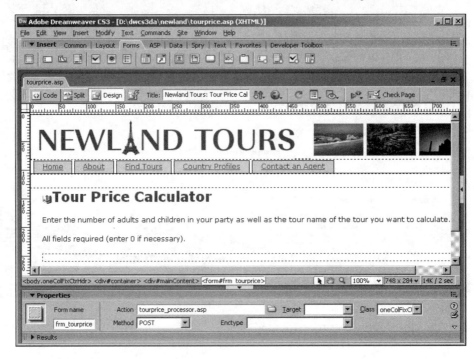

The dashed line represents form boundaries

2 With the insertion point inside the form, click the Insert Table button from the Common tab of the Insert panel. In the ensuing dialog, specify 4 rows, 2 columns, a width of 60 percent, a border of 0, cell padding of 3, and cell spacing of 0.

When you are finished, the form stretches to accommodate the new table that appears.

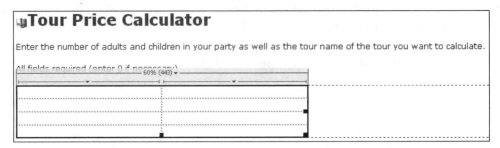

3 In the top three cells of the left column, enter *Number of Adults*, *Number of Children*, *Tour Name*. In the right column, from top to bottom, insert a text field, another text field, a list/menu, and a Submit button, using the Forms tab of the Insert panel.

✱ **NOTE:** Make sure each time when the accessibility dialog appears that you select No Label Tag, for reasons discussed in the previous chapter. From this point forward, you will not be using labels for form fields.

The Forms tab makes building Web forms a snap. However, you still need to configure each of the form elements.

Tour Price Calculator

Enter the number of adults and children in your party as well as the tour name of the tour you want to calculate.

All fields required (enter 0 if necessary)

60% (443)

Number of Adults	
Number of Children	
Tour Name	
	Submit

4 Select the first text field, and in the Property inspector name it *numAdults*. Give it an Init val of 0 and Max chars 3.

Text fields have a number of attributes that can be useful as you build your form. The Init val field in the property inspector sets the value attribute of the text field with a default value that will display in the text field when the page loads. In the body text we have told the user that each field requires a value and they should enter 0 rather than leave them blank. As a courtesy we have put in the zero for them. They can type over it should they want another value.

Form fields, in addition to being a wonderful way for your users to enter information, can also be entry points for those who may wish to compromise your system. Best practice dictates that we minimize the opportunities for such exploits. One simple step is to limit the number of characters to the maximum you might expect for the information being requested. Max char sets the maxlength attribute. In this case we are limiting the number of adults a user may enter into the form to three digits. Hopefully if the user wants a price for more than 999 adults they will call. The Char width field in the Property inspector sets the size attribute. It gives you control over the actual length of the input box. While we could restrict that to 3 characters as well, we will leave it at the default for aesthetic reasons.

✱ **NOTE:** The Char width only restricts the input box visually. Only Max chars will restrict the number of characters input. They are often used together.

5 Repeat the steps for the second text field. Name it *numChildren* and give it an Init val of 0 and Max chars 3.

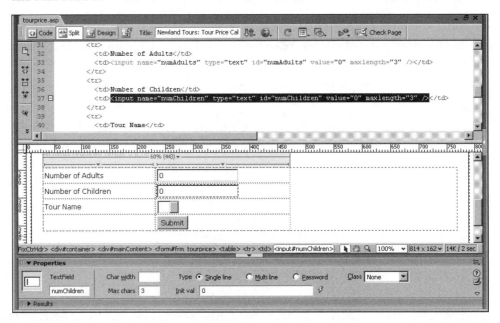

Remember, the field names are also the variable names that ASP/ColdFusion/PHP uses to extract the data, so it is important to give them meaningful names.

6 Select the menu, and in the Property inspector, name it *tourName* and then click the List Values button. In the List values dialog, click below Item Label, and type *Highlights of Argentina*. Press Tab and type *500*. Pressing Tab to continue, enter *Highlights of Western Canada*, *700*, *Egyptian Pyramids and More*, and finally *900*.

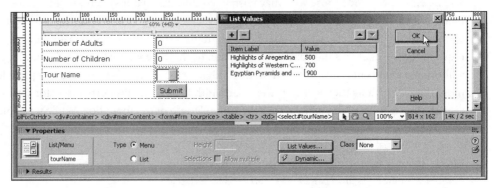

To understand what's happening in this step, let's compare form menus with text fields. When you create a text field, you give it a name. When the user types in the field, that information is the field's value. Thus, the firstName text field you created in previous lessons carried whatever value the user entered into it on the second page—the one that collects and displays the form data.

Menus work a bit differently than text fields. Like text fields, they're given names, and the data associated with them is stored with that name. Thus, on the page that processes this form, Request.Form("tourName") (ASP), #form.tourName# (ColdFusion), or $_POST['tourName'] (PHP) would retrieve this data.

But the similarity ends there. Drop-down menus are not as open-ended as text fields. With drop-down menus, users select from a finite number of options that the developer specifies. The options that the user chooses from are entered in the Item Label column of the List Values dialog. The Value column of the List Values dialog is the data value that is sent with the form. Thus, if a user chooses Egyptian Pyramids and More, then Request. Form("tourName") (ASP), #form.tourName# (ColdFusion), or $_POST['tourName'] (PHP) would retrieve 900. You'll use that value shortly when you perform the actual calculation.

The item label does not get submitted with the form to the next page. It remains in the form itself to enable the user to make a selection. The reason that the item label and values are separate is so that you can submit a value other than the label to the script. Since you are performing mathematical calculations, you need a numeric data value, rather than a text string.

Clearly, Newland Tours offers more than three tours. Entering them one by one would be tedious, to say the least. Worse, if you wanted to add or remove a tour, you'd have to revisit the List Values dialog to fix it. There is a better way: You can dynamically load the labels and their values from a database to automatically generate this menu on the fly. You'll see how to do that in Lesson 8. But for now, you'll hard-code these values just to build the core functionality.

Another problem with the current form might have occurred to you. Right now, if a user selects Egyptian Pyramids and More, only the value 900 is sent. You can multiply that by the number of adults or children, but there is no way to send separate values for each. The whole point of the application is to provide an estimate that reflects the values of both the price for adults and for children. You'll fix this problem as well in Lesson 8, by retrieving both figures from a database.

Before finishing your form you should style it to match the form on your contact page. A background color for the table is all you need.

7 Click anywhere inside the opening `<table>` tag in code view. In the Property inspector set the table's Bg color to #EEEEEE.

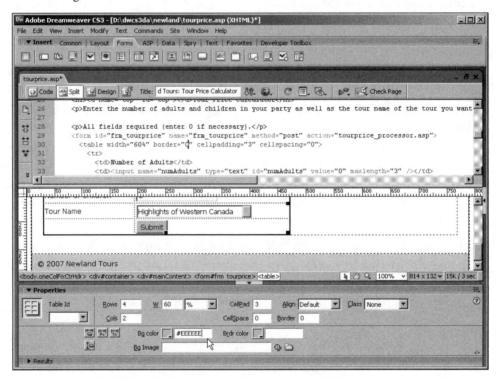

8 Save tourprice.asp, and press F12 to test it in a browser.

The form is complete and ready to use. Before moving onto the server-side code, however, you should test it in a browser to verify that it looks as expected. You can press Submit if you like, and tourprice_processor.asp should appear, but it won't look any different than before.

When you are finished, close tourprice.asp.

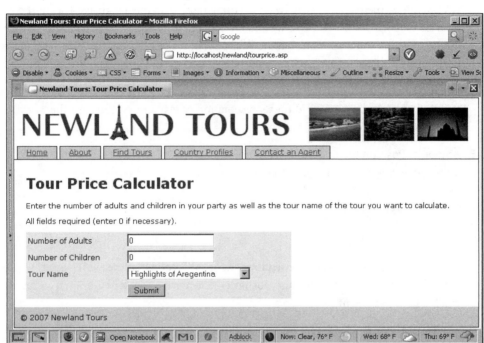

Collecting, Processing, and Displaying the Data

The stage is set, and now it is time to capture the data entered on the form and calculate the price based on the data the user entered. You are already familiar with collecting form data and displaying it on the page, so in this task you should focus on the calculation itself.

1 Open tourprice_processor.asp. If necessary, switch to split view or code view.

To perform the calculations, you need the data, which is available on the page specified in the form's action attribute.

The switch to code view is necessary for now, because you are about to do some hand-coding, and there is no way to do so in design view.

2 ASP only: Position the insertion point at the top of the document, before the opening <!DOCTYPE...> tag, press Enter/Return twice, return to line 1, and type:
<%@LANGUAGE="VBSCRIPT" CODEPAGE=" 65001" %>.

This line is necessary for two reasons. First, it tells the server that the scripting language used is VBScript. Remember, ASP can be coded using more than one language. The most common languages for ASP are VBScript and JScript, and with ASP.NET, you have even more options. ColdFusion users don't have to worry about this setting, because ColdFusion supports only ColdFusion Markup Language (CFML), so there is no possibility for confusion.

The second attribute, CODEPAGE, specifies the page's language. 65001 refers to Unicode (UTF-8), the industry standard for representation of text and symbols for the world's writing systems in e-mail and web pages.

3 ASP only: Position the insertion point in line 2 and press Enter/Return twice to add some more space. Beginning in line 3, type the following code:

```
<%
Dim numAdult, numChild, basePrice, tourPrice

%>
```

As you know from before, <% is used to mark up ASP code that the server needs to process. The extra space just above the closing %> is to leave room for additional script, which you'll add in a moment.

The second line may look a bit odd. In ASP, whenever you want to create a new variable, you must declare it. You declare new variables using Dim. Thus, the second line announces to the server that you are creating four new variables. These variables have not yet been assigned any values—you'll give them values momentarily.

✱ NOTE: Some languages do not require you to declare variables before you set their values. Neither ColdFusion nor PHP require you to declare variables before setting their values, so these scripts don't have equivalents for the *Dim* line.

By the end of this step, ASP users' code window should appear as in the following screen shot. ColdFusion and PHP users, just to reiterate, haven't done anything in this task yet, but that's about to change.

```
1   <%@LANGUAGE="VBSCRIPT" CODEPAGE="65001" %>
2   <%
3   Dim numAdult, numChild, basePrice, tourPrice
4   %>
5
6   <!DOCTYPE html PUBLIC "-//W3C//DTD XHTML 1.0 Transitional//EN" "http://www.w3.org/
7   <html xmlns="http://www.w3.org/1999/xhtml">
8   <head>
9   <meta http-equiv="Content-Type" content="text/html; charset=utf-8" />
10  <title>Newland Tours: Tour Price Calculator</title>
```

4 All users: Set three variables, numAdult, numChild, and basePrice, to the values entered in the numAdults, numChildren, and tourName form fields.

In ASP, insert the following code beginning in an empty line after the Dim line:

```
numAdult = Request.Form("numAdults")
numChild = Request.Form("numChildren")
basePrice = Request.Form("tourName")
```

In ColdFusion, enter the following code at the top of the document, before the opening <!DOCTYPE> tag:

```
<cfset numAdult = form.numAdults>
<cfset numChild = form.numChildren>
<cfset basePrice = form.tourName>
```

In PHP, enter the following code at the top of the document, before the opening <!DOCTYPE> line:

```
<?php
$numAdult = $_POST['numAdults'];
$numChild = $_POST['numChildren'];
$basePrice = $_POST['tourName'];
?>
```

You've seen Request.Form("fieldname"), form.fieldname, and $_POST['fieldname'] in earlier lessons. This time, rather than simply printing them on the page, as you did before, you are storing those values inside new variables. The reason for this is that what needs to be printed on the page is the output of the calculation. By storing these values in descriptively named variables, the calculation is easier to code (and read).

✱ NOTE: ColdFusion users might wonder why the form variables aren't surrounded by pound signs (##) as they were in previous lessons. Pound signs are always needed when ColdFusion variables are used outside or between pairs of ColdFusion tags, such as <cfoutput></cfoutput>. But they are not needed when used inside a ColdFusion tag, such as <cfset> unless the variable is inside quotation marks. Later in this lesson you will see variables used with functions. The variables themselves will not have pound signs around them, but the entire function, with the variable embedded, follows the rules outlined above. If it is between tags like <cfoutput></cfoutput> it will have pound signs. If it is inside a tag it will not.

5 Set a fourth variable, tourPrice, to equal the output of the calculation itself.

In ASP, insert the following code in the line below the `basePrice` line:

```
tourPrice = (numAdult * basePrice) + (numChild * basePrice)
```

In ColdFusion, insert the following code in the line below the `basePrice` line:

```
<cfset tourPrice = (numAdult * basePrice) + (numChild * basePrice)>
```

In PHP, insert the following code in the line below the `basePrice` line:

```
$tourPrice = ($numAdult * $basePrice) + ($numChild * $basePrice);
```

Assuming you survived seventh-grade math, you probably know what this line is doing. It is setting the value of tourPrice to equal the output of a simple calculation. The parentheses are used, as in arithmetic, to ensure that the calculations take place in the proper order.

When this line of code is resolved on the server, tourPrice has the final calculated dollar amount as its value. With that in place, all we need to do is output it into the HTML code where the XXX placeholder is, and the user will see the information that they need.

```
1   <%@LANGUAGE="VBSCRIPT" CODEPAGE="65001" %>
2   <%
3   Dim numAdult, numChild, basePrice, tourPrice
4   numAdult = Request.Form("numAdults")
5   numChild = Request.Form("numChildren")
6   basePrice = Request.Form("tourName")
7   tourPrice = (numAdult * basePrice) + (numChild * basePrice)
8   %>
9
10  <!DOCTYPE html PUBLIC "-//W3C//DTD XHTML 1.0 Transitional//EN" "http://www.w3.org/
11  <html xmlns="http://www.w3.org/1999/xhtml">
```

6 Still in code view, scroll down to the XXX placeholder (around line 35 in ASP, around line 31 in ColdFusion, and around line 33 in PHP). Delete XXX and in its place enter the following code to output the value of the tourPrice variable.

In ASP:

```
<% Response.Write(tourPrice) %>
```

In ColdFusion:

```
<cfoutput>#tourPrice#</cfoutput>
```

In PHP:

```
<?php echo $tourPrice; ?>
```

➤ **TIP:** If you don't like typing, you could always use the Bindings panel to create this variable and then drag it into the code, just like you did in Lesson 4. One of the instructional goals of this lesson is to eliminate any dependency on the Dreamweaver GUI so that you are comfortable monkeying with the code directly. Thus, there is an instructional advantage to typing the code by hand, but there is no code development or workflow advantage.

Outputting a variable value is familiar to you by now. The main difference between this instance of outputting a variable and what you did in Lesson 4 is that you don't need to specify an HTTP-compatible scope—URL/querystring, form, cookie, etc. The scope of this variable is the page itself as it is processed in ASP, ColdFusion, or PHP, and the variable will be resolved and removed before the code is ever sent over HTTP to the browser.

✳ **NOTE:** In ColdFusion local variables are actually in the implied "variables" scope—e.g., #variables.tourPrice#. Best practices dictate that you always scope your variables to avoid ambiguity for both the server and the coder. I have not added the scope to the ColdFusion variables here in order to maintain the parallel in the code examples. Your ColdFusion code will run fine and will serve the instructional purpose of the exercises.

```
33    <div id="mainContent">
34    <h1><a name="top" id="top"></a>Tour Price Calculator</h1>
35        <p>The estimated cost of your tour is <strong><% Response.Write(tourPrice) %></strong>.</p>
36
37        <p>Prices include hotel, accommodation, and travel expenses during the tour. They do not inc
38
39        <p><a href="tourprice.asp">Calculate</a> another tour.</p>
40
41        <p><a href="contact.asp">Contact</a> one of our qualified agents.</p>
42
43        <br clear="all" />
44    <!-- end #mainContent --></div>
```

7 Save and upload both tourprice.asp and tourprice_processor.asp. Select tourprice.asp in the Site panel, and press F12 to test it.

You should always test a page's functionality as soon as you can. These two pages are ready for testing. You'll add quite a few enhancements to this application, but its core functionality works—or should.

Try several different variations. Enter numeric values in each field, choose a tour, and press Submit. You should see the output page with the calculated amount in bold. Notice that the dollar amount appears, but nothing indicates that it's a dollar amount. ASP, ColdFusion, and PHP have built-in functions that enable you to output numbers in proper currency format, as you'll see in a moment.

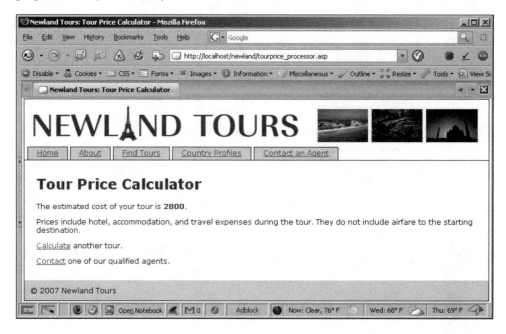

Once you have verified that it works in the best-case scenario, when you've properly entered numbers, try to break the application by entering bad data in the form. Submit it with one or both text fields blank, or enter a letter, such as D.

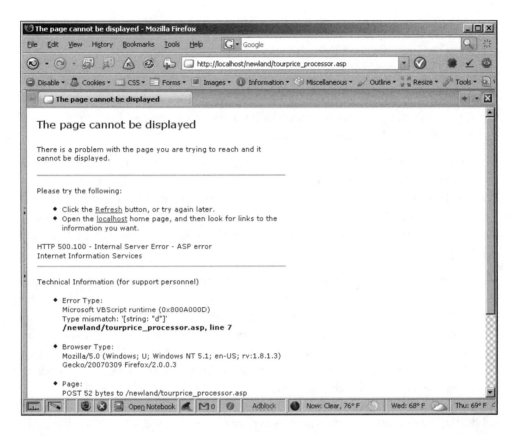

The page either returns an error message or tries to complete the calculation, anyway, returning a meaningless number. The reason is that your script multiplies and adds the contents of the form fields. If these fields have no content or contain non-numeric characters, it can't perform calculations. This application would benefit from a form validation enhancement that would ensure that users actually entered numbers in both fields, before it attempts to calculate a price.

8 Return to tourprice_processor.asp in Dreamweaver, and insert the function that converts the output number to the U.S. dollar currency format.

In ASP:

```
<% Response.Write(FormatCurrency(tourPrice)) %>
```

In ColdFusion:

```
<cfoutput>#DollarFormat(tourPrice)#</cfoutput>
```

In PHP:

```php
<?php setlocale(LC_MONETARY, 'en_US'); echo money_format('%i', $tourPrice); ?>
```

Functions are predefined actions that tell the interpreter how to do something. Computer languages generally have dozens of functions, if not more, built in for common tasks. Converting numeric figures to currency format is a common task, and so many languages have a function that performs this task.

Functions take the following format: FunctionName(Parameter). In some cases, there is no parameter, but the parentheses remain, as in the case of ColdFusion's Now() function, which returns the current time on the server. In the case of ASP's FormatCurrency() and ColdFusion's DollarFormat(), the lone parameter is the number that you want to format. Because the number is held in the tourPrice variable, you place that variable in the parameter.

The PHP function money_format() requires two parameters: The first indicates whether it should output the local or the international currency symbol (in the case of U.S. dollars, the local symbol is $, while the international symbol is USD); the second parameter is the number itself. But even before we can use money_format(), we need to use another function, setlocale(), which indicates which county's currency should be used in the first place; en_US refers to United States. International readers can look up their own locales using a search engine, such as Google.

✱ **NOTE:** There are two conditions under which money_format() will not work. If you are using PHP version 4.2 or earlier, which shipped with earlier versions of Mac OS X, such as 10.2 Jaguar, money_format() won't work, because it had not yet been introduced. The second condition is that some systems, including Windows, do not support the underlying system function that is required to perform the conversion. If you find yourself in either of these situations, you can use number_format() instead and hard-code the dollar sign (or local currency symbol) in the right place. <?php echo '$'.number_format($tourPrice, 2); ?>. Visit http://php.net for full details.

✱ **NOTE:** Rather than typing these functions manually, if you created a binding for the tourPrice variable, then you can choose a currency format from the drop-down menu on the right side of the Bindings panel (you may have to scroll to the right to see this option).

If you test the page now, the results are more satisfying.

Adding Server-Side Form Validation

As you discovered in the previous task, the application works well when the user enters numbers in both fields. But if the user leaves one blank or enters a non-numeric character, an unsightly error message or a meaningless number appears when she or he clicks Submit. Error messages such as the one shown earlier were meant to help developers debug applications; ideally, users should never see them.

To prevent the possibility of this error occurring, you can add form validation to ensure that the requisite numbers have been entered. You used form validation with the email form in Lesson 5. That was client-side form validation—using a Dreamweaver behavior, you added a JavaScript form validation script that fired as soon as the user clicked the Submit button. That was certainly easy to deploy, but as you'll remember, the JavaScript error pop-up that appeared when the form was not filled in correctly wasn't terribly helpful.

In this task, you will add form validation on the server-side; that is, you will write some ASP, ColdFusion, or PHP code to verify that numbers were entered. If they were not, a hidden region of the HTML page will appear indicating an error. Because the error will be coded in HTML, you can make it say whatever you want, and you can also format it however you want.

The process will be as follows: The user fills out the form and clicks Submit. The page tourprice_processor.asp is requested. At the top of that page is a small form validation script, written in ASP, ColdFusion, or PHP, which verifies that numbers were entered in both fields. If numbers were entered in both fields, then the page processes as normal. If numbers were not entered in both fields, the user is redirected back to tourprice.asp, and the once-hidden HTML region with an error message is revealed.

To create this functionality, we need to write the form validation script, which you'll do in this task. Then, in the next task, you'll create the HTML error region and hide it. Finally, you'll format the text in the HTML error region using CSS.

Now that you understand the big picture, let's sketch how this form validation script is going to work. First, we are using it for flow control. That is, depending on whether the user entered the proper data, the script needs either to continue to do the calculation or to redirect the user back to tourprice.asp. Handling flow control based on conditions is easy, using if…else constructs. The following pseudocode maps out the intended functionality of the script:

```
if the user entered a non-numeric or null value in either field
    redirect the user back to tourprice.asp
else
    continue as usual
end if
```

We'll further refine this script in two ways. The first is that you don't need to spell out the else portion if you just want to continue as usual. Thus, we really only need the if half of the script.

The second refinement is that you don't merely want to redirect back to tourprice.asp; you also want to send a trigger that will change the visibility of the hidden region. In this case, a querystring/URL variable will do the job. Then, you'll add a script that looks for the presence of that URL variable, and if it is there, it will display the region. If it is not, the region will be hidden. Don't worry if this seems abstract; you'll get plenty of practice with it by the end of this lesson. The final pseudocode for the form validation script looks as follows:

```
if the user entered a non-numeric or null value in either field
    redirect the user back to tourprice.asp with a querystring
end if
```

Now that we have a plan, let's write some code.

1 Open tourprice_processor.asp. Make some room at the top of the document, before the calculation script you wrote in the previous task, for a new script.

The form validation script should be at the beginning, because you don't want ASP, ColdFusion, or PHP to attempt the calculation when you haven't even verified that the proper form values exist.

ASP users: Be sure that space for the new code is below the `<%@LANGUAGE="VBSCRIPT" CODEPAGE="65001"%>` line, which should always remain the first line.

> **TIP:** When building script blocks, add some extra space above and below to help set them apart visually.

2 Create the outer shell of the script, using `if` and testing whether each of the form variables is numeric.

In ASP:

```
<%
If Not IsNumeric(Request.Form("numAdults")) or Not IsNumeric(Request.Form
➥("numChildren")) Then

End If
%>
```

In ColdFusion:

```
<cfif Not IsNumeric(form.numAdults) or Not IsNumeric(form.numChildren)>

</cfif>
```

In PHP:

```
<?php
(!(is_numeric($_POST['numAdults'])) or !(is_numeric($_POST['numChildren'])))

?>
```

The empty line in each code block is set aside for the code you'll add in the next step.

All three languages have a function, `IsNumeric()` or `is_numeric()`, which tests whether the enclosed parameter is numeric. If it is, it returns true. If not, it returns false. Because you want to redirect if the value is not numeric, you add the word `Not` (ASP and ColdFusion) or `!` (PHP) to invert the output of the `IsNumeric()` or `is_numeric()` function. Finally, because you are checking two fields, rather than one, they have to be listed separately, connecting them with `or`.

> ✱ **NOTE:** In PHP you will see the logical operators && and || used more often than their equiva-
> lents *and* and *or* respectively. While either set will work, the symbolic versions have a higher
> order of precedence than the word versions.

3 Add the inner action that is executed if the if clause evaluates to true.

In ASP, indented in the blank line beneath the if statement:

```
Response.Redirect("tourprice.asp?error=notnumeric")
```

In ColdFusion, indented in the blank line between the opening and closing <cfif> tags:

```
<cflocation url="tourprice.cfm?error=notnumeric">
```

In PHP, in the blank line beneath the opening if line:

```
{
    header("Location: tourprice.php?error=notnumeric");
    exit;
}
```

Response.Redirect() is an ASP function that sends the browser to the URL specified. Likewise, ColdFusion's <cflocation> and PHP's header("Location: …") also redirect the browser. In addition to specifying the URL, you've also added a querystring. You'll add a script back on tourprice.asp that looks for this querystring, using if…else to control the visibility of the error region.

```
1   <%@LANGUAGE="VBSCRIPT" CODEPAGE="65001" %>
2   <%
3   If Not IsNumeric(Request.Form("numAdults")) or Not IsNumeric(Request.Form("numChildren")) Then
4       Response.Redirect("tourprice.asp?error=notnumeric")
5   End If
6   %>
7
8   <%
9   Dim numAdult, numChild, basePrice, tourPrice
10  numAdult = Request.Form("numAdults")
11  numChild = Request.Form("numChildren")
```

4 Save and upload tourprice_processor.asp. Test tourprice.asp.

You'll see that if you don't enter numbers in both fields, not only are you stuck on tourprice.asp, but also the querystring variable appears in the Address bar. It's not being used yet, but it's there. Its presence enables both your server script and you to distinguish between when the page first loads, and when it loads because of an error.

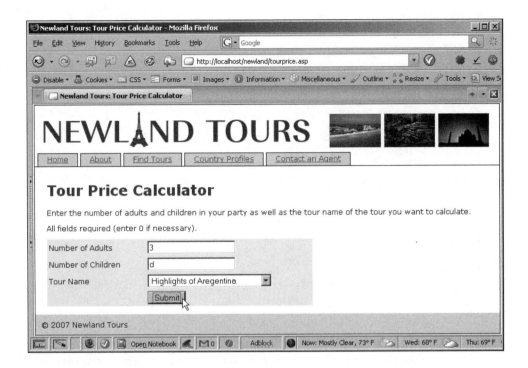

Creating the Conditional Region

The idea of a region of HTML that can be shown or hidden may sound fancy, but in fact you can do it using skills you have learned in this chapter. You simply embed standard HTML inside an `if` statement. If that evaluates to true, then the HTML is displayed. If it evaluates to false, then it skips the HTML and continues.

1 Open tourprice.asp in code view. Position the cursor before the opening `<form>` tag, and press Enter/Return a few times to make room for some new code.

You should find the opening `<form>` tag around line 38. By inserting the conditional region here, you cause the error message to appear in a prominent location when the page reloads.

2 As before, start with the outer shell, by writing the if statement.

In ASP:

```
<%
If Request.QueryString("error") = "notnumeric" Then

End If
%>
```

In ColdFusion:

```
<cfif url.error is "notnumeric">

</cfif>
```

In PHP:

```
<?php
if ($_GET['error'] == "notnumeric")

?>
```

The if statements here test to determine whether there is a querystring (or URL) variable called error, and if so, whether its value is set to notnumeric. When the page first loads, there is no querystring or URL variable named error, so this if statement would evaluate to false. As you have seen, however, if the page has been redirected back to tourprice.asp from the form validation script on tourprice_processor.asp, the querystring exists with that value.

3 Nested between the opening and closing if lines, insert the code that tells ASP/ColdFusion to output the desired HTML.

In ASP:

```
Response.Write("<p>*** Error! One or more fields was left blank or contained a
➥non-numeric character.</p>")
```

In ColdFusion:

```
<cfoutput><p>*** Error! One or more fields was left blank or contained a
➥non-numeric character.</p></cfoutput>
```

In PHP:

```
{
    echo "<p>*** Error! One or more fields was left blank or contained a
    ➥non-numeric character.</p>";
}
```

`Response.Write`, `<cfoutput>`, and `echo` can be used to output static or dynamic code. We've used them to output dynamic code thus far, but there is no reason why you can't put static code in there as well, or any combination of static and dynamic code.

```
28    <p>All fields required (enter 0 if necessary).</p>
29
30    <%
31    If Request.QueryString("error") = "notnumeric" Then
32        Response.Write("<p>*** Error! One or more fields was left blank or contained a
33    End If
34    %>
35
36    <form id="frm_tourprice" name="frm_tourprice" method="post" action="tourprice_proce
37      <table width="60%" border="0" cellpadding="3" cellspacing="0" bgcolor="#EEEEEE">
```

4 ColdFusion users only: Wrap the entire `<cfif>` script in another `<cfif>` script, so that the original `<cfif>` script only runs if the URL variable error actually exists.

```
<cfif isDefined("url.error")>
    <cfif url.error is "notnumeric">
        <cfoutput><p>*** Error! One or more fields was left blank or contained a
        ➥non-numeric character.</p></cfoutput>
    </cfif>
</cfif>
```

```
28    <p>All fields required (enter 0 if necessary).</p>
29
30    <cfif isDefined("url.error")>
31        <cfif url.error is "notnumeric">
32            <cfoutput><p>*** Error! One or more fields was left blank or contained a non-numeric
33        </cfif>
34    </cfif>
35
36    <form id="frm_tourprice" name="frm_tourprice" method="post" action="tourprice_processor.cfm">
37      <table width="60%" border="0" cellspacing="0" cellpadding="3">
```

The function `isDefined()` works much like `isNumeric()`, except that rather than testing whether the parameter is a number, it tests to see whether the parameter exists.

This extra code is necessary in ColdFusion, because ColdFusion assumes that if you are testing a variable (`<cfif url.error = "notnumeric">`), then that variable exists. If it does not exist, and you attempt to test it, ColdFusion displays an error message. The error URL variable exists only when the page loads as a result of a redirection from the form validation on tourprice_processor.cfm. Thus, when the page first loads, an ugly error message dominates the page. We solve the problem by testing to ensure that `url.error` is defined. If it is not, then ColdFusion ignores the directions that test whether error's value is set to notnumeric. If `url.error` is defined, ColdFusion continues with the test, as before.

ASP and PHP differ from ColdFusion in this instance, in that if `querystring.error` is undefined, then the interpreter knows error can't be equal to `notnumeric` and it proceeds as expected.

5 Save and upload tourprice.asp. Test it in a browser.

The error message now appears when you fail to enter numbers in both fields.

There's only one problem left: The error message isn't very conspicuous, is it?

Creating and Applying a Custom CSS Class

Making the error message more conspicuous is a matter of presentation. In XHTML, you should use CSS for presentation-related controls. XHTML has built-in styles for headings, body text, lists, and so forth, but XHTML lacks an `<errormessage>` tag that you can redefine with CSS. As you learned in Lesson 2, CSS enables developers to create custom styles, which can be applied to standard XHTML elements such as the `<p>` tag.

In this task, you will create a custom CSS style, also called a class, just for error messages.

1 In the CSS Styles panel, click the New CSS Style button. In the dialog, select Class (can apply to any tag), and enter *.error* as the name. Use the Define In field to verify that the new style is added to main.css. Click OK.

The period (.) before the word error is obligatory, so don't leave it out.

You went through this process several times earlier in the book, so it should be familiar. Just remember that rather than redefining an existing tag, you are creating a custom class.

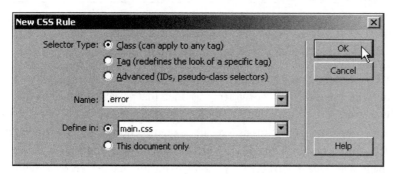

2 In the CSS Style Definition dialog, set the Weight as bold and the color as #990000, a deep red. Click OK.

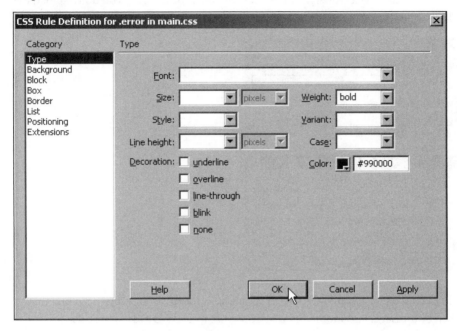

One of the advantages of CSS styles is that they inherit attributes of other styles that they don't explicitly contradict. This new class will be attached to the <p> tag that contains the error message. The <p> is already defined such that it uses a certain font, in a certain size, and so on. The .error class inherits all of that. When you create a CSS class, then, define only those attributes that are unique to that class—in this case, the fact that the text should be bold and red.

❋ **NOTE:** Depending on the settings in Dreamweaver Preferences, the CSS style sheet document may have opened in Dreamweaver. If so, you can close it.

Now that the style is created, you need to apply it.

3 Using the Site panel, upload main.css to the remote server.

Remember, the new .error style has been saved only locally, so if you don't upload the style sheet, you won't see any difference when you test the file.

4 Back in code view, scroll to the Response.Write, <cfoutput>, or <?php echo line that prints the error message, and modify its <p> tag so that it reads <p class="error">.

To apply a CSS style to a tag, use the class attribute. Notice that the period is omitted in the class attribute.

5 ASP and PHP users only: Add a second pair of quotation marks (ASP) or a backslash (PHP) in front of each of the quotation marks in the class attribute.

In ASP, the tag should now read <p class=""error"">, and in PHP it should read <p class=\"error\">.

The second set of quotes (ASP) or backslash (PHP) is necessary, because the entire HTML string is embedded in quotes. If you use a normal set of quotation marks, ASP/PHP gets confused. By adding the extra quotes/backslash, you are communicating to ASP/PHP that it should treat these quotation marks as a part of the text string, rather than as the boundaries of the text string.

This additional step is unnecessary in ColdFusion, because the output text string in ColdFusion is enclosed in <cfoutput> tags and not quotation marks.

```
28    <p>All fields required (enter 0 if necessary).</p>
29
30    <%
31    If Request.QueryString("error") = "notnumeric" Then
32        Response.Write("<p class=""error"">*** Error! One or more fields was left blank or contain
33    End If
34    %>
35
36    <form id="frm_tourprice" name="frm_tourprice" method="post" action="tourprice_processor.asp">
37      <table width="60%" border="0" cellpadding="3" cellspacing="0" bgcolor="#EEEEEE">
```

6 Save, upload, and test the file.

For such a simple application, it took a fair amount of work. But the extra polish shows: The application is useful and usable. Now that it works, you need to remove the dummy dollar values and use real data. That requires working with databases, which is introduced in the next lesson.

What You Have Learned

In this lesson, you have:

- Built a form using test field and drop-down menu elements (pages 169–175)

- Written a script that manipulates data the user entered (pages 175–180)

- Output the manipulated value and formatted it using a built-in function (pages 181–183)

- Written a script that performs server-side form validation (pages 183–186)

- Redirected the user to the first page, while appending a querystring (pages 184–186)

- Created and activated a conditional region, depending on the outcome of the server-side form validation (pages 187–190)

- Formatted the text in the conditional region using a custom CSS class (pages 190–193)

What You Will Learn

In this lesson, you will:

- Learn core database terms and concepts
- Learn how databases are used to support Web sites
- Tour the Newland database I have created for you
- Connect your copy of the site to the database
- Display a column of text pulled from the database on the site's homepage

Approximate Time

This lesson takes approximately 75 minutes to complete.

Lesson Files

Starting Files:

Lesson07/Start/newland_tours.mdb
Lesson07/Start/newland_tours.sql (for PHP/MySQL users only)
Lesson07/Start/newland/index.asp

Completed Files:

Lesson07/Complete/newland/index.asp

LESSON 7

Databases on the Web

Developing dynamic Web pages is more difficult than developing static pages. Whereas static Web page development uses only a handful of technologies—XHTML, CSS, and FTP—dynamic Web page development uses these and many more, including ASP, ColdFusion, PHP, databases, servers, ODBC, and SQL, among others. In addition, dynamic Web page development, as you have already experienced, involves quite a bit more coding.

Lessons 3 through 6 introduced you to server-side scripting. You learned about passing data between pages, manipulating data, using built-in functions, displaying dynamic data, flow control using **if...else** statements, form validation, and more. This four-chapter introduction culminated in the code-intensive Lesson 6, where you wrote a number of scripts to build a simple application. I threw all that code at you deliberately, to help you overcome any trepidation you might have about writing server-side code, as well as to get you accustomed to the concepts and syntax of ASP, ColdFusion, and PHP.

Data in a database is stored in tables, which, at first glance, look like Excel spreadsheets.

This lesson marks a turning point in the book. I will take for granted henceforth that you are comfortable with the concepts and techniques for sending data from one page to the other, though I will continue to explain every script you produce, whether you handwrite it or use a Dreamweaver behavior. In this and the next several lessons, you will focus on working with databases. You will learn how to connect to a database, display data pulled from a database, and build forms that save data in a database.

Few people realize how deep and complex a topic databases are, until they start working with them. This lesson mainly consists of a crash course in databases, including a tour of the database I have prepared for you to use in the rest of the book, and tasks that have you connect your site to the database and display a block of text dynamically pulled from a database. While the last lesson was heavy on code, this lesson is heavy on theory, so make mental adjustments accordingly.

A Crash Course on Databases

A tutorial-based book should keep you actively working, so I try to refrain from pausing the action for long-winded passages explaining esoterica. But you will not get very far developing dynamic Web sites if you do not have a solid familiarity (though not necessarily expertise) with databases. In this section, I'll introduce you to basic database concepts and vocabulary, using Microsoft Access as the running example. The layout of the data (and the data itself) in MySQL is the same as it is in Access. However, Access has a better user interface, so all the screenshots are from Access. I strongly encourage you to spend additional time learning to work with databases, as you continue to master dynamic Web site development. For now, this section should be enough to get you started.

Your WAMP and MAMP installers include graphical user interfaces for your MySQL data, such as phpMyAdmin. Though MySQL looks radically different from Access, all of the critical concepts still apply. Some of the following discussion is Access-centric, and where MySQL has no equivalent, I'll make a note of it.

Introducing Database Objects

In the simplest terms, a database is a system of storage for data. But in contemporary use, the term database generally means a lot more—certainly in the case of Microsoft Access, or an enterprise-level database system, such as MySQL, Microsoft SQL Server or Oracle. Each of these is a **relational database management system** (RDBMS). The RDBMS model was developed in the 1970s and 1980s to enable database managers to store data in a way that reflected relationships between different types of data. We'll return to the idea of relationships momentarily, but first you should understand the objects that make up databases.

Data in a database is stored in **tables**. At first glance, tables look like Excel spreadsheets, in that they are made of rows and columns. The columns, called **fields**, contain a single category of information. The rows, called **records**, contain a single set of information comprising one element of data for each field. For example, in a table called tbl_customers, you might expect to find fields for first name, address, city, state, postal code, phone number, and so on. Each individual customer would have her or his own record.

The accompanying figure shows a table from the Newland database as it appears in Access. This table contains basic information about countries. You can easily see each country listed in a row in the countryName field, and you'll see that each country has the same type of information listed. You can edit tables directly by clicking in a cell and typing away, but there is a better way, which is to use an interface, such as Access forms or a Web form.

	countryID	region	countryName	population	country_currenc	description	imageURL	imageALT
	1	1	Canada	30007094	Canadian Dollar	Country to the north of tl	vancouver.jpg	Vancouver skyline at
	2	3	Italy	57634300	Euro	With its mild, Mediterran	colosseum.jpg	The Roman Colosseu
	3	4	Taiwan	22370461	New Taiwan Dol	Once known as Formos;	chiang_kaishe	The Music Hall at Ch
	4	4	Japan	125931533	Yen	A country composed of i	miyajima.jpg	Island of Miyajima, Ja
	5	3	France	58804944	Euro	From Paris street cafes	paris.jpg	Paris at dawn
	6	3	United Kingdom	58970119	Pound Sterling	A nation comprising Eng	stonehenge.jp	England's enigmatic
	7	2	Peru	26111110	Nuevo Sol	Set on the west coast of	machu_picch	Incan ruins at Machu
	8	8	Mexico	98552776	Nuevo Peso	The United States' neigh	mexican_ruin	Mayan Ruins in the Y
	9	6	Namibia	1622328	Namibian Dollar	Formerly South-West Af	etosha.jpg	Etosha National Park
	10	5	Israel	5643966	New Israeli She	A state whose borders e	wailing_wall2.	The Wailing Wall, Jer
	11	6	Egypt	66050004	Egyptian Pound	Home of one of the most	sphinx.jpg	The Sphinx, with a py
	12	1	United States	270311758	American Dollar	Situated between Canad	dc.jpg	Washington, D.C., wi
	13	4	Thailand	60037366	Baht	Formerly known as Sian	mae_hong_so	Thailand's Mae Hong
	14	6	Morocco	29114497	Dirham	Situated in the northwes	mor_sahara.jr	The Sahara Desert, N
	15	2	Argentina	36265463	Nuevo Peso Arc	South America's second	fitzroy.jpg	The snow-capped pea
	16	7	India	984003683	Rupee	The world's seventh-large	ganges.jpg	Ganges River in Vara

Tables aren't the only type of object you can expect to find in databases. A desktop RDBMS such as MS Access includes handy tools such as forms, reports, and stored queries. **Forms** are used to insert new data and modify existing data. The form used to build the country table shown in the preceding screenshot can be seen in the following screenshot. Forms make it easy to insert and edit information, and you can also use them to control the type of information entered, which helps ensure the integrity of the data entered. At the bottom of the form is a group of record navigation buttons, which you can use to access the record you want to edit, or to create a new record from scratch. An enterprise RDBMS, while lacking these built-in tools, provides other valuable functionality such as views, stored procedures and triggers. These allow you to balance the workload between your application code and the database itself. If you take the skills learned in this book and move into the development of production Web applications you should learn what your RDBMS of choice can do. You will find the database a critical piece of the Web application equation.

> ✱ **NOTE:** MySQL handles the important part of database utility—data storage and access—arguably better than Microsoft Access, but MySQL's default interface is minimal, at best. Unless you download a separate graphical user interface (GUI), such as phpMyAdmin or MySQL GUI Tools, you control MySQL through a command line. The same is true for other enterprise RDBMS, but you should base the decision of what database to use on the database's capabilities, not its interface.

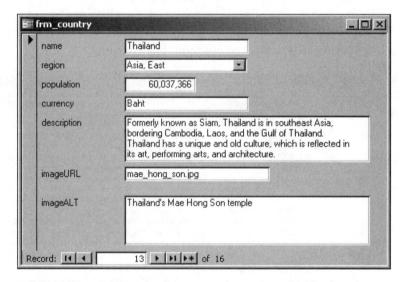

Whereas forms are a means of inputting information into tables, **reports** are a means of outputting that data. You probably noticed that it was difficult to read all of the information in the table directly, because the fields weren't wide enough to accommodate all the text. You can use reports to make data presentable. Better yet, you can selectively show only some data in reports, rather than showing all of it, which makes reports much more useful.

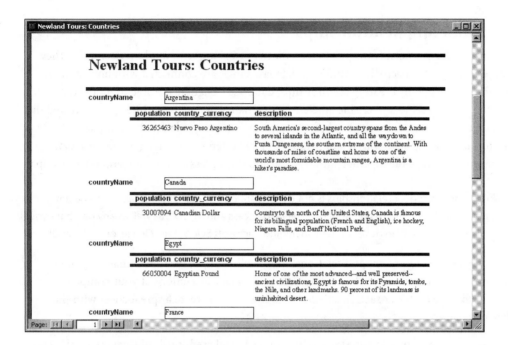

You use **queries** to show data selectively in reports. Queries are like searches: You provide certain criteria, and the database returns a report. For example, you could obtain a report of all the countries in the Newland database that begin with T, which would return Taiwan and Thailand. Queries are written in a language called SQL, or Structured Query Language. You will use SQL heavily when working with databases, beginning with this chapter, because you must use SQL to retrieve data from a database to make it available for Web pages via ASP, ColdFusion, or PHP. SQL is the primary means by which developers communicate with database systems. Access has a visual SQL editor, but you can't use it in Dreamweaver. In Dreamweaver, you can hand-code SQL or use Dreamweaver's visual SQL editor.

Familiarity with SQL is a prerequisite for dynamic Web application development. You'll learn a fair amount in this book, but for an easy-to-read and comprehensive introduction, check out *SQL: Visual QuickStart Guide* (Peachpit Press) or *Teach Yourself SQL in 10 Minutes* (Sams).

The SQL snippet in the accompanying screenshot retrieves all of the records in the countryName, population, country_currency, and description fields of the tbl_country table.

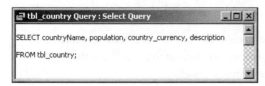

Understanding Relationships

Relationships are a crucial concept when it comes to working with modern databases. They enable developers to specify how different database tables are connected with one another through shared data. By creating relationships, database designers are able to model data into tables that reflect reality and enable efficient maintenance of data over time. I have created the database file you will use for the book, and it already has many relationships in place. While you won't be creating any more relationships, you will often need to retrieve and use data from more than one table together, and you can't do this unless you understand relationships.

✳ NOTE: The concept of relationships is not dependent on any particular database management system. That is, this discussion applies equally to Access and MySQL, as well as any database you are likely to use for Web development, including Microsoft SQL Server, Oracle, or PostgreSQL.

It is perhaps easiest to understand relationships by following an example. Imagine you use an Excel spreadsheet to store information about financial transactions at your company. You want to store each transaction as a separate row, so you create a spreadsheet with the following columns:

> f_name l_name str_add city state/prov country postal cred_card subtotal tax total

Over time, hundreds of records are added to this spreadsheet. Many of these records are for repeat customers. The problem is, each time a customer returns her or his address information is stored again. As time passes, some of these repeat customers move. Their new addresses are duly entered in the spreadsheet, but all of the former records have the old address. Chances are, sooner or later, someone will inadvertently use the wrong address. Updating these addresses is hard, because there are so many; and, unfortunately, in Excel there's not much you can do about this problem.

A more logical way to represent the transaction is to separate the customer from the transaction. One table would track individual sales, but the customer information would be stored in a separate table for customers. The customer table would have one and only one record for each customer. If a customer moved, you would need to update only the single record that applied to the customer, not all of the records of his or her transactions. Then, back in the transaction table, instead of listing all of the customer information, you would list a unique identifier that referenced the customer in the customer table. Databases enable you to create this type of relationship between tables.

▶ TIP: If you've ever wondered why catalog companies have product IDs or customer IDs that you have to refer to, this is why: Those IDs are unique numbers in their database that refer to you and only you, or to a given product and only that product.

Thus, the customer table would look as follows:

cust_ID F_name l_name str_add city state/prov postal credit_card

And the transaction table would look as follows:

transaction_ID cust_ID subtotal tax total

Notice that both tables have a field for cust_ID. The cust_ID in the customer table is a unique identifier in that table, also called the **primary key**. No two columns in this table will ever have the same cust_ID. It's possible that there will be two John Smiths, and it's possible that two people will reside at postal code 90210. But each row is guaranteed to be unique, because each row has its own unique primary key, cust_ID.

In contrast, the cust_ID in the transaction table could be repeated multiple times—this would mean that the same customer had ordered more than one time. When you use the primary key of one table as a field in a different table, it is referred to as a **foreign key**. By placing foreign keys in tables, you create relationships between tables. Again, the benefit of doing this is that you remove redundant information and better maintain the integrity of your data.

> ✱ **NOTE:** To facilitate the discussion, I've simplified these tables. For example, you would normally expect to see a third table to handle products (that is, an inventory table), with product_ID used as the foreign key in the transaction table. Also, this example assumes that a customer can have only a single credit card. Obviously, you can add new tables, fields, and relationships to handle these realities.

The following figure shows the relationships between the two tables described in this example. The line between the two tables indicates the relationship. The number 1 on the left side indicates that in the tbl_customers table, the cust_ID is unique, while the infinity character on the right indicates that cust_ID can appear many times. This is known as a one-to-many relationship.

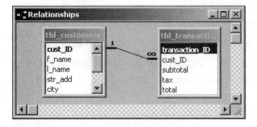

The power of relationships extends beyond preventing redundancy. For example, you can write a SQL query that pulls data out of both tables, using certain criteria. For instance, you could write a query that lists all of the first and last names of customers who spent over $100. You can also create forms that write to more than one table.

▶ **TIP:** A copy of this simple database can be found on the CD-ROM in Microsoft Access format, in Lesson07/Start/transactions.mdb.

Databases on the Web

Now that you have a sense for what databases look like and what they can do, you should be ready to understand how they work on the Web.

Database content is used on the Web in many different ways. The simplest way—which you'll do yourself at the end of this lesson—is to display the contents of a field on the Web. But you can display more than a simple string of text. You can also display multiple fields, populate menus, and handle user authentication. In addition to reading and displaying information, you can also collect it and store it in database tables. Using this technique, you can create user registration, surveys, quizzes, and content management systems.

▶ **TIP:** Content management systems let users add or modify site content without having to know any HTML, buy any special software, or worry about uploading files, using Web forms and databases. The user types the site content into a Web form. This content is then stored in a database and output to a different Web page.

If you compare database-driven Web pages to the Access database objects discussed earlier in the lesson, you'll realize that you can effectively use Web pages and Web forms as a surrogate for database reports and forms. Pages that output and display data are like reports, while pages with Web forms can perform the same function as database forms. The advantage to such a system is that users don't need Access or MySQL (or whichever RDBMS your organization uses) to maintain its content, and users can be distributed all over the world and still have access to the data storage, thanks to the Internet. Better still, because you aren't giving users direct access to the database, you decrease the likelihood of your data being compromised (maliciously or inadvertently).

So much for the cool features; now how does it all work? Just as you have access to files sitting on your hard drive, so a user has access to files sitting on a server's hard drive. An Internet user does not have permission to start modifying files on any server—that would be a security nightmare. But you can give applications on your system controlled access to certain files.

One way is to use Windows' Open Database Connectivity (ODBC), which enables you to create a data source name (DSN) that lets ASP or ColdFusion to read and write to your Access database. The relationship is depicted in the following figure.

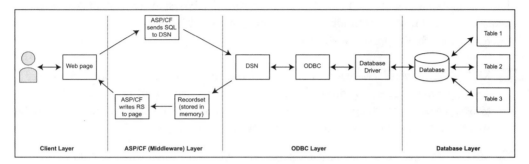

There's a lot going on in this figure. Before I deconstruct it, though, notice how far the user is from the actual data; this complex sequence enables the user to access data, but protects the data from convenient access, providing some measure of security.

Let's look at the figure in detail. You'll notice the figure is divided into four different regions: the client layer, the middleware layer, the ODBC layer, and the database layer.

The client layer includes static HTML interpreted by the browser. This static HTML may have been coded as static HTML, or as dynamic HTML, but as you know, by the time it is returned to the browser, it's all static HTML.

ODBC has all of the information needed to access the database, including the appropriate database driver and the path to the database. These two pieces of information are stored in ODBC and are referred to using the DSN.

Finally, the SQL reaches the database itself, and it looks in the proper table(s) and retrieves the appropriate information.

So much for the way in. On the way out, the data is sent back the same way it came in, until it gets to the middleware layer. At this point, the data retrieved is stored in the server's memory (RAM). It is not actually on the page yet. A set of data stored in memory as the result of a query is called a **recordset**. You use ASP or ColdFusion to output the recordset data (or any subset of it) inside the HTML, much as you did with form variables, so that the user can see it.

PHP/MySQL doesn't work exactly the same way, since it doesn't make use of ODBC. Instead, you provide the information the PHP processor needs to access the database directly in the code. I'll cover the details later in the chapter, but the gist is that PHP has a special function (`mysql_connect()`) used for connecting to a MySQL database. When you use this function, you provide a path to the database server as well as username and password credentials. Then you use another function (`mysql_select_db()`) to specify the name of the MySQL database that you want to access. MySQL can contain numerous databases; in contrast, in Access, each database is stored in its own *.mdb file. At any rate, though PHP and MySQL use a slightly different approach, the process is similar.

✱ NOTE: ODBC drivers for MySQL are available, but Dreamweaver doesn't use ODBC to connect PHP pages to MySQL, so you don't have to worry about installing ODBC drivers for MySQL. MySQL can be used with both ASP and ColdFusion as well. There is good documentation on the Web for setting up and using both these alternative configurations.

✱ NOTE: MS Access is useful for local development of Web applications with ASP, ColdFusion or even PHP. However Access is ultimately a desktop database application. Once you move your Web application into production online you should use a more robust database such as MySQL, Microsoft SQL Server or Oracle.

Database Security and the Web

Security is a major issue with dynamic applications that link to data sources. The integrity (and usually confidentiality) of a company's data is vital to that company's interests. If you read the news, you know that malicious users are out there who try very hard to hack into other organizations' databases and business logic. But, ironically, another dangerous threat comes not from malicious users at all, but rather from well-intentioned employees making mistakes while doing their job.

Security issues are largely beyond the scope of this book, but the following bullets offer suggestions for protecting the integrity of your database from yourself and/or end users. For more information, see Adobe's Security Development Center, a free resource containing dozens of articles, white papers, tips, tutorials, and more. It can be found at http://www.adobe.com/devnet/security/.

To maintain the integrity of your data, consider:

- Checking all user input for correct data type and format. That is, in a field that holds phone numbers, make sure that any data a user tries to enter is composed of digits and has the correct number of digits.

- Letting the database do manipulation of data (via SQL) rather than the application where possible.

- Setting proper constraints on tables and fields to prevent users from inputting bad data.

- Having users choose from a menu of permissible options rather than letting them input free-form text where appropriate.

- Restricting the rights of your dynamic application's connection to the database to the minimum necessary to get the job done. Typically these rights would be reading, updating, inserting and deleting records. Your application should not be capable of modifying the database structure by adding, removing or altering tables.

Implementing these features doesn't guarantee that data cannot be compromised, but it is a significant step in the right direction. As you develop, be sure to keep these considerations in mind throughout the project design and development phases.

Installing the Newland Tours Database in MySQL

MySQL can be used with both ASP and ColdFusion and Access can be used with PHP, but setting up those configurations is beyond the scope of this book. If you are using ASP or ColdFusion, skip to the next section, *Touring the Newland Database*.

The most popular tool for managing a MySQL database in a PHP environment is an application called phpMyAdmin. phpMyAdmin is a Web-based interface which lists all of the databases to which your account has access. It lets you view the data in your databases, see the SQL code used to generate each table, and it has a host of database maintenance features that make it easy to add new tables, modify existing ones, and delete tables and even whole databases.

One of the benefits of phpMyAdmin is that it lets users generate databases and tables using SQL stored in an external text file. You can use this feature to install the newland_tours database on a local or remote server running MySQL.

The WAMP (Windows) and MAMP (Macintosh OS X) installers used to set up PHP earlier in this book both include the MySQL RDBMS and phpMyAdmin. All that remains is to create the Newland Tours Database and populate it with data. The procedure will be the same for both with slightly different paths to phpMyAdmin.

Opening phpMyAdmin in a Local Windows Installation

Click the WAMP5 control panel in your system tray. Choose phpMyAdmin, near the top of the menu.

phpMyAdmin will open in your default Web browser.

Opening phpMyAdmin in a Local Macintosh Installation

1 Click Open start page in the MAMP control panel.

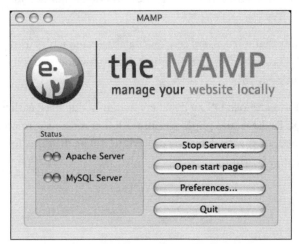

The MAMP start page will open in your default Web browser.

2 Click either of the phpMyAdmin links on the MAMP start page.

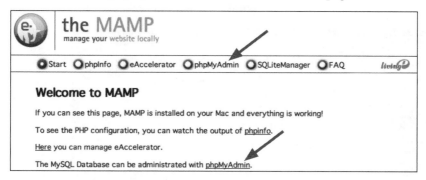

phpMyAdmin will open in a frame below the MAMP header.

Creating the Newland Tours Database on a Local Server

To create a new database, you simply import the SQL file included on the CD.

1 Click the Import link at the bottom of phpMyAdmin's Home screen.

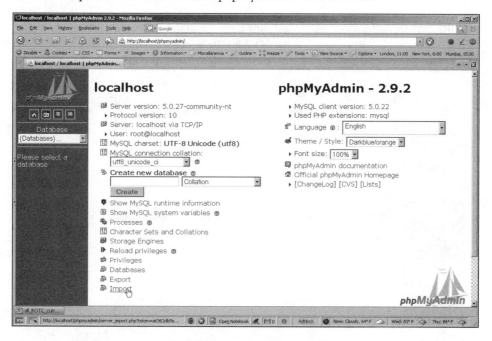

✱ **NOTE:** You can return to the Home screen by clicking the icon of the house at the top of the left navigation.

2 In the File to import section browse to the newland_tours.sql in the Lesson07/Start folder on the CD. Click Open. Click the Go button at the bottom of the screen.

The newland_tours database should now show up in the Database drop-down list on the left. You can select it to display a list of tables. By clicking on the name of a table you will display its structure. By clicking on the image to its left you will browse its contents.

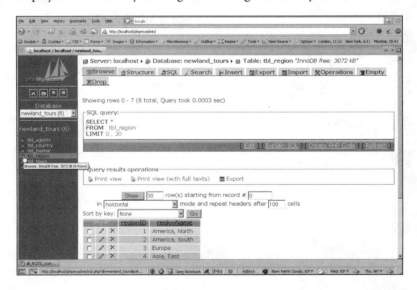

The newland_tours database is properly installed and running in MySQL. You can skip ahead to the section, *Touring the Newland Database.*

Creating and Populating the Newland Tours Database on a Remote Server

Unfortunately, I can't tell you how to install the newland_tours database into a remote MySQL server. There are too many variables, and you'll need to read your Web host's documentation or contract them to determine how to create the database. For example, some Web hosts will use phpMyAdmin; others have Web-based control panels. Whatever method your Web host uses, you will need to create a new database named newland_tours and populate it with data using the SQL script provided.

1 Copy the newland_tours.sql file from the Lesson07/Start folder on the CD to your computer. Open the file and delete the following three lines of code:

```
DROP DATABASE IF EXISTS newland_tours;
CREATE DATABASE newland_tours;
USE newland_tours;
```

The new first line of code should begin DROP TABLE IF EXISTS.

You will have already created the database on the remote server, either directly in phpMyAdmin or through some other means provided by your Web host, so these first three lines of code are redundant. Once the file is prepared, you can install the database using phpMyAdmin.

2 Log into phpMyAdmin on your remote server and select the newland_tours database. Click the Import tab near the top of the page.

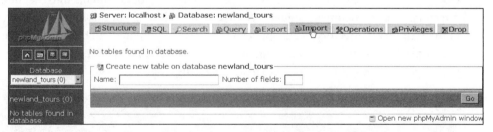

3 In the File to import section browse to the newland_tours.sql that you saved on your computer. Click Open. Click the Go button at the bottom of the screen.

The tables of the newland_tours database should now appear on the left. By clicking on the name of a table you will display its structure. By clicking on the image to its left you will browse its contents.

The newland_tours database is properly installed and running in MySQL

▶ **TIP:** phpMyAdmin is an active and successful open-source project. It is frequently updated. The most recent version can be downloaded for free, at the following URL: http://www.phpmyadmin.net/.

Touring the Newland Database

DSNs, SQL, ODBC, relationships, tables, queries, forms, reports, recordsets—that's a lot to absorb! Don't worry if you don't feel as if you've mastered all of this yet. You'll get lots of experience from here on until the end of the book. The important thing is that you understand the big picture: that data is stored in tables; that the Web can be used as a read/write interface for these tables; that tables may be related to one another; and that the connection between the Web and database tables happens through a combination of ASP, ColdFusion, or PHP; SQL code; and information to connect to the database, such as ODBC (ASP or ColdFusion) or a direct connection string (PHP/MySQL).

In this task, you'll get a quick tour of the newland_tours database that will drive the Newland Tours Web site. This tour uses Microsoft Access, because its interface makes it easy to understand the data and the ways it is structured.

✱ **NOTE:** Though the phpMyAdmin interface differs from that of Access , the structure of the data is exactly the same, so even if you are using MySQL, you should read through this section (without actually doing the steps.)

1 ASP and ColdFusion users only, copy the newland_tours.mdb file into an appropriate location on the server (see below for details).

If you are developing locally in Windows XP, create a new directory in the Shared Documents folder called *database*, and paste the newland_tours.mdb file into that new directory. Shared Documents might seem like an odd place to put this file—it's not even in the Web server directory!—but applications on your computer will have access to it, and by placing it in the Shared Documents folder, you also ensure that it will have the proper permission settings applied to it automatically.

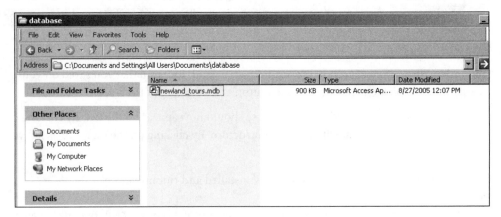

If you are developing ASP or ColdFusion and are using a remote server, such as an Intranet server or at your Web host via FTP, put the newland_tours.mdb file wherever the server administrator tells you to put databases. This varies by Web host.

✱ NOTE: It bears repeating that while MS Access is appropriate for development and training, once you move your Web application into production online you should use a more robust database such as MySQL, Microsoft SQL Server or Oracle.

2 If you have Access, open newland_tours.mdb, which is inside the database folder you just copied.

If you do not have Access, then follow along reading the text and looking at the screenshots.

When you open the database file, you see a window that lists several object categories on the left side, and a group of objects on the right. The object categories are the same as the ones discussed earlier in the lesson.

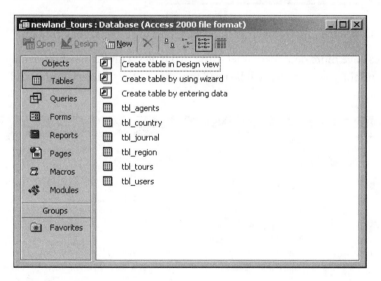

3 Click each of the objects listed on the left in turn, to see the objects that already exist in the database.

As you can see, six tables are in the Tables category, and a corresponding number of forms are in the Forms category. The remaining categories are empty.

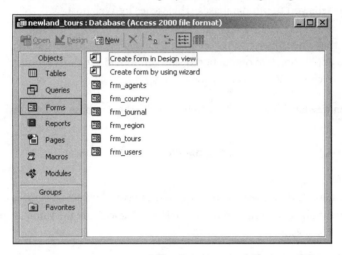

4 In the Tables group, double-click to open each of the tables to see what they contain.

Some of the tables have more data than others. The two tables with the most information are tbl_country and tbl_tours—these will be used to populate the Country Profile and Find a Tour segments.

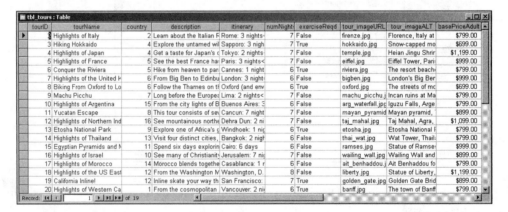

When you open tbl_journal, you'll see that it contains the text used in the Traveler's Journal section of the homepage.

The tbl_agents table is odd in that it contains only numbers, and no names as you might expect. The reason for this is that these numbers are actually foreign keys—the user is userID from tbl_users and the specialty is regionID from tbl_region.

The tbl_users table contains information used for logging in and authenticating at the site. When users register, their information is stored in this table. Notice that there are two categories in the userGroup field: admin and visitor. Users can access different areas of the site, depending on their userGroup category.

Close the tables window to return to the main screen.

5 In the Forms group, open each of the forms, navigating through records to see what they contain.

The forms, again, are convenient interfaces through which one can enter data into the tables. You won't use these in the Newland Tours site—forms aren't accessible through the Web, so you will create your own Web forms to replace them. But I used these to create the tables used in the site, and I left them in place, so you could explore them.

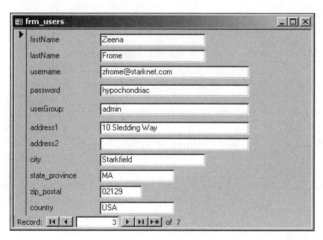

6 Click the Relationships button on the toolbar.

Access has a convenient visual interface that lets you view and modify relationships among tables.

Relationships button

7 Review the relationships among the different tables.

The bold field in each table is its primary key. Foreign keys are linked to primary keys by a line. Do you remember how tbl_agents had only numbers in it? Now you can see why. The table comprises a primary key (agentID) and two foreign keys (user and specialty). Notice also that tbl_journal isn't linked to any other tables. Not every table needs to be part of a relationship.

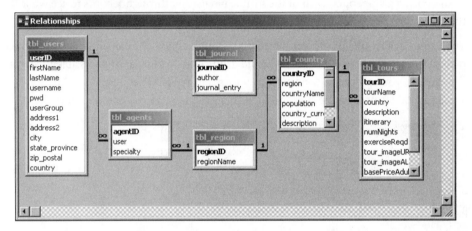

8 Do any further exploring without making any changes, and then close all open windows and Access.

You've now had a crash course in Access and familiarized yourself with a bona fide database.

Connecting to a Database

Enough theory and exploration: It's time to connect this database to your pages. As you must have gathered, a number of preliminary steps are involved to get everything set up. And the steps vary depending on how you are connecting to your server and the server technology (ASP, ColdFusion, or PHP) you are using.

For ASP and ColdFusion users, there are two steps you need to take to connect to a database. First, you have to create the DSN on the server, so you can take advantage of an ODBC connection. Remember, the DSN is simply a pointer to your database that you register on the server. Second, you have to get Dreamweaver to see this DSN, so it can ensure that scripts on individual pages can access the database through this DSN.

PHP/MySQL doesn't use ODBC or DSNs; instead, you provide the connection information—database location and name, as well as login credentials—directly in your PHP code. As you'll see, Dreamweaver lets you enter this information in a dialog, and then Dreamweaver writes a generic connection file, to which it refers every time you create a page that refers to your database.

The variations in configuring the database are so extreme that rather than attempting to create a generic set of instructions, I've separated them.

ASP Users (Running IIS Locally or Connecting to a Remote Server)

This section is for all ASP users, regardless of how they connect to their server.

In this section, you will configure Dreamweaver to connect to an existing DSN. ASP users who are working locally will need to first set up the DSN, and instructions to do so are included in this section. Then they will enable Dreamweaver to connect to that DSN.

ASP users who connect to a remote server must have the administrator for that server create a system DSN for them, using the following information: The DSN should be called newland. The database type is Microsoft Access (which uses the JET driver). The database is located in the newland/database folder in your directory. Assuming you have in fact copied the database folder to that directory, your server administrator has enough information to create the DSN for you. Unfortunately, you cannot continue until this DSN has been created. Once it has, you'll use the steps in this section to enable Dreamweaver to connect to that DSN.

1 Open index.asp.

It doesn't matter which page of your site is open when initially creating the connection. Dreamweaver creates the connection for the whole site. You've opened index.asp, because you will add dynamic content to that page, shortly.

2 Open the Databases panel, in the Application panel group. Click the Connection (+) button, and choose Data Source Name (DSN).

This opens the Data Source Name dialog, which is used to create a database connection for the site.

3 Users connecting to remote servers, skip to step 8 below. Users running IIS locally only: Click the Define button to begin the process of creating a System DSN.

The ODBC Data Source Administrator dialog opens. This is a Windows dialog, not a Dreamweaver dialog, which you can also access using the Control Panel.

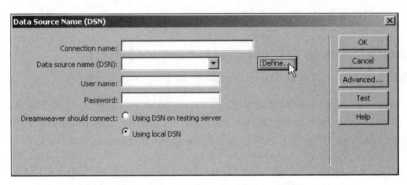

4 Click the System DSN tab.

To give Web access to your data source, you must add the DSN using the System DSN tab, and not the User DSN tab that appears by default.

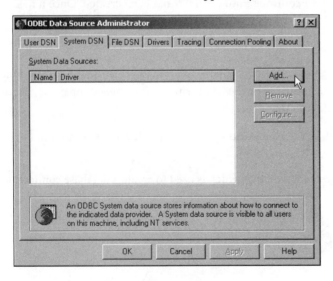

5 Click the Add button. In the Create New Data Source dialog, choose Microsoft Access Driver (*.mdb) from the dialog, and click Finish.

A DSN needs three pieces of information: The driver needed to communicate with the database, a name for the DSN, and the path to the database on the server. In this dialog, you provide the first piece of information.

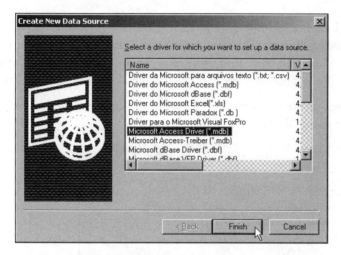

6 In the ODBC Microsoft Access Setup dialog that appears, type *newland* as the Data Source Name. Click the Select button, and in the Select Database dialog, browse to the newland_tours.mdb file, which should be in the following directory: C:\Documents and Settings\All Users\Documents\database.

In this step, you are supplying a name for the DSN and the path to the database.

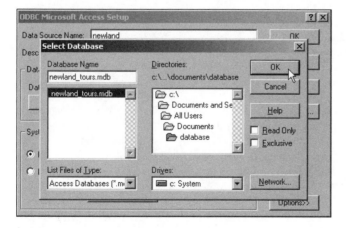

7 Click OK three times to close the windows and return to the Data Source Name dialog.

Now that the DSN is complete, you can return to Dreamweaver and use the new DSN to connect to your data source.

8 In the radio group at the bottom of the dialog, choose Using DSN on Testing Server, which erases all content in the dialog (this does not affect the DSN you created). Return to the top of the dialog, and in the Connection Name field, enter *conn_newland*. Enter *newland* as the Data Source Name. Click the Test button to verify the connection was made, and click OK.

By completing this dialog, you are providing Dreamweaver with sufficient information to connect to your database using ODBC.

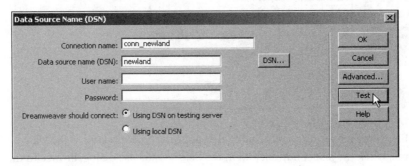

When you close the dialog, Dreamweaver creates a new folder in your site, called Connections, with a new file inside called conn_newland.asp. You should also notice that the Databases panel now has an expandable listing of the database and its assets.

9 Select the Connections folder in the Files panel, and click the Put button to upload it to the server.

You are ready to create a recordset and start binding database data. Skip ahead to the task, *Retrieving Recordsets and Displaying Database Information.*

ColdFusion Users (Running ColdFusion Locally or Connecting to a Remote Server)

This section is for all ColdFusion users, regardless of how they connect to their server.

ColdFusion users who connect to a remote server must have the administrator for that server grant them RDS login information—which consists of a password. Without RDS login, you will not be able to complete this book.

> ✱ **NOTE:** RDS should only be used in a development or learning environment. An administrator on a production ColdFusion server is unlikely to turn on RDS for you. This is one reason why many ColdFusion developers do most of their work on a local installation of ColdFusion server.

1 Open index.cfm.

It doesn't matter which page of your site is open when initially creating the connection. Dreamweaver creates the connection for the whole site. You've opened index.cfm because you will add dynamic content to that page in the next task.

2 Open the Databases panel, in the Application panel group. Click the Specify the RDS login for your ColdFusion server link, enter your password, and click OK.

RDS login grants developers permission to access the ColdFusion server, which is necessary for defining and using data sources.

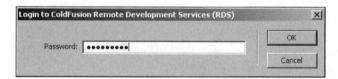

At the end of this step, if there are already many data sources existing on the ColdFusion server, they are all visible in the Databases panel.

The only problem is, the Newland database is not among them.

3 Click the Create a ColdFusion data source link (if it is available), or click the Modify Data Sources button on the right side of the Databases panel.

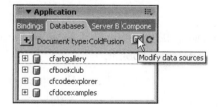

Regardless of whether you click the button or the link, after a moment, the ColdFusion administrator opens in a browser, to the Data Sources page. You will first need to enter the password to access the administrator.

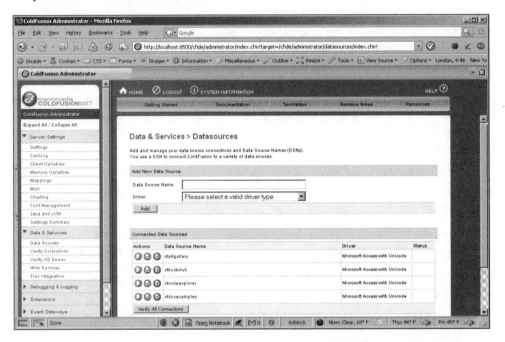

4 In the Add New Data Source box, enter *newland* as the Data Source Name. In the Driver drop-down menu, select Microsoft Access. Click Add.

A DSN consists of a name, a driver that enables the application to communicate with the database, and the path to the database. In this step, you have entered the first two of these three pieces of information.

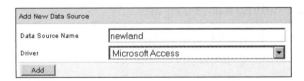

5 In the Microsoft Access Data Source box that appears, click the first Browse Server button and browse to the newland_tours.mdb file on the site. Click Submit.

Browse to the following directory: C:\Documents and Settings\All Users\Documents\ database\. This is the directory to which the shortcut Shared Documents points.

This step provides ColdFusion with the remaining information it needs to connect to your database.

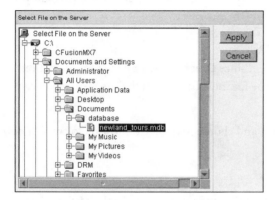

6 Close the ColdFusion Data Sources Web page to return to Dreamweaver. In the Databases panel, click the Refresh button beside the Modify Data Sources you clicked earlier. The newland DSN should show up. Click the + button beside it to expand it and explore the data source.

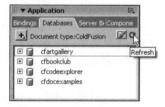

Now that you can see the contents of the newland_tours.mdb database, you know that Dreamweaver has successfully made the connection. You are ready to create a recordset and start binding database data.

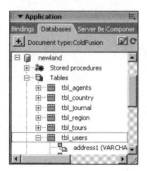

Skip ahead to the section entitled *Retrieving Recordsets and Displaying Database Information.*

PHP Users (Running PHP/MySQL Locally or on a Remote Server)

Because PHP doesn't make use of ODBC or DSNs, you can specify all the information you need to access your MySQL database right in Dreamweaver.

1 Open index.php.

It doesn't really matter which file is open, since Dreamweaver makes the connection available site-wide. However, at least one file must be open in the site, before you can create a connection to MySQL.

2 In the Databases tab, click the + button and choose MySQL Connection to create a new connection to MySQL.

The MySQL Connection dialog opens.

3 Specify the following information, so that Dreamweaver can make the MySQL data source available to your site.

Connection name: *conn_newland*

MySQL server: *localhost* (if developing locally) or whatever your server administrator tells you (if developing remotely)

User name and Password: the user name and password of the MySQL account that you use to access MySQL. For Windows users using the WAMP5 installer, the password is blank. For Macintosh users using the MAMP installer, the password is *root*.

✱ NOTE: Windows users developing locally will see a warning message about production databases requiring a password. While it is a very good warning, ignore it for your local development.

Database: *newland_tours*.

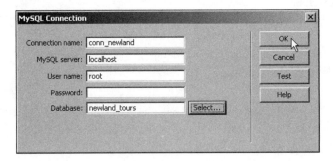

If you are developing on a remote server, only your server administrator will be able to tell you how to access MySQL from Dreamweaver/PHP. If you are developing locally, then just use the information you specified when you first installed MySQL. If you installed MySQL yourself and are unsure of your username and password, try root as the username and leave the password blank.

▶ **TIP:** Optionally, click the Test button to make sure that Dreamweaver can actually access MySQL.

4 Click OK.

Dreamweaver creates a Connections directory on your site, with a file in it called conn_newland.php. This file contains the information your pages will need to access MySQL. Whenever you call a database from PHP, Dreamweaver references this file.

5 Expand conn_newland in the Databases panel to explore the structure of the newland_tours database from within Dreamweaver.

Dreamweaver is actually accessing the database within MySQL and providing you with information about it. Albeit in a limited way, you can interface with MySQL via Dreamweaver.

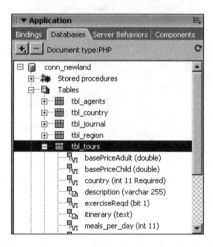

6 In the Files panel, click the Connections folder, and then click the Put button to upload it to the server.

The PHP/MySQL connection won't work unless this folder is uploaded.

Retrieving Recordsets and Displaying Database Information

It seems like a long time since you made any improvements to the actual site. You've done some theory, some exploration, and some configuration. But you haven't done anything to any pages yet. In this final task of the lesson, you'll cause the Traveler's Journal to load dynamically from the database. In the browser, the homepage will look the same as it did before, but in Dreamweaver, the difference will be unmistakable.

1 With index.asp open in Design view, select the text from "Teens Discover…" down to "…putting together" at the bottom. Do not select the yellow image icon beside the T in Teens (if it appears). Press Delete.

You're going to replace this text with dynamic text, so you are just making room in this step.

2 Click the Traveler's Journal image to select it. In the tag selector (in the bottom-left corner of the document window), right-click the <h3> tag just to the left of the <img> tag, and choose Remove Tag from the menu.

The journal entry in the database is already marked up in HTML. You need to remove the <h3> tag here, or the tags in the journal entry will be illegally nested inside the <h3> tag.

3 In the Bindings panel, click the New Binding (+) button, and choose Recordset (Query) from the menu.

At this point, you have connected your site to a data source, which means you have made it possible for Dreamweaver to write code for you that retrieves data from your database. However, you have not actually retrieved any data yet. In this and the next two steps, you'll create a recordset, which as you'll recall from the beginning of this lesson, is a collection of data that meets certain criteria and that is retrieved from a database using SQL.

Your goal is to display the journal entry, but you don't want to display all the journal entries, only the most recent. In order to facilitate this, each journal entry has been given a unique ID (a primary key). These IDs are numbered incrementally, as the records are added. Therefore the record with the highest journalID is the most recent. You'll need to sort the data, and then retrieve the contents of the latest journal entry in order to display it. You'll take the first steps toward doing this in the next step.

4 In the Recordset dialog, enter *rs_journal* as the Name. Choose conn_newland (or newland for ColdFusion users) from the Connection drop-down. Select tbl_journal from the Table drop-down. In the Columns section, choose the Selected radio button, and Ctrl-select (Windows) or Command-select (Macintosh) journalID and journal_entry.

In this dialog, you are creating a recordset, named rs_journal. The data in this recordset is retrieved using criteria specified in SQL. You may not realize it, but you have already begun the SQL statement.

Specifically, you have specified data in the data source stored in conn_newland (that connection specifies the newland DSN). Within that data source, you are specifying that the data is in a table named tbl_journal. Going a step further, you are specifying that you only want to retrieve the journalID and journal_entry fields from that table.

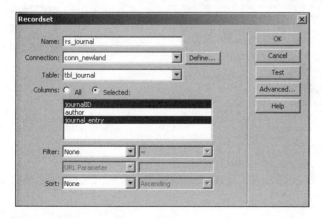

5 In the Sort drop-down menu, choose journalID, and then choose Descending in the next drop-down menu. Click OK.

This adds the SQL necessary to sort the entries from most recent to least recent. You have entered the information necessary to create the recordset.

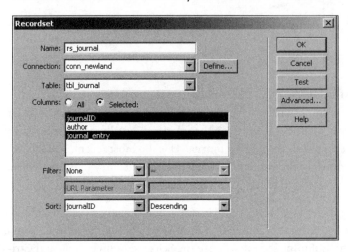

After you click OK, the recordset appears in the Bindings panel, much like form and URL variables did earlier in the book.

6 Expand Recordset(rs_journal) in the Bindings panel, and drag journal_entry so that it is just to the right of the image and release it.

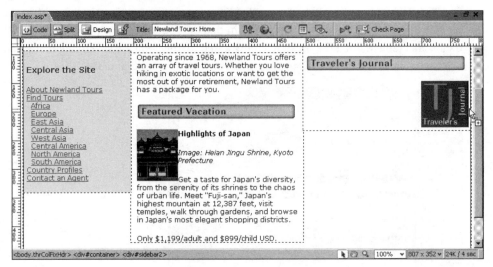

It may take some trial and error to order the dynamic text and the image correctly, so just keep trying till the image icon, the dynamic text, and the graphic itself look like they do in the screenshot.

7 Choose View > Live Data from the main menu.

You already know that when you want to test a dynamic page, you can press F12 to open it in a browser, running from the server. If that is too much trouble for you, you can also view Live Data from inside Dreamweaver. This is a very convenient feature, because you can see the effects of your work right in the Dreamweaver authoring environment. It is especially handy when you are trying to format dynamic content, and Dreamweaver's pseudocode placeholders don't give you a sufficiently visual idea of how the page will look.

Clearly, the recordset and display of the live data worked, because you can see the database data inside of Dreamweaver. You can also see that it is correctly formatted. The formatting is possible, because I entered HTML tags in the database itself, so when the data was placed on the page, the browser (or, in this case, Dreamweaver) correctly parsed and rendered the HTML tags.

✱ **NOTE:** The text is highlighted in yellow to show you that it is dynamic and cannot be edited like normal text. This yellow highlighting does not appear in the actual browser; it is merely a Dreamweaver authoring aid.

8 Choose View > Live Data again, to toggle it off. Save and upload index.asp. Press F12 to test it in a browser.

If you are seeing what's in the screenshot, then your system is fully configured, and from here forward it's all about the code.

What You Have Learned

In this lesson, you have:

- Learned about the objects a database comprises (pages 196–199)

- Learned about database relationships (pages 200–202)

- Discovered how database content is used on the Web (pages 202–205)

- Created and populated a database in MySQL on a Mac or PC (PHP users developing locally only) (pages 205–209)

- Explored the Newland Tours database in Access (pages 210–214)

- Configured your system so that Dreamweaver can connect to a database (pages 214–223)

- Displayed XHTML-formatted database content dynamically (pages 224–228)

What You Will Learn

In this lesson, you will:

- Dynamically populate a form menu with database data
- Filter a query using dynamic data
- Update the tour price calculation with live data
- Document your code with comments

Approximate Time

This lesson takes approximately 45 minutes to complete.

Lesson Files

Starting Files:

Lesson08/Start/newland/tourprice.asp
Lesson08/Start/newland/tourprice_ processor.asp

Completed Files:

Lesson08/Complete/newland/tourprice.asp
Lesson08/Complete/newland/tourprice_ processor.asp

LESSSON 8

Completing the Price Calculator

Back in Lesson 6, you began the tour price calculator application and created most of its functionality. As you'll recall, though, you lacked the actual data required to make it work. That data is stored in the newland_tours database (in Access or MySQL, depending on your setup). In this lesson, you will finish what you started, by working with information from the database, controlling what data is retrieved and how it is displayed.

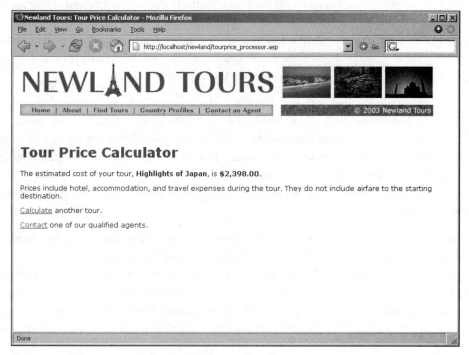

By the end of this lesson, the tour price calculator application will be fully functional with live data.

While there will be some hand-coding in this lesson, you will also make use of some of Dreamweaver's visual features for working with database data. For example, you will learn how to populate the drop-down list in the form on tourprice.asp with dynamic data using a simple dialog.

You'll also spend some more time working with SQL and creating queries. You'll see how to filter SQL queries using dynamic data, which enables you to deliver a truly customized experience to your users.

In addition, by the end of the lesson, both tourprice.asp and tourprice_processor.asp will have a number of server-side code blocks—enough to make them hard to read. You'll learn how to document these blocks using comments, making the scripts—and the documents as a whole—easier to read and maintain.

Dynamically Populated Drop-Down Menus

As you'll recall from Lesson 6, when the user submits the form on tourprice.asp, three pieces of data are sent: number of adults, number of children, and a dummy value for the cost of the tour. The ASP, ColdFusion, or PHP script in tourprice_processor then multiplies the number of adults by the dummy tour price and multiplies the number of children by the dummy tour price, adds the two results together, and outputs the number in HTML.

To replace the dummy values with real data takes a little work. To begin, you need to populate the drop-down menu in the form with real data. As you know, the drop-down menu can send only one piece of data, but you need to access two: the price for adults and the price for children. Therefore, rather than sending a dollar value, you'll send a unique identifier for the tour. On tourprice_processor.asp, you'll use that unique identifier to query the database for the adult price and child price for just that tour. You'll insert these values into the calculation, outputting the correct final value.

Now let's look more closely at the form menu element. As you know, each entry in a form menu has two attributes that need to be set: the label (the part users read, which is not submitted with the form), and the data (the information that is submitted as the value of the form element). It's easy enough to guess what the label should be: the tour name itself. Since there's a field in the database corresponding to the tour name, this should be easily retrieved. Now, how about the data? I said earlier that the data value that needs to be sent with the form should be the "unique identifier" for the tour. If you thought about tbl_tours' primary key when you read that, then you are thinking the right way. Remember, every database table has (or should have) a primary key, which contains a unique value for each row in that field (often this key is simply autonumbered). To summarize, each menu item's label will be the tour name, and its data value will be its primary key (tourID), both of which are stored in the tbl_tours table.

1 Open tourprice.asp. Click the New Binding (+) button in the Bindings panel, and choose Recordset (Query) from the list.

Before you can configure the menu you need to create the recordset that will make that data available so you can bind it to the form. Whenever you are working with database data, the first thing you have to do is create a recordset.

2 In the Recordset dialog, enter *rs_tournames* as the Name. Select conn_newland as the Connection. Select tbl_tours from the Table menu. In the Columns section, select Selected, and Ctrl-select (Windows) or Command-select (Macintosh) tourID and tourName.

✱ **NOTE:** ColdFusion users should select newland in the Connection field. ColdFusion does not require the separate conn_newland connections file that ASP and PHP do. In other words, whereas ASP and PHP reference conn_newland.asp/php to get directions to the newland DSN, ColdFusion accesses the newland DSN directly.

Up to this point in the dialog, you have specified most of the information you'll need to populate the menu. You are creating a script that creates a recordset called rs_tournames, which contains data obtained by going through conn_newland to find the appropriate database, and then finding the tbl_tours table, and retrieving all of the values stored in the tourID and tourName columns. You'll use the tourName data for the menu labels, and the tourID data for the menu data.

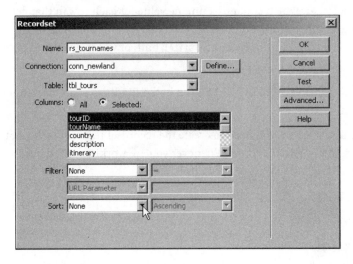

3 In the Sort drop-down menu, choose tourName, and verify that the box beside it is set to Ascending.

Unless you tell it otherwise, the database is going to display data in the order it appears in the database. However, the data was not entered in any particular order. By sorting the data by tourName ascending, you ensure that all of the tours are listed in alphabetical order, which will make it easier for your users to find the tour they want.

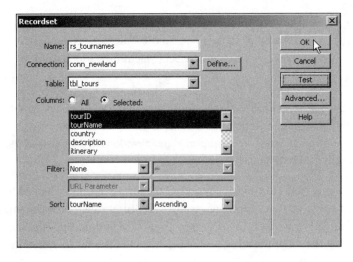

4 Click the Test button.

Clicking this button displays for you the contents (and order) of your recordset. Often, when you build queries you need to do some trial and error. Here, you can see that all 19 tours have been retrieved, and that they are ordered alphabetically by tourName.

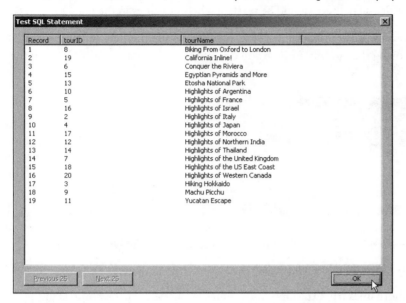

5 Click OK in the Test window to return to the dialog, and click OK.

The appearance of the document doesn't change, though if you look in the code, you'll see a new block that contains the code necessary to create the query. We'll look in more detail at this code later, but you can see it now by looking in code view—it should be just below the top of the document. The screenshot shows the code for ASP. ColdFusion users comparing their screens with the screenshot may be surprised at how much less code they have, as well as how much easier it is to read.

```
1   <%@LANGUAGE="VBSCRIPT"%>
2   <!--#include file="Connections/conn_newland.asp" -->
3   <%
4   Dim rs_tournames
5   Dim rs_tournames_cmd
6   Dim rs_tournames_numRows
7
8   Set rs_tournames_cmd = Server.CreateObject ("ADODB.Command")
9   rs_tournames_cmd.ActiveConnection = MM_conn_newland_STRING
10  rs_tournames_cmd.CommandText = "SELECT tourID, tourName FROM tbl_tours ORDER BY tourName ASC"
11  rs_tournames_cmd.Prepared = true
12
13  Set rs_tournames = rs_tournames_cmd.Execute
14  rs_tournames_numRows = 0
15  %>
```

6 Switch to design view, and click to select the menu in the form. In the Property inspector, click the List Values button to open the List Values dialog. In turn, select each of the label/data pairs, and click the Remove Value (minus sign) button. Once they have all been removed, click OK.

At the end of this step, there should be no item labels or values in the dialog.

You added dummy data in Lesson 6 just so you could build the functionality. In this step, you are removing the dummy data, so you can add the real data you just placed in the rs_tournames recordset.

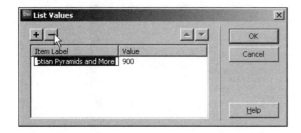

7 With the menu still selected, in the Property inspector, click the Dynamic button.

This opens the Dynamic List/Menu dialog, used to bind dynamic data to form menus.

8 Choose rs_tournames from the Options from recordset field. Specify tourID in the Values field, and specify tourName from the Labels field. Click OK.

Dreamweaver adds the code necessary to bind the data to the menu. One important thing to note is that the resulting ASP, ColdFusion, or PHP script loops through the data pulled from the database. In other words, just as you manually entered an item label and item value one at a time in Lesson 6, so each of the 19 tour label/value pairs must be loaded into the menu one at a time. Using a programming structure called a loop, ASP, ColdFusion, or PHP goes through each tourName/tourID pairing in the recordset and adds it to the menu item.

Obviously, in addition to the initial convenience—what you just did was a lot faster than manually entering 19 label/value pairs—you have the added bonus that if the database changes, this menu field is automatically and instantly updated. That means that as long as you maintain your database, Web maintenance will happen automatically.

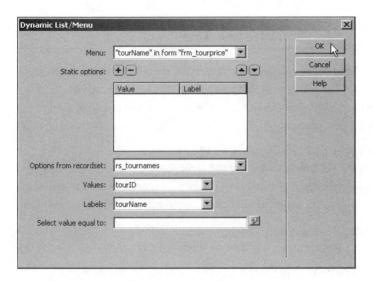

9 Save, upload, and test the page.

When you click the menu, you should see all 19 tours listed, in alphabetical order.

10 Complete the form and submit it.

The page, tourprice_processor.asp, should load and the calculation should still work. Of course, the tour price suddenly meets even the thriftiest of budgets. That's because the calculation is now using the tourID as the dollar amount, and all the tourIDs are under 20.

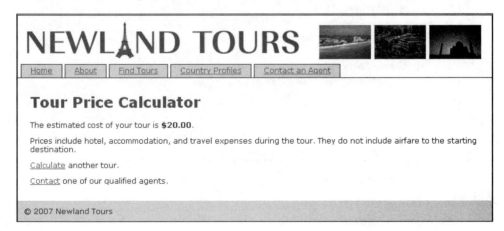

Undefined Index Error

PHP users may see an "undefined index" error: The error appears on only some implementations of PHP. The problem is that you're testing whether a variable ($_GET['error']) is of a certain value (notnumeric), without actually making sure the variable exists in the first place.

The solution is to use a nested if block (that is, an if block wrapped inside another if block). The outer if block determines whether the error variable exists in the URL. If it does, then it checks to see whether its value is equal to notnumeric. But if the error variable doesn't exist in the URL, the whole operation is skipped, and so the source of the problem is avoided.

If you experience this problem, amend the code in tourprice.php as follows.

Find the following code in tours.php.

```php
<?php
if ($_GET['error'] == "notnumeric")
{
echo "<p class=\"error\">*** Error! One or more fields was left blank or
contained a non-numeric character.</p>";
}
?>
```

Change that code block so that it reads as follows.

```php
<?php
if (isset($_GET['error']))
{
    if ($_GET['error'] == "notnumeric")
{
echo "<p class=\"error\">*** Error! One or more fields was left blank or
contained a non-numeric character.</p>";
}
}
?>
```

```
<div id="mainContent">
<h1><a name="top" id="top"></a>Tour Price Calculator</h1>
<p>Enter the number of adults and children in your party as well as the tour name of the tour you want to calculate.</p>

<p>All fields required (enter 0 if necessary).</p>

<?php
if (isset($_GET['error']))
{
    if ($_GET['error'] == "notnumeric")
    {
    echo "<p class=\"error\">*** Error! One or more fields was left blank or contained ?a non-numeric character.</p>";
    }
}
?>

<form id="frm_tourprice" name="frm_tourprice" method="post" action="tourprice_processor.php">
```

Creating Filtered Recordsets

Twice now, once each in this lesson and the preceding one, you have created recordsets and displayed their data. In both cases, you just retrieved all of the information stored in the database and bound it to the page. But you have a different problem now. To get the calculator to function properly, you need to plug in the adult and child prices for the selected tour—not all of the tours and not the first tour, but the one that the user selected.

How's that going to work? The user selected a tour from the menu on the form and submitted it. On tourprice_processor.asp, the tourID associated with that tour has been included as a form variable. Thus, when you query the database, you'll construct something along the following lines (in pseudocode):

```
Retrieve the adult price (basePriceAdult) and the child price (basePriceChild)
from tbl_tours where tourID equals the tourID submitted by the user on the form.
```

It is helpful to formulate your intentions very clearly before attempting any sort of programming, even if the programming (in this case SQL programming) is masked behind a graphic interface (in this case Dreamweaver's Recordset dialog).

1 Open tourprice_processor.asp. Use the Bindings panel to open the Recordset dialog.

When you create a recordset in Dreamweaver, it persists in the individual page only.

2 Enter *rs_tourprices_filtered* as the Name, *conn_Newland* as the Connection, *tbl_tours* as the Table, Selected in the Columns category, with the following fields selected: tourID, tourName, basePriceAdult, and basePriceChild.

As it stands (which you could see for yourself by clicking Test), this query returns data from all 19 records in tbl_tours in the four fields you specified. But you want the query to return only the data for the tour that the user specified in the form.

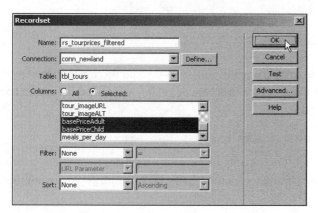

3 In the Filter category, create the following formula: tourID = Form Variable tourName by entering the appropriate choices in the four drop-down menus.

In this step, you are adding an additional criterion to the query. In pseudocode, you are saying, "Retrieve all the specified information from the table, but only from the record that matches the record the user selected in the form." The user's choice comes to this page in the form scope as a variable named tourName, its name on the page tourprice.asp.

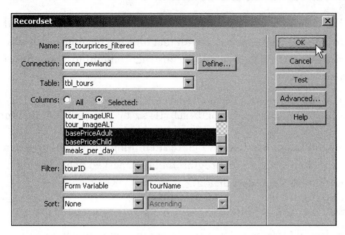

4 Click the Test button. Enter 9 in the Please Provide a Test Value dialog, and click OK.

The test this time works differently than it did in the past. This time, you must specify a test value. The reason is that the query needs a value to be sent from the form, but in the authoring environment, that data doesn't exist. So the dialog appears prompting you for a value.

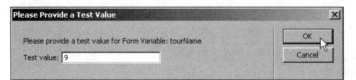

When the output window opens, only one tour is listed—Machu Picchu, if you entered 9. If you go back and enter different test values, you'll see different tour records that have been retrieved from the database.

5 Click OK to exit the test output, and click OK again to save the recordset.

Once again, the appearance and functionality of the page isn't changed, because creating a recordset only retrieves the data and stores it in the server's memory—you're not using it yet.

Revising the Calculation Script With Live Data

Both times before, when you output data from a database, you did so directly into HTML. You output the Traveler's Journal entry into the main page in index.asp, and you output the tourName/tourID pairing into a form menu element. In this step, you don't need to output the adult and child prices anywhere that the user can see them. In fact, they need to be output into the calculation itself. As you'll see, though, you output internally to a script the same way you do to XHTML.

Before you do that, though, let's add one more simple piece of functionality: Let's display the name of the tour that users just calculated, in case they forgot or chose the wrong one.

1 In tourprice_processor.asp, switch to design view. After the word tour in the first sentence, add the following text: , *XX*,. Select XX, and apply bolding to it, using the Property inspector.

Once again, the Xs are used as placeholder text. The advantage to using this text is that you can format it the way you want your dynamic content to appear, in this case, bold.

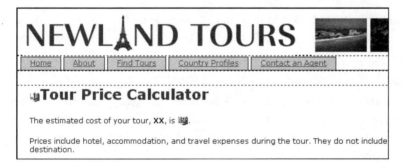

2 Select the XX text, and switch to the Data category of the Insert bar. Click the Dynamic Data button and choose Dynamic Text from the pop-up menu.

The Data tab is used to insert and manipulate common dynamic elements, such as dynamic text.

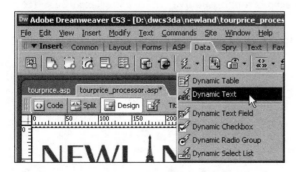

3 In the Dynamic Text dialog, expand Recordset (rs_tourprices_filtered), and click tour-Name. Click OK.

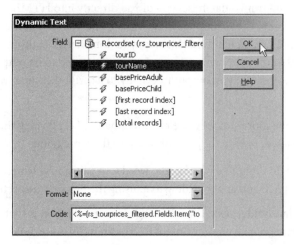

What you've just done is equivalent to dragging a binding from the Bindings panel onto the page. You should also be able to understand the code Dreamweaver outputs in the code window.

In ASP, the following is added where XX appeared before: <%=(rs_tourprices_filtered.Fields.Item("tourName").Value)%>. Remember, <%= (as opposed to <%) means <% Response.Write, so this is an output script. As you can probably guess from the rest, it is outputting the value of the tourName item, which is a field in the recordset rs_tourprices_filtered.

In ColdFusion, the following code appears: <cfoutput>#rs_tourprices_filtered.tourName #</cfoutput>. Again, the <cfoutput> tag is equivalent to ASP's Response.Write, and what is being output is the tourName value stored in rs_tourprices_filtered.

In PHP, the following code appears: <?php echo $row_rs_tourprices_filtered ['tourName']; ?>. The command echo is roughly equivalent to ASP's Response.Write and ColdFusion's <cfoutput>. As in the ASP and ColdFusion versions, this block is outputting the tourName value in rs_tourprices_filtered.

Reading and understanding the code is important, because in the next step, you'll have to do some hand-coding.

4 In code view, find the calculation script. Delete the line that sets the value of the base-Price variable to the form variable tourName.

The line in ASP that you are deleting is basePrice=Request.Form("tourName"), and it should be around line 34 (plus or minus) in code view.

The line in ColdFusion that you are deleting is <cfset basePrice = form.tourName>, and it should be around line 13 (plus or minus) in code view.

The line in PHP that you are deleting is $basePrice = $_POST['tourName'];, and it should be around line 53 in code view.

This line is no longer necessary, because you are not obtaining the base price from the form anymore, but rather from the database. In addition, there are two prices that you now need to use: the one for children and the one for adults.

```
29
30   <%
31   Dim numAdult, numChild, basePrice, tourPrice
32   numAdult = Request.Form("numAdults")
33   numChild = Request.Form("numChildren")
34 ▣ basePrice = Request.Form("tourName")
35   tourPrice = (numAdult * basePrice) + (numChild * basePrice)
36   %>
37
38   <!DOCTYPE html PUBLIC "-//W3C//DTD XHTML 1.0 Transitional//EN" "http://www.w3.org/TR/
```

5 Add two new lines of code to prepare to set the value of two new variables: basePriceAdult and basePriceChild.

In ASP:

```
basePriceAdult =
basePriceChild =
```

In ColdFusion:

```
<cfset basePriceAdult = >
<cfset basePriceChild = >
```

In PHP:

```
$basePriceAdult = ;
$basePriceChild = ;
```

All of these scripts create two new variables and set the values to the appropriate adult and child prices as retrieved from the database.

```
29
30   <%
31   Dim numAdult, numChild, basePrice, tourPrice
32   numAdult = Request.Form("numAdults")
33   numChild = Request.Form("numChildren")
34   basePriceAdult =
35   basePriceChild =
36   tourPrice = (numAdult * basePrice) + (numChild * basePrice)
37   %>
38
39   <!DOCTYPE html PUBLIC "-//W3C//DTD XHTML 1.0 Transitional//EN" "http://www.w3.org/TR/
```

6 Assign the correct values to the variables by dragging the basePriceAdult and basePriceChild variables from the Bindings panel into their respective lines of code view, just after the = sign.

Data in the Bindings panel can be added to either design or code views, so this step saves you some typing and prevents the headache of typos.

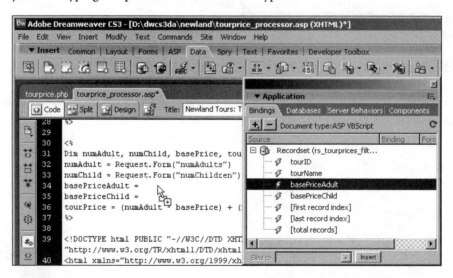

```
30   <%
31   Dim numAdult, numChild, basePrice, tourPrice
32   numAdult = Request.Form("numAdults")
33   numChild = Request.Form("numChildren")
34   basePriceAdult = (rs_tourprices_filtered.Fields.Item("basePriceAdult").Value)
35   basePriceChild = (rs_tourprices_filtered.Fields.Item("basePriceChild").Value)
36   tourPrice = (numAdult * basePrice) + (numChild * basePrice)
37   %>
```

✱ **NOTE:** Dreamweaver will add the pound signs (##) around the variable names when you drag them from the Bindings panel into the `<cfset>` statements. As we learned in Lesson 6, they are not necessary inside a ColdFusion tag. The code will work, but you should remove the pound signs to keep your code clean and consistent.

7 ASP users only: Remove `basePrice` from the `Dim` line and add `basePriceAdult` and `basePriceChild` to the list.

Since ASP requires explicit declaration of all variables, you have to remember to update that declaration whenever you change your variables.

8 Update the basePrice variables in the calculation line itself with the appropriate new variables.

In ASP:

```
tourPrice = (numAdult * basePriceAdult) + (numChild * basePriceChild)
```

In ColdFusion:

```
<cfset tourPrice = (numAdult * basePriceAdult) + (numChild * basePriceChild)>
```

In PHP:

```
$tourPrice = ($numAdult * $basePriceAdult) + ($numChild * $basePriceChild);
```

Now the calculation reflects the values that you have retrieved from the database.

```
30  <%
31  Dim numAdult, numChild, basePriceAdult, basePriceChild, tourPrice
32  numAdult = Request.Form("numAdults")
33  numChild = Request.Form("numChildren")
34  basePriceAdult = (rs_tourprices_filtered.Fields.Item("basePriceAdult").Value)
35  basePriceChild = (rs_tourprices_filtered.Fields.Item("basePriceChild").Value)
36  tourPrice = (numAdult * basePriceAdult) + (numChild * basePriceChild)
37  %>
```

✱ **NOTE:** If you prefer more minimalist code there is no reason you could not put the variables from the Bindings panel directly into the line where the calculation takes place (step 8) and skip the creation of local variables (steps 5 & 6). It would look like this: `tourprice = (numAdult * (rs_tourprices_filtered.Fields.Item("basePriceAdult").Value)) + (numChild * (rs_tourprices_filtered.Fields.Item("basePriceChild").Value))`. There is no functional difference. Some find it more elegant. Others find code produced by the steps above to be cleaner and easier to read.

9 Save and upload tourprice_processor.asp. In the Site panel, select tourprice.asp and press F12 to test the application.

The application outputs the correct calculation based on the information the user entered. Best of all, maintaining this application is as easy as maintaining the database. If a price goes up and the new value is added to the database, the calculator will reflect that immediately. If you add or remove an entire tour, that will be reflected in the application as well.

Documenting Your Code With Comments

You added quite a bit of functionality to make the tour price calculator application work. You can see the results of this work in all your Web pages. In my copy of tourprice_processor. asp, for example, the XHTML document proper doesn't start until line 39—everything above that is ASP scripts! Those using ColdFusion will discover that their XHTML documents start around line 17. For the most part, they have the same scripts that do the same things—it's just that ColdFusion requires fewer lines of code. PHP is in between—my XHTML document begins on line 58.

If you scroll through all that code at the top of tourprice.asp and tourprice_processor.asp, you should be able to interpret just about all of the scripts you'll find there (ASP and PHP users will have one exception, which I'll get to shortly). You can read these scripts not only because you are beginning to master ASP, ColdFusion, or PHP scripting, but also because they are fresh in your head. But if you came back in six months, or if someone just handed you this code today for the first time, you might not be able to look at it and know what everything is doing.

This is an important issue, because Web documents have a way of hanging around for years—often longer than the developers do. For your own sake, and the sake of your successor, you should document your code, so everyone knows what it's doing.

You document the code using comments, which are pieces of information added to code that tell readers what the code does, but which are ignored by computers interpreting the code. In this final section, you'll go through tourprice.asp and tourprice_processor.asp and comment the code blocks.

1 Open tourprice.asp. Add a comment just above the query.

In ASP, add a new line below the opening <% at the beginning of the query (just before Dim rs_tournames), and type the following:

```
' Creates a recordset of all the tour names and IDs from the tbl_tours table in
the database. This data is used later to populate the form drop-down menu.
```

In ColdFusion, type the following at the top of the document:

```
<!---Creates a recordset of all the tour names and IDs from the tbl_tours table
in the database. This data is used later to populate the form drop-down menu.
--->
```

In PHP, type the following just before the line that begins mysql_select_db, which should be around line 32:

```
// Creates a recordset of all the tour names and IDs from the tbl_tours table in
the database. The data is used later to populate the form drop-down menu.
```

In all three languages, comments are denoted in a special way. In ASP's VBScript, you use the single quote (') character. Everything from that character until the end of the line is commented out, or ignored by the interpreter. In ColdFusion, you wrap the comment in special comment tags. In fact, they are the same as HTML comment tags, except they use three dashes instead of two. ColdFusion comments can span multiple lines. Single-line PHP comments can be prefaced with two slashes (//) or a single hash mark (#). You can also create multiple-line comments in PHP, by wrapping the comment as follows: /* my comment */.

Because these comments are in the language of the server (VBScript, ColdFusion Markup Language, or PHP, as opposed to HTML), they are stripped out of the document before it is sent to the client. This means you can document your code as much as you like and not worry about users being able to see it.

```
1   <%@LANGUAGE="VBSCRIPT"%>
2   <!--#include file="Connections/conn_newland.asp" -->
3   <%
4   ' Creates a recordset of all the tour names and IDs from the tbl_tours table in the database. This data is used later to
5   Dim rs_tournames
6   Dim rs_tournames_cmd
7   Dim rs_tournames_numRows
8
9   Set rs_tournames_cmd = Server.CreateObject ("ADODB.Command")
10  rs_tournames_cmd.ActiveConnection = MM_conn_newland_STRING
11  rs_tournames_cmd.CommandText = "SELECT tourID, tourName FROM tbl_tours ORDER BY tourName ASC"
12  rs_tournames_cmd.Prepared = true
13
14  Set rs_tournames = rs_tournames_cmd.Execute
15  rs_tournames_numRows = 0
16  %>
```

2 Save and close tourprice.asp, and open tourprice_processor.asp.

Most of the scripts used in this application appear in tourprice_processor.

3 ASP and PHP users only: Add the following comment to the first block of code after the <%LANGUAGE declaration (ASP only) and the <!-include (ASP) or require_once (PHP) blocks, remembering to preface the comment with the ' (ASP) or // (PHP) character(s) as appropriate.

`A script generated by Dreamweaver to help with the dynamic query`

Make sure you always add comments in ASP or PHP inside the <% %> or <?php ?> block.

This script is probably unfamiliar to you, because Dreamweaver added it automatically, when you created the dynamic query (that is, when you filtered the data with the criterion: where tourID = form variable tourName). This comment will remind you what it's doing there and how it got there.

ColdFusion lacks this script, because it handled its functionality in a different—and simpler—way.

```
1   <%@LANGUAGE="VBSCRIPT" CODEPAGE="65001" %>
2   <!--#include file="Connections/conn_newland.asp" -->
3   <%
4   'A script generated by Dreamweaver to help with the dynamic query
5   Dim rs_tourprices_filtered__MMColParam
6   rs_tourprices_filtered__MMColParam = "1"
7   If (Request.Form("tourName") <> "") Then
8     rs_tourprices_filtered__MMColParam = Request.Form("tourName")
9   End If
10  %>
```

4 Find the script that creates the recordset, and add the following comment to it: Queries the database for the tour name, adult price, and child price; data is filtered so that the only record retrieved corresponds to what the user entered in the form.

In ASP, the query script begins with the declaration of its variables: Dim rs_tourprices_filtered.

In ColdFusion, the query script is easily identified, because <cfquery> tags surround it.

In PHP, look for the line that begins mysql_select_db.

Don't forget to use the proper comment syntax for your server technology.

```
1   <%@LANGUAGE="VBSCRIPT" CODEPAGE="65001" %>
2   <!--#include file="Connections/conn_newland.asp" -->
3   <%
4   'A script generated by Dreamweaver to help with the dynamic query
5   Dim rs_tourprices_filtered__MMColParam
6   rs_tourprices_filtered__MMColParam = "1"
7   If (Request.Form("tourName") <> "") Then
8     rs_tourprices_filtered__MMColParam = Request.Form("tourName")
9   End If
10  %>
11  <%
12  'Queries the database for the tour name, adult price, and child price; data is filtered so that th
13  Dim rs_tourprices_filtered
14  Dim rs_tourprices_filtered_cmd
15  Dim rs_tourprices_filtered_numRows
16
17  Set rs_tourprices_filtered_cmd = Server.CreateObject ("ADODB.Command")
18  rs_tourprices_filtered_cmd.ActiveConnection = MM_conn_newland_STRING
19  rs_tourprices_filtered_cmd.CommandText = "SELECT tourID, tourName, basePriceAdult, basePriceChild
```

5 Find the form validation script, and add the following comment: Form validation script; redirects user back to tourprice.asp if form fields do not have numeric values.

In ASP, this script begins If Not IsNumeric. In ColdFusion, it begins <cfif Not IsNumeric. In PHP, it begins if (is_numeric.

```
23  Set rs_tourprices_filtered = rs_tourprices_filtered_cmd.Execute
24  rs_tourprices_filtered_numRows = 0
25  %>
26  <%
27  'Form validation script; redirects user back to tourprice.asp if form fields do not have numeric values.
28  If Not IsNumeric(Request.Form("numAdults")) or Not IsNumeric(Request.Form("numChildren")) Then
29      Response.Redirect("tourprice.asp?error=notnumeric")
30  End If
31  %>
```

6 Find the calculation script, and add the following comment: Collects data for number of adults and children, and the prices for both adults and children; multiplies data to calculate total.

After all you've done with this script, you should be able to find it on your own.

When you are finished, don't forget to save and upload these files.

```
26  <%
27  'Form validation script; redirects user back to tourprice.asp if form fields do not have numeric v
28  If Not IsNumeric(Request.Form("numAdults")) or Not IsNumeric(Request.Form("numChildren")) Then
29      Response.Redirect("tourprice.asp?error=notnumeric")
30  End If
31  %>
32
33  <%
34  'Collects data for number of adults and children, and the prices for both adults and children; mul
35  Dim numAdult, numChild, basePriceAdult, basePriceChild, tourPrice
36  numAdult = Request.Form("numAdults")
37  numChild = Request.Form("numChildren")
38  basePriceAdult = (rs_tourprices_filtered.Fields.Item("basePriceAdult").Value)
39  basePriceChild = (rs_tourprices_filtered.Fields.Item("basePriceChild").Value)
40  tourPrice = (numAdult * basePriceAdult) + (numChild * basePriceChild)
41  %>
```

What You Have Learned

In this lesson, you have:

- Populated a menu with database data (pages 232–238)

- Created a dynamically filtered recordset (pages 239–240)

- Output the resulting data both in HTML and inside a server script (pages 241–246)

- Commented your code to make it more comprehensible (pages 246–250)

What You Will Learn

In this lesson, you will:

- Learn about an alternative for passing data to Web pages
- Create an application that filters and displays database data using Adobe Spry
- Expand Dreamweaver's built-in functionality using a custom extension
- Create dynamic Spry data regions
- Display images dynamically
- Hand-code SQL to combine filtered data from multiple tables
- Layout multiple elements populated with dynamic data and style them with custom CSS

Approximate Time

This lesson takes approximately two hours to complete.

Lesson Files

Starting Files:

Lesson09/Start/newland/profiles.asp
Lesson09/Start/newland/css/main.css

Completed Files:

Lesson09/Complete/newland/profiles.asp
Lesson09/Complete/newland/css/main.css
Lesson09/Complete/newland/countryDetailXML.asp

✱ **NOTE:** Dreamweaver and the Developer Toolbox create additional files, which are not listed here, because the file names differ depending on the language you are using.

Filtering and Displaying Data Using Ajax

One of the many benefits of using databases is that they are scalable. At the moment, the Newland Tours database contains profiles for 16 countries. However, over time the business could grow, and contain profiles of 40 or even 60 countries. But even at 16, the complete listing of country profiles on a single Web page is too much for most users to wade through. Users aren't usually interested in all the countries, but rather a subset—the ones they are considering visiting. The same applies to the tour descriptions themselves and even more broadly to most database data on the Web. Imagine using Amazon if you had to download and display millions of products on a single page!

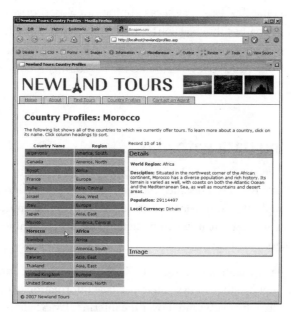

The profile of each country is pulled from an XML structure dynamically built from the database and formatted on the fly using Adobe Spry and CSS.

For this reason, it is important when developing dynamic Web sites to make it easy to filter data, so that users can see the data that they want to see. You can enable your site's visitors to filter data in many different ways, from simple URL parameters to full-blown search engines. In this, and the next two lessons, you'll build several different interfaces that give you control over how you display data to users.

In this lesson, you will learn to use a technique called Ajax, to create a richer, more engaging experience for your users. The users will be able to see the detailed profiles of the countries chosen without moving to another page or reloading the current page, making the user experience seem faster and the page seem more responsive.

Although there are many different ways to create Ajax functionality, Adobe has designed an easy-to-use Ajax library, called Adobe Spry. Adobe built Spry functionality into Dreamweaver CS3 and included a number of user interface elements. We'll therefore use Spry to create our Ajax functionality.

✳ **NOTE:** Because Spry works with XML datasets rather than standard query recordsets, Adobe also released an extension that will allow you to easily turn a standard recordset into an XML dataset for your application.

Much like the way you built the dynamic list of countries for a drop-down list earlier, here you will build a list of country names that will link to their individual profiles. The advantage to this approach is that once you've built the application, maintaining it is as simple as updating the database itself—no need to revise either page if a country is added, removed, or renamed (it happens).

Passing and Using Data with Ajax

Ajax or "Asynchronous JavaScript and XML", is a term that was coined in 2005 for a technique that's been available for over a decade. The Ajax technique is used to pass data to and from interactive Web applications. It helps you create Web pages that appear more responsive because the data passes between the user's computer and the server behind the scenes, without requiring the page to reload.

The two main technologies that make up Ajax are XML and JavaScript. Extensible Markup Language (XML) is a language that allows you to package information, such as a recordset, and maintain its structure while you send it over the internet. JavaScript is a scripting language that lets you manipulate objects, such as your recordset, in the user's browser.

> ✱ **NOTE:** There are accessibility concerns about Ajax. Some users browse with JavaScript disabled and some do not have JavaScript available to their browsers. These issues should be taken into consideration before deciding to use Ajax on your Website. A Web search will turn up further information on the specific problems and the most up-to-date work-arounds.

> ✱ **NOTE:** JavaScript is not to be confused with Java. The former is a scripting language primarily used for Web development. The latter is a powerful programming language that can be used for Web development but is primarily used for creating computer applications.

There are several Ajax libraries available, some with quite sophisticated capabilities. Each requires a different level of technical knowledge to use. Adobe created the Spry framework to make Ajax available to Web designers with minimal programming experience.

The Spry framework has a number of useful elements, including a photo gallery, a number of user interface "widgets", visual effects and form validation. It is designed to be easy to implement for anyone with a basic knowledge of HTML, CSS, and JavaScript. Spry, like most AJAX implementations, receives and sends its data as XML.

Dreamweaver CS3 shipped with Spry prerelease version 1.4. At the time of this writing Spry is at prerelease version 1.5. Each release includes new features and refinements. The latest release includes additional features we will take advantage of in a later chapter.

> ✱ **NOTE:** You can read more about Spry, see demos of the available functionality, and download the latest version on the Adobe Labs site at http://labs.adobe.com/technologies/spry/.

In this lesson, you will take the recordset created by querying the database for the country profiles, convert it to XML, and publish it as a page on the Web. This will serve as the data for your profile page application. You will then use Adobe Spry to create a table for the list of countries and their regions, and use the Spry Accordion to display details of the chosen country.

Expanding Dreamweaver with Extensions

While we could write code that would turn a recordset into XML using ASP, ColdFusion or PHP, there's a simpler solution. We'll use an **extension** to convert our basic recordset into XML format.

Extensions are tools that expand Dreamweaver's core functionality. The Adobe Dreamweaver Developer Toolbox (ADDT) is an extension that provides a number of server behaviors for ASP, ColdFusion and PHP development, including a behavior that gives Dreamweaver the ability to export standard recordsets in XML format and use them to create dynamic Spry XML datasets. As the data in the standard recordset changes, the server behavior will ensure that our XML data changes as well.

1 Using your Web browser, go to http://www.adobe.com/downloads/ and download the Adobe Dreamweaver Developer Toolbox from the Trial Versions section. Open the downloaded file to unpack the necessary files.

The downloaded file will expand to give you a folder and subfolders containing a ReadMe HTML file, documentation and the software itself, in the form of a .mxp fle.

2 Follow the installation directions in the ReadMe file in the Adobe folder created from the unpacked download. Close and restart Dreamweaver.

The installation uses the Adobe Extension Manager. This is one of the supporting applications installed when you install Dreamweaver.

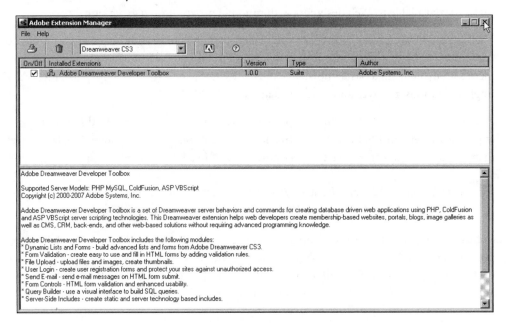

3 When Dreamweaver starts you will be asked to enter a serial number for the Developer Toolbox or begin a 30-day trial. Select the trial.

You will be presented with this choice each time you start Dreamweaver. Should you wish to remove the Developer Toolbox after we have used it, it can be uninstalled using the Extension Manager.

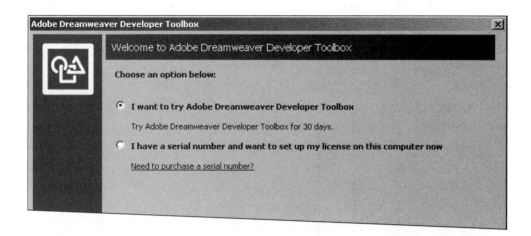

* **NOTE:** You can view the other Dreamweaver extensions at the Adobe Exchange Website at http://www.adobe.com/go/dreamweaver_exchange/.

* **NOTE:** If you are working offline, do not wish to download this extension or the extension has expired, XML files with the data used in this exercise have been included in the Lesson09/Start folder. Move the file countryDetail.xml from the chapter09/Start folder to your newland site folder, and skip ahead to *Connect Profiles Page to XML Data*.

Turning a Recordset into XML

Now that you have extended Dreamweaver to include the Developer Toolkit you are ready to produce XML data for use with Spry.

1 Choose File > New, and create a new dynamic page using ASP/VBScript, ColdFusion, or PHP.

The file you are creating will be like any of the other dynamic pages you have created except that it is unlikely to be viewed by a Web browser. It will be available for a browser to read, but its intended audience will be Spry.

2 In code view, select and delete everything from the opening <!DOCTYPE... to the closing </html> tag.

For ColdFusion and PHP you will delete everything on the page. The ASP page will be left with the language declaration <%@LANGUAGE="VBSCRIPT" CODEPAGE="65001"%> at the top.

3 Click the New (+) button in the Server Behaviors panel, and choose Recordset (Query) from the list.

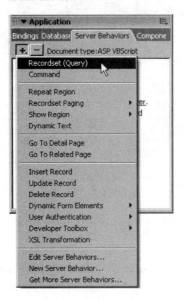

4 Name the recordset *rs_countryDetail*, set your Connection to conn_newland and Table to tbl_country. For Columns choose Selected. Click on countryID and then scroll down to the bottom of the list and shift-click on imageAlt. This should select all items in the list. Set the Sort to countryName and accept the other default values.

This query is pulling in all of the information about each country in your database. The recordset that is produced will contain the country name and ID, as well as details for each country as needed for the profile.

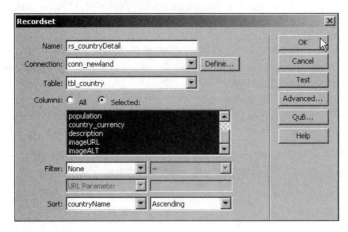

> **TIP:** Since the query is gathering all the information in the database, you might think it makes more sense to set the Columns field to All. While you could do this, it's more efficient for the query to know the names of the fields it's being asked to retrieve. With large datasets, efficient queries will run more quickly.

5 Save the file as *countryDetailXML.asp*.

Dreamweaver requires you to save the file before you can apply the next server behavior.

6 Click the New (+) button in the Server Behaviors panel, and choose Developer Toolbox > Export Recordset as XML from the list. Accept the defaults on the Basic tab. Click on the Advanced tab and set the Root node to countries and the Row node to country. Click OK.

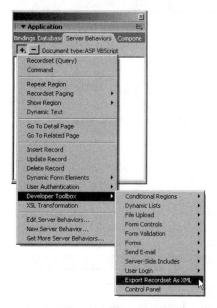
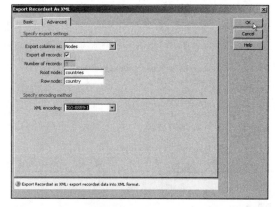

The Developer Toolkit extension writes the code for your recordset to be converted to an XML dataset for access on the server. It will also create a new folder called includes within your site. This contains the files that format the data as XML for your server model.

7 Save your changes. Upload countryDetailXML.asp and the includes folder to the server. Press F12 to view the results.

Most modern browsers can parse and display properly-formed XML. By setting the root and row nodes to countries/country respectively on the advanced tab of the Export Recordset as XML wizard, your XML structure will have meaningful names. The entire recordset is labeled <countries> with each individual record from tbl_country translated into a <country> in the XML file. The individual fields have carried their fieldnames over to the XML dataset. If you click the minus (-) sign next to an opening tag of any element that has multiple rows of content, it will collapse the element for greater ease of reading.

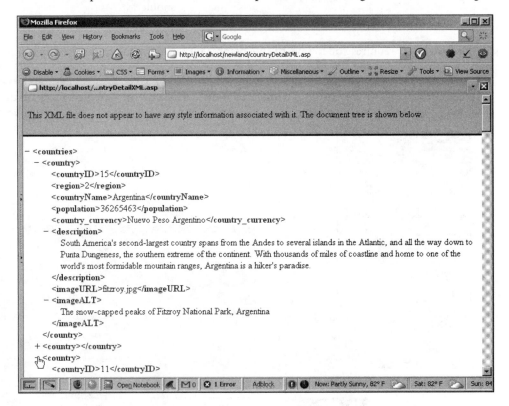

❋ **NOTE:** ColdFusion users: If you get an error stating "xml declaration not at start of external entity" it is because the server is adding whitespace at the start of your XML file. Move your remote site files up one level so that they are directly inside the wwwroot folder, and that should take care of the problem. You will need to modify your Dreamweaver site definition to reflect the new location.

Connect Country Profiles page to XML data

Currently, the Country Profiles page (profiles.asp) contains a listing in static HTML of the countries to which Newland offers tours. In order to create a page that is easy to maintain when new countries are added or changed, this information should come from the database. That means that just about all of the content on this page (excluding the banner and footer) is obsolete, so you need to delete it.

Once you have removed all of the old content, you'll need to add a list of links that will let users choose a country profile. This list will come from the XML dataset you created in the previous section. In this step you will pull that dataset into this page for use by Spry, both for the list and the detailed profiles.

1 Open profiles.asp in design view.

I find it much easier to delete page content while in design view, rather than hunting around for the proper start and stop points in code view.

2 Drag to select everything on the page starting from the horizontal rule just above Namibia all the way down to the bottom of the page to just include the words Nuevo Peso at the end of the profile of Mexico.

Be careful not to select any of the footer.

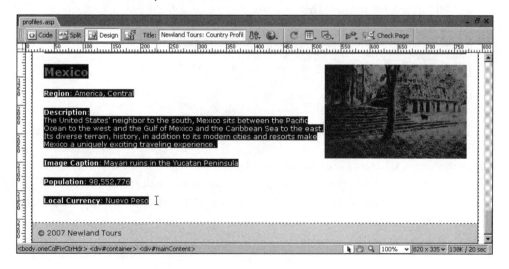

3 Press Delete.

The content is removed and the cursor is left in an empty <p> tag, visible in code or split view, at the bottom of the page.

4 Replace the first line of body text with *The following list shows all of the countries to which we currently offer tours. To learn more about a country, click on its name.*

Here, you are just changing the directions of the page to reflect the new functionality of the page.

5 In the Spry Insert menu, click the Spry XML Dataset button or click Insert > Spry > Spry XML Dataset.

For this step it does not matter where your cursor is placed. Dreamweaver is establishing a link to your XML dataset. That data will then be available throughout the page.

6 In the Spry XML Data Set dialog window leave the Data Set name ds1, and set the XML source to countryDetailXML.asp. (If you opted to use the static exercise file instead of generating a dynamic XML file, set the XML source to countryDetail.xml.) Click Get schema.

The schema is the description of the structure of the XML document. When Dreamweaver reads the schema it produces a generic outline of the structure, devoid of data.

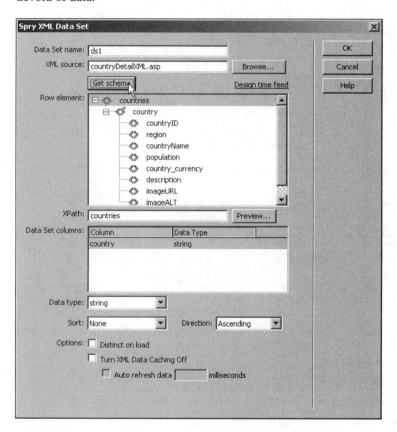

By default the top-most element in the XML schema is chosen. You will use the data one record, or country, at a time so you need to establish the country as your starting point.

7 Under Row element highlight country. You will see a change in the XPath to countries/country. Click Preview to see how it views the data at that level of the structure.

XPath is the addressing scheme in XML. It points to a specific spot in an XML document. In this case you are pointing to the starting point for individual records in your dataset. We want Spry to view each country as a single record.

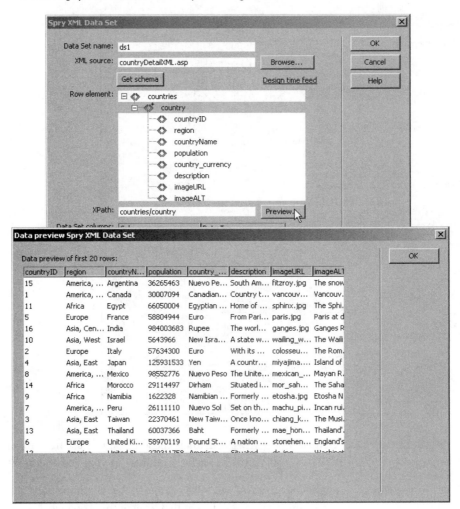

8 Click OK and save the file. Dreamweaver will notify you that it has copied two files to a new folder in your site called SpryAssets. Click OK.

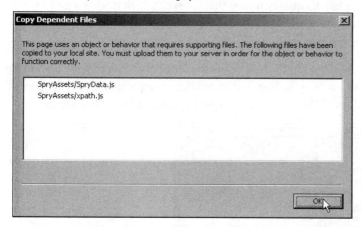

You will recall that Ajax uses JavaScript and XML. In order for Spry to use the XML file you just bound to profiles.asp, it needs some JavaScript functionality. Dreamweaver has moved copies of a couple of JavaScript libraries into your site and referenced them in <script> tags in the head of your document.

If you look in the Bindings panel you will see your full dataset ready for use. As with a recordset from a database query, these individual variables can be inserted on the page in order to display their dynamic content. You will do just that later in the lesson.

Building a Spry Table

In this task, you'll create the list of country names that users can click to view a given country profile. Spry makes this quite simple. First you will prepare the place in the document where you would like to use Spry and then you will build the list as a Spry table.

1 In design view place the cursor in the line below the lone paragraph of body text. In the Spry Insert menu, click the Spry Region button or click Insert > Spry > Spry Region. Accept the default values of Container: DIV, Type: Region and Spry Data Set: ds1.

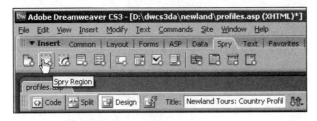

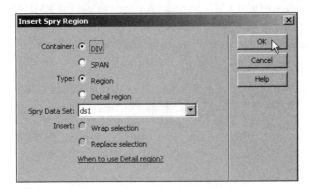

A Spry region is an area on a page that is bound to a dataset. This region is bound to our XML dataset, referred to here as ds1, the variable it was assigned to when first connected to the page. You will build your Spry table in this region.

2 Without moving your cursor from the highlighted text "Content for Spry Region Goes Here," insert a Spry Table from the Spry Insert menu or click Insert > Spry > Spry Table.

3 Remove all columns except region and countryName using the "–" next to Columns. Move countryName above region by highlighting the countryName row and clicking the up arrow. Highlight each column name in turn and check "Sort column when header is clicked." The value for Sortable will toggle from No to Yes. Finally, check "Update detail regions when row is clicked". Click OK.

The dialog window should look like the below screen shot before closing the window.

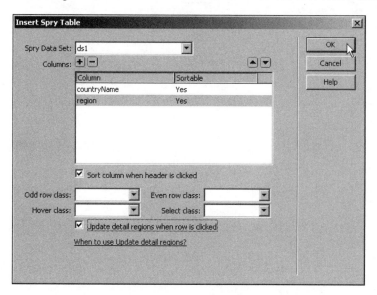

4 Add another sentence of instructions at the end of the text at the top of the page. Add *Click column headings to sort.*

You will add a visual indication that the column headings are clickable hotspots when you style the table, but some simple directions will also aid the users.

5 Save changes and upload both profiles.asp and the SpryAssets folder to the server. Highlight profiles.asp in your Files panel and press F12 to preview.

You should see the list of country names and region ID numbers. That was pretty easy, but what's so special about a Spry table? The columns are sortable. Check the functionality by clicking the column names to sort and reverse sort the records. Without Ajax, your users would have to refresh the page to sort the records.

The heading for the column with the names of the country reflects the name of the database field. Before you move on you should correct it by placing a blank space between Country and Name.

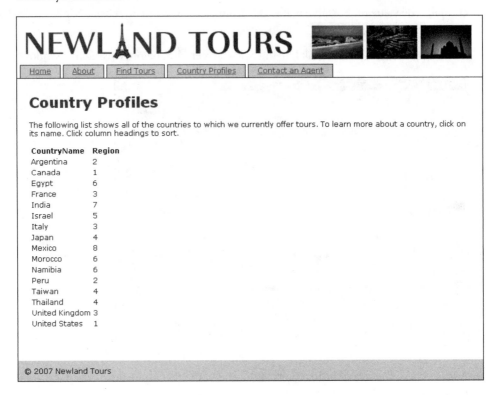

Styling the Spry Table

The table you created is more functional than your average table, but it could certainly be more attractive. You could give it a border and maybe even a background color. What about alternating the colors of the rows to make it easier for users to see distinct records? That sounds great, but you are building the table dynamically. How are you to color those rows on the fly?

Spry has some built-in attributes that will not only help you color alternating rows dynamically, but add some additional effects as well. While you can build the custom styles using Dreamweaver's tools as you have in previous lessons, you will have to do a little hand-coding to access some of these Spry features.

1 Return to profiles.asp. In the CSS panel, click the button for a new CSS rule. For Selector Type choose Class. Name your class .odd, for the odd-numbered rows. Click OK. Under the Background Category set a Background Color of #999999.

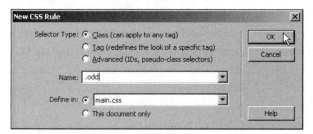

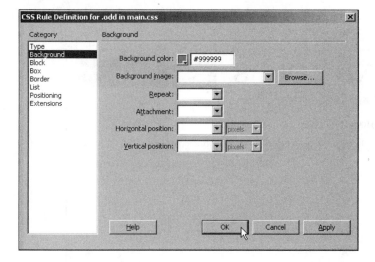

2 Repeat the same steps and create class selectors named .even with a background color of #CCCCCC, .rowHover with a background color of #FFFF99, and .rowSelect with a background color of #FFCC33 and a font weight of bold. Font weight is in the Type category.

These classes will be applied to rows in the table dynamically by Spry, adjusting for the number of rows and reacting to the user's mouse movements.

You will recall from Lesson two that simply creating the custom styles does not cause them to display. They have to be tied to an element in the structure of the main document. You can tie them to the rows of the Spry table using Spry attributes.

Change to either code or split view and examine the code for the Spry table. See if you can find where it binds the variables for the countryName and region. Spry uses curly braces {} to indicate its bindings.

3 Place your cursor just inside the closing bracket of the <tr> tag with the spry:repeat attribute (approximately line 40). Press the spacebar and type class="{ds_EvenOddRow}".

Spry has some built-in variables that mask the complexity of the programming logic necessary to dynamically alternate values based on the row number. The ds_EvenOddRow Spry variable will change the class name to either odd or even based on the current table sort. The rows will then render using the classes, odd and even, that you created above.

```
40    <tr spry:repeat="ds1" spry:setrow="ds1" class="{ds_EvenOddRow}">
41      <td>{countryName}</td>
42      <td>{region}</td>
43    </tr>
```

4 Save your changes. Upload profiles.asp and main.css to the server. Reload profiles.asp in your browser and view the changes.

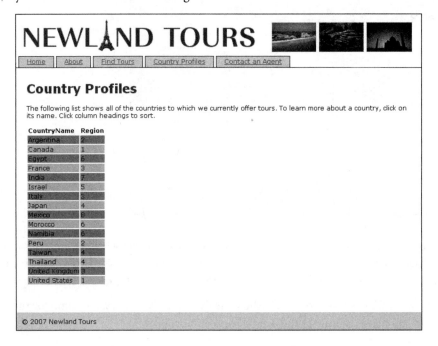

Spry has applied your odd and even classes to the rows. If you re-sort the columns the colors will dynamically change. But what of the other classes you created? How does Spry call the .rowHover and .rowSelect to affect the display?

As you look at the code you can see a pattern with how Spry affects the HTML display. Spry code usually starts with spry: followed by a specific function or attribute. You will use two more of these attributes which package some complex functionality in very little code.

5 Return to the `<tr>` tag you modified in step 3. Place your cursor just inside the closing bracket. Press the spacebar and type `spry:hover`. Note that Dreamweaver will start to present available options as you type. After typing `spry:hover` you will be presented with a list of class names. Choose `rowHover`.

6 Repeat the steps again, this time typing `spry:select`. For the value choose `rowSelect`.

The finished line of code should look like the screenshot below:

```
40    <tr spry:repeat="ds1" spry:setrow="ds1" class="{ds_EvenOddRow}" spry:hover="rowHover" spry:select="rowSelect">
41        <td>{countryName}</td>
42        <td>{region}</td>
43    </tr>
```

7 Save your changes. Press F12 to view the updated version.

Roll your mouse up and down over the rows. Click to select a row. The classes you created are being applied and you wrote remarkably little code.

There is one more subtle change worth making to improve the user's experience. Notice that when you mouse over the table headings your cursor remains an I-bar. If the cursor were a pointer, users would have a better visual cue indicating that the headings were clickable hotspots. You can change that behavior with CSS.

8 Return to profiles.asp. Create a new CSS rule. For Selector Type choose Class. Name it .sortHead. Make sure Define in: is set to main.css. Click OK. Under the Block Category set Text align to center. Under the Extensions Category look for Cursor. In the box next to it type *pointer*. Click OK.

There are many different values for the cursor, some with more support than others. I don't know why Adobe didn't include pointer in the drop-down list, but you can type in your value and Dreamweaver writes the appropriate code.

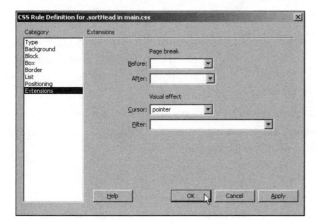

9   In design view, type a blank space to separate the words Country and Name in the table heading cell. Use the tag selector to choose the entire <th> tag. Using the property inspector, apply your newly created class sortHead to the table heading.

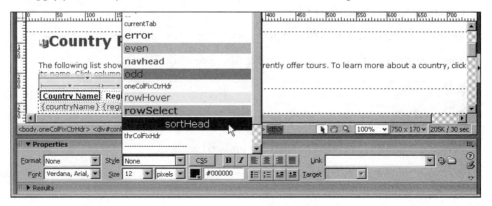

10   Repeat the previous step for the table heading containing the word Region. Save your file. Press F12 to view the changes.

Now when you mouse over the table headings your cursor changes to a pointer, indicating to the users that there is active functionality in those spots.

Creating Spry Regions

You have only just begun to tap the power of Spry. It was easy to make a table with sortable columns and remarkably simple to style the table and add some rollover functionality. Clicking on the rows in your Spry table can also act as a triggering event for other elements on the page. Rather than send users off to another page to view the details of the selected country or even back to the server for more information, you can use Spry to display the relevant information on this page in a quick, compact and visually pleasing way.

The table row that you modified in the previous section had a Spry attribute that might not have been entirely self-evident. spry:setrow="ds1" indicates that when a row is selected it will set any detail regions with a value of ds1 to be on the same row of data as the one selected. A detail region is a Spry area that displays the values for bound variables specific to the record selected in the main Spry region. We'll start with a simple example of this relationship between the selected row of the table and other data on the page.

1   Return to profiles.asp. Place your cursor after the closing </div> tag that follows the closing </table> tag. Press Enter/Return once to make space and enter the following code:

```
<p spry:detailregion="ds1">Record {ds_RowNumberPlus1} of {ds_RowCount}</p>
```

This code creates a paragraph that acts as a Spry detail region. Any Spry variables inside the paragraph respond when the user selects an element in the Spry region. ds_RowNumberPlus1 will display the currently selected row number and ds_RowCount displays the total number of rows in the dataset.

❈ **NOTE:** ds_RowNumberPlus1 represents an offset of one from the selected row. This is because JavaScript, like many computer languages, begins labeling records with zero, much like the coordinates on a map or graph start at zero. Since we are counting we add one to the JavaScript label to display the current row number.

2 Save your changes. Press F12 to preview the addition to the page.

As you select the various rows in the table, the detail region is updated. Even when you re-sort the table the detail region responds to the selected item's new position in the table and adjusts accordingly.

Country Name	Region
Argentina	2
Canada	1
Egypt	6
France	3
India	**7**
Israel	5
Italy	3
Japan	4
Mexico	8
Morocco	6
Namibia	6
Peru	2
Taiwan	4
Thailand	4
United Kingdom	3
United States	1

Record 5 of 16

Displaying with a Spry Accordion

The country list has been built and you have tested its ability to take user input and change a detail region. Now you need to create a detail region that will display all the details of the country the user chooses.

In order to keep the design compact you can use the area to the right of your table for your detail region. You could just output the variables in your dataset in a list, but Spry has a variety of user interface widgets and effects that allow you to display the data in a way that is more interesting for users. A Spry accordion will allow you to present the details and picture

of each country in an eye-catching way without taking up a lot of space. An accordion is a
series of panels that expand and collapse to reveal the content of one panel while concealing
the content of the other.

1 In design view, position your cursor in the whitespace below the Spry detail region you
inserted in the previous step. Choose Insert > Spry > Spry Accordion.

A two-panel accordion set has been inserted into the document. In your document code,
the files that style and add functionality to the accordion have been referenced. Once you
save your changes, copies of them will be moved to your site directory. You will upload
them to the server for testing later.

In order to make the accordion panels dynamic Spry elements, you need to identify the
areas you want to be Spry detail regions. Then you can populate the panels with the content you want to display. You will need to work in both design and code view, so you can
either toggle between the two or work in split view.

2 In code view, find <div class="AccordionPanelContent">. Add spry:detailregion="ds1".
Repeat the step for the second div.

You can quickly find the divs by selecting the text "Content 1" and "Content 2" in design
view. Dreamweaver's tag insight should help guide you as you type.

You have turned the accordion panels into Spry detail regions. The panels are now ready
to accept Spry variables that will respond to the user choices in the main Spry region,
your table.

```
48    <p spry:detailregion="ds1">Record {ds_RowNumberPlus1} of {ds_RowCount}</p>
49    <div id="Accordion1" class="Accordion" tabindex="0">
50      <div class="AccordionPanel">
51        <div class="AccordionPanelTab">Label 1</div>
52        <div class="AccordionPanelContent" spry:detailregion="ds1">Content 1</div>
53      </div>
54      <div class="AccordionPanel">
55        <div class="AccordionPanelTab">Label 2</div>
56        <div class="AccordionPanelContent" spry:detailregion="ds1">Content 2</div>
57      </div>
58    </div>
59    <p> </p>
60  <br clear="all" />
```

2 In design view, select the text "Content 1" in the first accordion panel and delete it. Type the following text into the first panel, pressing Enter/Return after each line. After typing each line, select the text and make it bold.

World Region:
Description:
Population:
Local Currency:

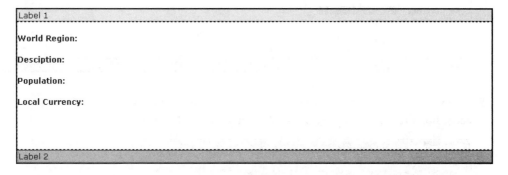

3 Position your cursor at the end of the World Region: line. Hit the spacebar to create a blank space, choose region in the bindings panel and click Insert.

4 Repeat for each of the four elements you have labeled, choosing the appropriate variable from the bindings panel for each.

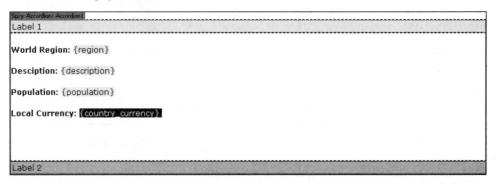

5 Save your changes. Dreamweaver will notify you that it is moving copies of the Spry accordion files into the Spry Assets folder in your site directory.

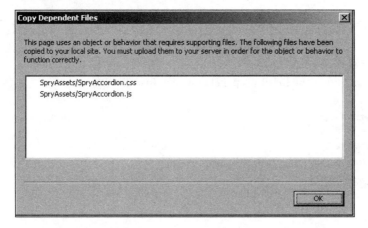

6 Press F12 to test the page. If you are not prompted to upload dependent files, upload the Spry Assets directory as well. Your server will need the files controlling the accordion element that Dreamweaver just copied to your site directory.

The information in the detail region should now respond to your choices in the country table. Click around a bit to test it. Re-sort your table and note that the details of the selected country do not change. Click on the title bar of the second panel, labeled "Label 2" and test the accordion functionality.

The accordion adds a nice effect, but you still have a lot of work to do before we can call the page complete. In the remainder of this lesson you will make a number of smaller changes to polish up the page. The second panel needs content. You will add the image associated with each country and its description to that panel. You will display the chosen country name more prominently on the page and replace the region number with its descriptive title. Finally you will make some changes to the CSS.

Adding Images and the Country Name

The country profile is basically functional, but you could add a little more information. In this task, you'll add an image and a description of the image and display the chosen country name more prominently. (You'll fix the region name problem later in the lesson.)

Each tour and each country has an image, all of which are located in the images folder. An extra field in the database holds the image's name and URL. To display an image, all you need to do is dynamically load its URL into an otherwise static <img> element in HTML.

1 Still in profiles.asp, switch to design view, mouse over the right corner of the accordion bar Label 2. An eye icon will appear. Click the eye to open the second panel. Select and delete the text "Content 2".

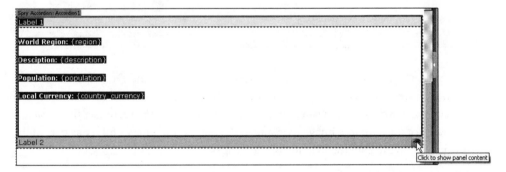

In a moment, you'll insert the image in this panel.

2 With your cursor inside the content area of the lower accordion panel, choose Insert > Image. In the Select Image Source dialog, select the Data Sources radio button at the top (Windows) or the Data Sources button near the bottom (Macintosh). Select imageURL for the field. Insert your cursor before the opening "{" in the URL field at the bottom of the dialog and type *images/*.

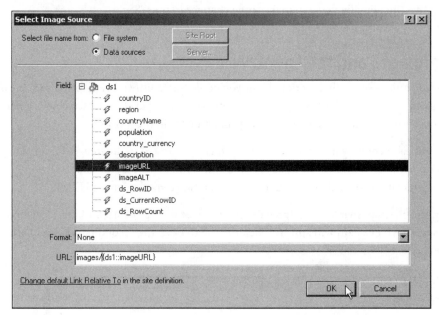

Normally, when you insert images, you browse to the image and Dreamweaver inserts the path. Because this is a dynamic image you are inserting, you don't want to choose an individual image. By choosing Data Sources, you gain access to the recordset that contains the name of the dynamic image. You added the path to the images folder as part of the image URL to indicate the location of the images.

3 When you click OK you will see the Image Tag Accessibility Attributes dialog box. Type *{imageAlt}* for the Alternate text. Click OK.

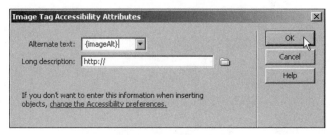

The imageAlt field carries a description of the image. In addition to adding it to the images alt attribute we will display it on the page.

✳ **NOTE:** You could hard code the path to the images folder into the imageURL field in the database, obviating the need to add it to the URL path in this step. However, site structure sometimes changes. Should you have to rename or move that folder it is much easier to go back and change the path to the images in one place in the code than to have to update the value for the imageURL in every country record in your database.

You will have a broken image placeholder graphic in the accordion panel. That is because you have modified the path to image. The important part is the dynamic image name that Spry will use when it renders the page.

4 Insert your cursor after the image icon in the lower accordion panel. In your bindings panel select the imageAlt field and click Insert.

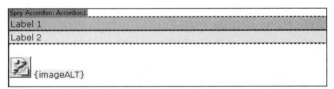

5 Select the image icon and use the Property inspector to change its alignment to Right.

When you are done with this step, the image icon appears on the right side.

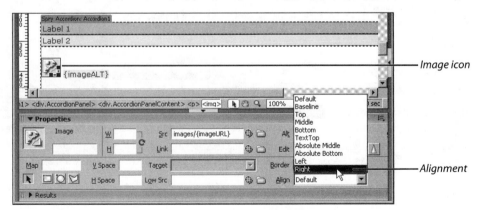

Image icon

Alignment

Before testing your changes, let's quickly take care of a few other data display issues. The name of the country your user selects does not currently display anywhere other than the table. You could add it to the other data in the accordion panel, but it merits a more prominent place on the page.

6 In code view, place your cursor just inside the closing bracket of the <h1> tag containing the page banner Country Profiles. This is approximately line 34. Press the spacebar and type spry:detailregion="ds1".

```
33      <div id="mainContent">
34        <h1 spry:detailregion="ds1"><a name="top" id="top"></a>Country Profiles</h1>
35        <p>The following list shows all of the countries to which we currently offer
```

A Spry detail region is necessary whenever you want to insert a Spry variable that you want to change based on the user selection from the Spry region. Now you can insert the country name.

7 Return to code view. Place your cursor after the word Profiles in the banner. Type a colon ":" and then a blank space. Next select countryName from the bindings panel and click Insert.

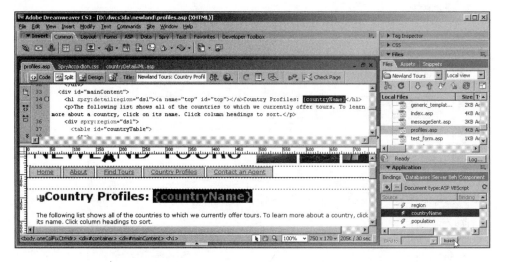

8 Save, upload, and test the file.

Click through the various country choices in the table. Observe how the country name changes at the top of the page. Click the second accordion panel to display the picture for each country. Choose another country and watch the picture and image description change.

NOTE: You did not format the population number. Ideally you would format it to display commas in the proper places but at the time of this the Spry team had not released formatting functions. Formatting functions in ASP, ColdFusion and PHP will not work because they do their work on the server and Spry changes the data on the user's machine, after the server has completed its work. There are possible work-arounds for this issue using other languages, but they are beyond the scope of this book. It is likely the Spry team will provide formatting functions, including one for numbers, in a future release.

Looking Up Foreign Table Data with SQL

There are still a few aesthetic issues to address, but before you take care of those, let's take care of one more data issue. I don't know about you, but the number in the region column has been bugging me. In order to correct this problem you'll have to rewrite some SQL code manually, but by doing so you will increase your understanding of the various working parts and improve your troubleshooting skills for future development.

Let's revisit the problem before attempting to solve it. Relationships are the cornerstone of most modern database management systems, such as Microsoft Access and MySQL. They enable people to organize their data in the most efficient format possible, by eliminating redundancy and simplifying data maintenance. Database developers put the unique key from a given table into another table as a foreign key. By doing so, developers can use a single query to assemble information from both tables correlated to any given record. In tbl_country there is a field for region and its value is the unique key taken from tbl_region's unique regionID field.

Let's be more concrete. In tbl_region, the record that contains North America has a unique key of 1. The record that contains East Asia has a unique key of 4. In tbl_country the records that contain Canada and the United States both have world regions of 1, which means both are in North America. Japan, Thailand, and Taiwan all have world regions of 4, meaning they are in East Asia. This relationship is shown in the following screenshot.

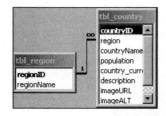

The catch, as you know, is that the only actual data from the region table is this unique key, and the key is not meaningful to regular users. What we need to do is combine the data from two tables (tbl_country and tbl_region) where they intersect. Thus, if the user selects Canada, not only will the query retrieve the selected fields of data from the Canada row in tbl_country, but it will also retrieve the data associated with the region value (1) in that table—and in the case of Canada, that data is North America.

Unfortunately, Dreamweaver's SQL builder is meant for relatively simple queries, rather than queries that combine data from two tables using a relationship. That means that you'll have to code some of the SQL by hand. Dreamweaver has an advanced SQL window that lets you hand-code SQL, but you can also edit it directly in the document.

The data for this page comes from the XML feed you created at the beginning of this lesson. That data for that XML dataset comes from a recordset you created in countryDetailXML.asp. That is where you need to go to modify the query.

> ❖ **NOTE:** If you chose to use countryDetail.xml as your XML source earlier in this lesson, move the file countryDetailWithRegionName.xml from the chapter09/Start folder to your newland site folder and rename it countryDetail.xml and skip ahead to *Refining Page Display Using CSS Styling and Positioning.*

1 Open countryDetailXML.asp. Find the SQL statement as it appears in the code, using the code listing below.

```
SELECT countryID, region, countryName, population, country_currency,
[description], imageURL, imageALT FROM tbl_country ORDER BY countryName ASC
```

✱ **NOTE:** Depending on the language you are working in you will note a slight variation in how Dreamweaver has written the field name "description". While it is a perfectly logical column name in our database, the word "description" is a reserved word in SQL. That means that it has a specific meaning in the language. In order to avoid confusion, it sets the term off in a special way. This is known as escaping the word. ASP escapes it using square brackets [], ColdFusion using double quotes "" and PHP using single back quotes ``.

2 Inside the query's FROM clause, replace tbl_country with tbl_country, tbl_region, being careful to leave the remaining code intact.

Originally, the query was retrieving fields only from tbl_country. By making this change, you are telling it to retrieve fields from both tbl_country and tbl_region.

3 Without moving your cursor from the previous step, insert the following code, being careful not to change the subsequent code.

```
WHERE tbl_region.regionID = tbl_country.region
```

This is the code that maps the region foreign key value in each individual country record in tbl_country to the correct regionID field in tbl_region. This allows you to pull in the correct regionName from tbl_region. In other words, when the Canada record is retrieved from tbl_country, SQL will use the record's region value (in the case of Canada, 1) to retrieve the regionName "America, North" from tbl_region.

The connection has been made between the two tables and the data in tbl_region is available to you. You need to specify which field from the new table you would like to retrieve. Previously you were selecting region from tbl_country. You no longer need that value. Now you need regionName from tbl_region.

4 Return to your SQL statement. In the SELECT clause change the field region to regionName. In the Bindings panel, click the Refresh button to verify that region has been removed and replaced by regionName.

Your final SQL looks like the code listing below:

```
SELECT countryID, regionName, countryName, population, country_currency,
[description], imageURL, imageALT FROM tbl_country, tbl_region WHERE tbl_region.
regionID = tbl_country.region ORDER BY countryName ASC
```

Even though Dreamweaver's Recordset dialog doesn't let you build this code from a wizard, Dreamweaver understands it.

> **TIP:** If there had been fields from the two tables with the same name, SQL would have thrown an error. This ambiguity is easily avoided by prefixing the field names with the table names. For example, if you write SELECT tbl_region.regionName it is clear to SQL which field you are referring to. Prefixing all of the field names improves the efficiency of the SQL and will speed up your application.

The change to your query means a change to the resulting recordset. The code that exports the recordset to XML will need to be modified to reflect that change.

5 Return to countryDetailXML.asp. Find the statement as it appears in the code listings below. It will be below the section containing the SQL statement you were just working on.

In ASP:

```
xmlExportObj.addColumn "region", "region"
```

In ColdFusion:

```
xmlExportObj.addColumn("region", "region");
```

In PHP:

```
$xmlExportObj->addColumn("region", "region");
```

6 Replace the first instance of region with regionName.

This will change the value being pushed into the XML dataset. The second instance of region is the label used in the XML structure. If you were to change that, too, you would then have to modify your Spry dataset since it is expecting a variable named region in the XML. The added layer of separation has worked in your favor by allowing you to modify the underlying data without having to modify your application code.

All of the changes you have made to countryDetailXML.asp can be seen in the following screen shot.

```
10  rs_countryDetail_cmd.ActiveConnection = MM_conn_newland_STRING
11  rs_countryDetail_cmd.CommandText = "SELECT countryID, regionName, countryName, population, country_currency, [description],
    imageURL, imageALT FROM tbl_country, tbl_region WHERE tbl_region.regionID = tbl_country.region ORDER BY countryName ASC"
12  rs_countryDetail_cmd.Prepared = true
13
14  Set rs_countryDetail = rs_countryDetail_cmd.Execute
15  rs_countryDetail_numRows = 0
16  %>
17  <%
18  'Begin XMLExport rs_countryDetail
19  Dim xmlExportObj: Set xmlExportObj = new XMLExport
20  xmlExportObj.Init
21  xmlExportObj.setRecordset rs_countryDetail
22  xmlExportObj.addColumn "countryID", "countryID"
23  xmlExportObj.addColumn "regionName", "region"
24  xmlExportObj.addColumn "countryName", "countryName"
```

6 Save countryDetailXML.asp and upload it to the server. Press F12 if you would like to view the change to the XML dataset. Refresh profiles.asp to view the changes reflected on that page.

You now see the country's continent, rather than an arbitrary number in both the country table and the World Region section of the accordion panel. Note that the sort for the region column is now alphabetical, responding to the change you made to the data.

Country Name	Region
Namibia	Africa
Egypt	Africa
Morocco	Africa
Mexico	America, Central
Canada	America, North
United States	America, North
Argentina	America, South
Peru	America, South
India	Asia, Central
Taiwan	Asia, East
Thailand	Asia, East
Japan	Asia, East
Israel	Asia, West
United Kingdom	Europe
France	Europe
Italy	Europe

Refining Page Display Using CSS Styling and Positioning

The page is now fully functional and the data is accurate and complete. So your work here is done, right? Well, no, not really. Depending on their screen resolution, some of your users would have to scroll down after choosing a country in order to see the details of their selection in the accordion panel. When you choose a country with a vertical image like France, Peru or Thailand the user has to scroll down in the accordion panel itself to view the entire image. The information in the country table and the accordion panels is a bit crowded against the sides of their respective containers. The accordion panels need proper labels and perhaps most egregious of all, the colors of the panel tabs just don't work with the rest of the scheme. Believe it or not, all of these are easily fixed with a little digital spit and polish.

Some of these changes are dependent on one another, so the sequence in which we make them is important. In order to reduce user scrolling and make the best use of the available screen real estate you can move the accordion up alongside the table. But we need to fix the issues with the country table before you can be sure how much room you will have for the accordion, so let's start there.

Padding and Positioning the Country Table

1 Return to profiles.asp. In the CSS panel click the button for a new CSS rule. For Selector Type choose Advanced. Name it #countryTable and make sure Define in: is set to main. css. Under the Box Category set Width to 300 pixels, Float to left and uncheck the Same for all box under Margin. Add the following values—Top: 5, Right: 10, Bottom: 10 and Left: 0. All values are in pixels.

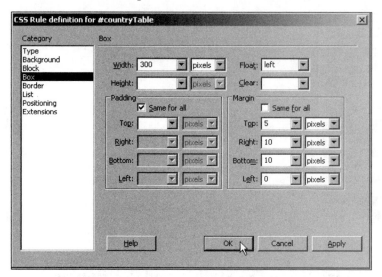

You have defined a custom CSS selector. The # indicates that it is an ID selector. You may recall from Chapter 2 that ID selectors are used for elements that are unique within a page. It is probably clear what setting its width will do, but what about the other values? I'll talk about float in a moment, but how about the margin? The CSS Reference built into Dreamweaver (Shift+F1) defines margin as "… the space that extends beyond the border of an element to provide extra empty space between adjacent or nested elements…" This means we've muscled out a little white space around our table so that other elements do not crowd it.

The important distinction between margin and padding, the other option in the Box Category, is that padding is the white space inside the border of the element and the margin is outside. That means that the 10 pixel margin you added to the right of the table element adds space to the 300 pixel width, making it total 310 pixels. Had it been 10 pixels of padding it would put those 10 pixels of white space inside your 300 pixel table element. These are two key components of what is referred to as the "Box Model" in CSS, the other component being the border. To see a clear demonstration of these differences, experiment by adding a 1 pixel border to the table so you can observe the edges of your element. Play with the margin and padding values and see where the space is added. Remove it when you are finished.

* **NOTE:** For years the various browsers have handled the Box Model differently. I would like to say that all browsers now render code in a consistent, standards-compliant way, but that is unfortunately not the case. It is difficult to make pixel-perfect layouts that are exactly the same in all browsers and you will see some variation in the results of your positioning efforts as you check the page in various browsers.

The other styling change you made is perhaps the most dramatic. You set float: left. That means that the element, in this case the table, will stick to the left side of its containing element while the rest of the page content flows around the table instead of being pushed down by it.

In order to see the effects of the ID selector style you have created you must add the proper ID to the country table.

2 In design view select the country table. If you are not sure you've chosen the table tag itself, click first in the table heading and then use the tag selector to choose the table tag. In the Property inspector choose countryTable from the Table ID list.

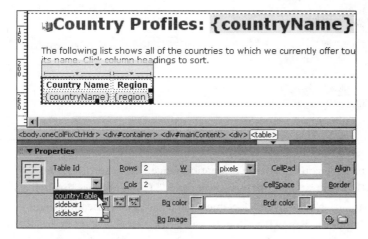

The ID countryTable was present in the list because you had already created the ID selector in the style sheet. You could also have typed countryTable into the Table ID box before creating the style.

You have now assigned the ID to the table and the styles you created are applied in design view.

3 Save your changes, upload both profiles.asp and main.css, and view the changes to profiles.asp through your browser.

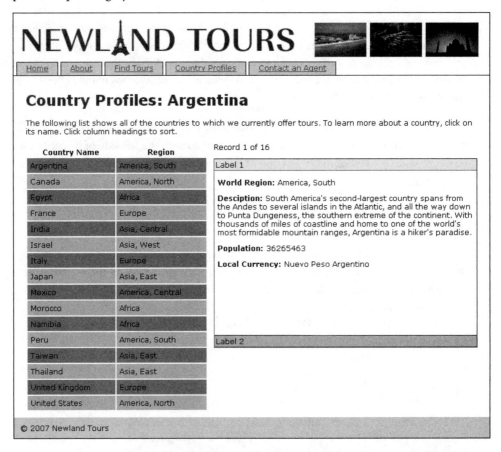

When you reload your page you see a fairly dramatic change. The accordion is now alongside the table. That is a testament to the power of CSS. Content flows through a Web page like water in a stream. Normally block elements like paragraphs, headings and tables disrupt that flow, acting like a dam. All content before block elements stays before them and content coming after block level elements occupy the space below them. By styling the table to float left it is as if the table grabs onto the left side of its container and allows the other content to swim in the water next to it. Now the "Record x of x" paragraph, as well as the accordion panels, are able to flow in the space next to the table rather than being pushed downstream below it.

Padding and Positioning the Accordion Panels

Now that you have the accordion panels in the right area of the page you can make final adjustments to their display. Let's begin by giving appropriate labels to the accordion panel tabs and making them more prominent.

1 Switch to code view. Locate the accordion panel. It should start around line 50. The label for the first tab is `<div class="AccordionPanelTab">Label 1</div>`. Change the text for the first panel tab from Label 1 to Details and change its tag from div to h3. Your code should now read:

```
<h3 class="AccordionPanelTab">Details</h3>
```

By changing the panel tab to an h3 you take advantage of h3's built-in font size and bolding. In code view you can make that change easily by simply editing the tag. If you make the change in design view Dreamweaver wraps an h3 tag around the label inside the div. This method puts too much space in the tab. I encourage you to test it out both ways and observe the results.

2 Repeat these steps for the second tab. Change Label 2 to Image and change the tag from div to h3. Save and upload profiles.asp to see your changes.

The remaining display modifications will be made to the style sheets. The accordion panels have their own CSS file, but you can access it easily through the CSS panel while you have profiles.asp open.

The vertically-aligned images used for countries like France and Thailand force a scrollbar in the panel. You can remedy this by making the panels' content cell taller.

3 Open the CSS panel and scroll to the bottom of the list of selectors where the styles from SpryAccordion.css are displayed. Single-click on .AccordionPanelContent. Its properties will be displayed in the Properties pane under the selectors list. Change the height attribute from 200 to 270.

If you double-click on a selector it will open its full editing window. This quick shortcut is handy, especially if the property already exists and you simply want to modify it.

Currently the content in the accordion panels rests against the sides of its panels. As we learned earlier, when you want to create white space on the inside of a container you use padding. Padding, like margin and border, is applied either as one value to the entire box or four values, representing each side of the box, starting at the top and moving clockwise around the element. In order to move the content off of the sides of the panel you can add padding to the left and right. There is no need to add any padding to the top or bottom as the elements inside the panels are all inside of <p> tags, block elements with built-in top and bottom margins that set them off from neighboring elements above and below.

4 Staying in the Properties pane at the bottom of the CSS panel, place your cursor after the padding value 0px, press the spacebar and then add 5px 0px 5px. The final value should read 0px 5px 0px 5px. Press Enter/Return or tab out of the field to make the change.

If you look at the .AccordionPanelContent class in SpryAccordion.css, around line 70, you will see padding: 0px 5px 0px 5px; listed among its properties. This form of CSS shorthand is the effective equivalent of the following:

```
padding-top: 0px;
padding-right: 5px;
padding-bottom: 0px;
padding-left: 5px;
```

Your final change to the page is to bring the colors of the panel tabs in line with the rest of the design. You can make these changes using the handy shortcut you learned in the previous steps or the traditional way by double-clicking and opening the edit window. I leave the choice up to you.

5 Locate the .AccordionFocused .AccordionPanelTab selector. Change its background color to #FFFF99. Next locate the .AccordionFocused .AccordionPanelOpen .AccordionPanelTab selector and change its color to #FFCC33.

These two selectors are considered advanced selectors. They reflect the relationship of elements much like the padding you added to the td that was a descendant of the countryTable earlier in the lesson. The first is for an element with the class AccordionPanelTab that is a descendent of an element with the class AccordionFocused. If you look in your code you will not see any element with the AccordionFocused class. Spry dynamically adds that class to the main accordion div when you click anywhere on the accordion.

The second advanced selector reflects yet another layer of ancestry, again with Spry dynamically adding the AccordionFocused and AccordionPanelOpen classes to the elements based on the user's mouse clicks. Nice functionality. Aren't you glad Spry has written it for you? It has saved quite a bit of time.

6 Save your changes and press F12 to preview. Make sure it uploads SpryAccordion.css with profiles.asp.

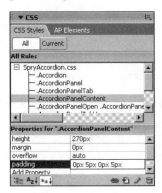

You have created a dynamic application for displaying the country profiles that not only provides your users with the information they need to learn about the countries your client's tours visit, but you did so in a way that provided a richer experience for the users. We will revisit Spry later in the book and I encourage you to keep an eye on the Spry development team's future releases on http://labs.adobe.com/.

What You Have Learned

In this lesson, you have:

- Created a recordset used to retrieve data to build a list of dynamically generated country names and regions (pages 257–259)

- Used a Dreamweaver Extension to generate XML datasets from standard recordsets (pages 259–260)

- Used the Adobe Spry implementation to convert XML data into dynamic content (pages 261–265)

- Created a compact layout using Spry user interface elements to display a country profile (pages 266–281)

- Modified SQL code by hand to combine and filter data from two different tables (pages 281–285)

- Used CSS to position page elements and style Spry elements with advanced custom selectors (pages 285–291)

What You Will Learn

In this lesson, you will:

- Plan the search and display application for the tours
- Create a recordset with handwritten SQL code
- Design the layout for tour descriptions, and populate it with dynamic data
- Apply recordset paging, to prevent too many descriptions from showing at once
- Integrate the tour descriptions intelligently with the tour price calculator
- Dynamically generate URLs

Approximate Time

This lesson takes approximately 2 hours to complete.

Lesson Files

Starting Files:

Lesson10/Start/newland/generic_template.asp
Lesson10/Start/newland/tourprice.asp
Lesson10/Start/newland/tourprice_ processor.asp
Lesson10/Start/newland/profiles.asp
Lesson10/Start/SpryURLUtils.js
Lesson10/Start/chapter10TypingHelp.txt

Completed Files:

Lesson10/Complete/newland/tours_detail.asp
Lesson10/Complete/newland/tourprice.asp
Lesson10/Complete/newland/tourprice_ processor.asp
Lesson10/Complete/newland/profiles.asp
Lesson10/Complete/newland/SpryAssets/SpryURLUtils.js

LESSON 10

Building the Tour Descriptions

When I was in college, I took a few years of Italian. On the first day of the second year, I asked the professor, "What are we learning this year?" The professor replied, "The same thing as last year, only this time I expect you to learn it." While the second year course covered much of the same grammar as the year before, it was different. We became more sensitive to nuances, more capable of expressing ourselves in the language; we began to internalize it and make it our own.

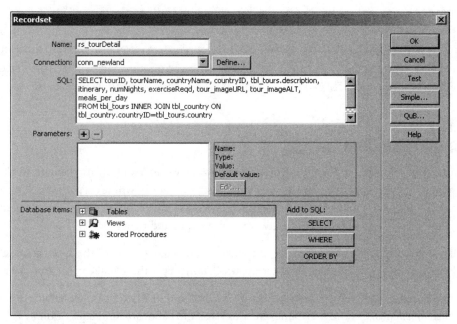

SQL can do a lot more than recall the data from a single table. In this lesson, you'll do some more advanced hand-coding in SQL, including using a structure called a join.

So it is with the application you'll build in Lessons 10 and 11. Much of what you'll do is already familiar, but this time around, you should both be internalizing the tasks and getting more ambitious. In the preceding three lessons, you worked with dynamic data pulled from databases, so you should be getting comfortable with the process of creating recordsets and outputting their values dynamically on pages. In addition to outputting simple text, you've output images dynamically and learned how to format numbers as currency. At the end of Lesson 9, you even looked up data from one table using criteria supplied by a different one. Such tasks are the substance of dynamic site development—things you will do again and again.

Lessons 10 and 11 build on this knowledge. You'll create a two-page mini-application that enables users to search and display tour descriptions. But the tours—they are, after all, the main feature of the Newland Tours Web site—need a slicker set of features. You'll implement three different means of accessing the tours (view all, view by region, or view an individual country). And you'll learn how to pass live data out of this application and into the country profile and tour price calculator applications to make this cluster of applications function a little more intelligently.

You'll push your skills in these lessons by writing your own SQL code, rather than relying on Dreamweaver's Recordset dialog. And the SQL code gets more sophisticated. You'll also start thinking more strategically about how to integrate dynamic data, server-side scripts, and SQL to accomplish certain feats. At the same time, you'll move data effortlessly among the scopes you have already learned: form, querystring/URL, local, and query. Finally, you should be comfortable intermingling XHTML and ASP/ColdFusion/PHP code in creative and diverse ways.

Planning the Application

Before you develop any application, you should have a clear idea of how it's going to work. As you build, potential enhancements and usability issues no doubt will present themselves, and your idea will evolve. But before you begin, you should know what you are building. Often, I draw flowcharts using flowcharting software or just paper and pencil.

For this application, you can go online and see the completed version of the application. Once you know where you are headed, the steps you will take to get there make a lot more sense.

1 In a browser, open *http://bobflynn.info/books/DWCS3DA/final/tours.php*, enter *osiris@ allectomedia.com* as the username, enter *osiris* as the password, and click Submit.

The log-in is something you won't implement for several more lessons.

2 Without clicking, roll your cursor over the world region links and the View all tours link in the status bar near the bottom of your browser window.

Notice that the page contains three different ways to access the tour descriptions. You can display all of the tours from a world region. You can display all of the tours for a given country. Or you can display all of the tours unfiltered by clicking the View all tours link.

When you roll over the links that filter by world region, you see that the URL parameter regionID=1 (or another number) is appended to the URL. Not surprisingly, the SQL statement on the descriptions page (tours_detail.php) filters using this parameter. But when you roll over the View all tours link, no URL parameter appears. Since no data filtering is taking place when users click this link, there is no need to send any special data to the next page.

As you have (hopefully) guessed, if you choose an individual country from the menu and click Submit, then that data is sent as a form variable and used to filter descriptions on the next page. The list of countries in this menu is, of course, dynamically generated, so that the list is always up-to-date.

* **NOTE:** If you do not see the status bar at the bottom of your browser window, turn it on by clicking View > Status Bar.

3 Click a few different links and submit the form a couple of times so you get the feel for how the search and display pages work together.

Pay special attention to the URL. Notice that it only contains URL parameters when you click one of the world region links. It has no parameters when you access the page through the form, and no parameters when you access the page through the View all tours link. Notice also that you can get tours to any given country to show up in each of the three ways.

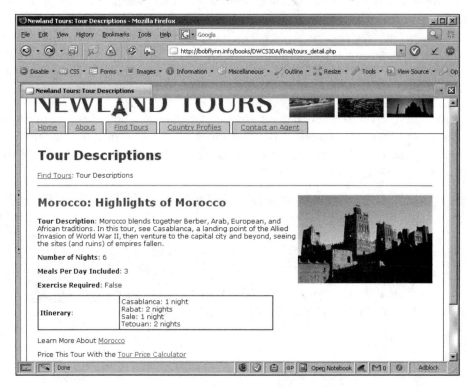

4 From any country's description, click the Tour Price Calculator link.

Notice that the drop-down menu that displays the tour names reflects the tour you were looking at before you clicked the link. That is, if you were reading the Highlights of Morocco tour description and click the Tour Price Calculator link, Highlights of Morocco will be preselected in the menu. This is possible in part thanks to the URL parameter (in the case of Highlights of Morocco, it's tourID=17).

In the lesson introduction, I mentioned that you would make the two applications—the search and display pairing for the tour descriptions and the tour price calculator—work together. You'll set up this collaboration later in this lesson.

Again, remember that as long as the database is maintained, the site will always display all of the tours Newland offers, and the display will meet whatever search criteria users select.

When you are finished exploring, close the browser and return to Dreamweaver.

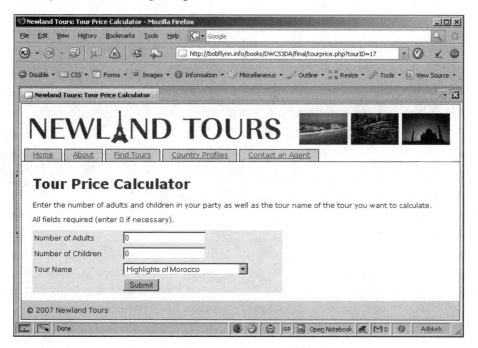

Creating Recordsets with Joins

In this task, you'll begin building the page that displays the tours. This is a new page in the site, so you'll start with generic_template.asp and go from there. This particular page is going to have lots of SQL—no less than three queries, in fact—and you'll build the simplest one in this lesson. This query will retrieve all of the information about all of the tours, without any filtering mechanisms.

When you create this query, you're going to use a SQL structure called a **join**. As you know, a relational database is split into many different tables that share different relationships. Sometimes, you will need a set of data from two or more tables that are related to one another. To collect all of this information, you use a join. If this sounds scary, don't worry: You've already done it! In Lesson 10 in the country profile page you created a join when you modified the SQL statement so that it retrieved the region name, rather than simply the region ID. (Remember the WHERE clause?)

The syntax you used in Lesson 10, which relied on WHERE, is no longer the preferred way to handle joins, though it is the easiest to understand and it will be supported in all major database management systems (like Access and MySQL) in the foreseeable future, so there is nothing wrong with using it. But there is a better way to join tables, which you will learn in this task.

1 Open generic_template.asp, use the toolbar to title the page *Newland Tours: Tour Descriptions*. Replace the placeholder title text with *Tour Descriptions*. Save the file as *tours_detail.asp*.

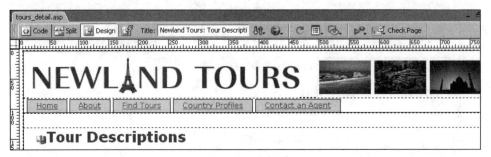

2 In the first line of body text, type *Find Tours: Tour Descriptions*. Highlight Find Tours and use the Property inspector to link it to tours.asp. Position the cursor at the end of the word Descriptions, and press Enter/Return twice to add two new lines. Copy the Find Tours line and paste it on the bottom line.

In these two steps, you are building the static part of the page. You'll place the tour descriptions between the two Find Tours links, so users can easily return to the tour search page from the detail page.

3 Add a new recordset to the page, using the following information:

Name: *rs_tourDetail*
Connection: conn_newland
Table: tbl_tours
Columns: Selected—Holding down the control/command key, select each column in the list *except* basePriceAdult and basePriceChild.

You need to create a query that will pull most of the fields from the tours table, so you can use it to build the descriptions. Since you will send the users to the calculator for pricing there is no need to pull in the prices. If you later wish to display the prices on this page you can simply add those fields to your SQL query.

As with the country profiles, one of the fields (country) contains a foreign key, which means that it will retrieve an arbitrary number (the country's primary key), rather than the country name, which is what you really want. You'll use a join to retrieve this information, but you can't do that in this simple interface, so in this step you are building the portion of the SQL query that you can use as the basis for the more advanced query you'll write in the next step.

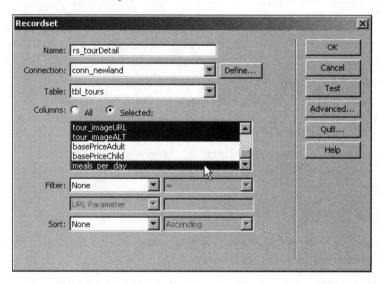

4 Click the Advanced button to open the advanced version of the Recordset dialog.

As you can see, this version of the dialog contains the SQL that you specified in the simple version of the dialog. You'll write the remaining code here in the SQL window.

▶ **TIP:** You can return to the simple version of the dialog by clicking the Simple button.

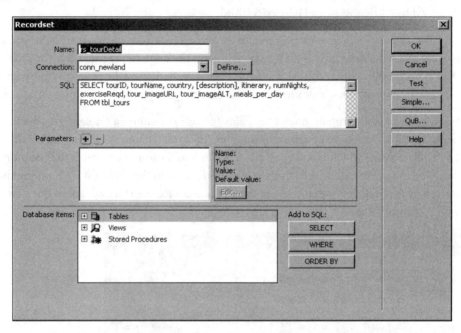

5 Change the SQL statement in the window so that it reads as follows:

```
SELECT tourID, tourName, country, [description], itinerary, numNights,
➥exerciseReqd, tour_imageURL, tour_imageALT, meals_per_day
FROM tbl_tours
INNER JOIN tbl_country
ON tbl_country.countryID=tbl_tours.country
```

The syntax for joins is hard to read for many people. However, this query does the exact same things as the following (easier to read) query:

```
SELECT tourID, tourName, country, [description], itinerary, numNights,
➥exerciseReqd, tour_imageURL, tour_imageALT, meals_per_day
FROM tbl_tours, tbl_country
WHERE tbl_country.countryID=tbl_tours.country
```

That is, it makes fields from both tables available. When it merges the two tables, it does so by matching the value in the country field of tbl_tours with the countryID field, which is the primary key of the tbl_country table. This ensures that the correct country's data is joined to each tour. In other words, the country Argentina (and all of its data as entered in tbl_country) is associated with Highlights of Argentina.

If you remember the fields in tbl_country from the last lesson you may see one problem with your SQL statement. Both tbl_tours and tbl_country have a field named description. SQL cannot deal with this ambiguity. You may also recall that we can clear up that ambiguity by prefixing the field name with its specific table name.

6 Remove the escape characters surrounding the description fieldname in the SQL statement. Add `tbl_tours.` before `description`. The resulting code should look like this:

`tbl_tours.description`

There are a couple of things left to do to your query before we close the recordset window. First, the country column is the foreign key in the region table. You can see from your JOIN syntax that country is what anchors your select statement to the primary key countryID and through it to the data in tbl_country (`ON tbl_country.countryID=tbl_tours.country`). You've made this connection to tbl_country in order to pull in the countryName field. You can further leverage tbl_country by ordering your records by countryName. Again, this is no different in its result than what you did in Lesson 9 with the region name. The only difference now is that you are using the best syntax (the `INNER JOIN...ON...`syntax) to retrieve this data.

7 Change the column country to countryName and add the column countryID. Be sure to add a comma after the new column name. At the end of the query, after `ON tbl_country.countryID=tbl_tours.country`, type a space and `ORDER BY tbl_country.countryName`. Your final SQL should read:

```
SELECT tourID, tourName, countryName, countryID, tbl_tours.description,
➥itinerary, numNights, exerciseReqd, tour_imageURL, tour_imageALT, meals_per_day
FROM tbl_tours INNER JOIN tbl_country
ON tbl_country.countryID=tbl_tours.country
ORDER BY tbl_country.countryName
```

✱ **NOTE:** Once you've entered this SQL code, you can no longer switch back to Simple view, because that view has no way of representing the sophisticated SQL statement you just created.

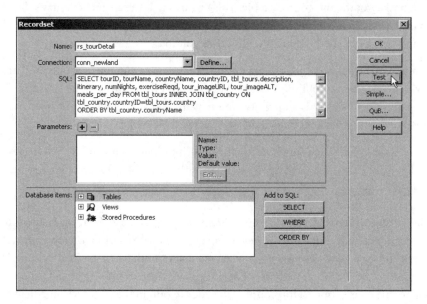

8 Click the Test button.

This brings up a large set of records. You'll need to scroll to the right to see most of the data, as it's off-screen to start.

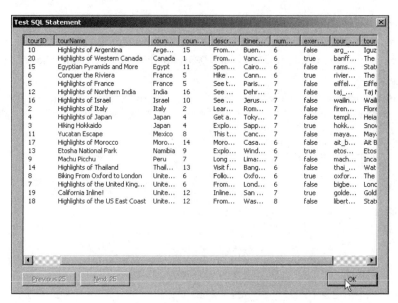

❋ **NOTE:** I have found that for some advanced queries the test button returns an unidentified error. If this happens, check the Bindings panel to ensure that all of your variables are listed. If they are, then Dreamweaver has correctly processed your SQL.

9 Click OK twice to close the Test and then the Recordset dialogs.

In the Bindings panel, you'll see the new recordset is in place. As noted earlier, although the simple version of the Recordset dialog can't handle this SQL, Dreamweaver can. The data is correctly represented in the Bindings panel.

❋ **NOTE:** If you double-click the recordset in the Bindings panel to edit it, you will be taken directly to Advanced view, because Simple view cannot represent the code.

The data is now available to the page, so you can begin laying out the tour descriptions.

Building the Descriptions

In this task, you will prepare the tour descriptions. As with the country profiles, this activity blends together both static and dynamic elements.

1 In design view, position the insertion point between the two Find Tours lines, and choose Insert > HTML > Horizontal Rule.

The horizontal rule will be used to separate each of the tour descriptions.

2 Type the following into the document:

XX Country Name: Tour Name XX
Tour Description:
Number of Nights:
Meals Per Day Included:
Exercise Required:
Itinerary:
Learn More About XX Country Name XX
Price This Tour With the Tour Price Calculator
All Photographs © PhotoDisc

Once again, you are entering the static content first, just to provide the page with its initial structure. In the coming steps, you'll insert dynamic content in appropriate places within the page.

To add the © symbol, choose Insert > HTML > Special Characters > Copyright.

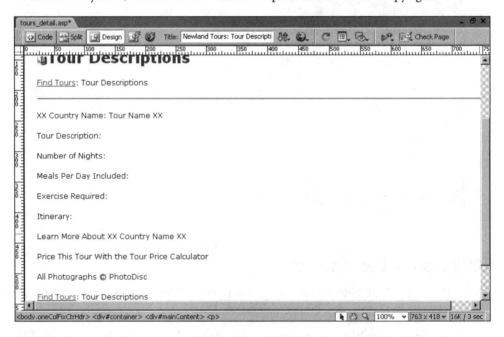

3 Click once in the XX Country Name: Tour Name XX line, and use the Property inspector's Format menu to change it to a Heading 2 element. One at a time, for each of the next five paragraphs, select the text up to (but not including) the colon, and use the Property inspector to apply bolding.

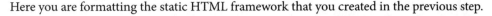

Here you are formatting the static HTML framework that you created in the previous step.

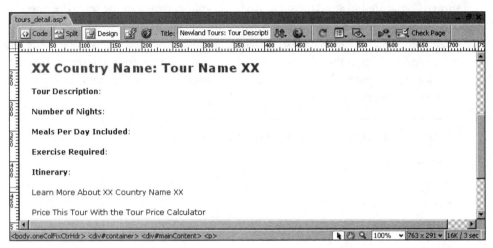

4 Select XX Country Name from the title, and replace it with countryName from the Bindings panel.

Dreamweaver replaces the placeholder text you typed with its own pseudocode to indicate the source of the dynamic text.

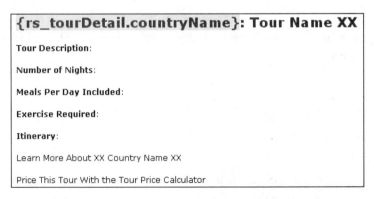

5 Select Tour Name XX, and replace it with tourName from the Bindings panel. Choose View > Live Data to verify that one country and tour are displaying correctly. Toggle off Live Data once you have verified that it's working.

I often toggle Live Data on and off during development just to make sure there are no surprises. You should see Argentina: Highlights of Argentina in the title. The interesting thing to point out is that not only is the title derived from two different fields in a record-set, but the different fields are also derived from two different database tables. The country name comes from tbl_country, and the tour name comes from tbl_tours. The fact that the country (Argentina) is correctly correlated with the tour (Highlights of Argentina) is further confirmation that the join in your query worked.

Argentina: Highlights of Argentina

Tour Description:

Number of Nights:

Meals Per Day Included:

Exercise Required:

Itinerary:

Learn More About XX Country Name XX

Price This Tour With the Tour Price Calculator

All Photographs © PhotoDisc

Find Tours: Tour Descriptions

---

6 Bind dynamic data after each of the following five items (the same five you bolded in step 3, as specified below:

Tour Description: description
Number of Nights: numNights
Meals per day included: meals_per_day
Exercise Required: exerciseReqd
Itinerary: itinerary

This is the meat-and-potatoes step of adding most of the dynamic content to the page. It is no different than what you have done before.

7 Toggle Live Data back on.

For the most part, it seems to be coming together pretty well. The itinerary part looks sloppy, however, because the second night is on a new line that doesn't line up with the first. A simple table will fix this.

Argentina: Highlights of Argentina

Tour Description: From the city lights of Buenos Aires to the resort city of Mar del Plata, this tour provides an excellent getaway. What begins with fashionable shopping and unique cuisine resolves into lounging on a beach in one of South America's best resort towns.

Number of Nights: 6

Meals Per Day Included: 2

Exercise Required: False

Itinerary: Buenos Aires: 3 nights
Mar del Plata: 3 nights

Learn More About XX Country Name XX

Price This Tour With the Tour Price Calculator

All Photographs © PhotoDisc

8 Place your cursor before Intinerary:. Toggle off Live Data and create a table with one row and two columns to separate the static text from the dynamic text. Give it the settings shown in the screenshot. Then drag Itinerary: into the left cell, and drag the dynamic block into the right.

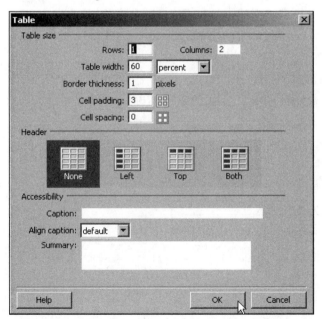

This way, when the itinerary is output on multiple lines, they'll line up properly. You'll need to toggle Live Data back on to see the results. You may be left with an extra blank line below your table. You can delete it.

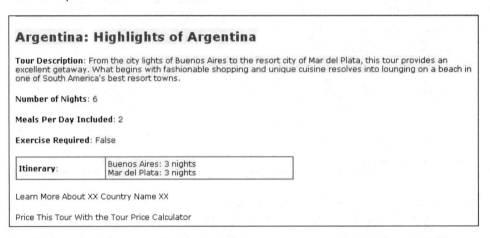

9 Select XX Country Name XX in the paragraph below the itinerary table, and replace it with countryName from the Bindings panel.

This will output the country name again. Later in this lesson, you'll add a link from this country name to its profile.

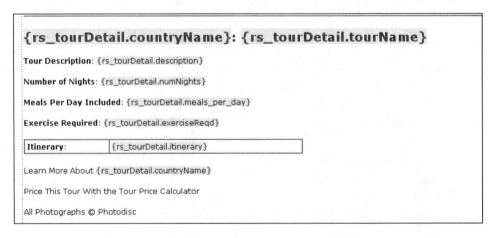

Inserting the Images and alt Attributes

The tour descriptions, like the country profiles, each have an image. In this task, you'll add those images (dynamically, of course), and you'll also add alt descriptions using information stored in the database.

1 Position the insertion point just before the country name {rs_tourDetail.countryName} in the heading near the top of the page.

The image will be positioned in the top-right corner of each tour description, much as it was with the country profiles.

2 Choose Insert > Image. In the Select Image Source dialog, click the Data sources radio button. Expand the recordset, and choose tour_imageURL in the list. Insert your cursor before the opening "{" in the URL field at the bottom of the dialog and type *images/*. Click OK. Cancel out of the accessibility dialog when it appears.

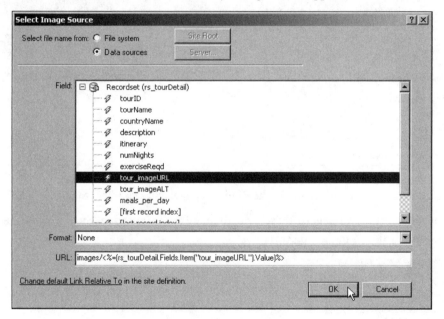

I had you cancel out of the accessibility dialog because in a moment I'll show you another way to make the site accessible.

Once again, the text string that contains the URL is stored in the database. When you insert a dynamic image, what you are really inserting is a dynamic string of text, which consists of a URL pointing to an image, inside of an <img> element.

An image icon appears in the document, where the insertion point was a moment ago.

3 With the image icon still selected, set its alignment to Right in the Property inspector.

The image icon moves to the right side of the page.

To make sure that the image works as expected, you can toggle on Live Data. You should see a photo of a series of waterfalls, with a rainbow and a lake in the foreground.

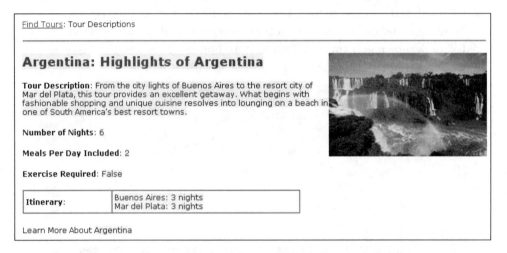

4 Select the image on the page, and in the Bindings panel, click to select tour_imageALT.

When you select tour_imageALT, the Bind To menu at the bottom of the panel becomes active, usually defaulting to img.src.

5 In the Bind To menu, change the selected option to img.alt. Click Bind.

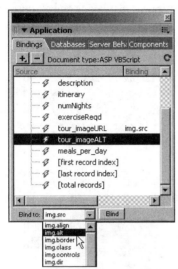

The image caption is now bound to the image as an alternate description. To confirm this, with the image selected, look in the Alt field of the Property inspector. You should see some dynamic code, and somewhere in that code, you should see rs_tourDetail. tour_imageALT.

6 Save, upload, and test the file.

The page should look pretty good in a browser at this point. Depending on your browser, if you hover your cursor over the image, a tool tip may appear displaying the alt description. Also, double-check that all of the dynamic text fields look right. For example, underneath the itinerary table, you should see "Learn more about Argentina."

Implementing Recordset Paging

Other than the two links near the bottom of the description, which link to other applications (the country profiles and tour price calculator applications), the description is complete. One glaring problem, however, is that Newland Tours appears to only offer one tour (the one to Argentina). You need to make the output loop so that it includes each of the tour descriptions, not just the first one returned.

You'll use a Repeat Region server behavior to output more than one description. The problem, though, is that you will be outputting an entire description, complete with an image. That could result in a long page and download time.

The functionality of the page would be better if you could limit the number of records shown, so that, for example, only five descriptions appeared at once, and users could navigate back and forth through them. This is possible—and quite easy—using a set of built-in Dreamweaver server behaviors. The Repeat Region behavior lets you limit the number of records (in this case, tour descriptions) that are displayed on a page. Another behavior, called Recordset Navigation Bar, automates the process of creating the First, Previous, Next, and Last links (or buttons) that enable users to access all of the descriptions. You'll use both behaviors in this task to create the desired functionality.

1 Toggle off Live Data View if you have not already done so. Drag to select everything from (and including) the horizontal rule through the "Price this tour with the Tour Price Calculator" paragraph.

This will be the repeated region. You don't want to include the copyright notice or the second Find Tours link in the repeated region—those should appear beneath all the tours.

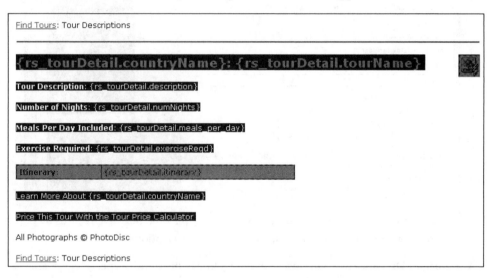

2 Use the Server Behaviors panel to add a Repeat Region behavior to the selection. In the Repeat Region dialog, enter 5 for the number of records to be shown at a time. Click OK.

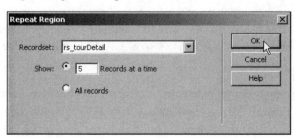

A Repeat Region square is drawn around the entire selection, indicating its boundaries.

3 Save, upload, and press F12 to test the page, to view it in a browser.

You'll see the first five records, listed alphabetically by country name. The first is still Highlights of Argentina, while the last record on the page should be Highlights of France.

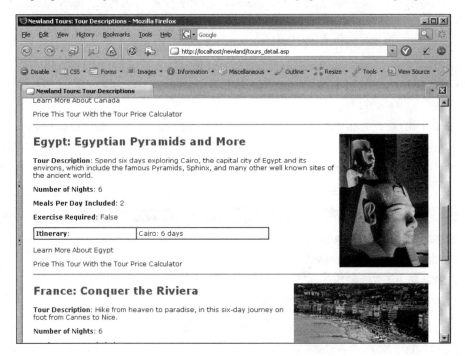

At this point, though, there is no way for you to display the next five records or skip to the end. You are stuck with only the first five tour descriptions.

4 Return to Dreamweaver, and insert an empty line beneath the Repeat Region area. With the insertion point in that empty line, choose Insert > Data Objects > Recordset Paging > Recordset Navigation Bar.

✱ **NOTE:** If you have difficulty getting the insertion point outside of the Repeat Region, switch to code view and insert your cursor immediately before `<p>All Photographs &copy; PhotoDisc</p>`. Insert an empty line and then proceed with inserting the Recordset Navigation Bar and then return to design view.

This "data object" is actually a group of server behaviors. It creates First, Previous, Next, and Last links or buttons (your choice). Each of these links tells ASP, ColdFusion, or PHP which five recordsets to show when they are clicked. In addition, if the user is viewing the first set of recordsets, the First and Previous links/buttons will be hidden, because they don't apply. Likewise, the Next and Last links/buttons won't be visible if the user is browsing the final set of records. All four links/buttons are visible in the middle.

5 In the Recordset Navigation Bar dialog, accept the defaults (rs_tourDetail as the Recordset, and Text as the Display Using option), and click OK.

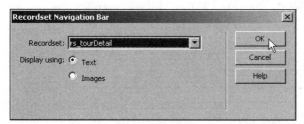

When you are finished, you'll see a new table added to the page, containing the four links. If you look in the Server Behaviors panel near the bottom, you'll also see several new behaviors, including several that begin, "Show if not…" and several "Move to XXX Record." Again, these are the individual behaviors created when you add a recordset navigation bar.

❊ **NOTE:** ASP users may see two server behaviors at the bottom of the panel with red exclamation marks beside them, indicating an error. In fact, there is no error on the page (it should work fine as-is) and you can safely disregard them, if they appear.

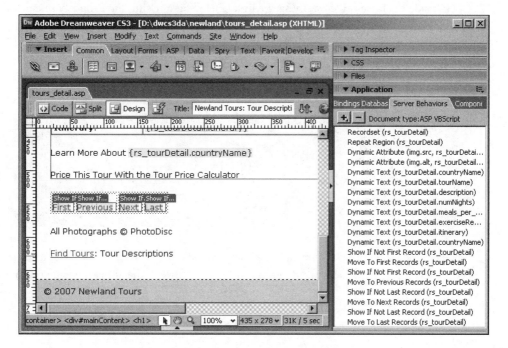

You can build this type of navigation bar manually, if you like, since all the server behaviors you need are individually available in the Server Behaviors panel, in the Recordset Paging and Show Region portions of the menu.

6 Click anywhere inside the table that contains the four links, select the `<table>` tag in the tag selector, and use the Property inspector to set the table's background color to a light gray, #EEEEEE. Set the width to 50% and align it to center.

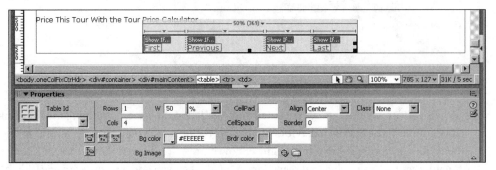

By default, the table that holds the links is invisible. Often, that's OK, but given how prominent other elements on the page are, the navigation bar is easily overlooked. By giving it a gray background, you make it stand out a bit more.

7 Click inside the table cell containing the link labeled First. Using the Property inspector change the horizontal (labeled "Horz") value to center. Repeat this for each of the four table cells.

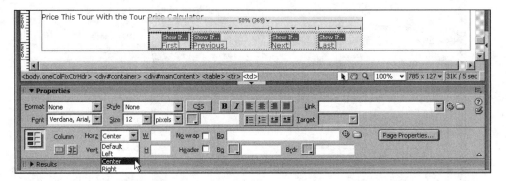

Since the four labels are of differing lengths it will look best if we center each in its own cell. You can play with the width of each cell to further tweak the appearance if you like.

8 Save, upload, and press F12 to test the page. Use the navigation bar to move backward and forward through the records.

The navigation works as expected. If the table holding the navigation bar looks a bit odd on the first and last pages it may be because HTML will not render table cells with no content. On the first and last pages, the conditional regions are suppressing the First/Previous or the Next/Last links, so the cells are empty. You can get around this by adding a blank space to each cell. If, after testing in multiple browsers and across platforms, it looks fine to you, then don't bother changing a thing.

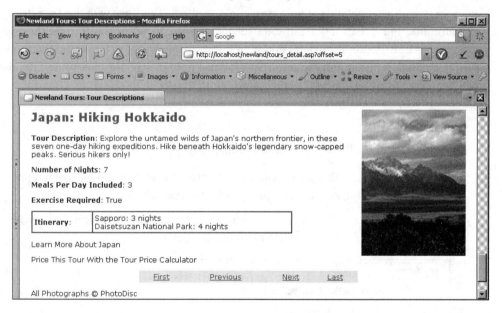

Passing Data to Other Applications

Users can now browse through all of the tour descriptions, five at a time. The descriptions are laid out and attractive, and the recordset navigation bar makes it easy to go back and forth through the recordsets. Before you wrap up the lesson, you need to add two more pieces of functionality.

At the bottom of each description should be two links. The first link is a country name that takes users to the country's profile on profiles.asp. The second link takes users to the tour price calculator (tourprice.asp). You can't simply create a link to these two pages, however. You need to pass data to both pages as well, so that the pages know which tour description the user was reading when she or he clicked the link.

In both cases you will pass a URL parameter that gives the receiving page the key needed to pull up the appropriate record. You will handle this functionality slightly differently for each of the two pages. In the case of the country profiles a URL parameter, countryID, will be used to determine which country to show. You'll need to add the same URL parameter to the link on tours_detail.asp. You'll add a small bit of additional Spry functionality to profiles.asp which will take the countryID and use it to select the record to display.

The tour price calculator link will also need some slight modification to handle the incoming data. That page has a dynamically generated drop-down menu listing all of the tours. But if the user is reading Highlights of Italy, then clicks the Price This Tour with the Tour Price Calculator link, and arrives at the tour price calculator form, he or she wants to see the price for Highlights of Italy (not the default option of Biking from Oxford to London). Again, the solution is similar to the country profile link—you just need to send the page some extra data. You'll take care of this (and a couple other issues) in this task.

Passing Data to Spry

First, let's take care of the link to the country profiles page.

1 Select the dynamic text that appears at the end of the "Learn more about" paragraph. In the Property inspector, type *abc* as a placeholder to create a link.

The placeholder URL will be replaced as soon as you attach dynamic data. But you need to put something there to create the link in the first place.

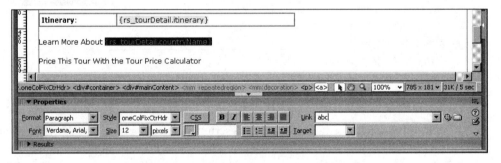

2 With the dynamic text still selected, click countryID in the Bindings panel, make sure that a.href is selected in the Bind To menu, and click Bind.

This step binds the value of countryID to the URL. Currently, the href attribute of the URL contains only a number. You need to go back and type in the main URL itself, as well as the variable name for the URL parameter.

3 With the link still selected, in the Link field of the Property inspector, position the insertion point at the very beginning, before the dynamic code, and enter *profiles. asp?countryID=*.

This is the link to the page itself, and after the server has resolved all the code, the countryID value will be appended just after the = sign. When a user clicks the link the browser will contact profiles.asp and pass it the value for the countryID of the chosen country. This takes care of the sending end, so now you need to prepare profiles.asp to read and use the passed value.

You will set profiles.asp up to "listen" for the incoming value and set the page to the appropriate row in your XML dataset. This requires a Spry library that was not included with Dreamweaver CS3. Not to worry, I've included the necessary file on your CD.

4 Move the file SpryURLUtils.js from the Chapter10/Start folder to the SpryAssets folder inside your newland site folder.

As the name may imply, this file contains a number of utilities that allow you to manage data that comes in on the URL. As mentioned earlier, Spry is a prerelease technology and new features are being produced all the time. This library was released after the Dreamweaver team had closed the door to additional features prior to the release of Dreamweaver CS3. Fortunately for us they have released it, because it is just what we need to make use of the value we have passed via the URL.

In order to take advantage of this functionality in the library you need to include the file in your document.

5 Open profiles.asp. Around line 7 or 8 you will see a series of <script> tags referencing the Spry libraries you are using. Make a blank line after the closing </script> tag for SpryAccordion.js. Insert a script from the Common Insert menu or click Insert > HTML > Script Objects > Script. For the Source field click the folder to browse to your SpryAssets folder. Choose SpryURLUtils.js and click OK twice.

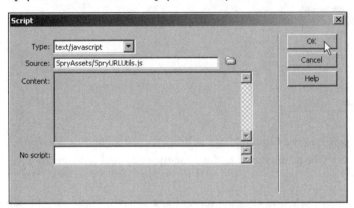

You can now make use of the full library of SpryURLUtils.js functions in profiles.asp. The function you need is has the cumbersome name of getLocationParamsAsObject(). The parenthesis indicates it is a function. If you can parse your way through its name you might guess that it takes the parameters on the URL string and turns them into an object of data that can you can use.

One of the benefits of using Spry is that it masks the complexity of the JavaScript necessary to produce the effects you see. Some functionality, like spry:sort and spry:repeat is really simplified. There will be times, however, when either Dreamweaver or Spry can't reduce the things you want to do to a button or wizard. At these times you have to take your gloves off and write a little code. You've already done that with ASP/ColdFusion/PHP and with SQL and now you'll do the same with Spry and JavaScript.

The code you'll write looks more technical than any other you will be exposed to in the book. Don't let it fool you: while it may look complicated, it is not.

6 Locate the line that starts var ds1 = new Spry.Data.XMLDataSet. It should be located on or around line 13. Press Enter/Return two times to clear some space immediately following that line, being careful to remain inside the <script> block and inside the <!-- //--> comment tags. Type the following code and explanatory comments. Bear in mind that JavaScript is case sensitive. I have included a file called chapter10TypingHelp.txt containing this code in the Chapter10/Start folder if you'd prefer to copy and paste.

```
    //Create a local variable and assign the URL parameters to it
var ourURLValues = Spry.Utils.getLocationParamsAsObject();
    //Set an observer so that when the data is loaded, we update the current row
    ➥to the url param value
ds1.addObserver({ onPostLoad: function(ds, type) {
    var matchingRow = ds1.findRowsWithColumnValues({"countryID":
    ➥ourURLValues.countryID }, true);
    // If we have a matching row, make it the current row for the data set.
    if (matchingRow)
        ds1.setCurrentRow(matchingRow.ds_RowID);
    }
});
```

```
5    <title>Newland Tours: Country Profiles</title>
6    <link href="css/main.css" rel="stylesheet" type="text/css" />
7    <script src="SpryAssets/xpath.js" type="text/javascript"></script>
8    <script src="SpryAssets/SpryData.js" type="text/javascript"></script>
9    <script src="SpryAssets/SpryAccordion.js" type="text/javascript"></script>
10   <script src="SpryAssets/SpryURLUtils.js" type="text/javascript"></script>
11   <script type="text/javascript">
12   <!--
13   var ds1 = new Spry.Data.XMLDataSet("countryDetailXML.asp", "countries/country");
14
15       //Create a local variable and assign the URL parameters to it
16   var ourURLValues = Spry.Utils.getLocationParamsAsObject();
17
18       //Set an observer so that when the data is loaded, we update the current row to the url param value
19   ds1.addObserver({ onPostLoad: function(ds, type) {
20       var matchingRow = ds1.findRowsWithColumnValues({"countryID": ourURLValues.countryID }, true);
21       // If we have a matching row, make it the current row for the data set.
22       if (matchingRow)
23           ds1.setCurrentRow(matchingRow.ds_RowID);
24       }
25   });
26
27   //-->
28   </script>
```

Let's examine the code a bit more closely. The first line creates a local variable named ourURLValues and assigns it the value returned by the function getLocationParamsAsObject(). This function, as described earlier, captures any values passed on the URL string. This means that ourURLValues now contains, well, our URL values! The next line of code creates an **observer** for our dataset ds1. An observer waits for a designated event to happen and then executes the code within its parentheses. In this case the event it is looking for is the moment the page is finished loading (onPostLoad). The code executed contains another aptly-named function, findRowsWithColumnValues(). This function is looking for a row with the column countryID that has the value on the URL string called countryID. The second argument the function takes is called firstMatchOnly. By passing it true you are telling the function to just find the first match of that value. The ID of the chosen row is then assigned to a variable called matchingRow. Finally, the if statement checks for a positive match. If there is one, it sets that row to be the row currently displayed in the dataset.

✱ **NOTE:** While the function names are specific, the variable names are arbitrary. I have tried to be descriptive, but you can name them whatever you like, bearing in mind that once you have created the variable you must maintain its spelling and case when you reference it.

7 Save your changes and upload them. Browse to tours_detail.asp. Click the Learn More About link for any country and it should take you to profiles.asp with the proper profile selected.

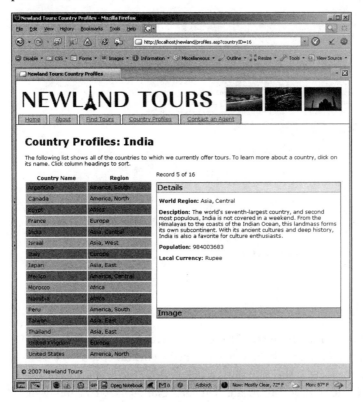

✱ **NOTE:** The country row in the table does not highlight the row of the selected country. The Spry action used to assign that highlighting was a mouse click function. The current release of Spry does not provide an easy way to replicate that functionality when selecting the row by other means.

Using Passed Data to Set a Form Value

By now you should be comfortable passing values for other pages to use. You've used those values to display on the page, calculate values and set the correct profile display in your Spry application. Sometimes the value you pass will be used only to make the user's life a little easier as they work their way through an application. In this section you will use the value passed on the link to the tour price calculator to set the drop-down menu on the calculator to the tour they chose on tours_detail.asp. This is a simple step that improves the user's experience on your site.

1 Return to tours_detail.asp in design view. In the final paragraph of the description, select the words Tour Price Calculator. Enter *abc* in the Property inspector's Link field to add a link. Using the same technique as before, use the Bindings panel to bind tourID to a.href in the Bind to drop-down menu.

Once again, abc is replaced with the tourID value. You still need to go back and add the rest of the URL.

2 Position the cursor at the beginning of the Property inspector's Link field, and type the following URL before the dynamic text: *tourprice.asp?tourID=*. Save and close tours_detail.asp.

Once you have completed this step, you have added the functionality that sends the tourID value to tourprice.asp. Unfortunately, nothing on that page is expecting that value, so nothing happens.

3 Open tourprice.asp, and open the Bindings panel. Add a new Request.Querystring (ASP) or URL (ColdFusion and PHP) variable called tourID.

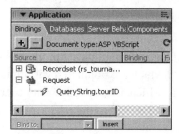

By creating this binding, you make the URL variable sent from tours_detail.asp available on this page. In the next step, you'll bind this information to the menu, so that the correct tour is highlighted automatically.

> **TIP:** In the ColdFusion and PHP server models, previously defined URL, form, and cookie variables tend to stick around for a long time, which can be useful or annoying, depending on whether you often reuse certain variables. For example, the mypet variable from the temporary widget that you built in Lesson 4 may still be listed in the Bindings panel. Old variables like these do no harm, but if the clutter starts annoying you, you might consider deleting them. To delete a binding, simply click and press the Delete key (or the Removing Binding [minus] button). If the binding you delete is the last or only binding in a category (e.g., cookie), then that whole category disappears. Deleting a binding from this panel does not affect any of the bindings you have dragged onto any page.

4 Click to select the drop-down menu in the form, beside Tour Name. In the Property inspector, click the Dynamic button.

You've already bound dynamic data to this menu. In fact, all of the items listed in the menu are dynamically added from a database. Your goal at this point isn't to add any more items—they're all present and accounted for—but rather to set the default to match the parameter sent in the URL.

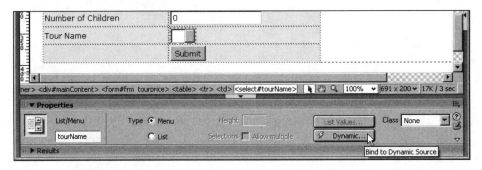

5 In the Dynamic List/Menu dialog, click the lightning bolt icon beside the Select Value Equal To field at the bottom to open the Dynamic Data dialog. In that dialog, select QueryString.tourID (ASP) or URL.tourID (ColdFusion and PHP), and click OK twice to save the settings.

As you probably recall from Lesson 8, the menu object has two main pieces of information that define it: its label (which humans can read and which are populated with tour names) and its values (which are sent with the form and which are populated with tour IDs). Here, you are setting the selected value (and hence label) to be equivalent to the value sent as a URL parameter.

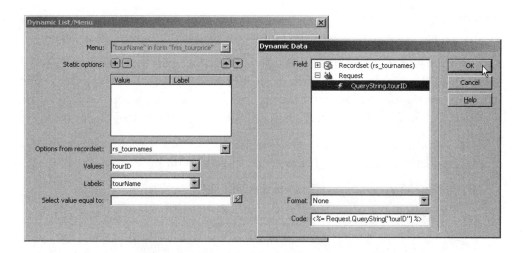

6 Save and upload tourprice.asp. Select tours_detail.asp in the Site panel, and press F12 to test it. Choose a random tour, and click both its country name link (which should take you to the correct profile) and its Tour Price Calculator link (which should load the proper tour name in the form menu).

Notice that the URL parameter is displayed at the bottom of the browser window, when you roll over the Tour Price Calculator link. The functionality is working pretty well, with one exception.

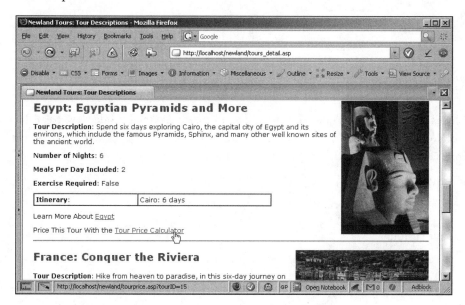

7 Still in the browser, click the Tour Price Calculator link from any tour. Remove one or both of the values for the Number of Adults or Number of Children, click Submit.

The form validation kicks in and reloads the page, displaying the error message. So far, so good. But notice that the Tour Name has reverted to Biking From Oxford to London. When the page was reloaded, the tourID URL parameter is no longer there, and so the menu fails to display the correct tour, and instead shows the first tour in the recordset.

Ideally, the form validation script on tourprice_processor.asp would send the tourID URL parameter back to tourprice.asp when it redirects the page.

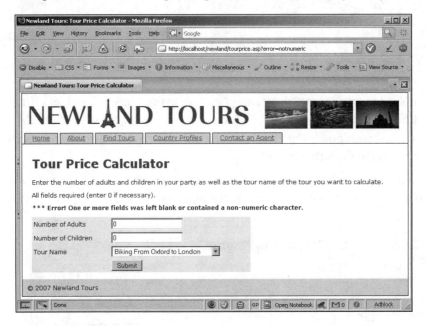

8 Close tourprice.asp, and open tourprice_processor.asp. Switch to code view. Near the top, look for the comment, Form validation script; redirects user back to tourprice.asp if form fields…. In that script, locate the following code:

In ASP:

```
Response.Redirect("tourprice.asp?error=notnumeric")
```

In ColdFusion:

```
<cflocation url="tourprice.cfm?error=notnumeric">
```

In PHP:

```
header("Location: tourprice.php?error=notnumeric"
```

This piece of code is where the form validation redirects back to tourprice.asp. As you can see, it is already appending a URL parameter. You might as well add another one, to complete the functionality.

9 Change the code you just identified so that it reads as follows:

In ASP:

```
Response.Redirect("tourprice.asp?error=notnumeric&tourID=" & Request.Form("tourName"))
```

In ColdFusion:

```
<cflocation url="tourprice.cfm?error=notnumeric&tourID=#form.tourName#">
```

In PHP:

```
header("Location: tourprice.php?error=notnumeric&tourID=".$_POST['tourName']);
```

You can probably already guess what the added code does. It appends a URL variable called tourID to the page when it is redirected. The value of this tourID variable is the value of form.tourName, which is the active tour when the Submit button was pressed. As you know, since you just programmed it in steps 6 to 8 above, tourprice.asp selects the correct tour in the menu based on a URL variable called tourID.

10 Save, upload, and test the files all over again.

This time, the whole transaction should work. You seamlessly transfer from one application to another, and the page responds appropriately, thanks to some simple data transfer and preparation.

What You Have Learned

In this lesson, you have:

- Learned the syntax for, and created SQL joins (pages 297–303)
- Laid out the tour descriptions, mixing static HTML and dynamic data (pages 303–308)
- Added images dynamically, and generated the contents of the alt attributes dynamically (pages 309–312)
- Applied the Repeat Region server behavior to enable display of multiple descriptions simultaneously (pages 312–314)
- Deployed the Recordset Navigation Bar server object (pages 314–317)
- Integrated three different applications intelligently by sending and receiving data (pages 317–327)

What You Will Learn

In this lesson, you will:

- Build a dynamic search interface that lets users search and filter data in three different ways

- Hand-code several SQL queries using joins, dynamically filtered data, and subqueries

- Show or hide the Recordset Navigation Bar, based on need

- Apply basic application security

- Temporarily disable code using comments for testing and debugging

- Use built-in functions to check for the presence of URL and form variables

- Use nested if...else blocks to create a sophisticated flow control structure

Approximate Time

This lesson takes approximately 150 minutes to complete.

Lesson Files

Starting Files:

Lesson11/Start/newland/tours.asp
Lesson11/Start/newland/tours_detail.asp
Lesson11/Start/newland/index.asp

Completed Files:

Lesson11/Complete/newland/tours.asp
Lesson11/Complete/newland/tours_detail.asp
Lesson11/Complete/newland/index.asp

Building Search Interfaces

It's time to complete the tour search application you began in Lesson 10. There, you built tours_detail.asp, which displays all of the tours in an unfiltered format. In this lesson, you will build a search page that enables users to search tours in three different ways: show all, show by world region, and show by country.

The challenge is to create three independent means of searching tours, all while showing the results on the same page (tours_detail.asp). The search page (tours.asp) will contain three ways of accessing tours_detail.asp. One way is a simple URL with no URL parameters, which will show tours_detail.asp unfiltered (that is, the way it currently exists). The second way will use a URL that has additional URL variables. And the third will access the page by submitting a form, which passes form variables. Both URL and form variables will be used to filter the recordset dynamically.

```
10
11   If IsEmpty(Request.Form("tourCountry")) Then
12       If IsEmpty(Request.QueryString("regionID")) Then
13           rs_tourDetail_cmd.CommandText = "SELECT tourID, tourName, countryName, countryID, tbl_tours.description, it:
14       Else
15           rs_tourDetail_cmd.CommandText = "SELECT tourID, tourName, countryName, countryID, tbl_tours.description, it:
16       End If
17   Else
18       rs_tourDetail_cmd.CommandText = "SELECT tourID, tourName, countryName, countryID, tbl_tours.description, itiner(
19   End If
20
```

In this lesson you will go behind the GUI once again and work extensively with code, especially SQL code.

To get these three different ways of getting tours_detail.asp to work, you need to set up a script in tours_detail.asp that reacts differently depending on whether it is accessed with no data (the first way), accessed with URL parameters (the second way), or accessed with form variables (the third way). The script will know how to filter the query that displays the tour description(s) based on the presence or absence of URL and form variables.

This may sound confusing at this early stage, but you have done most of the tasks involved in this lesson before—just never all of them together. But it's the ability to creatively combine the different techniques you learn, as well as the ability to tweak code by hand when necessary, that defines competence in ASP, ColdFusion, or PHP. In this lesson you will send and receive URL and form variables, hand-code SQL, write a nested **if...else** block to determine which of three SQL queries to run, use comments, and use **IsEmpty()** (ASP), **IsDefined()** (ColdFusion), or **isset()** (PHP) to determine the presence of variables.

Preparing the Search Page and Creating the Search All Link

In this task, you'll begin preparing the search page by removing now-obsolete content from the tours page. As it stands, tours.asp contains static listings of many of the tours. Now that you have built a dynamic listing of the tours (tours_detail.asp), this content is no longer needed on tours.asp. However, the navigation bars throughout the site point to tours.asp under the Find Tours link, so this page is perfect for containing the search interface.

The first activity, not surprisingly, is to delete all of the static tour listings. Next, you'll mock up the overall page layout. Finally, you'll create the first of three search interfaces, though in this case, "search interface" is an overstatement: It is a simple hyperlink to tours_detail.asp that causes the page to display all tours.

1 Open tours.asp, and change the Choose a Tour heading to *Find Tour*. Select everything after the heading through the end of the last itinerary at bottom of the page, and press Delete. Be careful not to select any of the footer. Enter the following text as body text beneath the new Find Tour page title.

Use this page to find the tour of your dreams. Once you've made a selection, check out the Tour Price Calculator.

Newland Tours offers many tours to different parts of the world. To find a tour to your desired destination, use the table below to browse by world region, by country, or view them all.

Though the page looks quite different at the end of this step, you haven't done much but replace obsolete static HTML with updated static HTML.

2 Link the text Tour Price Calculator to tourprice.asp.

Since no tour is specified, you can't send any URL parameters. But the tour price calculator application will still work; it just won't have a particular tour specified as the default in the form's drop-down menu when the page loads.

3 Create a new line beneath the second body text paragraph, and insert a table with three rows, two columns, width of 95 percent, border thickness of 1, cell padding of 3, and cell spacing of 0.

This table contains three rows, one for each kind of search. The left column will eventually contain a description of each search type, while the right column will enable the search itself.

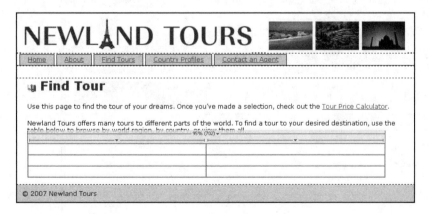

4 In order from top to bottom, type the following into the three cells in the first column: *By World Region*, *By Country*, and *View All Tours*. Drag the column divider to the left, so that the right column is wider than the left.

Once again, before you add dynamic content to a page, most often you'll build static content. Then you drop dynamic content into discrete locations within the page.

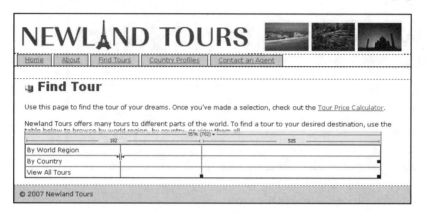

5 Drag to select View All in the View All Tours cell, and link the page to tours_detail.asp.

Clicking this link brings up the default version of tours_detail.asp—the version you completed in Lesson 11.

6 Save, upload, and test the file in a browser.

When you click the View All link, you'll be taken to tours_detail.asp, which should function as before. The important thing to remember for later is that when users click this link, no additional variables are sent as URL or form variables.

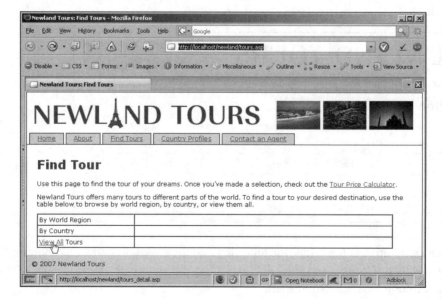

Searching by Region: Building the Interfaces

You are ready to create the first of the remaining two search options; searching by world region. When you are finished, you will have eight regions listed, each one linking to tours_detail.asp with a unique querystring appended containing a unique region ID. Back on tours_detail.asp, the SQL query that returns the tour descriptions will be filtered so that only the tours with that regionID will be displayed. Once you are finished, you will repeat the whole process in index.asp, to allow users to jump straight to tours in their favorite regions from the homepage. When you go to repeat the process in index.asp, I will encourage you to try to do so from memory, so as you follow the steps in tours.asp, try to internalize them.

1 Create a new recordset on tours.asp with the following settings:

Name: *rs_worldregions*
Connection: conn_newland
Table: tbl_region
Columns: Selected (regionID, regionName)
Filter: None
Sort: regionName, Ascending

This recordset retrieves all of the region names and their unique IDs. The region names will be used to create the list of regions, while their respective IDs will be passed as URL parameters. You used a strategy similar to this with the country profiles.

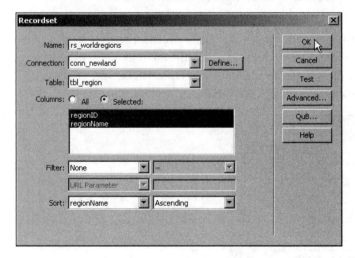

2 Position the insertion point in the empty cell to the right of By World Region. Use the Bindings panel to insert regionName into the cell.

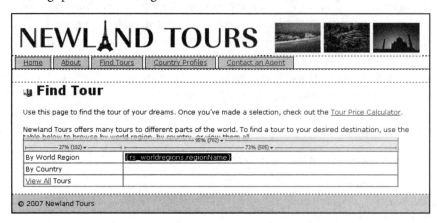

If you were to test this page now, the first region name (Africa) would be output onto the page. The rest would not, because you have not designated this output as a Repeat Region. Before you do that, however, you'll need to add the hyperlink to the dynamic text.

3 Click to select the dynamic text (in Dreamweaver pseudocode, you should see {rs_worldregions.regionName}). Click the Browse to File folder icon beside the Link field in the Property inspector, to open the Select File dialog. Click once to select tours_detail.asp.

In this step, you are linking to tours_detail.asp, using Dreamweaver's browse-to-link capability. Of course, it would be even easier to drag the Point to File to tours_detail.asp. But by browsing to the file, you get an added feature: Dreamweaver makes it easy to create a link that appends querystring/URL variables.

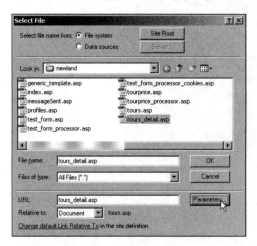

4 Still in the Select File dialog, click the Parameters button in the lower-right corner. In the Parameters dialog, type *regionID* as the name.

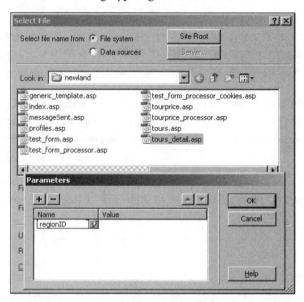

In this step, you are creating the regionID variable. At this point, Dreamweaver has enough information to generate the following code: <a href="tours_detail.asp? regionID=">. Of course, that's not enough. The regionID variable has to equal something, in this case, the current value of regionID.

5 Click the lightning icon in the Value category. Select regionID from the list and click OK to return to the Parameters dialog. Click OK two more times to return to the document.

In this step, you specify the value for the regionID querystring/URL variable.

If you look in the Property inspector's Link field at this point, you'll see tours_detail. asp?regionID=<%=(rs_worldregions.Fields.Item("regionID").Value)%> or an equivalent line in ColdFusion or PHP.

6 Click to select the dynamic code block, switch to split view. Look for the highlighted code. Select all of the code starting with <a href="tours_detail.asp?regionID= through the closing </a> tag. In the Server Behaviors panel, add a Repeat Region behavior, showing all records at once.

The Repeat Region behavior creates a loop that outputs each of the records retrieved by the query. There are eight regions in tbl_region, so each of them will be displayed now, and not just the first.

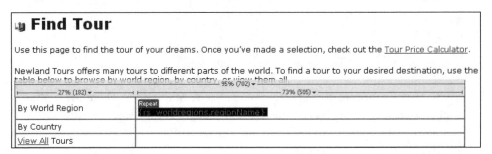

7 With the dynamic block selected, switch to split view if necessary. Look just after the highlighted code for the closing </a> tag. Immediately after that, enter a line break <br /> tag.

This is a repeat of a problem you dealt with in an earlier lesson: without this line break, all of the regions will be output on a single line. A <br /> tag, placed inside the loop, is sufficient to format it correctly.

```
55  s.EOF))
56
57  ions.Fields.Item("regionID").Value)%>"><%=(rs_worldregions.Fields.Item("regionName").Value)%></a><br />
58
59
```

Now that the line break is in place, the records will appear in a format that looks more menu-like.

8 Save, upload, and test the file in the browser.

You should see all eight regions displayed on the page. If you click any of the links, you should be taken to tours_detail.asp, which, aside from the new URL parameter, looks and acts like it did before.

The desired filtering hasn't taken place, because you haven't changed the query on that page, which currently is written to retrieve all of the tours.

9 Repeat steps 1 through 7 to create a dynamic menu on the index page, replacing the current list of regions, taking into account the notes and variations below.

Try to do this from memory, only referring to the steps if you get stuck. This is a good test to see how well you have absorbed this knowledge. Some points to remember:

- Don't forget to create a new recordset on the page, and name it rs_worldregions. A page can have multiple recordsets, as long as they have different names.

- When you add the Repeat Region behavior, make sure you specify the correct recordset (rs_worldregions) in the Repeat Region dialog; the wrong recordset will probably show up as the default. Specifying the wrong recordset in the Repeat Region dialog will cause an error message when you test the file in a browser.

- In addition to adding a <br /> tag inside the output loop just after the closing </a> tag, also insert two nonbreaking spaces (type   in code view to add each space) before the opening <a> tag, so that the list of regions is slightly indented.

- As you work on this step, the formatting of the navigation bar may look awful in Dreamweaver, because it can't fit all of its pseudocode and the Repeat Region box in the allotted design. This will go away of its own accord in a browser, so just ignore it!

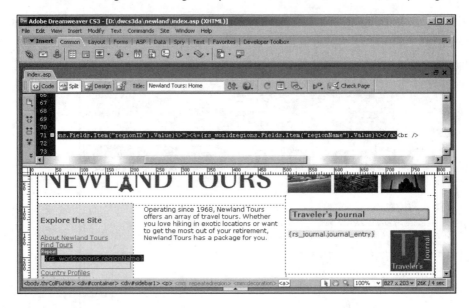

When you are finished, save, upload, and test the page in your browser, clicking a sampling of links to ensure both that you are redirected to tours_detail.asp and that a different URL parameter is appended to the URL each time.

Revising the Query and Commenting Code for Testing and Debugging

The region links send URL variables to tours_detail.asp, but that page has nothing set up that is able to do anything with those variables. In this task, you will put that functionality in place. But there is a catch.

Usually, when you bind a URL variable to the page, an error message will be displayed if a user accesses the page and that URL variable is not present. But in this case, when the user clicks the View All link, no URL parameter is sent. Later, once you've added the form that enables users to choose a country from the list, users will have another way of accessing tours_detail.asp without using URL variables. Therefore, you must set up the page in a way that does not depend on the presence of URL variables.

When you create applications—even applications as simple as a search and results page pair—it is incumbent on you to prevent errors from occurring. Prevention often requires some strategic planning, so let's think this through before we continue building. The goal is to find a way to enable the page to return the proper results based on the type of data that is (or is not) available to it.

If data is available to the page (such as URL or form variables), then that data will be used only in one place: inside the SQL query as a filtering mechanism. Nowhere else on the page depends on that data. To prevent errors, you need to prevent code from running that depends on variables that don't exist. You already know that if…else structures are good at preventing or enabling certain blocks of code. Therefore, one solution to the problem is to embed multiple SQL statements in an if…else structure, with one query for each type of search. The if…else structure will ensure that only the correct query will be executed, based on the presence or absence of variables that you specify.

You'll write the if…else structure at the end of this lesson. But for now, you need to create the SQL statement that will run if a URL variable (regionID) has been sent to the page. That statement will be different from the existing SQL statement, which simply returns all records. You still need that original query, though, in case no URL parameters are sent. So you will copy the existing SQL statement and revise it to work with URL variables.

But that leads to another problem: Your code will have two queries with the same name, which would produce an error. You'll fix that later with an if…else structure. But how do you work around the problem while you build and debug the new query? You will temporarily disable the existing query. This disabling will prevent it from running, but the code will still be there on the page when you need it for later. To create this win-win situation, you designate the original query as a comment. As you know from before, ASP, ColdFusion, and PHP ignore comments, so the code will still be there, but it won't interfere with the testing of your page. This technique, as you've learned previously, is called commenting out code, and it is a critical strategy when developing sophisticated applications.

> ❯ **TIP:** One strategy that programmers use is to write code to solve one neatly defined problem at a time. In this case you could try to create the new query and the if...else structure simultaneously, but if something goes wrong, you may not know which section of code is the culprit. Focusing on one task at a time makes it easier to debug your code.

In this task, you'll duplicate the original query, comment it out, and revise and test the copy.

1 Open tours_detail.asp in code view. Locate the query near the top of the page.

For me, in ColdFusion, the query code begins within the first few lines. In ASP, it occurs a little later, around line 12 and for PHP it begins around line 42 (look for mysql_select_db()). The goal in this step is to disturb the ASP, ColdFusion, or PHP code as little as possible, while trying to isolate the SQL code (which begins SELECT * FROM tbl_tours).

2 Find your server model below and follow the specified step.

For ASP users:

Select the entire line that begins rs_tourDetail_cmd.CommandText =. Copy this line, and paste it on the next line, so that you have two identical copies. Position the insertion point just before the first of these two lines, and enter a single quote (') character, to comment out that line.

You have copied the original query and temporarily disabled it. You are ready to start revising and testing the new query.

```
 9   Set rs_tourDetail_cmd = Server.CreateObject ("ADODB.Command")
10   rs_tourDetail_cmd.ActiveConnection = MM_conn_newland_STRING
11   'rs_tourDetail_cmd.CommandText = "SELECT tourID, tourName, countryName, countryID,
12   rs_tourDetail_cmd.CommandText = "SELECT tourID, tourName, countryName, countryID, t
```

For ColdFusion users:

Find the SQL statement enclosed inside the <cfquery> tags. Select the whole SQL statement through the end of the ORDER BY clause, copy it, and paste it on the next line. Select the whole original SQL statement again and choose Insert > ColdFusion Objects > Comment. Dreamweaver applies ColdFusion-specific comments around the SQL statement.

You have copied the original query and temporarily disabled it. You are ready to start revising and testing the new query.

```
4   <cfquery name="rs_tourDetail" datasource="newland">
5   <!--- SELECT tourID, tourName, countryName, countryID, tbl_tours.description, itir
6   FROM tbl_tours INNER JOIN tbl_country ON tbl_country.countryID=tbl_tours.country
7   ORDER BY tbl_country.countryName --->
8   SELECT tourID, tourName, countryName, countryID, tbl_tours.description, itinerary,
9   FROM tbl_tours INNER JOIN tbl_country ON tbl_country.countryID=tbl_tours.country
10  ORDER BY tbl_country.countryName
11  </cfquery>
```

For PHP users:

Select the entire line that begins $query_rs_tourDetail = "SELECT. Copy this line, and paste it on the next line, so that you have two identical copies. Select the whole original SQL statement again and choose Insert > PHP Objects > Comment. Dreamweaver applies PHP-specific comments around the SQL statement.

You have copied the original query and temporarily disabled it. You are ready to start revising and testing the new query.

```
41  mysql_select_db($database_conn_newland, $conn_newland);
42  /*$query_rs_tourDetail = "SELECT tourID, tourName, countryName, countryID, tbl_tours.descriptic
43  $query_rs_tourDetail = "SELECT tourID, tourName, countryName, countryID, tbl_tours.description,
44  $query_limit_rs_tourDetail = sprintf("%s LIMIT %d, %d", $query_rs_tourDetail, $startRow_rs_tour
45  $rs_tourDetail = mysql_query($query_limit_rs_tourDetail, $conn_newland) or die(mysql_error());
46  $row_rs_tourDetail = mysql_fetch_assoc($rs_tourDetail);
```

3 Just before the ORDER BY clause near the end of the statement, insert the following code:

In ASP:

```
WHERE tbl_country.region=" & clng(Request.QueryString("regionID")) & "
```

In ColdFusion:

```
WHERE tbl_country.region = <cfqueryparam value="#url.regionid#"
➥cfsqltype="cf_sql_numeric">
```

In PHP:

```
WHERE tbl_country.region = ". GetSQLValueString($_GET['regionID'], "int") ."
```

```
9
10  /ID=tbl_tours.country ORDER BY tbl_country.countryName"
11  ID=tbl_tours.country WHERE tbl_country.region=" & CLng(Request.QueryString("regionID")) & " ORDER BY tbl_cou
12
```

Notice that there should be a space after the closing quotes (") in ASP and PHP, and the closing angle bracket (>) in ColdFusion. That is, the word ORDER should not be directly against either the quotes or the pound sign.

Application Security

Whenever you create a Web application that relies on variables being passed to a page to be used in SQL queries you open yourself up to security concerns. A practice known as "SQL injection" can be used to pass extra SQL code to your page on the URL string or through a form. This code can be used to expose more information from your database than you intend or to damage or destroy your database. Client-side validation of user input can reduce user frustration and ensure cleaner data from well-intended users, but it can easily be bypassed by users wishing to compromise your system. You should not rely on it to secure your database.

There are a number of steps you can take to mitigate the threat, commensurate with the sensitivity and criticality of the data. In Lesson 7 I touched on some of these steps when you started working with databases, but they bear repeating.

- When you begin to create production applications you or your server administrator will create a set of login or connection credentials for your applications to connect to the database. This involves setting up a user with rights to your database. You can restrict the rights of this user to SELECT, INSERT, UPDATE and DELETE. The user should not have the ability to CREATE, DROP or ALTER your database tables. Even if your code is compromised, this will limit the damage that can be done.

- When you write the code to process the form or URL variables you should ensure that your page is getting the kinds of values it expects. If you are expecting an integer to be passed into the application on the URL string, as in the current exercise (regionID), you can check to make sure that is what you are getting. In ASP the clng() function ensures the variable is an integer. In ColdFusion the cfsqltype attribute of <cfqueryparam> allows you to designate the data type of the expected value. In PHP Dreamweaver has written a function GetSQLValueString() for you that checks the value of the variable against the type passed in, in this case "int". Use of such functions or tags should be a routine part of your development.

- If you take these measures, invalid input will produce an error. Application debugging information is an invaluable tool for application developers, but it should never be activated on a production system because error messages themselves can give information that provides clues for compromising your system.. ASP, ColdFusion and PHP have ways to test for and handle error messages gracefully. The methods used in this exercise for checking the data type of the passed value each have a different response to an invalid value.

⟩ TIP: Remember, in ASP, the & character is used to concatenate, or connect, text strings. The . character in PHP serves the same purpose. Concatenation is necessary in both cases because you are mixing literal strings (the majority of the SQL statements) that ASP or PHP should pass on without evaluating, and special ASP or PHP code that ASP/PHP should evaluate, such as ASP's Request.QueryString() and PHP's $_GET[] and the functions they are wrapped in. Strings are in quotes, while expressions are not. Combining the two requires you to concatenate—hence the use of & and . in these code blocks. ColdFusion doesn't have this problem, because it uses hash signs (#...#) or tags to mark up expressions that ColdFusion should evaluate.

So what does this addition to the query do? It creates another criterion, which further limits the original search. The original search retrieves all of the information needed to build all of the tour descriptions. This query does that, too, except it limits the set to those tours whose countries share the same regionID as the one passed as a URL parameter. For security reasons regionID is wrapped in a function or tag that ensures it is an integer. See the security sidebar for more detail.

Let's look at an example. Each tour has a field specifying its country. This country listing is, as you'll recall, a foreign key, which points to tbl_country. So both tours that take place in France have the countryID for France as one of their records. This shared field links the tours table to the country table, in this case, linking all tours in France to the record for the country France in tbl_country.

One of the fields that each country has is a foreign key for the region table. Thus, the record for France has a 3 in its region field, because 3 is the regionID for Europe, which contains France. Europe also contains the United Kingdom and Italy, so each of these countries' region fields also contains a 3. Japan's region value is 4, which is the regionID for East Asia. Therefore, all of the tours that list Japan as their country are related to a regionID of 4, and not of 1 or 3. Because Thailand is also in East Asia and has a regionID of 4, all of its tours are related to regionID 4.

To summarize, then, each regionID has a one-to-many relationship with countries. That is, each region may have several countries that belong to it. Likewise, each country has a one-to-many relationship with tours, which means that a single country can have multiple tours. However, no country can belong to multiple regions, and no tour can go to multiple countries. Therefore, you can write a query that retrieves tours where the tour's country belongs to a given region, and only those tours will be retrieved, and all others will be excluded.

That's what you've specified with this WHERE clause in the SQL statement. Test the file to make sure it works as expected.

4 Save, upload, and close tours_detail.asp. Select tours.asp in the Site panel, and press F12 to test that file.

You cannot test tours_detail.asp directly, because you would get an error. The SQL query that you just wrote needs the regionID URL variable to execute. If you test the page directly, that variable won't be available, which will break the SQL query and return an error.

5 Click any of the regions in the menu on the page.

After you click, you should see only tours from that region displayed on the page, so that part of the functionality works.

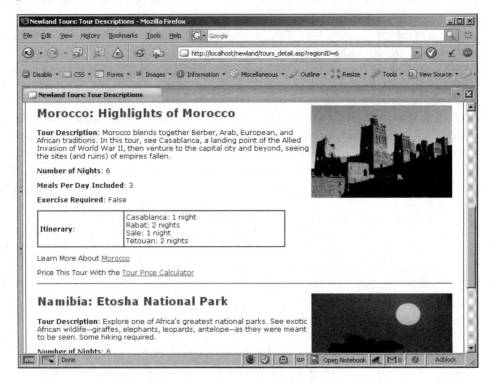

But there's some bad news as well: The Recordset Navigation Bar table is still visible. All of its cells are empty, because no region (at the moment) has more than five tours, so the page is always the first and last page. Remember, the Repeat Region server behavior on this page that displays the tours is limited to showing five records per page. It would be good to hide the Recordset Navigation Bar, when the page is the first and last page, that is, when five or fewer records are showing. But if that number ever exceeds five (say, for example, Newland adds tours to Germany, Norway, and Spain next year), the Recordset Navigation Bar needs to be made visible again.

Suppressing the Navigation Bar

As always, before you start coding, you should spell out exactly what it is you are trying to accomplish. You want to show the Recordset Navigation Bar, which is stored in a table, if the number of tours displayed on the page is greater than five (that is, six or more). Remember the page is set to show only five records at a time. However, if there are five or fewer, then the Recordset Navigation Bar can't be activated, and so you don't want it to appear.

As usual, the ASP, ColdFusion, and PHP code are different, but they all use the same concept. You can write conditional logic that will prevent the page from producing the navigation bar if there is no need for it.

1 Still in tours_detail.asp, using split view and the tag selector, select the table containing the Recordset Navigation Bar.

You have selected the entire table in both design and code views. You'll need to work in code view in the next step, but you have to isolate the table, because you'll need to add code above and below it to cause it to show conditionally. Here is a case where split view simplifies finding an element buried in code. You may want to add a few extra lines of white space above and below the table to help set it off.

2 In code view, just before the table begins, enter the opening half of the script that controls the visibility of the table based on the number of records.

In ASP:

```
<% If (MM_atTotal = false Or Not IsEmpty(Request.QueryString("offset"))) Then %>
```

In ColdFusion:

```
<cfif rs_tourDetail.recordcount gt 5>
```

In PHP:

```
<?php if ($totalPages_rs_tourDetail != 0) { ?>
```

When you create a recordset, not only is the data in the recordset itself stored in memory on the server, so too is some basic information about that data. One piece of information available to ASP, ColdFusion and PHP is the record count, or number of records retrieved by the query. In ASP and ColdFusion, the variable that holds the total number of records is RecordCount, accessed as follows: rs_myQuery.recordcount. PHP's equivalent is mysql_num_rows(), accessed as follows: mysql_num_rows($rs_myQuery). (In both examples, rs_myQuery is the fictional name of a recordset you hypothetically created.)

Any time you are dealing with looping through records or paging through records, the RecordCount variable (ASP and ColdFusion) or mysql_num_rows() (PHP) function can be a great help. In the immediate situation, there is a catch: Scripts generated by server behaviors that you've already applied are using these variables. If you use them again, your scripts may collide in unexpected ways. Thus, you worked around these problems in the ASP and PHP scripts by working with variables created by the server behaviors to which the original value of the recordcount are assigned.

Now let's look at the scripts themselves. In the ColdFusion version of the script, by far the most straightforward, you are telling the server that if the record count is greater than five (the number of records you can show onscreen at any given time), then execute whatever comes after this line. What comes after it is the table that contains the Recordset Navigation Bar. If the number of records is five or less (so that the if statement evaluates to false, then the script jumps ahead to the closing of the if structure (you haven't created the closing just yet) and continues. In other words, if the number of records is less than six, the table that contains the Recordet Navigation Bar does not appear. This flexible structure is convenient, because no matter what happens in the database—if new tours are added or removed—the Recordset Navigation Bar will be available if and only if it is needed.

The ASP version is written to make use of a pair of variables generated by the Recordset Navigation Bar object you inserted in the previous lesson. Understanding exactly how this line works presupposes some understanding of the VB code output by the Recordset Navigation Bar, and the nearly 300 lines of code that make up that script gets somewhat beyond the scope of what you are learning in this book. The condensed version is that the script detects when too many records were returned to fit on a page. If that's true, then the table holding the recordset navigation bar is displayed; otherwise, it is hidden.

```
352
353    <% If (MM_atTotal = false Or Not IsEmpty(Request.QueryString("offset"))) Then %>
354        <table width="50%" border="0" align="center" bgcolor="#EEEEEE">
355            <tr>
356                <td align="center"><% If MM_offset <> 0 Then %>
```

The PHP version of the script is a little more complex. An existing server behavior has created the $totalPages_rs_tourDetail variable, which the script uses to keep track of the total number of pages of records, a figure that is derived from the total number of records and the number of records displayed per page. This variable is also initialized to 0, which means (odd as it may seem) that if there is one page of records, its value is 0, and if there are three pages of records, then its value is 2. Thus, you know that if this value is not 0 (the operator != means "is not equal to"), then there are two or more pages, and the recordset navigation bar is needed. Conversely, if the value is 0, then the whole `if` block is skipped, and the recordset navigation bar is never displayed.

```
113
114         <?php if ($totalPages_rs_tourDetail != 0) { ?>
115         <table width="50%" border="0" align="center" bgcolor="#EEEEEE">
116           <tr>
117             <td align="center"><?php if ($pageNum_rs_tourDetail > 0) { // Show if not first page ?>
```

3 After the closing `</table>` tag of the table you highlighted in step 6, close the `if` block you opened in the preceding step.

In ASP:

```
<% End If %>
```

In ColdFusion:

```
</cfif>
```

In PHP:

```
<?php } ?>
```

This is the outer boundary of the `if` block. If the opening line evaluates to false, ASP, ColdFusion, or PHP looks for the closing of the block, so that it knows where to pick up again.

```
352
353    <% If (MM_atTotal = false Or Not IsEmpty(Request.QueryString("offset"))) Then %>
354        <table width="50%" border="0" align="center" bgcolor="#EEEEEE">
355          <tr>
356            <td align="center"><% If MM_offset <> 0 Then %>
357                <a href="<%=MM_moveFirst%>">First</a>
358            <% End If ' end MM_offset <> 0 %></td>
359            <td align="center"><% If MM_offset <> 0 Then %>
360                <a href="<%=MM_movePrev%>">Previous</a>
361                <% End If ' end MM_offset <> 0 %>
362            </td>
363            <td align="center"><% If Not MM_atTotal Then %>
364                <a href="<%=MM_moveNext%>">Next</a>
365                <% End If ' end Not MM_atTotal %>
366            </td>
367            <td align="center"><% If Not MM_atTotal Then %>
368                <a href="<%=MM_moveLast%>">Last</a>
369                <% End If ' end Not MM_atTotal %>
370            </td>
371          </tr>
372        </table>
373        <% End If %>
```

If you were to test the page at this point (remember to test through tours.asp or index. asp and click a region link), you will see that the Recordset Navigation Bar is suppressed.

If you want to be extra careful, you can comment out the second SQL statement and remove the comment from the first SQL statement and test the page unfiltered. You should see all of the tours listed, and the Recordset Navigation Bar should help you move back and forth through the tours. If you do test both ways, be sure to comment the first line of SQL back out and reactivate the second line of SQL.

ColdFusion and PHP users: Dreamweaver makes it easy to uncomment your code. Select your commented code line or code block and click the Remove Comment button in the sidebar.

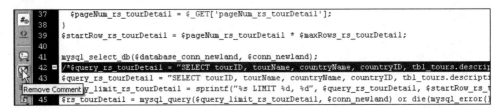

4 Save and close tours_detail.asp.

Searching by Country: Filtering by Form Variable

You have implemented the full functionality of the search by region. Implementing the search by country is similar, with a few variations. Rather than working with links and URL parameters, you will work with a form and form variables. As before, you'll create a new SQL statement to handle this filtering method.

1 Open tours.asp in design view, position the insertion point in the second row of the right-hand column, and insert a form with one list/menu element and a Submit button. Cancel out of the Accessibility Attributes dialogs.

You should at this point be comfortable mocking up form elements on the page.

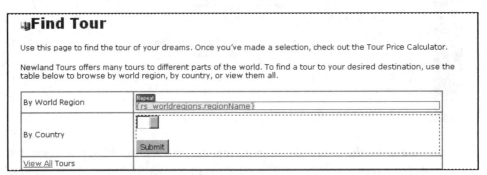

2 Select the `<form>` tag in the tag selector, and use the Property inspector to name the form *frm_bycountry*. Specify *tours_detail.asp* as the action. Specify POST as the method.

These settings apply to the form as a whole, and it is now ready to use. Of course, you still have to configure its elements, most notably, the menu element.

3 Use the Bindings panel to create a new recordset, using the following settings:

Name: *rs_countries*
Connection: conn_newland
Table: tbl_country
Columns: Selected, countryID, countryName
Filter: None
Sort: countryName, Ascending

If you press the Test button, you'll see that this recordset produces a list of all the countries in tbl_country in alphabetical order. You'll use this to build the drop-down menu in the form.

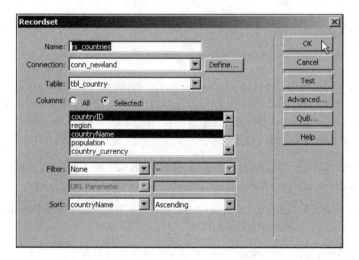

4 Click to select the menu, and in the Property inspector, name it *tourCountry*. Click the Dynamic button to open the Dynamic List/Menu dialog. Select rs_countries from the Options from recordset menu. Set the Values to countryID and Labels to countryName, and click OK.

You've done this before, so the consequence of these steps should not be a mystery. When the page is displayed in a browser, the country names will populate the menu in alphabetical order. When the user clicks Submit, tours_detail.asp will load (that was specified in the form's action attribute), and the name-value pair tourCountry=15 (if the user chose Argentina) will be sent as a form variable. While the user sees the name of the country in the list, the countryID is the value passed to tours_detail.asp. Unlike with the region links, form name-values pairs, like tourCountry, are not visible to the users, but they are available to the target page.

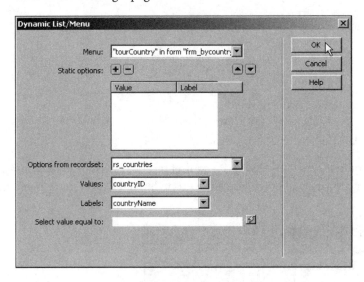

If you like, you can save and test the page in a browser, just to make sure that the menu is actually populated with country names. Don't press Submit, though, or you will either get an error or no records, because tours_detail.asp is expecting a URL variable called regionID, not a form variable called tourCountry.

5 Open tours_detail.asp in code view. Find the two queries (one should be commented out). Copy the second query and paste it on the next line. Comment out the second query.

Once again, you are making it possible to revise and test the new SQL statement, the one that will process the data submitted by the form.

```
8    Set rs_tourDetail_cmd = Server.CreateObject ("ADODB.Command")
9    rs_tourDetail_cmd.ActiveConnection = MM_conn_newland_STRING
10   'rs_tourDetail_cmd.CommandText = "SELECT tourID, tourName, countryName, countryID, tbl_tours.d
11   'rs_tourDetail_cmd.CommandText = "SELECT tourID, tourName, countryName, countryID, tbl_tours.d
12   rs_tourDetail_cmd.CommandText = "SELECT tourID, tourName, countryName, countryID, tbl_tours.de
13   rs_tourDetail_cmd.Prepared = true
```

6 Change only the WHERE clause in the statement so that it reads as follows:

In ASP:

```
WHERE tbl_country.countryID=" & clng(Request.Form("tourCountry")) & "
```

In ColdFusion:

```
WHERE tbl_country.countryID = <cfqueryparam value="#form.tourCountry#"
➥cfsqltype="cf_sql_numeric">
```

In PHP:

```
WHERE tbl_country. countryID= ". GetSQLValueString($_POST['tourCountry'], "int") ."
```

As before, make sure there is a space after the closing quotes (") in ASP and PHP, and the closing angle bracket (>) in ColdFusion and the next clause, which begins with ORDER BY.

For the most part, this version of the query should make sense to you. You are matching the country ID specified in the form with any tour that is associated with the same country name (though once again, you must go through the relationship between tbl_tours and tbl_country to access this ID).

✳ **NOTE:** If you had passed the countryName instead of countryID you would need to include single quotes (') to surround the dynamic content for ASP and PHP. (ColdFusion's <cfqueryparam> tag determines the need for quotes for you.) This is a SQL issue. Any time you are specifying a text string (as opposed to an expression or a number) it must be put in single quotes. Otherwise, the database attempts to interpret the text as if it's a function or some other special database command. By putting it in single quotes, you are telling the database not to interpret or evaluate it, but to match it with text stored in the database. Whenever possible pass numeric values, preferably primary or foreign keys, in order to avoid the complications presented by text strings.

```
 9
10   bl_tours.country ORDER BY tbl_country.countryName"
11   bl_tours.country WHERE tbl_country.region=" & CLng(Request.QueryString("regionID")) & " ORDER BY
12 ⊟ l_tours.country WHERE tbl_country.countryID=" & CLng(Request.Form("tourCountry")) & " ORDER BY th
13
```

7 Save and upload the file. Select tours.asp in the Site panel, and press F12 to test it. Select a country from the menu, and press Submit.

Most countries have only one tour, so you should see that tour listed when you choose a country. If you choose a country with multiple tours (France, Japan, United Kingdom, United States), you should see all of its tours.

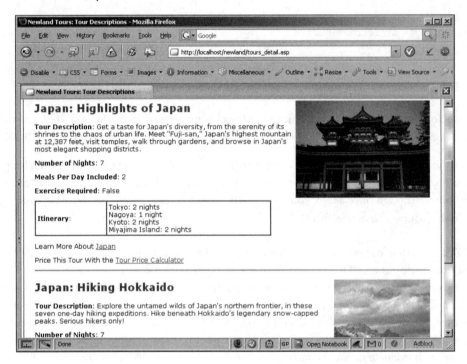

If you choose Taiwan, you'll see a blank page. The reason for this is that while Taiwan exists in tbl_country, it has no tours associated with it. In an ideal world, this discrepancy would never happen. However, it is possible that a tour to Taiwan is in the works and the person responsible for creating the country profile has already inserted this information into the database, but the tour description has not yet been finalized. In many databases, including Microsoft Access but not MySQL, you can account for this situation by retrieving only those countries that have tours associated with them in the query that populates the menu in tours.asp.

8 Open tours.asp. In the Bindings panel, double-click Recordset (rs_countries) to edit it. Click the Advanced button in the Recordset dialog. Between the FROM tbl_country and ORDER BY countryName ASC, enter the code that appears below.

```
WHERE EXISTS
(SELECT tourID FROM tbl_tours WHERE tbl_tours.country = tbl_country.countryID)
```

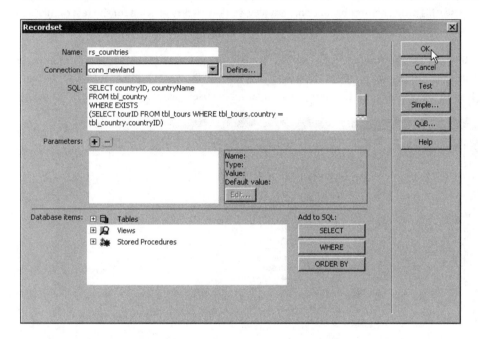

White space doesn't matter, so use line breaks as you like to make it more readable.

Let's talk about this SQL for a moment, because several things are going on. First, it uses a subquery, which is a query within a query, or more specifically here, a query used as a criterion within another query. The subquery is the part contained within the parentheses. That subquery looks for all the records from tbl_tours where there is a match between tbl_tours and tbl_country. All of the countries in the database, except for Taiwan, fall into this category.

The EXISTS keyword is used to check for the existence of rows in a subquery result. The actual values are not retrieved, because it is simply checking for their existence. Because it finds that 15 countries exist in both locations (tbl_tours and tbl_country), it includes them in the main SELECT statement. Since Taiwan doesn't exist in both places, it is excluded.

✱ **NOTE:** PHP Users: Although WHERE EXISTS and subqueries in general are a part of the ANSI standard for SQL, they are not supported in earlier versions of MySQL. If you enter this code in MySQL and get an error, return to the query and remove the WHERE EXISTS line and following subquery. The best solution in this case would be to have separate development and production databases and only upload data from development to production when it is ready. Of course, this project is entirely fictional anyway, so don't worry about it for the rest of this book—just don't follow the Taiwan link on tours.php.

Click the Test button to see the results. You should now see 15, rather than 16 countries listed. Taiwan is no longer in the group. If a tour to Taiwan is added to tbl_tours, then Taiwan will be listed in the menu once again, because it would meet the EXIST criterion.

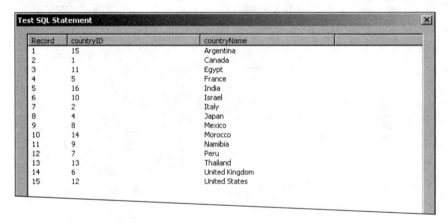

9 Save and close tours.asp.

Modifying SQL Statements According to Environmental Variables

You know from testing that each of the interfaces works—as long as two of the SQL statements are commented out. That setup is fine for testing, when you can open the document and apply the correct commenting based on your needs, but obviously it needs help before it can go into production. You need an automated way of switching the query based on the type of search. Your first task is to identify how tours_detail.asp will know which search type the user has chosen. Then, based on that, you need to swap in the proper SQL statement. An if…else construct is perfect for swapping the correct SQL statement in, but how does it know which search type the user submitted?

In lesson 6 you implemented server-side form validation. It checked to see whether a form variable called numadults or numchildren existed and was numeric. If it didn't exist, or it wasn't numeric, the user was redirected back to the form on the tour price page to fix the problem. I remind you of this because it provides a strategy for determining which search type the user selected: Check for the presence or absence of certain variables, as follows:

- If no form or URL variables are present, then the user clicked the View All Tours link.

- If a URL variable is present, then the user clicked one of the Region links.

- If a form variable is present, then the user selected a country from the form menu.

With this information, you can construct the logic for the script you need to write. The following pseudocode spells out the logic. Statements behind double slashes are the conclusions you can draw from certain information; however, these won't be explicitly written into the final script.

```
If no form variable exists //either the user clicked View All Tours or the user
clicked a region link
If no URL variables exist //the user clicked the View All Tours link
Run the first query
Else a URL variable does exist //the user clicked a region link
Run the second query
Else a form variable does exist //the user selected a country from the form menu
Run the third query
```

Looking at this pseudocode, you'll notice that it will require a pair of if…else structures, one nested inside the other. That's because one of the conditions—the absence of a form variable—can be true for two different reasons: because the user clicked the View All link and there are no URL variables, or because the user clicked a region link and there is a URL variable.

1 Open tours_detail.asp in code view. Find the three lines of SQL code, and remove the comments from all of them. Add a few line breaks above and below them, to isolate them in your code.

In this step, you are preparing to wrap the if…else script around these lines of SQL. You don't want to disturb the neighboring code. Once ASP or ColdFusion determines which SQL query to execute, it will be as if the other two never existed.

```
8   Set rs_tourDetail_cmd = Server.CreateObject ("ADODB.Command")
9   rs_tourDetail_cmd.ActiveConnection = MM_conn_newland_STRING
10
11
12  rs_tourDetail_cmd.CommandText = "SELECT tourID, tourName, countryName, countryID, tbl_tours.description, itinerary,
13  rs_tourDetail_cmd.CommandText = "SELECT tourID, tourName, countryName, countryID, tbl_tours.description, itinerary,
14  rs_tourDetail_cmd.CommandText = "SELECT tourID, tourName, countryName, countryID, tbl_tours.description, itinerary,
15
16
17  rs_tourDetail_cmd.Prepared = true
18
19  Set rs_tourDetail = rs_tourDetail_cmd.Execute
```

2 Just above the top line of SQL, write the line of code that tests for the existence of the form variable.

In ASP:

```
If IsEmpty(Request.Form("tourCountry")) Then
```

In ColdFusion:

```
<cfif Not IsDefined("form.tourCountry")>
```

In PHP:

```
if (!isset($_POST['tourCountry'])) {
```

Like all `if` statements, this can evaluate to true or false. If it's true (that is, the form variable does not exist), then the script still has to determine whether a URL variable exists. If it's false, then we know that the user has selected a country from the form, and we can execute the third query.

3 Select all three SQL statements and indent them at once, using the Tab key. Create a new line above the third SQL statement, and enter the script that will execute that line of code.

In ASP:

```
Else
```

In ColdFusion:

```
<cfelse>
```

In PHP:

```
} else {
```

When an `if` statement evaluates to false, the interpreter looks for any `else if` or `else` statements. If it sees them, it executes them. By adding this code here, you ensure that if the form variable is present, then the SQL statement that filters with that variable is run.

4 After the third line of SQL, close the `if...else` block.

In ASP:

```
End If
```

In ColdFusion:

```
</cfif>
```

In PHP:

```
}
```

```
8   Set rs_tourDetail_cmd = Server.CreateObject ("ADODB.Command")
9   rs_tourDetail_cmd.ActiveConnection = MM_conn_newland_STRING
10
11  If IsEmpty(Request.Form("tourCountry")) Then
12  rs_tourDetail_cmd.CommandText = "SELECT tourID, tourName, countryName, countryID, tbl_tours.description, itinerary, numNights,
13  rs_tourDetail_cmd.CommandText = "SELECT tourID, tourName, countryName, countryID, tbl_tours.description, itinerary, numNights,
14  Else
15  rs_tourDetail_cmd.CommandText = "SELECT tourID, tourName, countryName, countryID, tbl_tours.description, itinerary, numNights,
16  End If
17
18  rs_tourDetail_cmd.Prepared = true
```

You are halfway there. In fact, if you uploaded this page now and accessed it by selecting a country and clicking Submit in the form on tours.asp, it would work as expected. But if you tried to access the page any other way, you would get an error, because it would try to execute both of the other two queries at the same time.

5 Indent the top two lines of SQL one more time. Above the first line of SQL, enter an `if` statement that checks for the presence of the URL variable.

In ASP:

```
If IsEmpty(Request.QueryString("regionID")) Then
```

In ColdFusion:

```
<cfif Not IsDefined("url.regionid")>
```

In PHP:

```
if (!isset($_GET['regionID'])) {
```

If this, too, evaluates to true, then neither the form nor URL variable is present, and the broadest SQL query—the first one—should run. That query is directly below this line, so if it is indeed true, then that query will run.

If it is false, then the URL variable is present, and the second SQL query should run.

6 In a blank line between the top two queries, enter the code necessary to activate the second query.

In ASP:

```
Else
```

In ColdFusion:

```
<cfelse>
```

In PHP:

```
} else {
```

Again, the only way this code can be executed is if the form variable is not present, but the URL variable is.

7 In the line after the second SQL statement, enter a new line to close the nested if block.

In ASP:

```
End If
```

In ColdFusion:

```
</cfif>
```

In PHP:

```
}
```

These lines complete the nested if block.

```
10
11   If IsEmpty(Request.Form("tourCountry")) Then
12       If IsEmpty(Request.QueryString("regionID")) Then
13           rs_tourDetail_cmd.CommandText = "SELECT tourID, tourName, countryName, countryID, tbl_tours.description, it:
14       Else
15           rs_tourDetail_cmd.CommandText = "SELECT tourID, tourName, countryName, countryID, tbl_tours.description, it:
16       End If
17   Else
18       rs_tourDetail_cmd.CommandText = "SELECT tourID, tourName, countryName, countryID, tbl_tours.description, itiner:
19   End If
20
```

8 Save and upload this file. Test tours.asp in your browser, going back and forth trying every kind of search available.

The application should be pretty solid at this point. You should see all (and only) the tours that meet your search criteria. The Recordset Navigation Bar should show or hide, based on the number of records returned from your search. If you click a tour's country, you should see its profile. If you click a tour's Tour Price Calculator link, you should go to that application, and the tour should be preselected in the menu. In short, your users should now have a pretty slick interface through which to learn more about Newland Tours offerings.

What You Have Learned

In this lesson, you have:

- Prepared tours.asp so that it can accommodate three different kinds of search (pages 330–332)

- Built a dynamic menu that sends data to tours_detail.asp using dynamically generated URL variables (pages 333–338)

- Replicated that dynamic menu on another page (pages 339–344)

- Used code commenting as a strategy for testing and debugging isolated pieces of code (pages 340–341)

- Learned how to secure applications against SQL injection attack (page 342)

- Displayed or hid the Recordset Navigation Bar based on the number of records returned in a query (pages 345–348)

- Written an SQL query that filters data joined into two tables based on the value of a URL variable, and another that filters using a form variable (pages 348–352)

- Written an SQL query that uses the EXISTS keyword and a subquery (pages 353–354)

- Dynamically switched SQL queries based on the presence or absence of environmental variables using nested if…else structures in conjunction with IsEmpty() (ASP), IsDefined() (ColdFusion), and isset() (PHP) (pages 354–358)

What You Will Learn

In this lesson, you will:

- Learn about Web applications as entities distinguishable from pages
- Create a registration page
- Create a log-in page
- Make the log-in page intercept users who are trying to access a restricted page
- Ensure that after users log in, they are redirected to the page they tried to access

Approximate Time

This lesson takes approximately 90 minutes to complete.

Lesson Files

Starting Files:

Lesson12/Start/newland/generic_template.asp
Lesson12/Start/newland/index.asp
Lesson12/Start/newland/profiles.asp
Lesson12/Start/newland/tours_detail.asp
Lesson12/Start/newland/tourprice.asp
Lesson12/Start/newland/tourprice_ processor.asp
Lesson12/Start/newland/tours.asp

Completed Files:

Lesson12/Complete/newland/index.asp
Lesson12/Complete/newland/login.asp
Lesson12/Complete/newland/login_failed.asp
Lesson12/Complete/newland/profiles.asp
Lesson12/Complete/newland/register.asp
Lesson12/Complete/newland/registration_ failed.asp
Lesson12/Complete/newland/tours_detail.asp
Lesson12/Complete/newland/tourprice.asp
Lesson12/Complete/newland/tourprice_ processor.asp
Lesson12/Complete/newland/tours.asp
Lesson12/Complete/newland/Application.cfc (ColdFusion only)

LESSON 12

Authenticating Users

Implementing a framework that allows users to register (and log in) is one of the most common tasks for Web developers. Pages in the site are divided into those that are publicly accessible and those that require users to log in. A set of registration and log-in pages allows users to get through the barriers and access the pages requiring authentication. Creating a user authentication framework is the centerpiece of this lesson. Thanks to a series of Dreamweaver server behaviors, creating an authentication framework is much easier than you might think.

In this lesson, you'll create a complete registration and log-in system, taking into account both when things go right and when they go awry.

You might be wondering why Newland Tours would even have user authentication. Newland distinguishes three groups of users:

- Visitors who first arrive at the site and are determining whether they are interested in Newland Tours

- Visitors who are serious about travel and want to learn specific information about certain tours

- Newland Tours employees who are authorized to maintain site content

The first group can access the home, about, and contact areas of the site. To access the tour descriptions, country profiles, or tour price calculator, users first need to register to access the site. The registration is free, and Newland Tours only uses the information for marketing and promotional reasons—learning more about the users, and so on. The third group of users has access to the content-management system features of the site. This system, which you'll build later in the book, will enable Newland Tours employees to fill out Web forms to publish new content to the site, without the need to code in HTML or transfer files via FTP.

User Authentication as a Web Application

As always, before we jump in and start using new server behaviors, it's important to understand at least conceptually how they work. You will be creating an authentication framework. Users can only access restricted pages once they've successfully logged in. To log in, a user supplies a username and password combination. ASP, ColdFusion, or PHP queries the database to see if any records contain both the username and the password together. If one does, the log-in is successful, and the user is flagged as having logged in (more on that in a moment). If there are no records with both the username and password, the log-in fails, and the user is redirected to a page indicating that log-in has failed.

Each restricted page has a script at the top that checks to verify that the user is logged in, and if so, processes and displays the page. If the user is not logged in, she or he is typically redirected to a page that enables log-in, and the restricted page never actually loads.

With one exception, you can probably understand how all this could happen in ASP, ColdFusion, or PHP. That exception is the notion of flagging a user as logged in and checking for that flag across multiple pages. Because of the nature of the HTTP protocol the server forgets the user in between every page. Consequently setting and checking for the existence of the logged-in flag is problematic. You've overcome the server's forgetfulness in previous lessons by sending URL (or querystring) and form variables between pages. But these solutions are temporary, requiring you to manually send data to every page that needs it. What's needed is something more persistent.

You already worked with one type of persistent variable: the cookie. As you'll recall, a cookie is a name-value pair stored on the user's hard drive and sent to the server when the user makes an HTTP request. Using this technique, you can simulate the effect of the server remembering a user across multiple pages, simply by having pages use and respond to cookie data.

In large part to facilitate applications that need to keep track of users and data over time, ASP, ColdFusion, and PHP have special built-in features that handle much of this work for you. These features include, among others, two variable scopes: application variables and session variables. Variable scopes are virtual containers which you can store information (variables) in.

- Application-scoped variable data: Application-scoped variable data includes any variable information that you want to set for the entire application, regardless of user. For example, if you want to specify a contact person on every page of the site, rather than hard-coding that person's name and email address onto every single page, you can define the name and address once as an application variable and bind that value to every instance of a contact address in the site. Then, if that person is replaced, you need only to change the name in one place, and the rest of the site is updated. Only ASP and ColdFusion explicitly have the application scope, though it can be simulated easily in PHP.

- Session-scoped variable data: Session variables contain information for a single user in a single session. If the user leaves the site or closes the browser, the session ends and the information is flushed from memory.

✱ NOTE: Different programming languages define scopes in different ways and therefore some languages have more scopes than others. While I do not cover other scopes in this book, you will find it beneficial to understand and use the various scopes available to you in the language of your choice.

Clearly, the session variable is perfect for handling the log-in flag. That is, once a user successfully logs in, a session variable is set indicating the successful log-in. Each page that restricts access needs merely to check for the presence of this session variable to determine whether to grant access to the page or redirect the user to a different page.

The critical concept here is persistence. Through these enhanced application features, ASP, ColdFusion, and PHP enable developers to create sites where data persists for a certain period of time, overcoming the intrinsic limitation of the stateless HTTP protocol. This persistence is crucial in many applications, not just user authentication. Imagine a Web shopping cart that forgot who you were between the pages where you entered your shipping address and credit card information! You could pay for merchandise that is then sent to someone else.

For the data to be persistent, it must be stored somewhere. Where it is stored depends on the scope of the variable. Application-scoped variables are stored on the server, typically residing in memory. For this reason, you should keep your application-scoped variables to a minimum.

Session variables, in contrast, are typically stored as cookies on the user's computer and matched to temporary session variables stored on the server. The storage of data in two locations and its subsequent matching is usually invisible to the developer; that is, while you may set and retrieve session variables, for example, you won't be both setting and retrieving server and cookie variables, because that happens behind the scenes.

To enable all of this functionality, ASP, ColdFusion, and (to a certain extent) PHP recognize the collection of pages that make up your site as a single entity, an application. Different pages are part of an application when they have access to the same session and application data. You can't see the whole application anywhere—it's not a tangible entity—but it's there. Web applications consist of sets of files that ASP, ColdFusion, or PHP manages as a group.

Both ASP and ColdFusion have a special page where you can put application-related data and scripts. ASP has global.asa, and ColdFusion has Application.cfc. Although these two files are different in many particulars, their roles are comparable. Both handle application-scoped variables and events, as well as session management. Any variable, script, or functionality you add to global.asa or Application.cfc is included in and available to every ASP or ColdFusion site within the same application. In most cases, global.asa or Application.cfc resides in the site's root directory and therefore the application's scope is the entire site.

PHP lacks a direct equivalent to global.asa and Application.cfc. However, their functionality is reasonably easy to simulate in PHP. For example, one of the most important uses of Application.cfc is that it enables sessions, session-scoped variables, and session management. The ColdFusion developer enables session management in Application.cfc, and ColdFusion essentially prefixes this file to every single page requested within the application. In other words, what makes ColdFusion session management work is that in the final analysis, after ColdFusion prefixes each file with the contents of Application.cfc, the session-enabling code is inserted into every page at the top. In PHP (4.1 and higher), you can insert the equivalent code, a method called session_start(), at the top of any page to enable sessions. Or, you can create an include file with this method, and include that file at the top of every page. Thus, even though PHP isn't exactly the same as ASP or ColdFusion, the similarities are far more fundamental than their differences.

From even this brief overview, you can understand why a session management framework is so important to authentication. It enables a single entry through a log-in page to provide access to multiple pages, without requiring the developer to manually create scripts that send the data from each page to the next.

Building the Registration Pages

Log-in presupposes a collection of valid usernames and passwords in the database. The best way to get those combinations into the database is to create a registration form that inserts them there. This is a departure from the database interaction you have been working with for the past several lessons. In those lessons, you retrieved data from the database and filtered and manipulated it for the user. Here, you are making it possible for the user to insert information into the database. Fortunately, Dreamweaver has a behavior that makes that insertion easy.

But merely inserting information is not enough. You also need to check to ensure that two people didn't use the same username. To prevent this problem, you'll use one of an entire suite of user authentication server behaviors: Check New Username. If it succeeds, the user is registered and redirected to the log-in page. If it fails, the user is redirected to a registration failed page.

1 Open generic_template.asp. Save it as *register.asp*. In the Toolbar, give it a title of *Newland Tours: Register*. Replace the placeholder heading with *Please Register to Use the Site*. Replace the placeholder text with *All fields required*.

Now the page has a basic identity.

2 Insert a form below the text you just entered. Use the Property inspector to name the form *frm_register* (leaving the action and method attributes alone for now). With the insertion point inside the form, insert a table with 10 rows, 2 columns, a width of 95%, a border thickness of 0, a cellpadding of 3, and a cellspacing of 0.

The table will be used to structure the elements in the form.

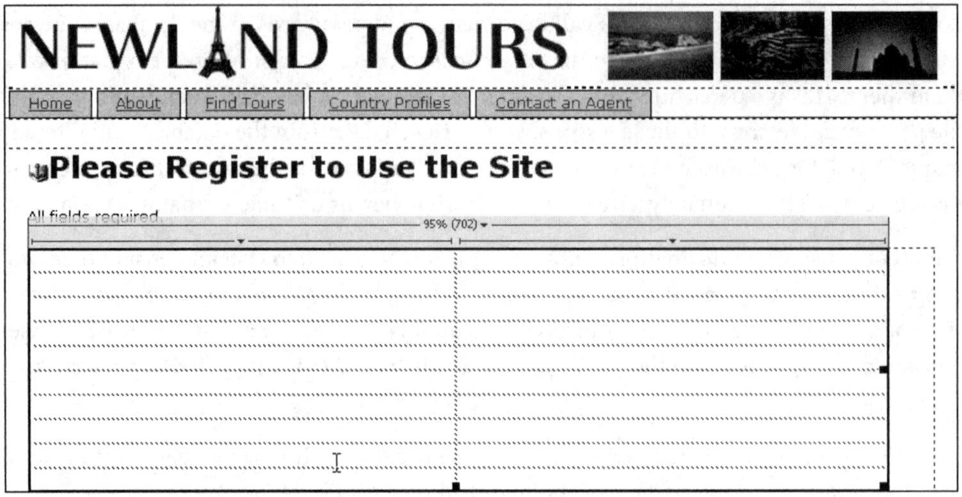

3 Insert text fields and a submit button as shown in the screenshot. Use the Input Tag Accessibility Attributes dialog to give IDs to the text fields as you create them. Alternatively you can use the Property inspector after the text field has been created. Name the fields as follows:

firstName
lastName
username
pwd
address1
city
state_province
zip_postal
country

Don't take any shortcuts in this step. You will be very sorry if you leave the text fields with their default names (textfield1, textfield2, etc.). You should always use descriptive names for every field, or it becomes nearly impossible to create the scripts that make use of the data from these fields. In addition, the names listed above correspond to the fields in the database where this data will go, which makes it much easier to add the server behavior that inserts the records.

Make sure the pwd text field is set to the Password type in the Property inspector. Use the Char width setting in the Property inspector to lengthen or shorten the text fields. For example, I set address1 to 60 characters wide, to make additional room in that field.

You can drag the column divider to the left, to make extra room for the right column, if needed.

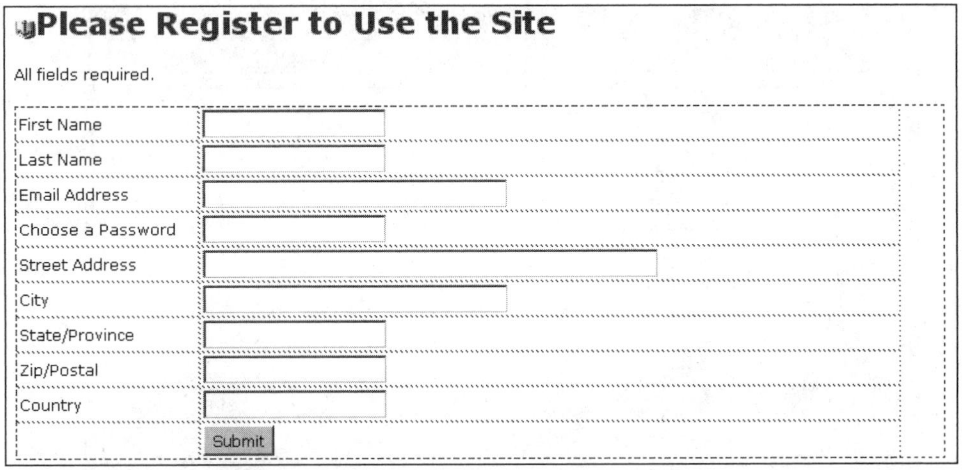

Please Register to Use the Site

All fields required.

First Name	
Last Name	
Email Address	
Choose a Password	
Street Address	
City	
State/Province	
Zip/Postal	
Country	
	Submit

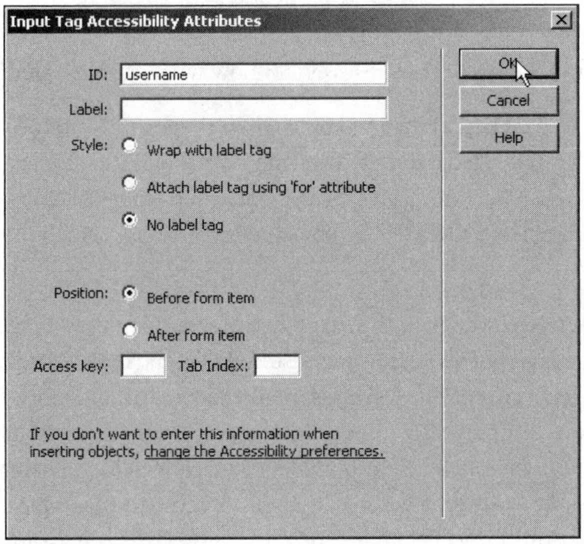

Input Tag Accessibility Attributes

ID: username

Label:

Style: ○ Wrap with label tag

 ○ Attach label tag using 'for' attribute

 ⊙ No label tag

Position: ⊙ Before form item

 ○ After form item

Access key: Tab Index:

OK

Cancel

Help

If you don't want to enter this information when inserting objects, change the Accessibility preferences.

4 Position the insertion point in the empty cell to the left of the Submit button. From the Forms tab of the Insert panel, insert a hidden field element. Name it *userGroup*, and type *visitor* as its value.

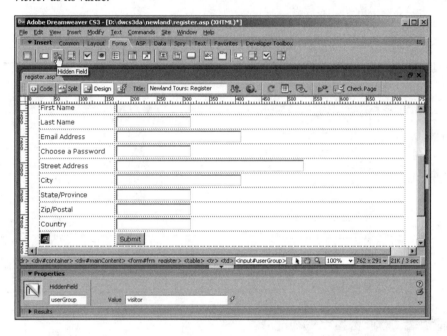

The purpose of this step is not immediately clear, unless you know what's going to follow.

Hidden fields are used in forms to pass predetermined data when the form is submitted. In this case, when the form is submitted, along with name value pairs such as firstName=Lyra and lastName=Bellacqua, the form will also pass userGroup=visitor. Unlike the firstName and lastName fields, the userGroup value is read-only, which means users won't be able to edit it.

You're probably wondering what userGroup is in the first place. Remember, the site will be set up to enable three different levels of visitors: nonregistered visitors, registered visitors, and Newland Tours employees. Two of these groups, registered guests and employees, will have different permissions. Employees will be able to access a whole set of admin pages that registered guests cannot. The catch is that both sets of users will log in using the same form. So the log-in script needs some way to distinguish between the different types of users. The way it does this is by checking which group they've been assigned to—a setting stored in their record in tbl_users of the database. But you obviously don't want users to be able to make this decision themselves—you need to ensure that everyone who registers with the public form is set up as a visitor.

To add employees to the admin group, you'll either need to build a second log-in page or existing employees will have to modify a new employee's record in the database. In the next lesson, you'll build a simple interface in the admin section of the site that enables employees to change a person's profile to be in the administrator group.

⊞ **NOTE:** Hidden fields are a convenience for passing read-only data and are appropriate for many development uses. However they should not be used for sensitive data because their value can be seen by viewing the page source in your browser. Furthermore hidden fields, like any other form data, can be spoofed by ill-intentioned users. A production application would likely only use such a form for collecting information, not for setting access levels. A better strategy might to be set "visitor" as the default userGroup at the database level for all new records. There are a number of possible approaches. As mentioned previously in this book, security should always be a concern when putting applications into production and further study on the topic and how your chosen language deals with it is strongly encouraged.

5 Click to select the Submit button, and in the Server Behaviors panel, click the Add Server Behavior (+) button to add an Insert Record behavior.

The Insert Record behavior matches data entered in the form to fields in the database, creating a new record in the database and populating it with the user-entered data.

This form will add a record to tbl_users, which you will later use in the log-in script to verify that the user is registered, as well as to determine which user group the user is a member of.

6 In the Insert Record dialog, select conn_newland as the Connection, tbl_users as the Table. In the After inserting, go to field, type *login.asp*. In the Get values from field, make sure frm_register is selected.

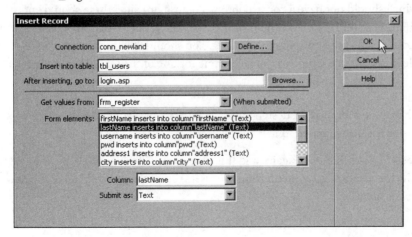

You are familiar enough with building queries that a lot of this dialog should already be comfortable (especially the Connection and Insert Into Table settings). Like the Recordset dialog, the Insert Record dialog builds a SQL query. But unlike the Recordset dialog, the query built here does not retrieve data, but rather inserts it.

✱ NOTE: ColdFusion and PHP users will notice that their version of the Insert Record dialog looks slightly different than the one shown here, for ASP. However, the differences are mostly cosmetic, and all variations are noted in the text, where appropriate.

Inserting data, as mentioned earlier, is a matching activity: One item of data from a form is matched to one field in the destination table. That matching is what the lower half of the dialog is all about. Each of the items should follow this syntax: (for ASP) item_x inserts into column "item_x" (Text) or (for ColdFusion and PHP) item_x Gets Value From 'FORM.item_x' as 'Text'. One instance of item_x is the field from the form (on the left in ASP, and on the right in ColdFusion and PHP). The other is the column name in the table (on the right in ASP, and on the left in ColdFusion/PHP). The Text part refers to the variable type (e.g., text, date, integer, etc.).

In your dialog, all of the items on the left should match the items on the right, and they must be the same type. That is, if the database is expecting a number, then ASP, ColdFusion or PHP must insert a number; otherwise the application server will display an error message. In this case, the form names and the database field names match, but they don't have to: you can name your form fields differently than your database table fields. However, if they have the same name, Dreamweaver does the matching for you. If their names differ, you'll have to manually match the form fields with their corresponding table fields.

If you have any fields that don't have a corresponding column (besides userID and address2, which should not have a corresponding column or value; these should appear on for ColdFusion and PHP), select them, and choose the proper Column or Value from the drop-down menu at the bottom of the dialog. You shouldn't have any stray fields, though, unless you entered a typo as the field name for one of the text fields in the form.

7 Click OK.

The Server behavior is applied. In design view, the form turns cyan, indicating that a Server behavior has been applied to it.

8 Click to select the Submit button again, and this time add a Check New Username server behavior, which appears in a submenu from the User Authentication section of the new Server Behavior menu.

This Server behavior ensures that the username entered in the form is unique.

9 In the Check New Username dialog, select username (or FORM.username, as ColdFusion is likely to display it) from the Username field drop-down menu, and type *registration_failed.asp* in the "If already exists, go to" field. Click OK.

Here, you are ensuring that the value entered in the username field doesn't already exist. Since you asked for the user's email address to use as their username, this shouldn't be a problem for legitimate users.

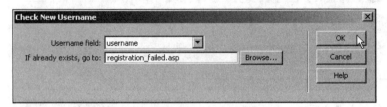

10 Back on the main page, select the Submit button once again, and from the Behaviors (not Server Behaviors) panel, add a Validate Form behavior. Make each of the fields required. In addition, make sure the username field will accept only Email Address.

Whenever you create a form, make sure you deploy some sort of form validation, whether it's a client-side JavaScript behavior such as the one used here, or a server-side script like the one you wrote earlier in the book.

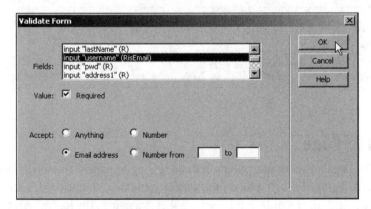

11 Save, upload, and close register.asp.

You don't need to test it now, since, whether you are successful or unsuccessful in your registration, you will be redirected to a page that doesn't yet exist.

12 Starting with generic_template.asp, create a new page called *registration_failed.asp*. Use the Toolbar to title it *Newland Tours: Registration Failed*. Make it look like the page shown in the screenshot. The link should point to register.asp. Save and close the page.

Users are redirected to this page if the Check New Username Server behavior detects that the username already exists.

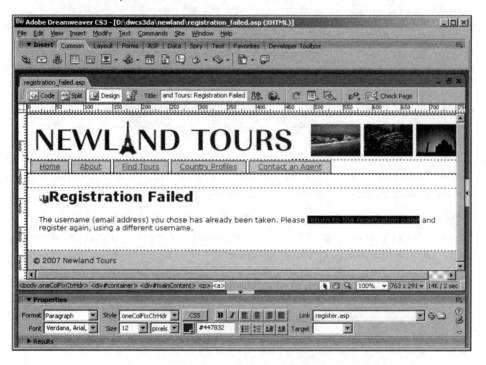

Building the Log-in Page

Now that your registration page is functioning, you can build the log-in page. Remember, the role of the log-in page is to obtain (through a form) the user's username and password. Then it will compare these values with the records in tbl_users. If there's a match, the log-in script sets a session variable indicating that the user is logged in. If there is no match, the user is redirected to a log-in failed page.

1 Starting with generic_template.asp, create a new file, login.asp. Title it *Newland Tours: Log In*. Type *Please Log In* as its heading.

Now you've created the basic page framework.

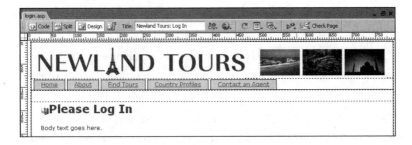

2 Replace the placeholder body text with a form. Call the form *frm_login*. Inside the form, insert a table with 3 rows, 2 columns, a width of 95%, a border of 0, a cellpadding of 3, and a cellspacing of 0.

Once again, the table inside the form is used to structure the form elements. Also, as before, you don't specify the action or method attributes of the form. These are both required, but they will be completed automatically for you when you add the Server behavior, so you can leave them alone for now.

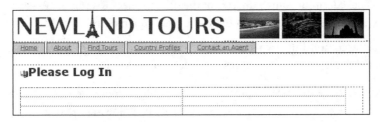

3 Insert the text labels, text fields, and Submit button shown in the screenshot. Name the text box beside Email Address *username*, and name the one beside Password, *pwd*. Make sure the pwd text field is set to the Password type in the Property inspector. In the Property inspector modify the Char width of the Email Address field to match the value you used for it in register.asp.

The form is built, but it doesn't do anything yet.

4 Click to select the Submit button, and use the Server Behaviors panel to add a User Authentication > Log In User behavior.

This behavior will do all the work of verifying that the user's credentials match a pair in the database; setting a session variable if the log-in was successful; and redirecting the user to an appropriate location, based on whether the log-in was successful.

5 In the top quarter of the Log In User dialog, verify that frm_login is the selected form, that username is set as the Username Field, and that pwd is set as the Password field. In the second quarter of the dialog, choose conn_newland as the Connection, tbl_users as the Table, username as the Username Column, and pwd as the Password Column.

With these settings, you are providing the parameters the script needs to compare the authentication entered into the log-in form with the list of registered users in the database.

6 In the third quarter of the Log In User dialog, enter *index.asp* for the successful log-in redirection, and *login_failed.asp* for the failed log-in redirection. Make sure that Go To Previous URL is checked. In the fourth quarter of the dialog, select Username, Password, and Access Level, and choose userGroup in the Get Level From menu. Click OK.

In this step, you are accomplishing two goals. First, you are specifying where the user should be redirected depending on the success or failure of the log-in.

The Go To Previous URL setting needs some explanation. There are two ways that users will access this log-in page. First, they can access it directly by following the Log In link on the homepage. But they'll also see this page if they try to access a page that requires log in, and they haven't logged in yet. That is, the log in page may intercept their progress in the site. Upon successful log in, users won't want to be redirected to the homepage— not when they clicked a link to access tours or country profiles. By checking this option, you add functionality to the script that ensures that once these users have logged in, they are redirected to the page they attempted to load before they logged in.

The second goal you are accomplishing is to create the separate user group functionality discussed earlier. This will enable you to distinguish between registered users who have logged in and employees who have logged in. Since these access levels are stored in the userGroup field of tbl_users, you specify that information in the Get Level From menu.

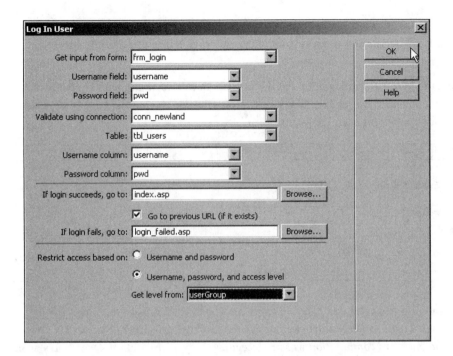

7 Click the Submit button, and add a Form Validation behavior that makes both fields required. Make sure the username field will accept only Email Address.

Just about every form needs some mechanism for validation.

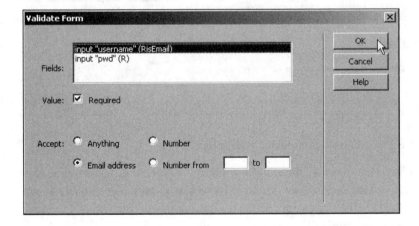

8 Beneath the form, in regular body text, enter the following: *If you don't already have an account, please register for a free account.* Link the word register to register.asp. Save, upload and close the page.

Because the log-in page may intercept the user's path to information, and because the user may not even have realized that registration is required, adding a simple explanation with a link is a helpful usability feature.

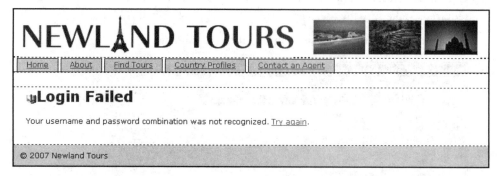

9 Starting with generic_template, create *login_failed.asp*. Title it *Newland Tours: Login Failed*. Type *Login Failed* as the heading. Type the following as the body text: *Your username and password combination was not recognized. Try again.* Link the words Try again to login.asp.

![NEWLAND TOURS — Home | About | Find Tours | Country Profiles | Contact an Agent. Login Failed. Your username and password combination was not recognized. Try again. © 2007 Newland Tours]

Static pages are passé, I know, but they have their uses.

ASP and PHP users can test the whole log-in application. Open register.asp, and create a profile. Then log in with your username and password. As always, try to break the application as well. Register the same name twice. Try logging in with the wrong password. Try typing your phone number instead of your email. And so on.

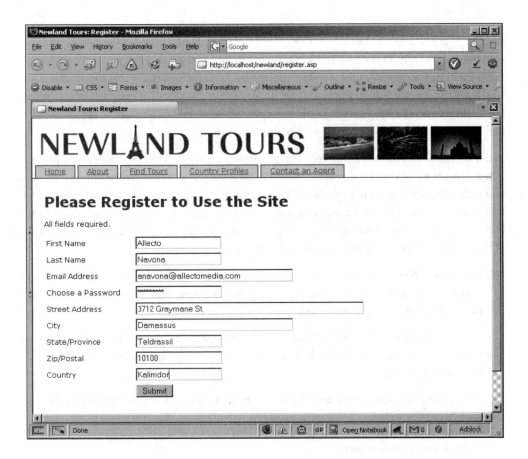

❋ NOTE: If ASP users get an error stating "Operation must use an updateable query" after submitting the registration form it could be because your Access database file is not writable by the built in IUSR_MACHINE, the Internet guest account that IIS uses to connect to Access. This can be corrected by granting that account the correct permissions.

ColdFusion users have a quick chore to do before they can test the application: They need to create the Application.cfc file that governs the Web application framework. ASP users don't have to worry about creating a global.asa file—ASP will handle session management just fine without it.

Creating Application.cfc (ColdFusion Only)

One of the functions of the Log In User server behavior is that it creates a session variable when the user successfully logs in. The problem is, the session scope is inactive by default, which means that the log-in page won't work. You'll have to activate session management in the ColdFusion Web Application Framework. Doing so is a simple matter of creating a new file (Application.cfc), and entering a single line of code.

You'll note that this file has a different file extension (.cfc) from normal ColdFusion pages (.cfm). This is a ColdFusion Component or CFC. CFCs serve as libraries or collections of custom code. Application.cfc is a special CFC that runs at the start of each .cfm in its directory. It is used to set variables and conditions for your site or application. It has a number of useful built in functions that allow you to globally manage error-handling and events related to some of the variable scopes. You will only scratch the surface of its uses.

1 Click File > New and create a new page of type ColdFusion Component. Dreamweaver creates a CFC skeleton with template code for writing functions. You will not be writing any functions, so delete all of the code in between the opening and closing `<cfcomponent>` tags.

Application.cfc is not a regular Web page, and so it does not have the usual HTML tags you would expect to see. All code in a CFC must be inside the opening and closing `<cfcomponent>` tags.

2 Create a blank line after the opening `<cfcomponent>` tag and type the following code:

```
<cfscript>
    this.name = "newlandTours";
    this.sessionManagement = true;
    this.setClientCookies = true;
    this.sessionTimeout = createTimeSpan(0,0,20,0);
</cfscript>
```

Code inside a `<cfscript>` block is written with a more traditional programming syntax. It is an alternative method for writing ColdFusion code and in most cases is completely equivalent. I use it here because it clearly lays out the values you are setting for your application.

This.name names your application and in doing so enables your application to use the Web application framework, including the session management. The other variables set here enable session management, enable the setting of cookies, and create a session timeout.

You'll note that rather than specifying a simple period of time in the sessionTimeout variable, there is a function, CreateTimeSpan(). This function takes four parameters, standing for days, hours, minutes, and seconds. Thus, the sessionTimeout is set for 20 minutes. In other words, if a user is inactive or leaves the site to browse on other pages for more than 20 minutes, all session variables associated with that user are flushed. In practical terms, it means the user would have to log in again.

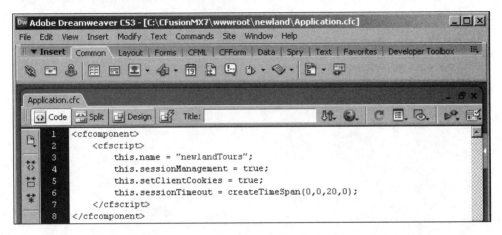

✱ NOTE: Application.cfc was introduced in ColdFusion version 6.0. Prior to that release you would have used Application.cfm to set up session management. Application.cfm can still be used, but it is not nearly as robust as Application.cfc.

3 Save, close, and upload Application.cfc.

At this point you can test the registration and log-in features you've added in this lesson. As mentioned earlier, try to break the application, by entering every variation you can think of.

Restricting Access to Pages

By now, you should have tested your registration and log-in pages, and they should work as expected. Still, until you implement page restriction features to the pages you want to block access to, your registration and log-in framework is not very useful. In this task, you will add the server behaviors that prevent users from accessing pages, unless they've first logged in.

1 Open profiles.asp.

This is one of the pages that users must log in to see.

2 Click anywhere on the page, and insert a Restrict Access to Page server behavior, found in the User Authentication submenu of the Server Behaviors menu. In the Restrict Based On group, choose Username, Password, and Access Level.

This dialog not only lets you restrict access to the page; it also lets you restrict access to a page based on a user's access level.

Of course, no such levels are defined in the Select Level(s) area, so you'll need to define some.

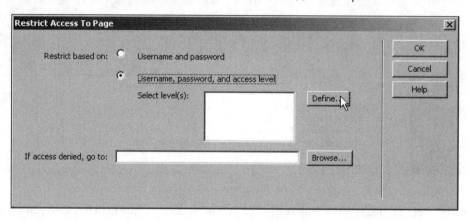

3 Click the Define button. In the Define Access Levels dialog, place the cursor in the Name field, type *visitor*, and press the + button. Repeat the process to add *admin*. Click OK.

Dreamweaver won't check to make sure these groups actually exist; it takes your word for it, so make sure you spell them correctly. These correspond to the available values in the userGroup field of tbl_users. Once it knows their names, Dreamweaver can grant access to pages to users in either or both groups, and deny access to users not in either.

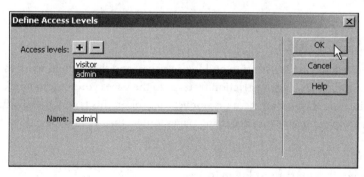

4 Back in the Restrict Access to Page dialog, Ctrl-click (Windows) or Command-click (Mac) to select both visitor and admin from the Select Level(s) area. In the If Access Denied, Go To field, enter *login.asp*. Click OK.

You've done two things in this step. You've granted access to the page to users in either the visitor or admin group. Had you wanted to grant access to this page to only one of those groups, you would have selected only the one group. Once you've created the admin section of the site, you'll use this dialog and let in only members of the admin group.

The other thing you've done is redirect the user to login.asp if access is denied. This is how that interception described earlier happens. A user tries to access a restricted page without logging in, and she or he sees the log-in dialog. Once log-in is achieved, the restricted page she or he was trying to access appears.

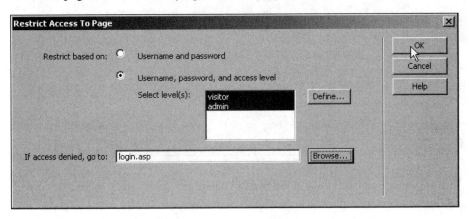

5 Repeat steps 1 through 4 for each of the following files: tourprice.asp, tourprice_processor.asp, tours.asp, and tours_detail.asp.

Each of these pages now requires authentication as well.

6 Save and upload all of the pages you have worked on in this lesson, and, starting from the homepage (index.asp), try accessing the tours and the country profiles.

The authentication framework is fully functional. If you try to access a protected page, the login screen should appear. If you've created a registration account, use it. Or you can use username: osiris@allectomedia.com and password: osiris to test. Once you've logged in, you should automatically be redirected to the page you first requested.

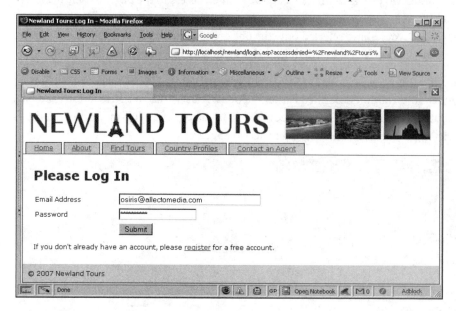

7 Open index.asp, and add links at the bottom of the left navigation bar, Register (Free!) and Log In, connecting to register.asp and login.asp respectively.

Since users will be intercepted if they attempt to enter restricted pages, and since you took the time to add a link from the log-in page to the registration page, users should find everything even without these links. Still, their presence here makes it that much easier for visitors and employees alike to use the site.

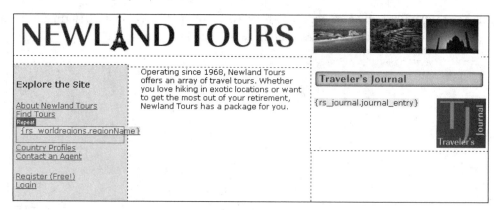

WHAT YOU HAVE LEARNED

In this lesson, you have:

- Learned about persistent data (pages 362–364)

- Created a registration page, using the Insert Record and the Check New Username server behaviors (pages 365–372)

- Built a log-in page, using the Log In User behavior (pages 372–377)

- Created pages to handle registration and log-in failures (pages 376–377)

- Applied Restrict Access to Page server behaviors to each secured page in the site (pages 379–382)

What You Will Learn

In this lesson, you will:

- Empower non-technical users to add formatted content to a Web page instantly

- Create an admin section for the site, including a new template

- Use and customize a text area form element

- Track user activity with session variables and hidden fields

- Learn about SQL's INSERT statement

- Use the Insert Record server behavior

Approximate Time

This lesson takes approximately 45 minutes to complete.

Lesson Files

Starting Files:

    Lesson13/Start/newland/generic_template.asp
    Lesson13/Start/newland/index.asp

Completed Files:

    Lesson13/Complete/newland/admin_template.asp
    Lesson13/Complete/newland/admin_index.asp
    Lesson13/Complete/newland/admin_update_tj.asp
    Lesson13/Complete/newland/index.asp

Managing Content with Forms

A content management system, as its name suggests, is an interface that facilitates the maintenance of content, including the addition of new content, the modification of existing content, and the removal of unwanted content. In this and the next two lessons, you will make steps toward building a content management system (CMS) for the Newland Tours site. You won't build a fully comprehensive CMS, which is an ambitious and often redundant task, making it of limited value for learning. But you will build enough of it to get a sense of how they work and the know-how to start building your own.

By inserting some HTML as the default text in a text area, you can provide users a template for creating formatted text.

How do CMSs work? You can look at this question as a functional question (how can Web content be maintained over the Web?) or as a technical question (how do we use available technologies to make this possible?). Whenever you face a problem like this, answer the functional question first, and then worry about the technical answer.

In practice, CMSs typically include several pages with forms on them. When users fill out the forms, whatever they entered appears on the site. You don't want these forms to be accessible to the public, which is why you created the log-in framework first. You have probably guessed how this process from form to Web works: database connectivity. You know that the contents of a Web page can be populated with database data, and you know that you can capture user-entered information from a form and put it in a database. Put two and two together, and voila! You have a content management system.

In 2002, Macromedia released software called Contribute. Now Adobe Contribute CS3, the software enables non-technical users to maintain site content in a friendly, office productivity tool-like environment. Contribute has both advantages and disadvantages compared to a CMS using a database and ASP, ColdFusion, or PHP. As a Web editor, Contribute enables users to format content much more robustly and easily than the best database-driven CMS. And unlike database-driven sites with ASP, ColdFusion, or PHP, Contribute doesn't require significant programming up-front to achieve the most basic functionality. Because it works mainly with static sites, Contribute is generally a less expensive solution. On the down side, Contribute doesn't work with live database content. And whereas updating a database-driven Web site requires a browser and Internet access, updating a site with Contribute requires Internet access and a copy of Contribute, which, though inexpensive, is not free.

As a rule, use Contribute for text- and image-heavy static sites whose contents need occasional updating, and use dynamic pages and a database for highly structured or data-oriented sites whose contents change frequently, or on sites whose contents need to be searchable. Many enterprise sites make use of both databases and server-side scripting (such as ASP, ColdFusion, or PHP) and Contribute—using each according to its strengths.

Back to the CMS we'll begin in this lesson. Content maintenance implies three abilities: inserting content, modifying content, and deleting content. If you know SQL, you are probably aware of the INSERT, UPDATE, and DELETE statements, which make it possible to insert, modify, and delete data from a database. If you don't know SQL, don't worry: you'll get practice with each of these statements in this and the next two lessons. You will use these in your queries, rather than simple SELECT statements, to make content manageable.

The primary task remaining is to create form interfaces that serve as the front-end for the work going on in the background. Some of these, especially those for inserting data, are quite easy to create. In fact, by building the registration form, you've already created one. Updating and deleting data are a little trickier, because you have to retrieve data from the database and make it available to the user, so she or he can send the requisite queries back to the database to do the actual updating or deleting.

In this lesson, you will create the simplest portion of the CMS: the form that Newland Tours employees can use to update the Traveler's Journal on the homepage. This functionality requires only a single page, a single form, and a single server behavior (Insert Record).

Creating the Admin Section

By the time the site is complete, employees will be able to do a number of administrative tasks, which include inserting new Traveler's Journal articles, maintaining the country profiles, and maintaining the tour descriptions. All of these activities will be limited to those in the admin user group. It is a nice touch to create an administrative homepage—a single page that links to all of the different tasks that administrators can accomplish with the site.

In addition, creating the CMS features will mean creating several new pages. Each of these pages needs to have the Restrict Access to User server behavior applied to it in such a way that only members of the admin user group can get in. That could get monotonous, so to avoid that, you'll create a special admin-only template, called admin_template.asp, which is nearly identical to generic_template.asp, except that it'll have the Restrict Access to User server behavior already applied.

1 Open generic_template.asp. Use the toolbar to change the title to *Newland Tours: Admin*, and save the file as *admin_template.asp*.

You know your template is useful when you use it to create other templates!

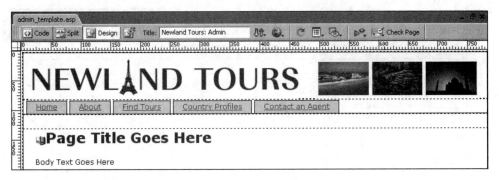

2 Use the Server Behaviors panel to add a Restrict Access to Page behavior. In the dialog, restrict based on Username, Password, and Access Level, and make sure that only admin is selected in the Select Level(s) area. Specify login.asp in the If Access Denied field, and click OK.

All of the admin pages should require that the user log in as a member of the admin user group, so you might as well attach the Restrict Access to User behavior directly to the template.

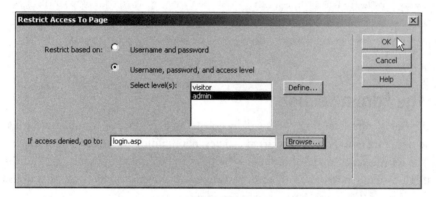

3 Choose File > Save.

You've made a change to the template, so you need to save it.

4 Choose File > Save As, and save the file as admin_index.asp. Change the page title to *Newland Tours: Admin Home*, and change main heading to *Admin Home*.

Employees will use this page as a starting point for administrative tasks. You'll also enable them to log in directly to this page.

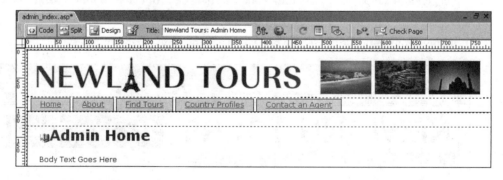

5 In the body section, replace the placeholder text with the following lines:

Choose an administrative task from the list below. If you have any questions or problems, please contact the webmaster.
Update the Traveler's Journal
Add or remove a registered user to/from the Admin group
Add a new tour description
Modify or remove an existing tour description
Add a new country profile
Modify or remove an existing country profile

This is the main menu for the page. You'll add actual links as you go, but now you have the framework.

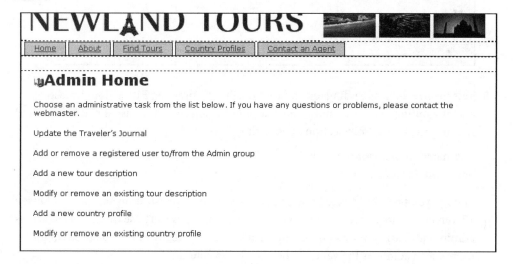

6 Link the word webmaster to your own email (don't forget the `mailto:` prefix). Save and close admin_index.asp.

Whenever you deploy a content management system, make sure you provide explicit directions and contact information, in case its users have any problems.

▶ **TIP:** Developers often put admin files in a separate folder, which has different permissions. For the sake of simplicity, we'll keep everything in one place and prefix all admin pages with admin_. As previously discussed, the topic of Web application security is important but beyond the scope of this book. It is not a topic you should take lightly when you start developing dynamic applications in the real world.

7 Open index.asp, and just below the Log In link, add a new link called Admin, which links to admin_index.asp.

Now all users—visitors and employees alike—can access what they need through the site's front door.

8 Test the new link (including log-in functionality) by pressing F12 with index.asp open and attempting to access admin_index.asp. At the log-in screen, use the following credentials to access the admin section of your site.

Username: *zfrome@starknet.com*
Password: *hypochondriac*

Though you probably created one or more of your own registration accounts in Lesson 12, remember, those are set to the visitor user group. You can't use them (yet) to access admin_index.asp. The credentials supplied above are already in the database (in tbl_users), with admin as the value in the userGroup column.

You might try logging in with your own username and password, just to verify that you *don't* get in. If you don't have a username and password, you can use osiris@allectomedia.com as the username and osiris as the password, since this user account has the visitor status.

Formatting Content Stored in a Database

Now that you have a basic framework for the admin section, you can start building its functionality. In this task, you will create a form that enables users to input new Traveler's Journal entries, which take effect immediately. The form outputs to tbl_journal, which is the same table whose contents index.asp retrieves to display the Traveler's Journal.

Teens Discover the Mayans

By Ellen Olenska

Newland Tours recently took two dozen students of Bart Township High School to Chichen Itza, Mexico. While on the tour, students saw ancient Mayan ruins and artifacts. They learned the latest on the "mystery of the Mayans."

The Mayans were one of the world's most advanced civilizations when they mysteriously disappeared centuries ago. While archaeologists don't know exactly what happened to the Mayans, evidence points to war as one possible explanation. Bart Township High School students are using the experience as the basis for a series of reports that teams of participants are putting together.

But if you look at the Traveler's Journal, you'll notice that its contents are formatted. The title is in a heading (<h3>, to be specific), the author line is in a <p> tag with the author class applied, and each subsequent paragraph is in its own set of <p> tags. How can you capture content so that it can be marked up and formatted? You can take two approaches:

- Separate each of the elements. With this approach, you create a field for the title in the form and in the database table. Then you dynamically populate an <h3> element with the contents of that record. You then add another pair of fields for the author, and so on. This is how the country profiles and tour descriptions were formatted so precisely.

- Embed HTML markup in the database table. With this approach, part of the text stored in the database is HTML markup. When the record is retrieved, so is the markup. Since the server inserts this text as a part of the page, the browser doesn't know that it is dynamically generated HTML, and it renders just like it would any other HTML.

Each approach has different advantages and disadvantages, and they are not exclusive, so you can use a hybrid approach if you like. The advantage to separating the elements is that HTML tags are hard-coded in the document, and they don't appear in the database. One disadvantage of this approach is that it's limited to paragraph-level styles. That is, it is easy to store the entire title and bind it to an <h3> element, but it would be hard to italicize one of the words in the title. Another disadvantage is that it requires more fields in both the database and the form. If someone typed the Traveler's Journal in a word processor and wanted to transfer it to a form, they would have to transfer one piece at a time.

The embedded HTML approach has its own strengths and limitations. One strength is that you can format the content to your heart's content. You can italicize words, make them bold, turn them pink, and magnify them to 100 pixels if you want. The weakness of this approach is that it requires users to hand-code HTML. One of the goals of a CMS is to make it possible for non-technical people to maintain content, so requiring them to hand-code HTML defeats a key purpose of having a CMS.

Some CMSs include basic formatting GUIs, which enable users to format using HTML without ever seeing it—they just highlight text and click a B button to make the selection bold. Such a feature set is again beyond the scope of this book, but it is possible.

> ✴ **NOTE:** The Traveler's Journal is one element that would benefit from Adobe Contribute: users could replace it directly and quickly, and format it as they please. We'll go ahead and build a CMS for it, because doing so will give you exposure to concepts and techniques that you'll use over and over again.

In this task, you will take a compromise approach, in which users have to see some HTML markup, but they don't actually have to write any. They just overwrite descriptive placeholders in an already marked-up block of text that you set up as the default in a text area.

Creating the Form Interface

Most CMSs are form-based, so building them involves creating lots of forms. The key to developing forms is to analyze the structure of your data in the database, and make the forms match accordingly. In this case you will be inserting a new record into a table that has only three fields, including one that's a primary key. So this form will be easy, containing only two elements and a Submit button. In this task, you'll mock up the visible part of the form.

1. Open admin_template.asp, title the page *Newland Tours: Admin Update Traveler's Journal*, change the heading to read *Update Traveler's Journal*, and save the file as admin_update_tj.asp.

   As usual, you begin a page by mocking up its core elements.

2. Replace the placeholder body text with the following two paragraphs:

   Use the form below to update the Traveler's Journal. Be sure not to overwrite any of the HTML, only rewriting the content in between the HTML tags.

   Tip: To add a new paragraph on a new line, type <p>New Paragraph</p>. To remove a paragraph, remove not only the text, but also the <p> and </p> tags that precede and follow it.

Again, when you create a CMS, it is incumbent on you to document its use and train its users. Adding page directions is a simple way to meet user needs.

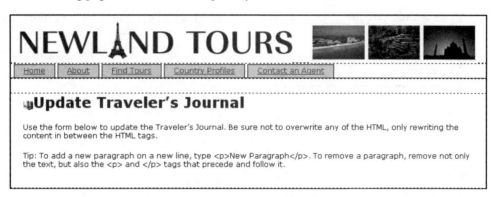

3 Below the directions, insert a new form (frm_update_tj). Inside, place a text area and a Submit button.

The text area form element is used to enable users to enter longer blocks of text than are generally allowed in a text field.

TIP: When using text areas that output to an Access database, make sure the target field's type is Memo. The normal Access Text type is limited to 255 characters and defaults to 50. The Memo type allows 65,535 characters.

Update Traveler's Journal

Use the form below to update the Traveler's Journal. Be sure not to overwrite any of the HTML, only rewriting the content in between the HTML tags.

Tip: To add a new paragraph on a new line, type <p>New Paragraph</p>. To remove a paragraph, remove not only the text, but also the <p> and </p> tags that precede and follow it.

Submit

4 Select the text area, and in the Property inspector, name it *journal_entry*, set its Char Width to 55 and its Num Lines to 9.

These settings give the text area a name and make it a bit larger, so users have more space to write.

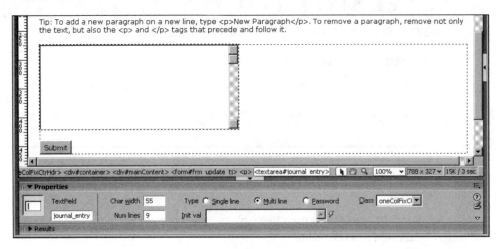

5 With the text area still selected, switch to split view (if you are not already there). Between the opening and closing <textarea> tags, add the following HTML.

```
<h3>Enter Headline Here</h3>
<p class="author">By FirstName LastName</p>
<p>First Paragraph</p>
<p>Second Paragraph</p>
```

This HTML will be the default text that appears in the text area when the page loads. Thus, the only thing users have to do is type over "Enter Headline Here" to enter a new headline, and as long as they don't disturb the surrounding tags, the new headline will appear in the <h3> format.

* **NOTE:** You can also enter default text in the Property inspector. To do so, select the text area, and type directly in the Init Val field. This technique is fine for two or three words, but you'd better have a strong pair of bifocals if you want to type much more.

```
49        <form id="frm_update_tj" name="frm_update_tj" method="post" action="">
50          <p>
51            <textarea name="journal_entry" id="journal_entry" cols="55" rows="9">
52  <h3>Enter Headline Here</h3>
53  <p class="author">By FirstName LastName</p>
54  <p>First Paragraph</p>
55  <p>Second Paragraph</p>
56            </textarea>
57          </p>
58          <p>
59            <input type="submit" name="button" id="button" value="Submit" />
60          </p>
61        </form>
```

✱ **NOTE:** Dreamweaver's Design View doesn't show the <h3> and <p> tags, even though you entered them in code view. However, they will show up properly in a browser.

6 Back in Design view, notice the highlighted </p> tag error on the page. To fix it, switch back to code view and remove the opening and closing <p> and </p> tags that surround the <textarea> tags.

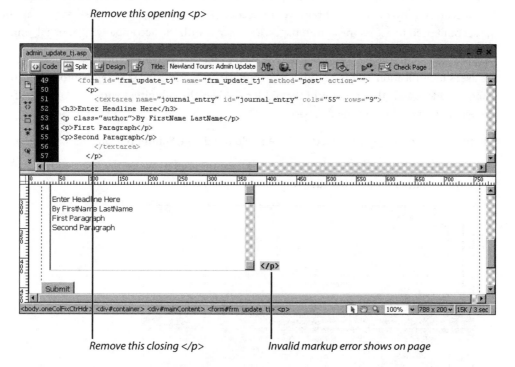

Remove this opening <p>

Remove this closing </p>   Invalid markup error shows on page

The problem occurs because the text area is inserted inside <p> tags, which in itself isn't a problem, except that the default text in the text area also has <p> tags. This confuses Dreamweaver, which causes the error. The fix is simply to remove the <p> tags that surround the <textarea> block element.

7 Open admin_index.asp, select Update the Traveler's Journal, and link it to admin_update_tj.asp.

Once you've created new pages, don't forget to add links to them. Save and close admin_index.asp, and save admin_update_tj.asp.

Using Session Variables and Hidden Fields to Track Users

One concern administrators have about a content management system is the potential for abuse. If someone manages to access the form that enables users to add a new Traveler's Journal for malicious purposes, you want to know who did it. Or, more specifically, you want to know whose account was used to do it. That way, you can identify the responsible employee (if it was an employee) or at least remove the account (if it was not). In this task, you'll capture the account used to access the admin pages, and save it with the accompanying journal_entry.

The technique you will use—and this is explained in more detail as you do it—is to capture the user's identification as it is stored in a session variable, and copy that value into the form using a hidden field. The contents of the hidden field will be submitted with the contents of the text area, and stored in the database.

1 In admin_update_tj.asp, insert a hidden field beside the Submit button. Name it *author*.

This hidden field will store the name of the account used to access the page. At this stage, though, it has no value, because you haven't bound any data to it.

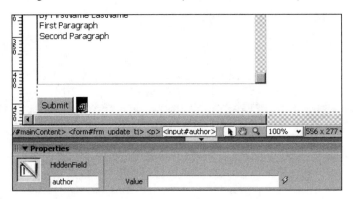

The question is, how do we find out whose account has been used? To answer that, think about what data is available to the page. This page has a Restrict Access to Page behavior attached to it. This behavior checks for the presence of a session variable set when the user successfully logged in. If that variable exists, it checks to see if its user is in the admin group. In other words, for a user to be on this page, she or he must not only be logged in with an admin account, but the page must know the account. Since this information is already available to the page as a session variable, all you have to do is bind that value to the hidden field and it will be written into the database along with the form.

2 Use the Bindings panel to add a new session variable binding. In the Session Variable dialog, enter *MM_Username*, and click OK.

MM_Username is the session variable that is set when the user logs in. It is created automatically when you use the Log In User server behavior.

One thing to remember about the Bindings panel: The bindings it lists are limited to ones that you enter. In other words, even though MM_Username has been available all along as a session variable, as a part of the Restrict Access to Page server behavior, it is not listed in the Bindings panel unless you explicitly put it there.

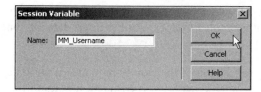

3 Select the hidden field, if necessary, then select Session > MM_Username in the Bindings panel, and click Bind.

This binds the value of MM_Username (that is, the account name used for this session's log-in) to the hidden field. You now submit the author data along with the journal entry itself.

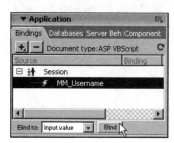

Inserting the Record

The form is now ready, except that nothing is set to happen when the Submit button is pressed. In this task, you'll use the Insert Record server behavior to insert the data stored in the form into tbl_journal of the database, also causing the instant updating of the site.

Thanks to Dreamweaver's Insert Record server behavior, all of the SQL code will be written for you. Still, you should be familiar with the basic syntax of the INSERT statement, in case you ever need to edit it.

```
INSERT INTO tbl_table(
    fieldname1,
    fieldname2,
    fieldname3)
VALUES(
    'value1',
    'value2',
    'value3');
```

You might think of the Insert Record dialog (and for that matter, the Update Record dialog, though you haven't seen it yet) as a matching exercise, where you match form elements to table fields. The underlying SQL reveals why the dialog behaves this way. You specify a table in the INSERT INTO line, and then you list each of the table fields you want to insert data into one at a time, in the order you want data inserted, in parentheses.

Then you use the VALUES statement to specify the data itself that you want to insert; this data too goes inside a set of parentheses. Each piece of data that is a text string (as opposed to a number or an expression) is placed within single quotes. The individual pieces of data are separated by commas. The values at the bottom are matched in order to the fields listed at the top, so not only do the number of fields and the number of values have to match, but also you have to make sure you list them in the correct order.

▶ **TIP:** One of the most common typos when building INSERT INTO SQL statements is to add a comma after the last field name or the last value. The last value should not be followed by a comma. If it is, you will see an error message.

1 Click to select the Submit button, and begin the process of adding an Insert Record server behavior.

This server behavior will be used to input the text area (journal_entry) and the hidden field (author) into tbl_journal's journal_entry and author fields.

2 In the Insert Record dialog, specify conn_newland as the connection, tbl_journal as the Insert Into Table, and index.asp as the After Inserting, Go To. Verify that the lower half of the dialog provides Dreamweaver with the instructions it needs to insert journal_entry into journal_entry and author into author.

This is the matching exercise part, where you specify which field of which database table is populated with which field of the form. Since you gave the form elements the same names as their destination table field names, Dreamweaver correctly matches everything for you.

You specify index.asp as the redirection page, so that users can verify that what they entered is now showing on the homepage.

Again, ColdFusion and PHP users will note that the dialog they see, though functionally the same, varies cosmetically from the one shown in the screenshot.

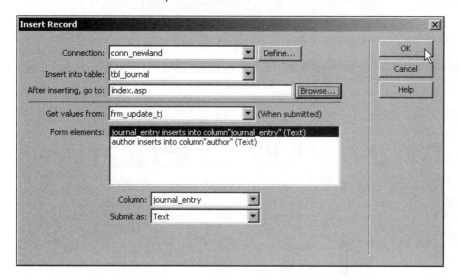

3 Test the new functionality, making sure to log in as an administrator.

The homepage now contains whatever you entered, formatted using the specified HTML.

If you look in the tbl_journal table of the database, you will see both the first line of the text you entered (text entered after line breaks is not displayed in Access' table view) and zfrome@starknet.com, because that is the account you used to log in, and that identity was stored as a session variable and passed through the form to the database.

	journalID	author	journal_entry
▶	1	lseldon@mirth.r	\<h3>Italy Tour was a Hit!\</h3>
	2	eolenska@frees	\<h3>Teens Discover the Mayans\</h3>
	3	zfrome@starkne	\<h3>Florentine Art Show Floors Art Lovers\</h3>
*	(AutoNumber)		

What You Have Learned

In this lesson, you have:

- Created an admin section that makes administrative tasks conveniently accessible to users (pages 387–390)

- Repurposed generic_template.asp into a special template for the admin section (pages 390–392)

- Built a form using a text area element with HTML-formatted default text (pages 392–396)

- Designed a system to capture the identity of users updating the Traveler's Journal (pages 396–397)

- Inserted the data using the Insert Record server behavior (pages 398–401)

What You Will Learn

In this lesson, you will:

- Plan for a master-detail set, by analyzing the data needed for the application
- Create a master-detail page set, using the admin template created in the previous lesson
- Learn about SQL's UPDATE statement
- Convert the detail page to a dynamically populated form capable of updating, rather than merely displaying, contents in the database

Approximate Time

This lesson takes approximately 60 minutes to complete.

Lesson Files

Starting Files

Lesson14/Start/newland/admin_template.asp

Completed Files

Lesson14/Complete/newland/admin_addUser_master.asp
Lesson14/Complete/newland/admin_addUser_detail.asp

LESSON 14

Building Update Pages

In this lesson, you will build an interface that lets employees change a registered user from one user group to another (from visitor to admin, or vice versa). This implies a certain work-flow: To add an employee to the admin group, the employee must first register at the site, and then another employee must go in and change her or his user group. Likewise, if an employee leaves Newland Tours, another employee can easily change the former employee's user profile back to visitor. The interface will use two pages—one where the employee selects the user whose profile will be changed, and one to actually update the profile.

You'll enable users to update database data using a Web form, SQL's UPDATE statement, and Dreamweaver's Update Record server behavior.

Two-page applications that use this structure are referred to as master-detail page sets. A master-detail page structure is one of the most common—and useful—structures that you will master as a Web developer. The first page is the master page, because it lists many records in a summary format. Users browse this summary, and then select the record they want to learn more about or modify/delete. The second page is the detail page, because it contains detailed information about the selected record. On this page, users can learn more about a product or modify/delete a record. To summarize, the master page lists a small sampling of fields from multiple records within a database, while the detail page displays many fields from a single record.

You'll enable users to update database data using a Web form, SQL's **UPDATE** statement, and Dreamweaver's Update Record server behavior.

You've already built two variations on the master-detail theme in the course of the book: the tour description page set is an example in two pages and the country profiles page is a master-detail example in one. But in both cases, the detail piece only displayed data. In this lesson, you'll use the detail page to update data.

Updating data is slightly more complex than inserting new data, which you did in Lessons 12 and 13. When you insert new data, you identify a table and specify which data to write to which fields in that table. When updating data, you have to do the same thing to a particular, existing record; you can't just append information as a new record at the end of the table. SQL has a command—**UPDATE**—that you can use to accomplish this task, and Dreamweaver has an Update Record server behavior that makes it even easier.

In this lesson, you will combine the master-detail page structure with the update-record page structure. You will use several Dreamweaver behaviors to make it happen. It is vital in this lesson that you understand the big picture about what is happening: Dreamweaver behaviors sometimes make it easy for us to not worry too much about the mechanics of what's going on, but in the next lesson, you are going to replicate this structure using a more ambitious hands-on approach, so you need to nail down the concepts now.

Preparing the Pages

To insert a master-detail page object, you must open the page that will become the master. In the course of completing the dialog that creates the page set, you specify the name of the detail page as well. If you haven't yet created the detail page, Dreamweaver can create one for you. But it's hard to go back and apply your template to that page. Thus, in this task, you will create the master and detail pages used in this set.

1 Open admin_template.asp, title the page *Newland Tours: Admin Add User to Admin Group*, change the heading to *Add User to Admin Group*, and save the file as *admin_ addUser_master.asp*.

This page will be the master page, holding summary information about each of the registered users.

2 Replace the placeholder body text with the following. Save the file.

To add a registered user to the Admin group, select her or his name from the list, and change the permission group to admin on the following page.

Again, providing directions now enhances the efficacy of the site and reduces tech-support calls and frustration later.

3 Open admin_template.asp, title the page *Newland Tours: Admin Add User to Admin Group*, change the heading to *Add User to Admin Group*, and save the file as *admin_ addUser_detail.asp*.

This page will be the detail page, which will contain the form that employees can use to actually change a user's permission group.

4 Replace the placeholder body text with the following. Save the file.

Use the drop-down menu in the form below to change a user's permission group. Click Submit to make the changes take effect.

You have now built the basic page shells to which you will add the Master-Detail Page Set object.

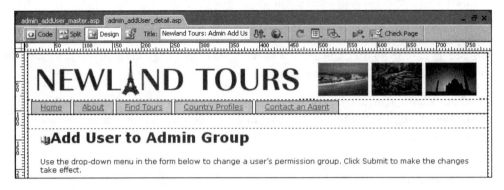

5 In admin_index.asp, link the "Add or remove a registered user" line to admin_addUser_master.asp. Save and close admin_index.asp.

Now users have convenient access to the new page set.

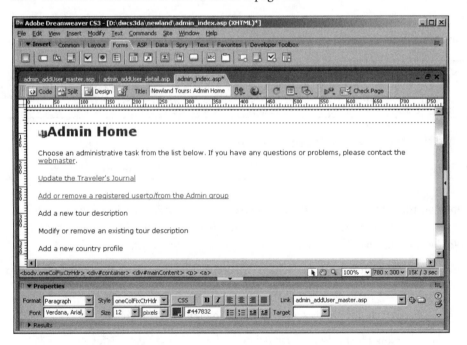

Planning for the Master-Detail Pages

As you saw from your earlier experiences developing the tour description master-detail page set, creating these sets often requires quite a few server behaviors and other dynamic elements working in unison.

- You create a recordset to populate the menu on the master page.

- Because you are dealing with multiple records, you often need to create a Recordset Navigation Bar, which itself is made of several behaviors, including the behaviors from the Show Region group as well as from the Recordset Paging group.

- You output records using Dynamic Text, and apply the Repeat Region server behavior to ensure that all of the records are output.

- If the records are hyperlinked, you bind a unique querystring or URL parameter to the href attribute.

- A SQL statement that uses a dynamic value in a WHERE clause filters the recordset using criteria the user supplied on the master page.

Building master-detail pages by hand can be slow and tedious. Dreamweaver speeds up the development of this common structure with a special data object that adds all of the needed server behaviors and creates the pages for you. This server object is called a Master-Detail Page Set, and is available in the Insert > Data Objects menu. This is a very convenient tool, as you'll see in this lesson.

The Master-Detail Page Set object works by collecting all of the relevant information needed to build the page set. Some of this information is derived from a query, so you'll have to create a recordset first. All told, the data object requires quite a bit of information, and a single mistake derails the entire process. For this reason, you should figure out what you want in advance. (When writing this lesson, it took me several tries in the dialog before getting it right, because I tried to cut this corner.)

The main thing you need to sort out is what information you want to appear on the master page, and likewise what information you want to appear on the detail page. This information is all retrieved from a database, so what you are doing here is determining what you should retrieve in your initial recordset.

For this master-detail page set, you want the master page to contain the following information as a menu, which should be sufficient for the employee to find and select the correct user account.

Last Name   First Name   Username   Current User Group

The detail page should include the following information.

Last Name   First Name   Current User Group

In this case, ironically, the detail page contains less information than the master page. But remember, the purpose of this detail page is not to display lots of information about the record (as you would with a product description in an online catalog), but rather to offer extended functionality to the record (in this case, the power to update the record).

At the very least, you will need to make the information shown above available to the page (via a recordset). But these four elements do not represent a complete listing of information needed from the database. Do you remember when you created the master-detail page set for the tour descriptions that when users clicked the link a URL parameter was appended to the URL? This data for this URL parameter is needed to filter the query on the detail page, so it can display only the desired record. In this case, you need some piece of information that can cause the detail page to display one unique record. And any time you need to use something unique to identify a database record, you should immediately think of the table's primary key, in this case, userID.

To summarize, then, the recordset on which your master-detail page set will be built will require the following fields from tbl_users:

userID
firstName
lastName
username
userGroup

In addition, this data will need to be ordered alphabetically by last name to facilitate lookup, so you will need to sort on last name, ascending. Go ahead and create this recordset now.

1 In admin_addUser_master.asp, add a new recordset, called *rs_registeredUsers*, according to the specifications just outlined.

By creating this recordset, you have made available the data needed to build the master-detail page set.

Remember, it's always a good idea to click the Test button in the Recordset dialog, just to make sure you are getting everything you need, and in the right order.

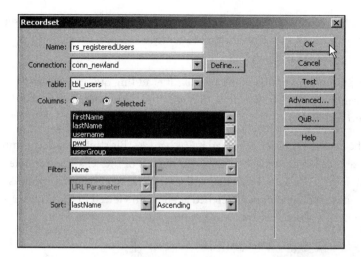

2 Position the cursor on a new line below the directions, and choose Insert > Data Objects > Master Detail Page Set.

Selecting this option opens a large dialog.

3 In the Insert Master-Detail Page Set dialog, make sure that rs_registeredUsers is selected as the recordset. In the Master Page Fields section, select userID and click the minus button to remove it. In the Link to Detail From menu, choose username. In the Pass Unique Key field, choose userID. Check Show 20 Records at a time.

The top half of the dialog, which you have just completed, is used to control the appearance and functionality of the master page. The Master Page Fields section represents all of the fields of each record that you want shown. The four selected here correspond to the four discussed in the introduction to this task. That is, they will appear on the page as four columns, making up a menu for the user.

The Link To Detail From menu lets you specify which field's data will be hyperlinked to the detail page. The field username is a good choice, because it is unique.

The Pass Unique Key menu lets you specify which piece of data will be used to filter the data on the detail page. Again, that should be unique, so the table's primary key, userID, is the right choice.

When you choose to show 20 records at a time, you are providing Dreamweaver with the information it needs to insert a Recordset Navigation Bar server object for you. Given that the number of registered users will likely grow to many, a recordset navigation bar is a good idea. Otherwise, employees are forced to download potentially hundreds of records all at once.

4 In the lower half of the Master-Detail Page Set dialog, type or browse to admin_addUser_detail.asp. Select userID and click the minus button to remove it. Select username and click the minus button to remove it. Click OK.

Dreamweaver may take a moment at this point, because it is adding quite a few server behaviors to two different pages. When it is done, though, the master-detail page set should be complete and functional.

The master page may be quite a bit wider now than it was before. This stretching accommodates the pseudocode strings Dreamweaver has inserted in each of the cells (for example, rs_registeredUsers.lastName). The actual data that will go in these fields is not as wide as the pseudocode, so the page will not appear stretched at all when viewed in the browser, so just disregard the stretching in Dreamweaver. Most important, do not try to fix it.

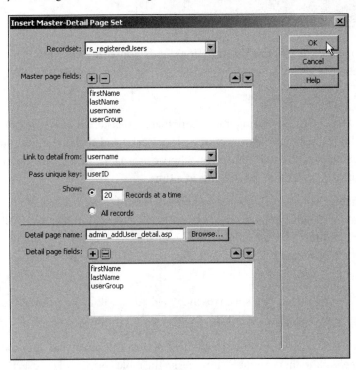

5 Switch to admin_addUser_detail.asp. If necessary, move the new table so that it is inside the main page table, just below the directions.

Dreamweaver has to guess where to put the table on the page, and it doesn't always guess correctly. Moving the table won't affect any functionality, so this change is entirely cosmetic.

6 Save and upload both files. Test their functionality.

You'll be intercepted by the log-in screen first. Use the following credentials to get in:

Username: *zfrome@starknet.com*
Password: *hypochondriac*

The master page contains a table with the four columns you specified. In addition, the usernames are all hyperlinked, and if you roll over the links, you'll see the URL of the detail page with the unique userID appended as a URL parameter in your browser's status bar (if it is visible).

Also, you'll see Records 1 to 6 of 6 (or however many records you have at this point in your database). This is created with the Recordset Navigation Status data object (Insert > Data Objects > Display Record Count > Recordset Navigation Status), which is inserted automatically as a part of the Master-Detail Page Set data object.

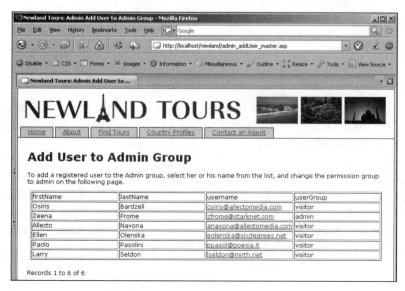

Once you've clicked one of the usernames, you'll see the detail page, with a small table containing the information that you specified in the dialog. While the data in the table is hyperlinked, the links don't go anywhere. You can't update it yet, but you can at least see that the correct record has been retrieved.

One thing you probably noticed on both pages is that the column/row headers were neither prominent nor meaningful.

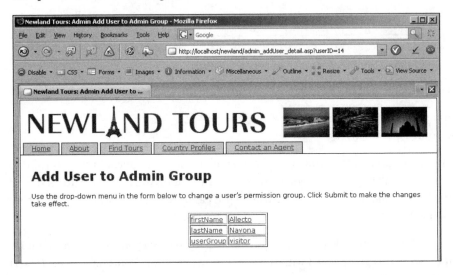

7 On admin_addUser_master.asp, one at a time, select firstName, lastName, username, and userGroup, and make them bold. Then replace each as follows:

firstName: *First Name*
lastName: *Last Name*
username: *Email Address*
userGroup: *Current User Group*

When it generates the table, Dreamweaver uses the database column names as the default table headers. But the database was structured to hold data, not to serve as column headings. These changes make the table easier to understand and use.

▶ **TIP:** Customizing table headers also improves security. Had you not changed them, malicious users such as hackers could glean a fair amount of information about your database schema just by looking at table headings. Of course, if hackers are viewing your admin pages, you have bigger security problems than table headings! Still, obscuring database field names from users is a good practice.

8 On admin_addUser_detail.asp, remove any hyperlinks from the fields in the table cells by selecting the text and deleting #top from the Link box in the Property inspector.

When Dreamweaver creates the Master-Detail page set it sometimes generates these links because of the named anchor next to the page heading. The detail form will have a submit button so any other navigation in the form would just confuse users.

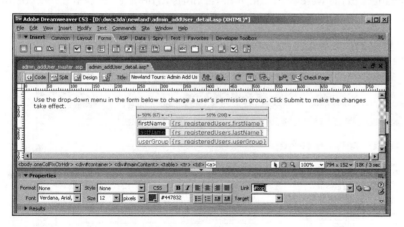

9 Make the three row headers bold, as in the previous step, and replace the text as follows:

firstName: *First Name*
lastName: *Last Name*
userGroup: *Current User Group*

You are making these changes for the reasons described in the preceding step.

▶ **TIP:** You can drag the line that separates the two columns to the right to create more space for the row headers. You might also need to increase the size of the table by dragging its right edge.

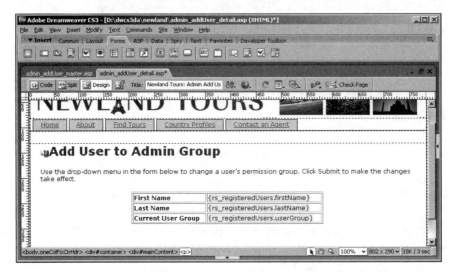

10 Save, upload, and test the pages again, to make sure they look right.

Though the changes made were cosmetic, it never hurts to double-check the effect before moving forward.

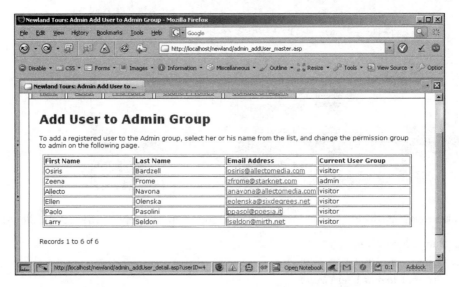

Making the Detail Page Updateable

Other than the convenience of using a ready-made object to create master-detail pages, nothing you have done is terribly new, since you've deployed most of the functionalities aggregated on these two pages during the course of the book. But what you'll add in this task is new: You'll use the filtered display as a means of identifying the row to update.

This task should be easy, since you are merely adding a simple server behavior to a form that will have a single field. But it's not that simple. All three versions of the server behaviors wind up not working as expected, though for different reasons. The ASP version of the server behavior sends a superfluous querystring parameter that creates a conflict with another querystring. And the ColdFusion and PHP versions of the server behavior give a URL parameter an unexpected name, which might cause you to mismatch a pair of values.

I must emphasize that neither of these issues matter if you are applying the Update Record behavior to a simple page. But as you know, admin_addUser_detail.asp is not a simple page—it is a part of the great complexity of server behaviors and dynamic elements that is the Master-Detail Page Set data object.

Both sets of problems are fairly easy to fix. The important point to realize is that once again you can't rely entirely on the convenient server behaviors: You must deal with code, both to create functionality that the server behaviors can't create or to customize (and in this case fix) the code that the server behaviors generate.

1 In admin_addUser_detail.asp, create a new form (*frm_updateUser*), and place the users table inside it.

You've used tables to structure form content through the book. Here, you are including dynamic content within that table, but the presence of dynamic content makes no difference to the form. The only portions affected by the form itself are form elements, and you haven't added them yet.

2 Position the insertion point anywhere in the bottom row. Choose Modify > Table > Insert Rows or Columns. In the dialog, specify 2 rows below the selection, and click OK.

The newly created fourth row will contain a menu enabling users to change user groups, and the fifth row will hold the Submit button.

3 In the left cell of the fourth row, type *New User Group* and make it bold. In the right cell, insert a menu element. Name this element *userGroup*. Click the List Values button, and enter *Visitor* and *visitor* as the first row's item label and value, and *Admin* and *admin* as the second row's item label and value. Click OK. Back in the Property inspector click Visitor in the Initially Selected area.

This menu makes it possible for the user to specify only one of two user group options. Its values are static, and if Newland Tours ever renamed or added a new user group, the HTML would have to be modified. This could be handled dynamically, of course, but that would require a new database table, joins, and all sorts of code. Sometimes, hard-coding is simply more cost-effective than doing everything dynamically.

✱ **NOTE:** Make sure you do not misspell either of the values, or the affected users won't be able to log in at all!

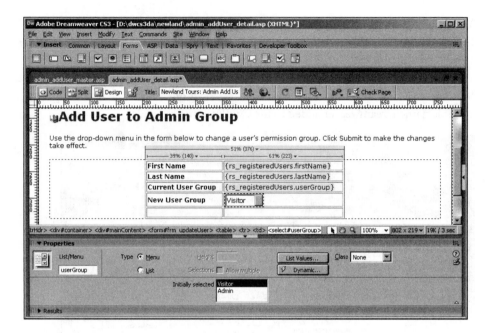

4 Place the insertion point in the right cell of the bottom row, and insert a Submit button.

Most forms don't do much without one of these.

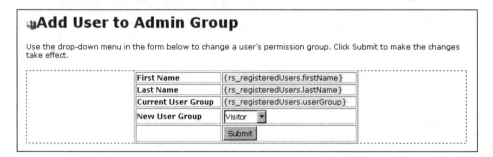

5 ColdFusion and PHP Users Only: In the cell to the left of the Submit button, insert a hidden field element and call it *userID*. Use the Bindings panel to add a new URL variable called *recordID*. Select the hidden field in the form, and bind the new URL variable to that hidden field.

The ColdFusion and PHP versions of the Update Record server behavior require that you pass the primary key to the field you are updating. The ASP version, in contrast, requires that you do *not* pass this value.

You would think that the URL parameter passed to this page would be called userID, because that is, in fact, the value being passed, as you specified in the Insert Master-Detail Page Set dialog. In ASP, that is the name. For some reason, the ColdFusion and PHP versions of the server behavior name the URL parameter recordID, rather than userID. So when you bind the URL parameter to the userID hidden field, you have to specify the variable name Dreamweaver added to the ColdFusion/PHP code.

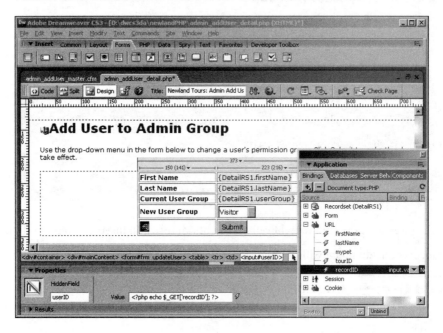

6 Click to select the Submit button, and initiate an Update Record server behavior from the Server Behaviors panel.

Updating records requires a special SQL command, called UPDATE. You have used both SELECT and INSERT in the course of this book, but you haven't looked at UPDATE yet. The server behavior will generate all of the SQL for you, but you should at least be generally familiar with the UPDATE syntax, which is as follows:

UPDATE tbl_table
SET fieldName = 'New value for this field'
WHERE keyID = '123456';

When you update a record, you specify a table. Then, you use SET to specify the new value. Finally, you use the WHERE clause to identify which row. Optionally, you can specify multiple fields to update in the SET clause; to do so, just separate each field name-new value combination with a comma.

✱ **NOTE:** Use caution. If you use UPDATE without a WHERE clause that specifies the row, you'll end up changing the value of every row.

Though you won't need to in this lesson, sometimes you need to modify the SQL, and it's important to learn SQL as you learn dynamic Web site development.

The ASP, ColdFusion and PHP versions of the Update Record dialog are sufficiently different cosmetically that I'll break them down separately.

7 ASP Users Only: In the Update Record dialog, choose conn_newland as the connection, tbl_users as the Table To Update, rs_registeredUsers in the Select Record From menu, userID as the Unique Key Column (the Numeric checkbox should remain checked). In the After Updating, Go To field, enter *admin_addUser_master.asp*. Verify that the Form Elements area contains this text: userGroup updates column "userGroup" (Text).

With this information, you are telling Dreamweaver to write a SQL query that will update tbl_users' userGroup field with the information stored in the userGroup form element, in the row whose primary key matches the one retrieved in the rs_registeredUsers query.

Once users submit the form, they are redirected to admin_addUser_master.asp, where, as you'll recall, the summary lists each user's current user group, enabling users to make sure that the change went through.

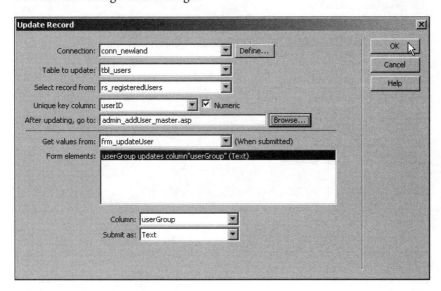

ColdFusion and PHP Users Only: In the Update Record dialog, choose newland as the Data Source (ColdFusion) or conn_newland as the Connection (PHP) and set tbl_users as the Update Table. In the Columns area, make sure that the following two statements appear: 'userID' Selects Record Using 'FORM.userID' as 'Numeric' (or as 'Integer'); 'userGroup' Gets Value From 'FORM.userGroup' as 'Text'; and the rest say Does Not Get a Value. Lower in the dialog, in the After Updating, Go To field, enter *admin_addUser_master.cfm*. ColdFusion users only: Make sure that Pass Original Query String is unchecked.

With this information, you are telling Dreamweaver to write a SQL query that will update tbl_users' userGroup column with the information stored in the userGroup form element, in the row whose primary key matches the one stored in the form's userID (hidden field) element.

Once users submit the form, they are redirected to admin_addUser_master.cfm, where, as you'll recall, the summary lists each user's current user group, enabling users to make sure that the change went through.

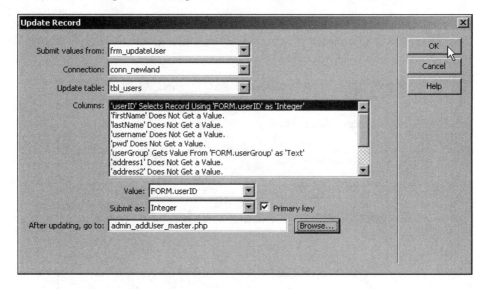

8 Save and upload the page. Then, test the page set, starting from the master page.

You should be able to select a user, change their status on the detail page, and see the change reflected when redirected to the master page. The application works to this point. There's still a problem with the ASP version, but ColdFusion and PHP users are finished with the lesson.

Once again, the login information is as follows:

Username: *zfrome@starknet.com*
Password: *hypochondriac*

ASP users: Once you've tested the page pairing once, go ahead and try it again. The second time you try it, you get an error message. The problem is easy to spot—just look at the URL. Somehow, the querystring contains userID=# twice. This is tripping up the ASP interpreter. Click the Back button, and you'll see that one instance of userID=7 is present on the master page. But that shouldn't be there. The master page is supposed to send the

URL variable, but it is not supposed to have a URL variable of its own. Why is this happening? When the form is submitted on the detail page, it passes back a URL variable to the master page. In ColdFusion, a checkbox called Pass Original Query String lets you determine whether to pass the URL variable back or not: in ASP, however, Dreamweaver assumes you want the querystring to be passed, even though you don't.

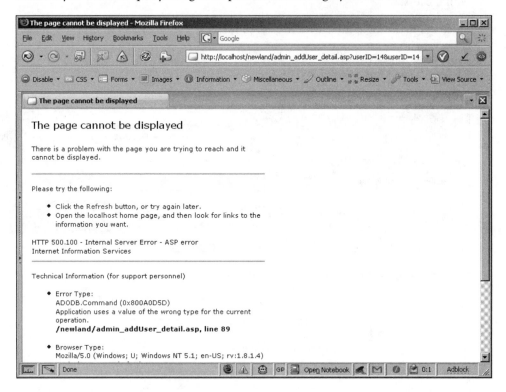

There is no way to fix this problem in a dialog or wizard. You'll have to fix it in the code itself.

9 ASP Users Only: In admin_addUser_detail.asp, switch to code view. Look for a comment, `'append the query string to the redirect URL`. Skipping the two lines that create and set the MM_editRedirectUrl, insert an apostrophe before the next seven lines to comment them out.

In my version of the page, the offending code begins in line 62. If you have trouble finding it, use Edit > Find.

You'll see a nested pair of if statements. These do the work of appending the querystring, so you want to deactivate them. You could just delete them, but it's safer to comment them out, just in case you need them at some later point.

Make sure you don't inadvertently comment out the third End If, because it belongs to the parent block of code, not the portion you are commenting out. Your code should match the screenshot.

```
58
59        ' append the query string to the redirect URL
60        Dim MM_editRedirectUrl
61        MM_editRedirectUrl = "admin_addUser_master.asp"
62 '      If (Request.QueryString <> "") Then
63 '        If (InStr(1, MM_editRedirectUrl, "?", vbTextCompare) = 0) Then
64 '          MM_editRedirectUrl = MM_editRedirectUrl & "?" & Request.QueryString
65 '        Else
66 '          MM_editRedirectUrl = MM_editRedirectUrl & "&" & Request.QueryString
67 '        End If
68 '      End If
69        Response.Redirect(MM_editRedirectUrl)
70      End If
71 End If
72 %>
```

Once you've commented out these lines of code, test the page set again, multiple times. It should work as expected.

What You Have Learned

In this lesson, you have:

- Created the basic layout for each of the pages in advance (pages 405–406)

- Planned the precise data to be used in the master-detail page set (pages 407–408)

- Created a recordset sufficient to handle both pages (pages 408–411)

- Inserted a Master-Detail Page Set data object, based on the recordset (pages 409–411)

- Converted the detail table to a form (pages 412–414)

- Applied the Update Record server behavior (pages 415–421)

- Applied fixes to ASP to make the Update Record server behavior work alongside the Master-Detail Page Set data object (pages 421–423)

What You Will Learn

In this lesson, you will:

- Build a coordinated content management system, enabling users to insert, update, and delete data
- Develop the code with minimal reliance on Dreamweaver's GUI
- Hand-write your own code to make database connections
- Make use of SQL's INSERT, UPDATE, and DELETE statements

Approximate Time

This lesson takes approximately 180 minutes to complete.

Lesson Files

Starting Files:

Lesson15/Start/newland/admin_template.asp

Completed Files:

Lesson15/Complete/newland/admin_cp_insert.asp
Lesson15/Complete/newland/admin_cp_insert_processor.asp
Lesson15/Complete/newland/admin_cp_master.asp
Lesson15/Complete/newland/admin_cp_update.asp
Lesson15/Complete/newland/admin_cp_update_processor.asp
Lesson15/Complete/newland/admin_cp_delete_processor.asp

LESSON 15

Hand-Coding a Basic CMS

As the final activity in the book, you'll build a content management system for the country profiles. Using it, Newland Tours employees will be able to insert new country profiles, and modify or delete existing country profiles, using simple HTML forms as their interface. You've already used UPDATE and INSERT SQL statements to manage content, so the only new SQL in this lesson is the DELETE statement.

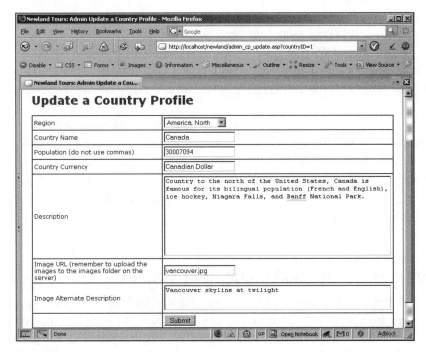

You will hand-code a complete content management system from the ground up, enabling users to maintain site content using Web forms.

In this lesson, in contrast to the previous lessons where you built pages that inserted and updated data, you will not rely on Dreamweaver server behaviors. There is nothing wrong with using server behaviors, but one of the primary goals of this book is to give you the conceptual underpinnings and experience working with code that will empower you to create your own dynamic sites. And as I've stressed throughout the book, building dynamic sites usually requires some level of competence with ASP, ColdFusion or PHP code.

Although server behaviors are convenient, some of them effectively mask what's going on, enabling you to add functionalities that you don't understand. That's great for rapid development, but not good for learning. And the code generated by the server behaviors is often incredibly complex—too complex for someone new to dynamic development to read. This complexity is often due to Dreamweaver's need for a given server behavior to work under a tremendous variety of circumstances, rather than the task itself. But it means that you often can't deconstruct the server behaviors that you add. (ColdFusion users are more likely to understand Dreamweaver's server behavior code than ASP or PHP users, due to the intrinsic nature of each language.) Avoiding server behaviors in this lesson will teach you more than you would otherwise learn.

Much of what you'll do in this lesson is not new. You'll build a group of pages that work together to handle certain functionalities. You'll create forms that collect information from the user. You'll use SQL to retrieve data from and send it to a database. You'll have a master-detail page pairing. The difference is that you'll put it all together in one lesson, and you will do all of it manually.

At the same time, the directions will be a little more high level. That is, for certain tasks you have done over and over again in this book (such as creating new pages and mocking up form interfaces), I will not provide detailed step-by-step instructions, but will assume you can manage with comparatively less guidance. That will enable the lesson to focus on the more challenging aspects of the job—connecting ASP, ColdFusion, or PHP to a database and writing the queries that will make the CMS work.

Preparing the Content Management System

Though it is often tempting to open Dreamweaver and start building pages right away, when you are developing a Web application, you are better served by thinking through exactly what you want to create, and at least outlining the major file assets that you need. The goal of this content management system is to create a group of pages that let users insert new country profiles, and modify or delete existing profiles.

You already should see a distinction between these two processes: When inserting a new record, you can just create a form that collects the data to be inserted, but to allow users to delete or modify existing records the users need to be able to specify a record. In other words, the insert page doesn't require a master-detail page pairing, but both of the other two functionalities do. There's no reason, though, that the pages that enable users to modify versus delete records can't share the same master page.

Each of the three functionalities requires a script to do the actual work of inserting, updating, or removing records. The easiest way to implement these scripts is to put them on their own pages, using the _processor suffix we have used throughout the book. Once a given script is processed, we'll redirect users to the master page, so they can verify that the correct action has been taken. These pages are hidden because they are active for only the split second required to process the script before redirecting the user to another page.

✱ **NOTE:** Though it is easy to store these scripts in hidden files, many developers actually put them on the same page as the form, and have the page submit the form to itself. An if...else structure near the top determines whether the form variables are present, and if so, processes the script. If not, it skips over the script and displays the page. This approach reduces the number of files on the server and keeps all the scripts that create a certain functionality in one file, but there are some advantages to keeping scripts separate. First, a good programmer can write reusable scripts, using the same script for multiple pages. Second, you can place scripts in a special folder, with special permissions on it to enhance security.

The following figure summarizes the pages needed to create this application.

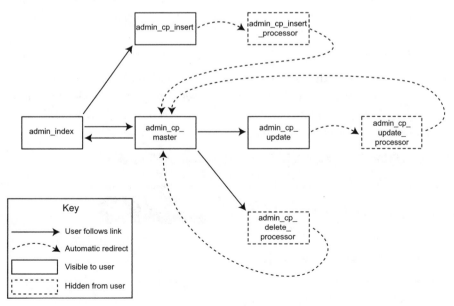

Starting from admin_index.asp, users can choose either to insert a new country profile (in which case, they are redirected to admin_cp_insert.asp) or modify/delete an existing country profile (in which case, they are redirected to admin.cp_master.asp).

The admin_cp_insert.asp page contains a blank form. Users will fill out this form when they want to create a new country profile. When they submit the form, the data is sent to admin_cp_insert_processor.asp, where it is inserted into the database and users are redirected to the master page. The new country's presence on the master page is proof that the insert action was successful.

Once on admin_cp_master.asp, users can click a link to modify an existing record, in which case they are taken to admin_cp_update.asp, which contains a form whose contents are already filled in with existing data. They can modify this data, and when they submit it, a script (on admin_cp_update_processor.asp) updates the database with the new data and redirects users back to the master page. They can view the profile again to verify that the update was successful.

Alternatively, from the master page, users can choose to delete a country profile. When they click this link, they are redirected to admin_cp_delete_processor, which contains a script that deletes the selected country and redirects users back to the master page. This process takes a fraction of a second and appears to users as if they never left the master page—it simply updates with the selected country removed.

Now that you have a firm grasp of the basic layout of the content management system, you can start building it.

1 Using admin_template.asp as the source, create the first two pages that the user will see, as follows.

admin_cp_insert.asp

admin_cp_master.asp

These two pages are visible to the user, so don't delete the code and be sure to customize each accordingly. Add a page title in the toolbar, and overwrite the placeholder heading at the top of the page with something appropriate, such as *Insert a New Country Profile*, and *Select a Country Profile to Modify or Delete*.

2 Create each of these hidden pages as well, saving three files (as follows). Be sure to delete all the HTML code from these pages (starting with the <!DOCTYPE declaration), while in code (not design) view. Do not delete the ASP, ColdFusion, or PHP code for the Restrict Access to Page server behavior.

admin_cp_insert_processor.asp

admin_cp_update_processor.asp

admin_cp_delete_processor.asp

These pages should never be displayed to the user, and so they should not have any HTML code in them. They will contain only the code needed to perform the function (insert a new record, update a record, and so on.).

> **TIP:** The easiest way to complete this step is to create a new file, strip out the code, and save it three times with different filenames.

Though users won't ever see them, these will be some of the most powerful pages on the site, because they will contain the scripts that change the contents of the database. Without ensuring login, a hacker who knows the page name could easily wipe out the Newland database—*without logging in*!

You now have six new files. Granted, they are empty, but now that they exist, it will be easier to link to them as you build the application itself.

```asp
<%@LANGUAGE="VBSCRIPT"%>
<%
' *** Restrict Access To Page: Grant or deny access to this page
MM_authorizedUsers="admin"
MM_authFailedURL="login.asp"
MM_grantAccess=false
If Session("MM_Username") <> "" Then
  If (false Or CStr(Session("MM_UserAuthorization"))="") Or _
        (InStr(1,MM_authorizedUsers,Session("MM_UserAuthorization"))>=1) Then
    MM_grantAccess = true
  End If
End If
If Not MM_grantAccess Then
  MM_qsChar = "?"
  If (InStr(1,MM_authFailedURL,"?") >= 1) Then MM_qsChar = "&"
  MM_referrer = Request.ServerVariables("URL")
  if (Len(Request.QueryString()) > 0) Then MM_referrer = MM_referrer & "?" & Request.QueryString()
  MM_authFailedURL = MM_authFailedURL & MM_qsChar & "accessdenied=" & Server.URLEncode(MM_referrer)
  Response.Redirect(MM_authFailedURL)
End If
%>
```

Building the Form and Hand-Coding a Recordset

In this task, you'll create the form that employees can use to insert new country profiles. You'll have the form submit its data to admin_cp_insert_processor.asp, where you'll also write the code necessary to insert the new record.

1 In admin_cp_insert.asp, create a form (Form Name: frm_insertProfile; Action: admin_cp_insert_processor.asp, Method: post), and insert a table inside of it with eight rows, two columns, and a border of 1, as shown in the screenshot.

The seven items listed in the left column correspond to seven of the eight fields in tbl_country (the eighth is the autogenerated primary key).

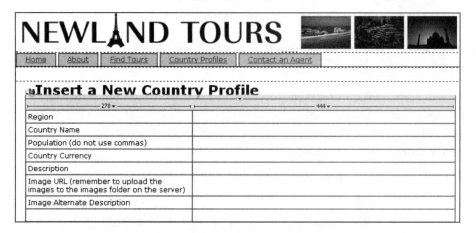

2 Add form elements into the right column, according to the following table:

Element Type	Element Name	Notes
List/Menu	region	Leave its type at the default, Menu, in the Property inspector
Text field	countryName	
Text field	population	
Text field	country_currency	
Text area	description	Provide enough room for users to enter a description, by setting its Char Width to 55 and its Num Lines to 9 in the Property inspector.
Text field	imageURL	
Text area	imageALT	This doesn't need to be as large as the one for description. Give it a Char Width of 55 as well, but leave the Num Lines blank.

Once again, the element names are the same as the field names in the corresponding table, making it easier to match the two. This time, you'll be hand-coding the SQL, so you won't be using Dreamweaver's Insert Record dialog, but it's nonetheless easier if the form fields match the database table fields.

The form is almost ready, but it lacks one critical piece: The menu at the top doesn't have any data in it. It should be populated by data from tbl_region, which means you'll have to create a recordset.

Insert a New Country Profile

Region	[▼]
Country Name	[ ]
Population (do not use commas)	[ ]
Country Currency	[ ]
Description	[ ]
Image URL (remember to upload the images to the images folder on the server)	[ ]
Image Alternate Description	[ ]
	Submit

3 Switch to code view, and scroll to the portion of the document after the Restrict Access to Page server behavior but before the opening <!DOCTYPE...> tag. Type the code necessary to create a connection to the database.

In ASP:

```
<%
'Create connection object
Dim dbConn
Dim rs_regions
set dbConn = server.CreateObject("adodb.connection")
'Connect to database via DSN
dbConn.open("newland")

%>
```

In ColdFusion:

```
<cfquery name="rs_regions" datasource="newland">

</cfquery>
```

In PHP:

```php
<?php
// Set up connection to MySQL
$host = "localhost";
$user = "[enter your username]";
$pwd = "[enter your password]";
$dbConn = mysql_connect($host,$user,$pwd);
// Connect to newland_tours database
$database = "newland_tours";
mysql_select_db($database);

?>
```

```
15      If (InStr(1,MM_authFailedURL,"?") >= 1) Then MM_qsChar = "&"
16      MM_referrer = Request.ServerVariables("URL")
17      if (Len(Request.QueryString()) > 0) Then MM_referrer = MM_referrer & "?" & Request.QueryString()
18      MM_authFailedURL = MM_authFailedURL & MM_qsChar & "accessdenied=" & Server.URLEncode(MM_referrer)
19      Response.Redirect(MM_authFailedURL)
20   End If
21   %>
22   <%
23   'Create connection object
24   Dim dbConn
25   Dim rs_regions
26   set dbConn = server.CreateObject("adodb.connection")
27   'Connect to database via DSN
28   dbConn.open("newland")
29
30   %>
31   <!DOCTYPE html PUBLIC "-//W3C//DTD XHTML 1.0 Transitional//EN" "http://www.w3.org/TR/xhtml1/DTD/xhtml1-tr
32   <html xmlns="http://www.w3.org/1999/xhtml">
33   <head>
34   <meta http-equiv="Content-Type" content="text/html; charset=utf-8" />
```

This code is sufficient to open a connection to the database. However, it doesn't actually do anything once the connection is established. You still need to add a SQL statement to make anything happen.

Let's look at the code for a moment. ColdFusion users have it fairly easy: They use the <cfquery> tag, give their query a name (rs_regions) and specify the data source (newland). ColdFusion figures out the rest.

ASP requires a bit more legwork. The word Dim is used to declare a new variable. Two are created here: dbConn and rs_regions. The variable dbConn will be used to create the database connection itself, and rs_regions will be used to hold the recordset. Both of these names are arbitrary, and you can call them whatever you want. The line after the Dim lines, which begins set dbConn =, tells ASP to create a new database connection object, whose name is dbConn. The next line then instructs ASP to actually open that connection to the DSN named "newland."

✱ **NOTE:** ASP and PHP users might wonder why they enter (respectively) "newland" and "newland_tours" rather than "conn_newland" as they have throughout the book. In the case of ASP, the reason is that "newland" is the DSN name that exists on the server and points to the Newland Tours database. In the case of PHP, newland_tours is the name of the database on the MySQL server. For both ASP and PHP, conn_newland, in contrast, is a connection created in Dreamweaver that uses the newland DSN (ASP) or newland_tours database (PHP) but is separate from it. Since you are coding by hand, and not going through Dreamweaver server behaviors, you specify the DSN (ASP) or the MySQL server newland_tours database directly.

Part of the ASP framework is a group of ready-made objects designed to handle common tasks. ASP has many such objects, and you have made extensive use of them through the book (though you may not have realized it). These include the Request, Response, Session, and Application objects, among others. The Connection and Recordset objects are a part of ActiveX Data Objects, or ADO. The topic of object-oriented programming, or OOP, is beyond the scope of this book, but suffice it to say for now that you can reliably use the code developed in this lesson as a template for connecting to a database.

The PHP code, although the most verbose in the group, is fairly easy to read. The built-in mysql_connect() function is used to help PHP find the MySQL server. As the code indicates, it takes three parameters: the host, username, and password of the account you want to access. This username and password combination is the same pairing that you entered in the MySQL Connection dialog earlier in the book. Be sure to enter it in the code, where you see [enter your username] and [enter your password] in this step's code listing. Once PHP can find the MySQL server, it needs to find the database itself. To do that, you use the built-in mysql_select_db() function, whose sole parameter is the name of the database on the MySQL server.

✱ **NOTE:** The value of $host in PHP may be different than "localhost" if you are working on a remote server. Compare it to $hostname_conn_newland in your Connections/conn_newland. php file. They should be the same.

✱ **NOTE:** You will be using this code to open a database connection in several more files in this lesson so you should mark this step to refer back to later.

4 Add the code necessary to retrieve the desired records in the blank line you left in the preceding step.

In ASP:

```
Set rs_regions = dbConn.Execute("SELECT regionID, regionName FROM tbl_region
➥ORDER BY regionName")
```

In ColdFusion:

```
SELECT regionID, regionName FROM tbl_region ORDER BY regionName
```

In PHP:

```
$query_rs_regions = "SELECT regionID, regionName FROM tbl_region ORDER BY
➥regionName";
$rs_regions = mysql_query($query_rs_regions);
$row_rs_regions = mysql_fetch_assoc($rs_regions);
```

This particular SQL should pose no challenge to you by this point in the book. It retrieves the regionID and regionName fields in all of the records in tbl_region, and orders them alphabetically by the name of the region.

Again, the surrounding ASP and PHP code might be somewhat confusing. I'll start with the ASP. Remember, dbConn is the connection object, not the recordset. This line of code creates the recordset by creating a recordset object whose contents are equal to whatever is retrieved from the query executed through the connection.

```
19      Response.Redirect(MM_authFailedURL)
20    End If
21    %>
22
23    <%
24    'Create connection object
25    Dim dbConn
26    Dim rs_regions
27    set dbConn = server.CreateObject("adodb.connection")
28    'Connect to database via DSN
29    dbConn.open("newland")
30    Set rs_regions = dbConn.Execute("SELECT regionID, regionName FROM tbl_region ORDER BY regionName")
31    %>
32
33    <!DOCTYPE html PUBLIC "-//W3C//DTD XHTML 1.0 Transitional//EN" "http://www.w3.org/TR/xhtml1/DTD/xhtml
34    <html xmlns="http://www.w3.org/1999/xhtml">
35    <head>
```

The first two lines of the PHP code query the database, as you probably guessed. And you probably also guessed that the results of the query would be a recordset stored in the $rs_regions variable. But there you would be wrong. When querying a MySQL database in PHP using mysql_query(), the result is not the recordset, but rather a

resource identifier or number, which points to the data. The data itself is not returned. Instead, it sits in a limbo area of memory. Now, to get this data out of that area, you must **fetch** it, using `mysql_fetch_assoc()` (or one of its variants). This function retrieves the data from limbo and constructs an array to contain it. That array, in this block, is named `$row_rs_regions`. Once the data is in the `$row_rs_regions` array, it acts much like a recordset in ASP or ColdFusion—to access it, you reference `$row_rs_regions`.

This code is sufficient to create the recordset and make the data available to the page. If you look in the Bindings panel, you won't see this recordset listed. Dreamweaver doesn't realize it's there. Unfortunately, this also means that you won't be able to bind the recordset to the form object. You'll have to code it manually.

5 Still in code view, scroll down until you see the form. Just a few lines below it, inside the table, look for the `<select>` element, which is the menu. Press Enter or Return a few times to make some space between opening and closing tags.

The `<select>` tag creates the menu itself. To populate the menu, you use the `<option>` tag. Each option tag results in one more option in the menu. It uses the following syntax:

```
<option value="data">Label</option>
```

In this example, `Label` is what appears in the menu that humans can read, while `data` is the value that is submitted with the form. We need to bind regionName to the label and regionID to the value attribute.

```
58    <form action="admin_cp_insert_processor.asp" method="post" name="frm_insertProfile">
59       <table border="1" cellspacing="0" cellpadding="3">
60          <tr>
61             <td width="278">Region</td>
62             <td width="444">
63             <select name="region" id="region">
64
65
66             </select>
67             </td>
68          </tr>
```

6 In the empty space between the `<select>` tags, type the code needed to bind database data to the `<option>` tag.

In ASP:

```
<%
Response.Write("<option value=""" & rs_regions("regionID") & """>" &
➥rs_regions("regionName") & "</option>")
%>
```

In ColdFusion:

```
<cfoutput>
<option value="#rs_regions.regionID#">#rs_regions.regionName#</option>
</cfoutput>
```

In PHP:

```
<?php
echo "<option value=\"".$row_rs_regions['regionID']."\">"
➥.$row_rs_regions['regionName']."</option>";
?>
```

```
58    <form action="admin_cp_insert_processor.asp" method="post" name="frm_insertProfile">
59      <table border="1" cellspacing="0" cellpadding="3">
60        <tr>
61          <td width="278">Region</td>
62          <td width="444">
63          <select name="region" id="region">
64            <%
65               Response.Write("<option value=""" & rs_regions("regionID") & """>" & rs_regions("r
66            %>
67          </select>
68          </td>
69        </tr>
```

You've bound regionID to the value attribute, and regionName appears as the label in the menu.

The ASP and PHP code blocks, as usual, need additional explanation. As you know from before, Response.Write() and echo are the ways ASP and PHP respectively output text to the browser. In this line, you are telling the server to output a line of HTML for the <option> tag. When you want ASP or PHP to output a string of text, you enclose that string in quotation marks. The complication is, you don't want ASP to literally write into the browser <option value=" rs_regions("regionID")>rs_regions("regionName")</option> (or PHP the equivalent). You want ASP to evaluate rs_regions("regionID") and rs_regions("regionName"), and you want PHP to evaluate $row_rs_regions['regionID'] and $row_rs_regions['regionName']. Once these have been evaluated, you want ASP and PHP to write their results ("6" and "Africa," respectively) into the browser. But if you leave that portion of the script inside quotes, ASP or PHP would simply write, rather than evaluate, and output the code.

To get around this problem, you use a technique called concatenation, which refers to the building of strings out of different pieces. Here, the pieces are string literals, such as "<option value=" and expressions, such as rs_regions("regionID") and $row_rs_regions['regionID']. You glue together these pieces with the ampersand (&) character in ASP and the period character (.) in PHP. ASP/PHP then knows to evaluate the expressions and then glue the values into the string. ColdFusion uses the pound signs (#) to distinguish between string literals and expressions, eliminating the need to concatenate elements.

So the final output to the browser of this code, whether you use ASP, ColdFusion, or PHP is `<option value="6">Africa</option>`.

ASP and PHP have another complication: Quotation marks are used in two different ways in this block of code. Like most programming languages, ASP and PHP use quotes to distinguish between strings and expressions. Everything inside of the quotes ASP and PHP ignore and output as-is. Unfortunately, the string that ASP and PHP need to output contains quotation marks: The proper syntax for the valid XHTML attribute is `<option value="XYZ">`. In the final output of this code, the number output by `rs_regions("regionID")` and `$row_rs_regions['regionID']` should appear in quotes, as in, `<option value="6">`. ASP and PHP get confused when they see the quotation marks used in the `value` attribute, and think that you are marking the end of the string, which in fact you are not. To solve this problem, when you want to tell ASP and PHP to write quotation marks, rather than interpret them, you insert two sets of quotation marks (ASP) or precede the quotation marks with a backslash (\) (PHP). Thus, in the ASP code you just entered, `"<option value="""` &, where you see three quotation marks in a row, the first two indicate the quotation marks that ASP should write into the HTML, and the third indicates the end of the string. Likewise in the PHP code you just entered, `"<option value=\""`., the `\"` tell PHP to output one pair of quotes, while the next set of quotes (immediately preceding the period) indicated to PHP the end of the string.

Save, upload, and test the file, and look at the menu. You'll see right away that Africa has loaded, and it is alphabetically the first region in the database table. That's good. But we've got a problem. Africa is the only option in the menu! You need to cause ASP, ColdFusion, or PHP to create a new `<option>` tag for each record in the database. This calls for a programming structure known as a **loop**. In a loop, the same block of code is executed over and over until a condition is met. In this case, we need to create a loop that will output the `<option>` line over and over until it runs out of records.

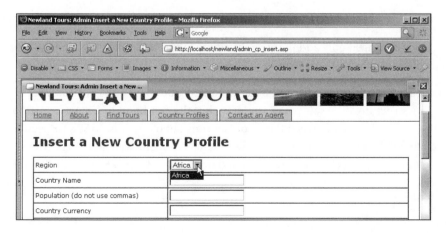

7 Amend the block of code you added in step 6 so that it incorporates a looping structure.

In ASP:

```
<%
Do Until rs_regions.EOF
        Response.Write("<option value=""" & rs_regions("regionID") & """>" &
        ➥rs_regions("regionName") & "</option>")
        rs_regions.MoveNext
    Loop
%>
```

In ColdFusion:

```
<cfoutput query="rs_regions">
<option value="#rs_regions.regionID#">#rs_regions.regionName#</option>
<cfoutput>
```

In PHP:

```
<?php
do
{
    echo "<option value=\"".$row_rs_regions['regionID']."\">"
    ➥.$row_rs_regions['regionName']."</option>";
}
while ($row_rs_regions = mysql_fetch_assoc($rs_regions));
?>
```

```
62      <td width="444">
63      <select name="region" id="region">
64      <%
65          Do Until rs_regions.EOF
66              Response.Write("<option value=""" & rs_regions("regionID") & """>" & rs_regions("re
67              rs_regions.MoveNext
68          Loop
69      %>
70      </select>
71      </td>
```

ColdFusion users need only add the query attribute to the <cfoutput> tag, and the loop is created automatically for them, behind the scenes.

ASP and PHP users, as usual, have a harder time. ASP's Do Until and PHP's do...while are looping structures. The sole parameter of each is the condition that must be met to break the loop, in both cases when the recordset runs out of records. (ASP's EOF stands for End of File.) The next line constructs the <option> element, as before. PHP uses curly braces {} to identify which code is to be looped over. ASP's MoveNext method tells ASP to advance to the next record. ASP's last line, Loop, sends ASP back to the Do Until line, while PHP's last line, with the while statement, provides the loop-breaking condition for the do half of the loop.

Test the file again in a browser, and click the menu. You'll see all of the regions listed now.

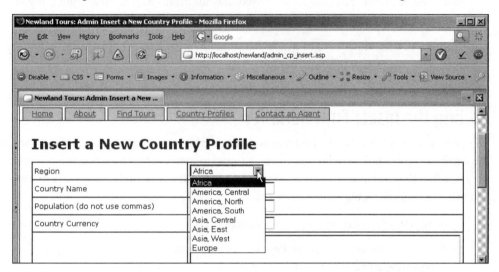

8 ASP and PHP users only: In code view, scroll all the way to the bottom of the document, and after the last line of code, </html>, insert the following script, to close and destroy the recordset.

In ASP:

```
<%
rs_regions.Close()
Set rs_regions = Nothing
%>
```

In PHP:

```
<?php
mysql_free_result($rs_regions);
?>
```

At the top of the document, you opened a connection and created a recordset. This recordset exists in the server's memory. Unless you tell it to go away, it might stay in the server's memory. Over time, you could overwhelm your server with useless recordset data that is no longer being used. The ASP code block removes all of the records from the recordset (`rs_regions.Close()`) and then destroys the recordset object itself (`Set rs_regions = Nothing`). The PHP version simply clears the `$rs_regions` recordset array. You add this script to the bottom of the page, of course, so that the rest of the page is processed before the recordset is destroyed. It wouldn't do your form any good if you destroyed the recordset before you had a chance to populate the menu with its data!

ColdFusion users don't have to worry about this step, because it happens automatically behind the scenes any time you deploy `<cfquery>`.

Adding the Insert Functionality

The form is now fully ready. The problem is that no script yet exists to write the form data into the database. In this task, you'll write the script used to insert data. The script you'll write has the same functionality as the Insert Record behavior, but the code will be somewhat leaner, and this time around, you'll understand it.

1 Open admin_cp_insert_processor.asp in code view.

Aside from the Restrict Access to Page server behavior, the file should be empty of all code, including and especially HTML code.

Before adding code, let's review what this page should do. It should retrieve the data entered into the form and insert it as a new record into tbl_country. Once that's complete, it should redirect the user to admin_cp_master.asp.

2 Insert the code that creates the connection to the database. Refer to the exercise earlier in the lesson where you created the connection in admin_cp_insert.asp for the basic code you will need. Make the following modifications:

In ASP, you only need one variable declaration, `Dim dbConn`.

In ColdFusion, set the `cfquery` name attribute to `rs_insertCountry`.

In PHP, you must start the connection code on the line immediately following the end of the Restrict Access server behavior. If you leave even one line of blank space between the two code blocks, you will see an error message indicating that headers have already been sent.

This is essentially the same code used in the previous task to create the recordset that was used to populate the form menu. The difference here is that you don't even need to have a recordset returned. You are inserting data into the database, but you are not retrieving a recordset.

> **TIP:** Because we typically use the same code over and over to connect pages to your database, many developers store the basic code for connecting to a database in a separate file, which they then include in every document. This could be a special include file, such as Application.cfm or a regular include file, accessed using something like PHP's require_once(). In fact, this is exactly what Dreamweaver does in the ASP and PHP models, when you "define a connection." In other words, the conn_newland source ASP and PHP users have used throughout this book is simply an include file with the basic information needed to connect to the newland_tours database.

You will recall from Lesson 11 that when you write code that takes user-entered variables, either via a form or URL string, and uses them in SQL queries, you must take special measures for security. In order to prevent SQL injection attacks, you must prevent the escape character—the single quote—from appearing in a text string. Of course your users may want to enter a single quote or apostrophe and it does not seem very user-friendly to tell them they can't. The challenge is to allow it as input while preventing it from adversely affecting your SQL.

3 Write the code that inserts the data into the table in the blank space you left in the previous step.

In ASP:

```
Dim region_cleaned, countryName_cleaned, population_cleaned,
➥country_currency_cleaned, description_cleaned, imageURL_cleaned, imageALT_cleaned
region_cleaned = CLng(Request.Form("region"))
countryName_cleaned = Replace(Request.Form("countryName"),"'","''")
population_cleaned = Replace(Request.Form("population"),"'","''")
country_currency_cleaned = Replace(Request.Form("country_currency"),"'","''")
description_cleaned = Replace(Request.Form("description"),"'","''")
imageURL_cleaned = Replace(Request.Form("imageURL"),"'","''")
imageALT_cleaned = Replace(Request.Form("imageALT"),"'","''")
dbConn.Execute("INSERT INTO tbl_country (region, countryName, population,
➥country_currency, description, imageURL, imageALT) VALUES ('" & region_cleaned
➥& "', '" & countryName_cleaned & "', '" & population_cleaned & "', '" &
➥country_currency_cleaned & "', '" & description_cleaned & "', '" &
➥imageURL_cleaned & "', '" & imageALT_cleaned & "')")
```

In ColdFusion:

```
INSERT INTO tbl_country
(region, countryName, population, country_currency, description, imageURL,
➥imageALT)
VALUES (<cfqueryparam cfsqltype="cf_sql_integer" value="#form.region#" />,
➥<cfqueryparam cfsqltype="cf_sql_varchar" value="#form.countryName#" />,
➥<cfqueryparam cfsqltype="cf_sql_varchar" value="#form.population#" />,
➥<cfqueryparam cfsqltype="cf_sql_varchar" value="#form.country_currency#" />,
➥<cfqueryparam cfsqltype="cf_sql_longvarchar" value="#form.description#" />,
➥<cfqueryparam cfsqltype="cf_sql_varchar" value="#form.imageURL#" />,
➥<cfqueryparam cfsqltype="cf_sql_varchar" value="#form.imageALT#" />)
```

In PHP:

```
$query_rs_insertCountry = "INSERT INTO tbl_country
(region, countryname, population, country_currency, description, imageURL,
➥imageALT)
VALUES (".mysql_real_escape_string($_POST['region'])."; '".mysql_real_
➥escape_string($_POST['countryName'])."; '".mysql_real_escape_string($_POST
➥['population'])."; '".mysql_real_escape_string($_POST['country_currency']).";
➥'".mysql_real_escape_string($_POST['description'])."; '".mysql_real_escape_
➥string($_POST['imageURL'])."; '".mysql_real_escape_string($_POST['imageALT'])."')";
$rs_insertCountry = mysql_query($query_rs_insertCountry);
```

```
23  <%
24   'Create connection object
25   Dim dbConn
26   set dbConn = server.CreateObject("adodb.connection")
27   'Connect to database via DSN
28   dbConn.open("newland")
29
30   Dim region_cleaned, countryName_cleaned, population_cleaned, country_currency_cleaned, description_clean
31   region_cleaned = CLng(Request.Form("region"))
32   countryName_cleaned = Replace(Request.Form("countryName"),"'","''")
33   population_cleaned = Replace(Request.Form("population"),"'","''")
34   country_currency_cleaned = Replace(Request.Form("country_currency"),"'","''")
35   description_cleaned = Replace(Request.Form("description"),"'","''")
36   imageURL_cleaned = Replace(Request.Form("imageURL"),"'","''")
37   imageALT_cleaned = Replace(Request.Form("imageALT"),"'","''")
38   dbConn.Execute("INSERT INTO tbl_country (region, countryName, population, country_currency, description,
39
40  %>
```

To understand these lines first recall the basic syntax of an INSERT statement in SQL:

```
INSERT INTO tbl_table
  (field1, field2, field3)
VALUES
  ('value1; 'value2; 'value3')
```

The ASP, ColdFusion, and PHP code blocks are constructing SQL statements that use this syntax. Each is using a different method to clean up the passed values before it inserts them into the database.

In the ASP code you once again use `CLng()` to clean the numeric variable and then the `Replace()` function to replace a single quote with two single quotes in the string variables. Just as the combination of two double quotes produces a literal double quote in HTML, so too does two single quotes result in a literal single quote being sent to the SQL query. The cleaned values are then used to construct the INSERT statement.

PHP and ColdFusion provide a function and tag respectively for cleaning up the values of the variables going into your SQL query. They escape the single quote and prevent hackers from using it to inject SQL. They also prevent SQL from misinterpreting legitimate apostrophes and causing errors.

> **TIP:** ASP and PHP users should use code coloring to their advantage. The coloring typically changes the moment you enter an error, making it easy to spot problems before you test the page. ASP: In all cases, `Request.Form` should be purple, while the form field name should always be green. The ampersands (&) used to concatenate should always be blue. In PHP: In all cases, string literals (including all commas and single quotes) are red, $_POST is always light blue, while periods and square brackets are always dark blue.

> **NOTE:** Both the ASP and PHP versions use both double quotes (") and single quotes ('), which can be confusing. Content enclosed in double quotes is a part of ASP/PHP, specifically, string literals that ASP/PHP should pass without evaluating. Content enclosed in single quotes belongs to SQL and represents the values being inserted into the database.

4 Insert the code that redirects the user to the master page once the insert is completed.

In ASP, before the closing %>:

```
Response.Redirect("admin_cp_master.asp")
```

In ColdFusion, after the closing </cfquery>:

```
<cflocation url="admin_cp_master.cfm">
```

In PHP, before the closing ?>:

```
header("Location: admin_cp_master.php");
```

Because ASP, ColdFusion, and PHP will display an error message if they experience problems, the redirect line will only be executed if the insertion is successful.

Test the page to make sure it works (you can just make up the details about your country). Once you insert your data, you'll be sent to an as-yet incomplete admin_cp_master. asp. But there's an easy way to see whether the insertion was successful: Go to the country profiles. Updating the country profiles is the whole point of this application. You should find your newly inserted country there. Don't worry about nonsense data—you'll be building a delete application later in the lesson, and you'll need a bogus country or two to test it, so just leave your creation in the database for now.

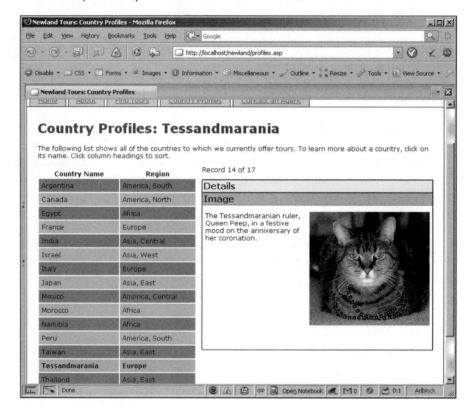

✱ NOTE: Unless you upload an image to the images folder with the same name as the one you enter in the form, the image link will be broken.

Creating the Master Page

A master-detail page pairing is necessary for the update and deletion functionality, because you have to allow the users to select which country they want to update or delete. In this task, you'll create a simple master-detail page consisting of a table with each country's name, a link to modify the country, and a link to delete the country in a row. As before, each of these links will pass a URL parameter identifying the country that the user has selected.

1 Open admin_cp_master.asp, and switch to code view.

As before, you'll create the recordset before laying out the page, and since you'll hand-write the code necessary to create the recordset, you need to be in code view.

2 Between the Restrict Access server behavior code and the beginning of the document itself (just before the <!DOCTYPE> tag), enter the code that creates the connection to the database. As in the previous exercise, refer to the steps taken earlier in the lesson when you created the connection in admin_cp_insert.asp for the basic code you will need. Next enter the code necessary to create a recordset ("rs_countries") that retrieves the country name and ID of every record in tbl_country.

Make the following modifications:

In ASP declare a variable for the recordset Dim rs_countries. Your query should be:

```
Set rs_countries = dbConn.Execute("SELECT countryID, countryName FROM
➥tbl_country ORDER BY countryName ASC")
```

In ColdFusion set the cfquery name attribute to rs_countries. Your query should be:

```
SELECT countryID, countryName FROM tbl_country ORDER BY countryName ASC
```

In PHP your query and recordset should be:

```
$query_rs_countries = "SELECT countryID, countryName FROM tbl_country ORDER BY
➥countryName ASC";

$rs_countries = mysql_query($query_rs_countries);
$row_rs_countries = mysql_fetch_assoc($rs_countries);
```

```
19      Response.Redirect(MM_authFailedURL)
20   End If
21   %>
22
23   <%
24   'Create connection object
25   Dim dbConn
26   Dim rs_countries
27   set dbConn = server.CreateObject("adodb.connection")
28   'Connect to database via DSN
29   dbConn.open("newland")
30   Set rs_countries = dbConn.Execute("SELECT countryID, countryName FROM tbl_country ORDER BY countryName ASC")
31   %>
32
33   <!DOCTYPE html PUBLIC "-//W3C//DTD XHTML 1.0 Transitional//EN" "http://www.w3.org/TR/xhtml1/DTD/xhtml1-trans
```

Aside from the details of the SQL statement, this code is identical to that used earlier in this lesson, so you should understand it. The query itself is also easy to read: It retrieves the country name and unique ID, ordered by country name.

3 ASP and PHP users only: Add the code to close and destroy the recordset at the end of the document.

In ASP:

```
<%
rs_countries.Close()
Set rs_countries = Nothing
%>
```

In PHP:

```
<?php
mysql_free_result($rs_countries);
?>
```

Again, this code prevents the recordset from wasting memory on the server.

```
66   </body>
67   </html>
68   <%
69   rs_countries.Close()
70   Set rs_countries = Nothing
71   %>
```

4 Switch to design view, and type the following two lines of text. Make the word "Caution" bold for emphasis.

Select a country to modify or delete.

Caution: Deleting is instant and permanent.

Again, providing directions for the user is critical to the success of your applications.

5 Return to code view, and below the paragraphs you just created, add the code to create a new table with one row and three columns.

```
<table width="98%" border="1" cellspacing="0" cellpadding="3">
   <tr>
      <td>XX</td>
      <td>XX</td>
      <td>XX</td>
   </tr>
</table>
```

This creates the basic framework for the table. When you are done with it, its contents will be dynamically generated, with each record being mapped to a single row. Since you can't know the number of rows in advance, you'll have to loop through the recordset, creating a new row for each record.

6 Enter the appropriate code needed to create a looping structure that encloses the <tr> tag. The code should wrap outside the opening and closing <tr> tags.

In ASP:

```
<%
   Do Until rs_countries.EOF
%>
<tr>
   <td>XX</td>
   <td>XX</td>
   <td>XX</td>
</tr>
<%
   rs_countries.MoveNext()
   Loop
%>
```

In ColdFusion:

```
<cfoutput query="rs_countries">
   <tr>
      <td>XX</td>
      <td>XX</td>
      <td>XX</td>
   </tr>
</cfoutput>
```

In PHP:

```php
<?php
   do {
?>
<tr>
   <td>XXX</td>
   <td>XXX</td>
   <td>XXX</td>
</tr>
<?php
   }
   while ($row_rs_countries = mysql_fetch_assoc($rs_countries));
?>
```

In this step, you are in effect creating a repeat region—you just aren't using the Dreamweaver behavior. And in spite of their cosmetic differences, all three server models use remarkably similar logic. Each has a block of code before and after the section to be looped over (the <tr> section). Each specifies a query and creates a loop that breaks only when the recordset runs out of records: ASP's EOF accomplishes this explicitly; the record-set loop is implied in ColdFusion, when you specify the query attribute in a <cfoutput> tag; and PHP tests using mysql_fetch_assoc().

Next, you need to build the contents of the table cells, which will contain a mix of HTML and ASP, ColdFusion, or PHP code.

```
60       <table width="98%" border="1" cellspacing="0" cellpadding="3">
61       <%
62       Do Until rs_countries.EOF
63       %>
64       <tr>
65           <td>XX</td>
66           <td>XX</td>
67           <td>XX</td>
68       </tr>
69       <%
70           rs_countries.MoveNext()
71           Loop
72       %>
73       </table>
```

7 Create the static HTML structure using placeholders for the content inside the <td> tags.

```
<td>Country Name</td>
<td><a href="admin_cp_update.asp?countryID=CountryID">Modify this country's
➥profile</a></td>
<td><a href="admin_cp_delete_processor.asp?countryID=CountryID">Delete</a></td>
```

This code is the same for ASP, ColdFusion, and PHP (except that the file extensions in the href attribute for ColdFusion/PHP should be *.cfm/.php* rather than *.asp*), because it is merely static HTML. We're using placeholders (such as "Country Name" in the first cell) to ensure that we get the HTML syntax right, before adding the dynamic code.

```
60    <table width="98%" border="1" cellspacing="0" cellpadding="3">
61    <%
62    Do Until rs_countries.EOF
63    %>
64    <tr>
65        <td>Country Name</td>
66        <td><a href="admin_cp_update.asp?countryID=CountryID">Modify this country's profile</a></td>
67        <td><a href="admin_cp_delete_processor.asp?countryID=CountryID">Delete</a></td>
68    </tr>
69    <%
70        rs_countries.MoveNext()
71        Loop
72    %>
73    </table>
```

8 Replace the three placeholders with dynamic output, as follows.

In ASP:

```
<td><%=rs_countries("countryName")%></td>
<td><a href="admin_cp_update.asp?countryID=<%=rs_countries("countryID")%>
➥">Modify this country's profile</a></td>
<td><a href="admin_cp_delete_processor.asp?countryID=<%=rs_countries
➥("countryID")%>">Delete</a></td>
```

In ColdFusion:

```
<td>#countryName#</td>
<td><a href="admin_cp_update.cfm?countryID=#countryID#">Modify this country's
➥profile</a></td>
<td><a href="admin_cp_delete_processor.cfm?countryID=#countryID#">Delete</a></td>
```

In PHP:

```
<td><?php echo $row_rs_countries['countryName']; ?></td>
<td><a href="admin_cp_update.php?countryID=<?php echo $row_rs_countries
➥['countryID']; ?>">Modify this country's profile</a></td>
<td><a href="admin_cp_delete_processor.php?countryID=<?php echo
➥$row_rs_countries['countryID']; ?>">Delete</a></td>
```

You've seen plenty of ASP, ColdFusion, and PHP output code in the course of this book, so the code should be easy to read, especially if you remember that <%= in ASP is equivalent to <% Response.Write().

```
60    <table width="98%" border="1" cellspacing="0" cellpadding="3">
61    <%
62    Do Until rs_countries.EOF
63    %>
64    <tr>
65        <td><%=rs_countries("countryName")%></td>
66        <td><a href="admin_cp_update.asp?countryID=<%=rs_countries("countryID")%>">Modify this country's profile</a></td>
67        <td><a href="admin_cp_delete_processor.asp?countryID=<%=rs_countries("countryID")%>">Delete</a></td>
68    </tr>
69    <%
70        rs_countries.MoveNext()
71        Loop
72    %>
73    </table>
```

9 Save, upload, and test the file in a browser.

The table has as many rows as tbl_country has records. If you hover your mouse over one of the links, you'll see not only the URL, but also the countryID parameter attached with the correct country ID.

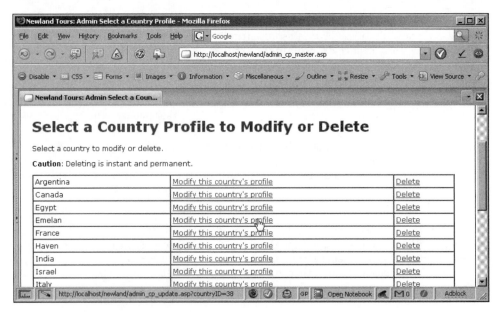

You can close admin_cp_master.asp.

Creating the Update Record Detail Page

The master page is ready, so the next step is to create the detail page. In this task, you'll build the detail page used for updating records. You won't actually need a detail page for deleting a record, because users don't need to see any details about the page—they just need a script to process the deletion.

The update page that you are about to create looks quite a bit like the page that you built enabling users to insert new country files. In fact, the page will use a modified version of the same form. The only differences are that on the update page, the form fields will already be filled in, and of course when the user submits the form, a database record will be updated, rather than a new one created.

1 Open admin_cp_insert.asp. Choose File > Save As, and save it as admin_cp_update. asp. Change the page heading to *Update a Country Profile*, and change the page title to *Newland Tours Admin: Update a Country Profile*.

In doing so, you preserve the form you created as well as the rs_regions recordset, which retrieves all of the regions and their IDs, and populates the Region drop-down menu.

When you use this technique, you must keep in mind all of the things you will need to change. In this form, each of the fields must be automatically populated with appropriate data from the database for the chosen country; a new recordset will need to be created to facilitate this change. The action attribute of the <form> tag needs to point to admin_ cp_update_processor.asp, rather than the insert processor page, and the form ought to be renamed.

2 In code view, find the opening <form> tag, and set its attributes, as follows.

action: admin_cp_update_processor.asp

method: post (same as before)

name: frm_updateProfile

id: frm_updateProfile

This is an easy step to overlook, so it's best to get it done right away.

```
59    <h1><a name="top" id="top"></a>Update a Country Profile</h1>
60    <form action="admin_cp_update_processor.asp" method="post" name="frm_updateProfile" id="frm_updateProfile">
61        <table border="1" cellspacing="0" cellpadding="3">
```

When this page first loads, the countryID variable appears in the URL sent from the master page. A query relies on this variable, so that it knows which country the user wants to modify. Now, the actual updating of the database will be done on a different page: admin_cp_update_processor.asp. However, that page, too, needs to know which record it should update.

3 Create a new recordset, rs_countryDetail, which retrieves all of the information stored about the country profile selected on the master page.

In ASP, inside the dbConn block, in a new line just below the line that begins
Set rs_regions = :

```
Set rs_countryDetail = dbConn.Execute("SELECT countryID, region, countryName,
➥population, country_currency, description, imageURL, imageALT FROM tbl_country
➥WHERE tbl_country.countryID=" & CLng(Request.QueryString("countryID")))
```

In ColdFusion after the closing </cfquery> of the previous query:

```
<cfquery name="rs_countryDetail" datasource="newland">
SELECT countryID, region, countryName, population, country_currency,
➥description, imageURL, imageALT
FROM tbl_country
WHERE tbl_country.countryID=<cfqueryparam cfsqltype="cf_sql_integer"
➥value="#url.countryID#" />
</cfquery>
```

In PHP, at the end of the existing query block, just before the closing ?>:

```
$query_rs_countryDetail = " SELECT countryID, region, countryName, population,
➥country_currency, description, imageURL, imageALT FROM tbl_country WHERE
➥tbl_country.countryID=".mysql_real_escape_string($_GET['countryID']);
$rs_countryDetail = mysql_query($query_rs_countryDetail);
$row_rs_countryDetail = mysql_fetch_assoc($rs_countryDetail);
```

```
23  <%
24  'Create connection object
25  Dim dbConn
26  Dim rs_regions
27  Dim rs_countryDetail
28  set dbConn = server.CreateObject("adodb.connection")
29  'Connect to database via DSN
30  dbConn.open("newland")
31  Set rs_regions = dbConn.Execute("SELECT regionID, regionName FROM tbl_region ORDER BY regionName")
32  Set rs_countryDetail = dbConn.Execute("SELECT countryID, region, countryName, population, country_c
33  %>
34
35  <!DOCTYPE html PUBLIC "-//W3C//DTD XHTML 1.0 Transitional//EN" "http://www.w3.org/TR/xhtml1/DTD/xht
36  <html xmlns="http://www.w3.org/1999/xhtml">
```

```
46   <?php
47   // Set up connection to MySQL
48   $host = "localhost";
49   $user = "root";
50   $pwd = "";
51   $dbConn = mysql_connect($host,$user,$pwd);
52   // Connect to newland_tours database
53   $database = "newland_tours";
54   mysql_select_db($database);
55   $query_rs_regions = "SELECT regionID, regionName FROM tbl_region ORDER BY regionName";
56   $rs_regions = mysql_query($query_rs_regions);
57   $row_rs_regions = mysql_fetch_assoc($rs_regions);
58   $query_rs_countryDetail = " SELECT countryID, region, countryName, population, country_
59   $rs_countryDetail = mysql_query($query_rs_countryDetail);
60   $row_rs_countryDetail = mysql_fetch_assoc($rs_countryDetail);
61   ?>
```

Once again, most of this code should look familiar to you. It's worth deconstructing the SQL statement, though. Remember, tbl_country contains the information that Newland tracks about a country. The SQL statement does not retrieve all of the country profiles—only the one that the user selected on the master page, the ID of which was sent as a querystring/URL variable.

✱ NOTE: ASP users should also Dim the new variable, rs_countryDetail, near the top of the script where the other Dim statements appear. The code should still work without it, but it's good practice to declare all variables.

You now have all of the information about the selected country that Newland keeps. You'll use this information to populate the form on the page with live data from the database. When users submit the form, a script will replace existing database data with the information in the form. Now that this data is available, you need to bind it as the default value of each respective form element.

4 In code view, find the countryName form <input> element. Give it a value attribute, as follows:

value="XX"

This is standard HTML, so it is the same for ASP, ColdFusion, and PHP. If you were to test the page now, the letters XX would appear in the Country Name field.

▶ TIP: If you do test this page during the lesson, remember that it is expecting a querystring/URL parameter. If one is not supplied (and one never is when you press F12), you will see an error. To solve this problem, at the end of the URL in the Address/Location bar in your browser, type the following: ?countryID=3 and press Enter/Return. Doing so provides the necessary information for the query to run and the error is removed.

5 Replace the XX placeholder with the dynamic value, as follows:

In ASP:

```
<%=rs_countryDetail("countryName")%>
```

In ColdFusion:

```
<cfoutput>#rs_countryDetail.countryName#</cfoutput>
```

In PHP:

```
<?php echo $row_rs_countryDetail['countryName']; ?>
```

This way, when the page loads, the proper country name appears by default in the field. If users modify it, then the country's name will be updated in the database. If the user leaves it alone, then strictly speaking, the form value will still replace the value in the database, but since they are the same, nothing will change.

```
76   d>Country Name</td>
77   d><input type="text" name="countryName" id="countryName" value="<%=rs_countryDetail("countryName")%>" /></td>
78   >
```

6 Using the correct ASP, ColdFusion, or PHP syntax, repeat steps 4 and 5 for each of the remaining text field <input> elements, using the following information (provided in pseudocode):

Population: rs_countryDetail.population

Country Currency: rs_countryDetail.country_currency

Image URL: rs_countryDetail.imageURL

Now the four text fields are ready for use. You still need to take care of the two text areas.

```
80   as)</td>
81   pulation" id="population" value="<%=rs_countryDetail("population")%>" /></td>
82
83
84
85   ntry_currency" id="country_currency" value="<%=rs_countryDetail("country_currency")%>" /></td>
86
87
88
89   ' id="description" cols="55" rows="9"></textarea></td>
90
91
92   ad the images to the images folder on the server)</td>
93   ageURL" id="imageURL" value="<%=rs_countryDetail("imageURL")%>" /></td>
94
95
96   :/td>
```

In order for the processing page to know which record to update, it will need the countryID of the record you are submitting.

7 Scroll to the end of the form. In the empty table cell to the left of the submit button insert a hidden field with the value of the countryID from the recordset.

In ASP:

```
<td><input type="hidden"name="countryID"value="<%=rs_countryDetail
➥("countryID")%>"></td>
```

In ColdFusion:

```
<td><input type="hidden"name="countryID"value="<cfoutput>#rs_countryDetail.
➥countryID#</cfoutput>"></td>
```

In PHP:

```
<td><input type="hidden"name="countryID"value="<?php echo $row_rs_countryDetail
➥['countryID'];?>"></td>
```

```
 99             <tr>
100               <td><input type="hidden" name="countryID" value="<%=rs_countryDetail("countryID")%>"></td>
101               <td><input type="submit" name="button" id="button" value="Submit" /></td>
102             </tr>
103           </table>
104         </form>
```

8 Between the two sets of opening and closing <textarea></textarea> tags (for description and imageALT), insert the code necessary to output dynamic data as their default values.

In ASP:

```
<%=rs_countryDetail("description")%>
<%=rs_countryDetail("imageALT")%>
```

In ColdFusion:

```
<cfoutput>#rs_countryDetail.description#</cfoutput>
<cfoutput>#rs_countryDetail.imageALT#</cfoutput>
```

In PHP:

```
<?php echo $row_rs_countryDetail['description']; ?>
<?php echo $row_rs_countryDetail['imageALT']; ?>
```

```
 92     <td>Image URL (remember to upload the images to the images folder on the server)</td>
 93     <td><input type="text" name="imageURL" id="imageURL" value="<%=rs_countryDetail("imageURL")%>" /></td>
 94     >
 95
 96     <td>Image Alternate Description</td>
 97     <td><textarea name="imageALT" id="imageALT" cols="55"><%=rs_countryDetail("imageALT")%></textarea></td>
 98     >
 99
100     <td><input type="hidden" name="countryID" value="<%=rs_countryDetail("countryID")%>"></td>
101     <td><input type="submit" name="button" id="button" value="Submit" /></td>
```

The <textarea> tag uses slightly different syntax than other form element tags. Rather than having a value attribute, you place the default value between the opening and closing tags. The syntax for the ASP, ColdFusion, or PHP code is the same, though.

When you are done, save and upload the file so you can test it.

9 Select admin_cp_master.asp in the Site panel, log in, and click to select any non-African country.

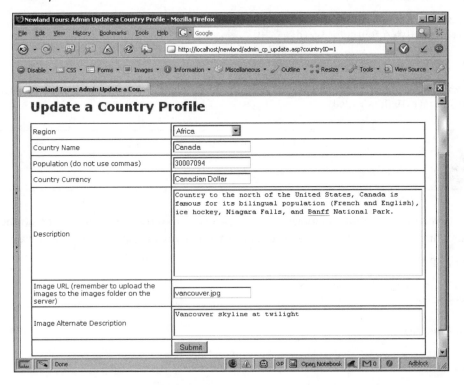

The update form appears, and all of its default values are already supplied. However, as long as you chose a non-African country, you'll see a problem: The country's region is listed as Africa. This occurs because a different recordset (rs_regions) is populating the drop-down menu, and Africa is the first region in the recordset, so it appears by default. You could change the menu, so that it displays data from rs_countryDetail, but since that has only one record, only one region would be displayed, making it impossible to change the region. And while it is unlikely that Italy will relocate to South America, you should preserve the flexibility to change regions, in case someone at Newland Tours decides to use a different regional division logic than continents, such as Northern Europe and Southern Europe, rather than simply Europe.

You could consider specifying to employees that they have to change this drop-down menu every time as appropriate, but that's poor usability. Sooner or later, an employee will forget to change it, and a country such as Mexico will be listed in Africa. The consequences of this mistake are significant: Remember that users can search by region, so they won't see Mexico if they search under Central America. And imagine the blow to credibility that a travel agent will suffer if it declares that Mexico is in Africa! This is a problem in need of a solution.

But the solution is going to take some work. At the moment, the code sent to the browser (that is, after it has been processed by the ASP, ColdFusion, or PHP interpreter) for this menu element looks as follows:

```
<select name="region" id="region">
    <option value="6">Africa</option>
    <option value="8">America, Central</option>
    <option value="1">America, North</option>
    <option value="2">America, South</option>
    <option value="7">Asia, Central</option>
    <option value="4">Asia, East</option>
    <option value="5">Asia, West</option>
    <option value="3">Europe</option>
</select>
```

As you may be aware, the <select> element has an additional attribute, selected, which you can use to specify which item appears by default. So in the following list, Asia, Central would be the element that appears by default in the browser (bolding applied to make the change easier to spot).

```
<select name="region" id="region">
    <option value="6">Africa</option>
    <option value="8">America, Central</option>
    <option value="1">America, North</option>
    <option value="2">America, South</option>
    <option value="7" selected="selected">Asia, Central</option>
    <option value="4">Asia, East</option>
    <option value="5">Asia, West</option>
    <option value="3">Europe</option>
</select>
```

What you need, then, is to insert the attribute selected into the code for the region corresponding to the active country. Now, the complication you face is that your menu is not hard-coded, but is rather populated by a loop, which inserts a new <option> line for each record in the rs_regions recordset.

The solution to the problem is this: Each time through the loop that populates the drop-down menu, a script will test to see whether the current record's regionID matches the region in the rs_countryDetail recordset. If it does match, then the script will output the word selected into the code. If it does not match, the script will proceed as usual. Here's how the block looks in pseudocode:

```
Loop the following code until rs_regions runs out of records
   Write the <option> line, using rs_regions.regionID as the value attribute,
   ➥and rs_regions.regionName as the label
   If the active rs_regions.regionID equals rs_countryDetail.region
      Write the attribute 'selected="selected"' into the code
   End If
Go back to beginning of loop and start next iteration
```

That's a lot to absorb conceptually, but once you understand the idea, the actual code is not that hard to write.

10 Update the code between the opening and closing <select></select> tags for the region, as follows:

In ASP:

```
<%
   Do Until rs_regions.EOF
%>
<option value="<%=rs_regions("regionID")%>"
<%
   If rs_regions("regionID")=rs_countryDetail("region") Then
      Response.Write(" selected=""selected""")
   End If
%>
><%=rs_regions("regionName")%></option>
<%
   rs_regions.MoveNext
   Loop
%>
```

In ColdFusion:

```
<cfoutput query="rs_regions">
   <option value="#regionID#"<cfif (rs_regions.regionID EQ rs_countryDetail.region)>
   ➥selected="selected"</cfif>>#regionName#</option>
</cfoutput>
```

In PHP:

```php
<?php
   do {
?>
   <option value="<?php echo $row_rs_regions['regionID']; ?>"
      <?php
      if ($row_rs_regions['regionID'] == $row_rs_countryDetail['region']) {

         echo " selected=\"selected\"";
      }
      ?>
   ><?php echo $row_rs_regions['regionName']; ?></option>
<?php
   }
   while ($row_rs_regions = mysql_fetch_assoc($rs_regions));
?>
```

I bolded the opening and closing portions of the <option> tag just to make them easier to read—especially the closing angled bracket (>), which looks orphaned in ASP, ColdFusion, and PHP. (That bracket, by the way, should be orange in the code editor for all three server models.) The reason for this is that selected="selected" must be written before that closing bracket, so that bracket alone goes on the right of the if section of code, while the remainder of its tag goes on the left of the if section.

You will recall from the beginning of this lesson that ASP uses "" and PHP \" in order to output literal quotes.

```
64              <td width="444">
65              <select name="region" id="region">
66                 <%
67                    Do Until rs_regions.EOF
68                 %>
69                 <option value="<%=rs_regions("regionID")%>"
70                 <%
71                    If rs_regions("regionID")=rs_countryDetail("region") Then
72                       Response.Write(" selected=""selected""")
73                    End If
74                 %>
75                 ><%=rs_regions("regionName")%></option>
76                 <%
77                    rs_regions.MoveNext
78                    Loop
79                 %>
80              </select>
81              </td>
```

Pay close attention to spacing when you type this code—it is important that there is a space before the selected attribute, so that it does not run into the value="X" that precedes it.

ASP and PHP users may note that this section uses different syntax for the <option> state-ment than it did in the menu you built in the insert form at the beginning of the lesson. Rather than a single ASP/PHP block that concatenates multiple elements to construct the <option> line, it uses multiple ASP/PHP blocks, using the ASP (<%...%>) or PHP delimiters (<?...?>). There is no functional impact to this change. The main difference is that the code is easier to understand once you add the if section, when broken out like this.

11 Save and upload the file. Test admin_cp_master.asp, and select a non-African country, as before.

The correct region is selected by default, and yet all of the other regions are available as well.

The update form is complete, and the worst is over.

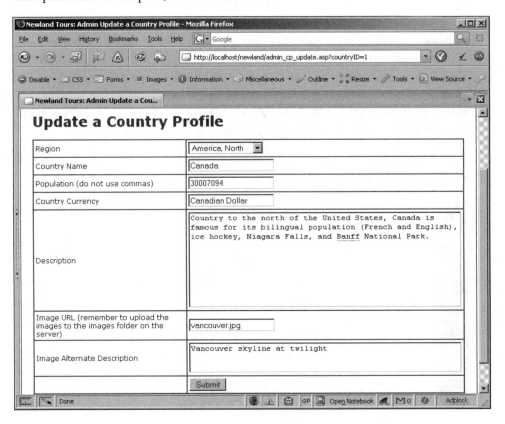

Adding the Update Functionality

After the preceding task, the last two tasks will be anticlimactic. In this task, you'll create the update processor page.

1 Open admin_cp_update_processor.asp in code view.

Once again, the restrict access server behavior aside, you'll be starting from a blank slate when producing this script-only page.

2 Just below the restrict access server behavior code, write the code that creates the database connection. Make the following modifications:

In ASP you only need one variable declaration for now, Dim dbConn. You will add more momentarily.

In ColdFusion set the cfquery name attribute to update_cp.

In PHP users must start the connection code on the line immediately following the end of the Restrict Access server behavior.

Now that you've got your connection, you can add the SQL.

3 Enter the code necessary to update the database in the blank line you left in the preceding step.

In ASP write your query on a line following dbConn.open("newland") and before the closing %>:

```
Dim countryID_cleaned, region_cleaned, countryName_cleaned, population_cleaned,
➥country_currency_cleaned, description_cleaned, imageURL_cleaned,
➥imageALT_cleaned
countryID_cleaned = CLng(Request.Form("countryID"))
region_cleaned = CLng(Request.Form("region"))
countryName_cleaned = Replace(Request.Form("countryName"),"'","''")
population_cleaned = Replace(Request.Form("population"),"'","''")
country_currency_cleaned = Replace(Request.Form("country_currency"),"'","''")

description_cleaned = Replace(Request.Form("description"),"'","''")
imageURL_cleaned = Replace(Request.Form("imageURL"),"'","''")
imageALT_cleaned = Replace(Request.Form("imageALT"),"'","''")
dbConn.Execute("UPDATE tbl_country SET region='" & region_cleaned & "',
➥countryName='" & countryName_cleaned & "', population='" & population_cleaned
➥& "', country_currency='" & country_currency_cleaned & "', description='" &
➥description_cleaned & "', imageURL='" & imageURL_cleaned & "', imageALT='" &
➥imageALT_cleaned & "' WHERE countryID=" & countryID_cleaned)
```

In ColdFusion:

```
UPDATE tbl_country
SET region=<cfqueryparam cfsqltype="cf_sql_integer" value="#form.region#" />,
    countryName=<cfqueryparam cfsqltype="cf_sql_varchar"
    ➥value="#form.countryName#" />,
    population=<cfqueryparam cfsqltype="cf_sql_varchar"
    ➥value="#form.population#" />,
    country_currency=<cfqueryparam cfsqltype="cf_sql_varchar"
    ➥value="#form.country_currency#" />,
    description=<cfqueryparam cfsqltype="cf_sql_longvarchar"
    ➥value="#form.description#" />,
    imageURL=<cfqueryparam cfsqltype="cf_sql_varchar" value="#form.imageURL#" />,
    imageALT=<cfqueryparam cfsqltype="cf_sql_varchar" value="#form.imageALT#" />
WHERE countryID=<cfqueryparam cfsqltype="cf_sql_integer"
➥value="#form.countryID#" />
```

In PHP:

```
//Update database
$query_updateCountry = "UPDATE tbl_country
SET region=".mysql_real_escape_string($_POST['region']).";
    countryName='".mysql_real_escape_string($_POST['countryName'])."';
    population='".mysql_real_escape_string($_POST['population'])."';
    country_currency='".mysql_real_escape_string($_POST['country_currency'])."';
    description='".mysql_real_escape_string($_POST['description'])."';
    imageURL='".mysql_real_escape_string($_POST['imageURL'])."';
    imageALT='".mysql_real_escape_string($_POST['imageALT'])."'
WHERE countryID="mysql_real_escape_string(.$_POST['countryID']);
    $updateCountry = mysql_query($query_updateCountry);
```

Again, use code coloring to your advantage, especially ASP and PHP users. Also, make sure you don't inadvertently add a comma at the end of the element just before the WHERE clause.

```
23  <%
24  'Create connection object
25  Dim dbConn
26  Dim rs_regions
27  set dbConn = server.CreateObject("adodb.connection")
28  'Connect to database via DSN
29  dbConn.open("newland")
30
31  Dim countryID_cleaned, region_cleaned, countryName_cleaned, population_cleaned, country_currenc
32  countryID_cleaned = CLng(Request.Form("countryID"))
33  region_cleaned = CLng(Request.Form("region"))
34  countryName_cleaned = Replace(Request.Form("countryName"),"'","''")
35  population_cleaned = Replace(Request.Form("population"),"'","''")
36  country_currency_cleaned = Replace(Request.Form("country_currency"),"'","''")
37  description_cleaned = Replace(Request.Form("description"),"'","''")
38  imageURL_cleaned = Replace(Request.Form("imageURL"),"'","''")
39  imageALT_cleaned = Replace(Request.Form("imageALT"),"'","''")
40  dbConn.Execute("UPDATE tbl_country SET region='" & region_cleaned & "', countryName='" & countr
41
42  %>
```

4 Insert the line of code needed to redirect the user back to the master page.

In ASP, in the line above the closing %> tag:

```
Response.Redirect("admin_cp_master.asp")
```

In ColdFusion, in the line after the closing </cfquery> tag:

```
<cflocation url="admin_cp_master.cfm">
```

In PHP, just before the closing ?> tag:

```
header("Location: admin_cp_master.php");
```

This returns the user to the master page, so she or he can conveniently verify that the modifications took place.

```
38    imageURL_cleaned = Replace(Request.Form("imageURL"),"'","''")
39    imageALT_cleaned = Replace(Request.Form("imageALT"),"'","''")
40    dbConn.Execute("UPDATE tbl_country SET region='" & region_cleaned & "', countryName='"
41  ▣ Response.Redirect("admin_cp_master.asp")
42    %>
```

5 Save and upload the file. Test the master page (F12), click a country, modify it, and click Submit. Return to that country's update page to change the value back.

The update functionality is complete and functional.

Adding the Delete Functionality

Writing the script for the delete processor page is even easier than writing the script for the update processor. Remember, users will access this page from the master page, which you have already built, so all that remains is to add the script that deletes the record from the database.

1 Open admin_cp_delete_processor.asp in code view.

Once again, this page will contain only a short script and a redirect elsewhere, so it needs no HTML code at all.

2 Add the code that creates the connection, below the server behavior code. Make the following modifications:

In ASP you only need one variable declaration, Dim dbConn.

In ColdFusion set the cfquery name attribute to delete_country.

In PHP users must start the connection code on the line immediately following the end of the Restrict Access server behavior.

Now you can insert the code that executes a SQL statement.

3 Add the code that deletes the record specified in the URL parameter, in the space you left in the preceding step.

In ASP (all in one line):

```
dbConn.Execute("DELETE FROM tbl_country WHERE countryID=" &
➥CLng(Request.QueryString("countryID")))
```

In ColdFusion (may be on multiple lines):

```
DELETE FROM tbl_country
WHERE countryID=<cfqueryparam cfsqltype="cf_sql_integer"
➥value="#URL.countryID#" />
```

In PHP:

```
$query_deleteCountry = "DELETE FROM tbl_country WHERE
➥countryID=".mysql_real_escape_string($_GET['countryID']);
$deleteCountry = mysql_query($query_deleteCountry);
```

With SQL's DELETE statement, you don't have to specify each field singly, because it deletes from all fields, making it much more convenient to write. It also makes it easy to inadvertently wipe out your entire table if you forget to specify the WHERE clause!

4 Add the redirection back to the master page, in the appropriate location.

In ASP, in the line above the closing %> tag:

```
Response.Redirect("admin_cp_master.asp")
```

In ColdFusion, in the line after the closing </cfquery> tag:

```
<cflocation url="admin_cp_master.cfm">
```

In PHP, before the closing ?> tag:

```
header("Location: admin_cp_master.php");
```

This returns the user to the master page, so she or he can conveniently verify that the deletion took place.

```
23  <%
24  'Create connection object
25  Dim dbConn
26  set dbConn = server.CreateObject("adodb.connection")
27  'Connect to database via DSN
28  dbConn.open("newland")
29  dbConn.Execute("DELETE FROM tbl_country WHERE countryID=" & CLng(Request.QueryString("countryID"))
30  Response.Redirect("admin_cp_master.asp")
31  %>
```

5 Save and upload the file. Press F12 to open admin_cp_master.asp in a browser, and delete the country you inserted earlier in the lesson.

As promised, the country disappears instantly and permanently—don't bother trying the Back button!

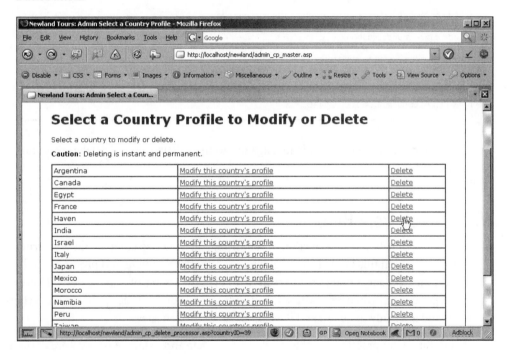

Update the Links on the Admin Page

You have finished the country management section of your CMS. In order to make it easy to access, you will need to link the pages to your administrative index page.

1 Open admin_index.asp and create the following links from the text listed:

Add a new country profile: admin_cp_insert.asp

Modify or remove an existing country profile: admin_cp_master.asp

---

⸬Admin Home

Choose an administrative task from the list below. If you have any questions or problems, please contact the webmaster.

Update the Traveler's Journal

Add or remove a registered user to/from the Admin group

Add a new tour description

Modify or remove an existing tour description

Add a new country profile

Modify or remove an existing country profile

Authorized staff can now quickly manage the country listings in the database and on the site.

Where to Go from Here

With the completion of this portion of the CMS, you have also completed the instruction contained in this book. Learning dynamic Web development and programming is a significant task, one too big for a person to do over the course of a single book. However, if you got this far, you have mastered the fundamentals of dynamic application development and are ready to go out and develop database-driven sites.

If you want extra practice, use the Newland Tours site and database—they were designed specifically for learning. For example, if you want more practice building a CMS, build one for the tour descriptions.

If you are ready to return to the real world, then revisit the sites for which you are responsible, and try to identify how they might be more efficient and easier to maintain if they used dynamic scripting. You have seen and written plenty of ASP, ColdFusion, and/or PHP code in this book, and you can probably start solving problems right away. For more ambitious jobs, go to the bookstore or look online for ASP, ColdFusion, or PHP books or tutorials. You may be surprised at how much easier they are to read, now that you've built the Newland Tours site.

What You Have Learned

In this lesson, you have:

- Designed a CMS application, including each of its pages and data flows (pages 426–427)
- Created a recordset without relying on Dreamweaver's Recordset dialog (pages 431–440)
- Written a script that inserts a new record based on a Web form (pages 440–444)
- Constructed a drop-down menu form element using a two recordsets, a loop, and an if statement (pages 444–460)
- Written a script that updates an existing record based on a Web form (pages 461–463)
- Written a script that deletes an existing record from a database table (pages 463–465)

Index